Kundalini
RISING

Kundalini
RISING

EXPLORING THE ENERGY
OF AWAKENING

GURMUKH KAUR KHALSA KEN WILBER SWAMI RADHA
GOPI KRISHNA JOHN WHITE

SOUNDS TRUE
Boulder, Colorado

Sounds True, Inc.
Boulder, CO 80306

Cover and book design by Rachael Murray

Printed in the U.S.A.

ISBN-13: 978-1-59179-728-9

Contents

Introduction *Tami Simon*   ix

Part I   **THE EXPERIENCE: Personal Accounts
and Findings from Those Who Have
Experienced Kundalini**

Kundalini and the Mystic Path
Dorothy Walters, PhD   3

Kundalini: The Role of Life-Force Energy
in Self-Realization *Bonnie Greenwell, PhD*   21

Kundalini: Unfolding the Human Design
Penny Kelly   37

Kundalini Yoga *Stuart Perrin*   47

Deep Light and the Great Retruthing
Whitehawk   55

Beyond Kundalini Awakening *John Selby*   73

Part II **KUNDALINI AND YOUR HEALTH:
Accounts from Health Experts, Therapists,
Scientists, Researchers, and Clinical Surveys
of Kundalini Experiences**

Kundalini Yoga as Therapy: A Research
Perspective *Sat Bir Singh Khalsa, PhD*   87

Kundalini and Health: Living Well with
Spiritual Awakening *Olga Louchakova*   97

The Yogic Brain *Andrew B. Newberg, MD*   117

Kundalini Awakening *David Lukoff, PhD*   127

Mental and Emotional Health in the Kundalini
Process *Barbara Harris Whitfield*   141

Spiritual Energy: Perspectives from a Map of the
Psyche and the Kundalini Recovery Process
Charles L. Whitfield, MD   161

Near-Death Experiences and the
Physio-Kundalini Syndrome *Bruce Greyson, MD* 173

Healing Through the Three Channels
Shanti Shanti Kaur Khalsa, PhD   185

Part III **KUNDALINI AT LARGE: Kundalini
in a Historical, Philosophical, and
Cultural Context**

Are the Chakras Real? *Ken Wilber*   195

Kundalini: Sex, Evolution, and Higher
Consciousness *John White*   207

Kundalini: Her Symbols of Transformation
and Freedom *Lawrence Edwards, PhD*   225

On Being Moved: Kundalini and the
Complete Maturation of the Spiritual Body
Stuart Sovatsky, PhD   247

An Illuminated Channel from the Ocean
of Consciousness *Gene Keiffer*   269

The Goal of Consciousness Research
Gopi Krishna   277

Part IV **KUNDALINI IN MOTION: Kundalini
Yoga and Musings from Yogis**

Thoughts on Kundalini *Swami Sivananda Radha* 299

Heart *Swami Sivananda Radha*   305

Let Your Presence Work Through the Power
of Kundalini Yoga and Meditation
Gurmukh Kaur Khalsa   313

Kundalini Yoga and Meditation as Taught by
Yogi Bhajan *Gurucharan Singh Khalsa, PhD*   319

Notes   337

Contributors   349

Credits   363

Index   365

Introduction

═══════════════

In 1984, I needed the book *Kundalini Rising*, and it didn't exist. I was twenty-two years old and I had just returned home from participating in a series of intensive meditation retreats in Sri Lanka, India, and Nepal. I was in a very strange condition (at least *I* thought it was strange). I had developed a case of the "shakes," which meant that my body would twitch and contort of its own accord. The shakes would get worse whenever I meditated, to the point where I would find myself shaking and then twisting into weird positions during sitting practice. I consulted with various teachers, and I was told that what I was experiencing was the natural releasing of blocked energy in the body. I should simply relax and let the process unfold. A couple of meditation teachers mentioned that what I was experiencing was sometimes associated with "kundalini" beginning to awaken in the body, and again, I should just relax.

Relax? I wanted to know everything there was to know about kundalini. Was it a good or bad sign that I was shaking and contorting? Why did some people say that the awakening of kundalini could be dangerous? Why was kundalini so often compared to a snake coiled at the base of the spine? Was the "rise" of kundalini just a metaphor, and if so, a metaphor for what transformative process?

What I discovered at the time was that there were few comprehensive resources available on the topic of kundalini. Mostly what I found were yogic texts that had been translated from Sanskrit and felt to me ancient and distant, their meaning hard to decipher. I also found some individual accounts of kundalini awakenings that were quite fascinating to read but didn't help me contextualize or map the process in a way that enabled me to understand my own experience. What I wanted was a contemporary resource guide, a book on kundalini that could help me understand the experience in Western language and from many different vantage points.

Here is the book I wish I'd had twenty-five years ago. Gathered into one volume, *Kundalini Rising* comprises twenty-four essays on different aspects of the kundalini experience, including what transpersonal psychologists have to say about kundalini; understanding the yogic brain from a scientific perspective; the relationship between near-death experiences and kundalini awakening; understanding the relationship between kundalini energy and sexual energy; yogic exercises to catalyze the kundalini process; the role that kundalini awakening plays in the unfolding of our highest human potential; and more.

It is now time for our understanding of kundalini to be broad and multi-disciplined, for our discussions about kundalini to come out of the realm of esoterica and to enter ordinary discourse. The primary reason for this is that more and more of us are experiencing spiritual awakenings of all kinds, identity-shattering experiences that leave us open to the mystery of being beyond name, shape, or form. These intense experiences "re-wire" us; they bring with them changes not just in our mental self-structure (our mental sense of who we are) but in our *energetic* self-structure (our felt sense of who we are). When we experience intense spiritual openings, movements and changes occur in our subtle body; at the energetic level of our being, kundalini begins to stir, and rise.

It is my belief that kundalini is on the rise, literally—that more and more people are having experiences of spiritual awakening. I base this belief on reports that I hear from contemporary spiritual teachers along with the increased public acceptance and growing popularity of practices such as meditation, energy healing, and kundalini yoga—all practices that are designed to dissolve our solid sense of self and open us to the transformative power of awareness. Such spiritual awakenings are inevitably accompanied by openings in the energetic channels of the body. It is as if our physical body, our energetic body, and our sense of boundless being are all synced up, interpenetrating and affecting one another in every way.

While kundalini is most often associated with the snake (the term itself is Sanskrit for "that which is coiled"), in traditional Hindu mythology, kundalini is sometimes referred to as a goddess—a fierce and powerful energy that works according to her own sense of timing and the evolutionary needs of the situation. Her movement through the body can be thunderous, destroying whatever energetic attachment is obstructing her free flow.

When this energy began to awaken in me, I felt afraid. (All these years later I sometimes still shake during meditation, but the good news is that I no longer feel worried when this happens.) What I have since learned is that the experience of shaking and involuntary movements (called *kriyas* in yogic literature) is a perfectly normal part of the awakening process. Kundalini is intense energy moving through the body and clearing out energetic blockages. There was never any reason for me to be panicked or afraid. And yet at the time, I lacked information. My hope is that this collection of essays on "kundalini rising" will help demystify the kundalini experience for you, providing you with the helpful information and contextual understanding you need to support your own process.

I have one further hope for this collection of essays. It is my experience that reading about kundalini can actually help catalyze the awakening process. It is as if once we understand the energy that lies within us and the pathways through which it can travel in our subtle body, we have an ability to visualize and flow with the process with heightened sensitivity. May *Kundalini Rising* help activate this natural unfolding of our expanded human potential in you, for the sake of the whole.

PART I

The Experience

*Personal Accounts and Findings from Those
Who Have Experienced Kundalini*

Kundalini and the Mystic Path

DOROTHY WALTERS, PHD

In 1981 at the age of fifty-three, Dorothy Walters experienced intense and spontaneous kundalini awakening, and the subsequent unfolding has been the center of her life ever since. With little preparation and with no external guide or mentor to lead her, she followed the promptings of her "inner guru," or what she calls "Kundalini consciousness," which led her safely through the many challenges she faced, including episodes of extreme bliss as well as pain. She describes her awakening experience, along with reflections on the kundalini process, in her book Unmasking the Rose: A Record of a Kundalini Initiation.

Now, amazed by how rapidly kundalini awareness and awakening are occurring throughout the world, Dorothy strongly believes that we are in the midst of planetary initiation into a new level of consciousness, with kundalini as the primary engine for this evolutionary leap. A retired professor and author of Marrow of Flame: Poems of the Spiritual Journey *and* A Cloth of Fine Gold: Poems of the Inner Journey, *she shares her experience in the following essay, which begins and ends with two of her poems. Here, Dorothy introduces such questions as: Does kundalini's activation of bliss and awareness, doubt and pain prepare us for another level of conscious development? Do we all have the ability to experience kundalini?*

What the heart wants
is to follow its true passion,
to lie down with it,
near the reeds beside
the river,
to devour it in the caves
between the desert dunes,
to sing its notes
into the morning sky
until even the angels wake up
and take notice
and look around
for their beloved.

THE YEAR WAS 1981. I was sitting in my living room on an elm-lined street in Kansas, reading a book that made passing reference to a phenomenon I had heard of but knew almost nothing about. The phenomenon was named *Kundalini*, said to be a "snake" that resided at the base of the spine and whose journey upward—instigated through the practice of ancient yogic techniques—would lead, ultimately, to the opening of the crown and even enlightenment. I decided to give it a try. I was in a time of personal crisis, but something inside said that I could raise these energies, even though I had never practiced yoga or meditated or, for that matter, even had a massage. Indeed, I did not even know anyone who engaged in such esoteric pursuits. As a university professor of English and women's studies, I had lived primarily in my head, with virtually no awareness of the inner energies and the life of the spirit they engaged.

I sat quietly in my chair and breathed deeply, focusing on an image of the god and goddess in union in the volume I had been reading. Suddenly I felt a ball of rapturous energy in my lower abdomen. And then, within seconds it seemed, these energies rushed upward into my head.

I felt an influx of ecstatic energy streaming into my skull while my very brain was infused with rapture. As my crown opened, it felt like "a thousand petals unfolding," just as the ancient texts describe. The experience lasted for several minutes, and, as long as I did not think about what was happening, it continued. Suddenly I realized that I was not, in fact, a separate, autonomous, self-individuated being, but merely a tiny spark in a great, indescribable, inscrutable force, the unnamed source of all that is, that which animates and powers the universe in overwhelming love. I was a fiction I told to myself, a myth I had invented. Finally, I decided to end my "experiment," since I really was not sure what was actually happening to me.

But this was not the end of the experience at all. Rather, it marked the beginnings of a long journey, which was sometimes daunting and at other times filled with rapture, one which would take me into realms I had not dreamed of and whose ends I could not foresee.

What had occurred to me on that now-distant day was "spontaneous Kundalini awakening," prompted primarily by the stress of my immediate psychological crisis and a curious convergence of circumstances. I had been catapulted into a new level of awareness, transformed in a quantum leap of staggering proportions. In Katherine Anne Porter's phrase, it was truly "the moment that changes everything."

In the days that followed, I seemed to be led forward by a consciousness beyond my own. I experienced inner visions of initiatory rites, both Tibetan Buddhist and yogic in nature, though I had no real background in either of these traditions. I held the *vajra* and the bell (the text I had been reading mentioned these sacred implements, which were unfamiliar to me—I found a reasonable facsimile of the former in the house and then a tiny bell, the only one I had). When I stood before a mirror, I saw the light around my body and saw my lips move as I heard (internally) my new name, a Sanskrit word that I did not then know but which I later interpreted to mean "truth speaker." At the same moment, I was also told that an additional part of my life's purpose was to be a healer. Kundalini itself seemed to lead me forward. But what was Kundalini?

Even now, there are few universally agreed-upon definitions or descriptions of this mysterious power. Kundalini arrives in various kinds of packaging and affects each person in a highly individual way. For each, it carries its own scent and brings its own signature. However, a few observations may be made with some confidence. Those most informed on the subject hold Kundalini to be the bioelectrical energy of the physical body (and the creative energy of the universe as a whole). It also operates as a connecting force in the various layers of the subtle energy fields that enfold the physical body. For most people, this energy typically operates by itself, well below the threshold of consciousness. It is the elemental life force, what keeps us going for as long as we are alive.

Once the Kundalini "awakens," bodily sensations and impulses come into awareness in a way not experienced before. We become incredibly sensitive to both pleasure and pain, as if the cells themselves are firing in awareness as small (or large) explosions of joy or discomfort. Generally, it is believed that pain results when there are "blockages," that is, constrictions in mind, body, emotions, or psyche. People with major unresolved psychological issues, as well as those with serious physical challenges, may be especially at risk. As the Kundalini works through the system, it flushes out these hidden blockages, and presses on until they are cleared.

This process can be difficult and troublesome, even for the most seemingly balanced and normal person. There may be episodes of intense bliss alternating with periods of severe pain. Saints are said to sustain near constant bliss, but even these exalted ones undergo episodes of suffering. For almost all of us, the two states mingle and intermix. It all depends on the subject herself. It is almost as if the Kundalini has an intelligence of its own as it presses forward—its promptings may be strong or weak at various times, but it generally continues until the task is completed.

But Kundalini is much more than an ongoing series of novel sensations. For the committed aspirant, it awakens a deep sense of connection with the divine essence, the ultimate mystery of creation itself. Often, especially during the bliss states, we feel as though these visitations come from a heavenly source, almost as if the angels have descended and enfolded us in boundless love. As one observer remarked, "Kundalini is God moving through your body." During this time, we may feel as though the Beloved Within is a real lover, who awakens each part of the self to sensuous, tender rapture or even ecstasy. We may feel hugely blessed, even though no one can say for certain what is actually taking place or where the process will lead.

As I was carried day after day into such blissful states, I had no spiritual teacher or guide to direct me or to explain what was happening. At that time, Kundalini was virtually unknown in the West, and certainly no qualified teacher or guru was to be found in the part of the country where I lived. In fact, I knew no one who had had such an experience or, for that matter, had even heard of Kundalini. I had one book on the subject, the famous work in which Gopi Krishna describes his own experience. As far as I knew, he and I were the only people on the planet who had undergone Kundalini awakening. I was on my own.

For me, this unforeseen event (in a process that continued to unfold day by day) was the holiest of holies, the most sacred of all possible human experiences. It told me that the divine was all, and that I was but a minute particle in an ongoing and unfathomable process of an unknown vastness, ultimate love itself pouring through and maintaining the entire structure of the cosmos.

Though I had no human mentor, I soon realized that I was being led by a special awareness within, an "inner guru" who utilized my own intuition and the consciousness of Kundalini itself to lead me on my way. I seemed to know instinctively what to do, how to construct a personal devotional practice, how to move, how to feel. Everything seemed right. I let myself be led by this unnamed reality into experiences that were untried yet strangely familiar. It was as though I had at last, after years of struggle and effort, finally come home.

In ancient India, yogis prepared for years for the ultimate experience of "enlightenment." They followed strict ascetic disciplines, ate a carefully controlled diet, performed obscure rituals of cleansing and purification, and mastered extreme yogic techniques. By these rigorous means, they hoped, eventually, to enter "nirvana," release from the wheel of human suffering and pain. Kundalini, carefully cultivated and controlled, was the driving force behind these efforts.

I knew nothing of such practices. Initially, I felt that I had no real preparation for the dramatic shift that had erupted in my life. But after much reflection, I realized that my life path had in fact laid a foundation for such an expansion of consciousness.

Certainly, I had been on the "seeker's path" for many years, reading such writers as Joseph Campbell (*The Hero's Journey*), Carl Jung, Mircea Eliade, T. S. Eliot, W. B. Yeats, and others who explored the fundamental questions in a serious way. And like many other spiritual explorers in that era (the sixties and seventies), I had investigated certain metaphysical and esoteric areas, such as tarot, caballa, extrasensory perception, precognition, telepathy, astrology, and even ouija work. I knew the writings of Carlos Castaneda and Jane Roberts (the Seth books) and had drenched myself in the lore of the Western goddess and felt her influence strongly in my life. I had contemplated Taoism, the connection of yin and yang, male and female, intuitive and receptive, wave and particle, the various opposites whose union is central to many initiations. (Such information is now commonplace, but in 1981 these were still fresh areas of discovery.)

So from one point of view, I had in fact prepared for this major transformation in my life on the mental and psychological levels.

And, though I did not have an outer guide to lead me, I did have one book that proved invaluable: Evelyn Underhill's classic work entitled *Mysticism*. In it, she outlines in meticulous detail the journey of the Western mystic, a description based primarily on the experience of the devoutly religious of the Christian tradition. This is not an easy book to read. It is like a reference book one returns to again and again, each time grasping a bit more of her erudite message. But this book became my guide even though she makes scant reference to Kundalini as such, for the broad stages of the mystical journey are much the same for initiates of various traditions, and the patterns of the saint are often reflected in the less celebrated ventures of the humble seeker.

Traditionally, the Western mystic path is divided into three primary stages: purgation, illumination, and union. But Underhill offers five principal stages in the mystic progression, adding awakening or conversion as the first stage, and surrender or the "Dark Night" as the next to last:

1. Awakening or conversion
2. Self-knowledge or purgation
3. Illumination
4. Surrender or the Dark Night
5. Union

Each section in her text offers invaluable insight and understanding, but she emphasizes that the stages do not always follow one another in a neat, linear progression, instead frequently overlapping or oscillating back and forth in a pattern unique to each aspirant. For modern seekers, especially those destined to follow the Kundalini path, I believe a somewhat different terminology and arrangement will be more helpful.

YEARNING AND PREPARATION

Anyone beginning a journey must first possess the desire for such an undertaking. The Sufis call this initial stage "yearning."

Spiritual yearning is indeed the sign of the serious student, one who acknowledges that something is lacking in her or his life and wishes to discover what this may be. The desire may not be pointed directly toward Kundalini arousal as such; nonetheless it is an important step in the overall process if Kundalini is to be more than a fleeting bodily sensation.

I have already described the kinds of incidental "preparation" I followed before my own key experience. Today, workshops and spiritual teachers, meditation instruction, even classes called "Kundalini Yoga" abound, so that the eager student can find many ways to expand consciousness. Practices once considered esoteric are now commonplace. Information formerly confined to a select few is now readily available, often rewritten in transparent language for the ordinary reader. And, though some of the current efforts are somewhat superficial or blatantly commercial, some see this current wave of interest as leading toward worldwide expansion of consciousness and planetary initiation.

AWAKENING

Whatever the preliminaries, the moment of deep awakening into fuller awareness, whether that of the Christian convert or the Kundalini initiate, entails an abrupt shift in worldview and sense of self. This is the time of "unselfing," the swallowing up of the limited sense of identity into the larger awareness of an Absolute that knows no limits. We realize that this ineffable source, this indefinable reality that has so swiftly torn down all defenses and poured into our very selves, is, in fact, all that is, for we are mere indiscernible atoms in this immeasurable process, and we are humbled by this knowledge. For some, this is not welcome information—they resist giving up the ego's claim to selfhood. For others, this is the time to revel in the new sense of beauty, of Oneness, of the splendor of all that makes up our perceived reality. We are in a very literal sense reborn, made new, and we emerge from our encounter wearing new garments in which to greet the world. At last, our being is complete. Finally, we know who we are.

This blissful opening may persist as a state of unbroken joy and exultation for weeks or months, with ecstatic energies bringing daily rapture to the engaged practitioner. This is the time when the senses may become eerily acute, and new capacities such as long-distance sight and hearing may occur. The disciple may sense wondrous odors or hear beautiful music within. Everything seems fresh and new. The world has been remade, and we reside in a newfound Garden of Eden, the original paradise of mythology. These are universal symptoms of the awakened mystic.

If the Kundalini is flowing, the daily love-play with the inner paramour tells us that the Beloved Within in not merely a symbol or myth, but a reality experienced as fully as if a human lover were involved. Merely lifting an arm or breathing in a certain pattern can stimulate remarkably sensuous delight. Music may convey sensations of rapture beyond the power of description. This, then, is heaven on earth.

It is during this time that the initiates of many traditions may recapitulate the ancient themes of the divine lover come to pursue the human partner on earth. Myth and archetypes from across the world tell a universal story of gods and goddesses descending to lure and seduce the human below. We think of Zeus and his wanton escapades, Krishna and the maidens, the goddesses East and West who enrapture their human partners. The most familiar of these narratives is that of the Virgin, impregnated by the Holy Spirit in order to bear the Divine Child. Even nuns are said to be brides of Christ.

Likewise, when we are in the throes of intense Kundalini arousal we may, in our imaginations, become love partners of various divine beings, from angels to assorted goddess/god figures to Christ himself. This state resembles (and for the aspirant is) the mystic marriage, the ultimate union of human and divine such as that described by St. Teresa of Avila and St. John of the Cross.

BALANCING: BLISS INTERMINGLED WITH PAIN

As the system adjusts to the new frequencies now at play within, there are often oscillations between times of pleasure and episodes of suffering. Periods of ecstatic love-play may be abruptly interrupted by sessions of discomfort or distress such as massive headaches, digestive problems, eyestrain, seeming heart irregularities, dizziness, anxiety, and other disorders for which no physical basis can be found. The distress may occur now here, now there, moving from organ to organ, system to system, as if the Kundalini were indeed clearing the overall organism, purging and releasing in search of a stable point of balance. Underhill points out that even the high saints may undergo such trials.

Many have noted that when the suffering becomes too intense, at the moment when they think they can bear no further stress, the Kundalini-begotten pressures will withdraw and allow a period of rest before the next challenge appears. It is as if the Kundalini is conscious of our limits and knows when to back away and when to resume.

For the committed mystic of the traditional path, this period of "purgation" is often a time of deep introspection, of examination of the soul to root out all its imperfections and weaknesses. Extreme ascetics of both East and West sometimes resort to rites of mortification, or severe regimens of fasting and prayer, to bring the soul into a state of perfection. Sins are brought to light and rituals of penance imposed.

However, for the modern aspirant, it is often psychological issues or lifestyle practices that call for attention. Now is the time to seek meaningful psychological help for all the lingering wounds of childhood or societally imposed traumas, to deal with what has been repressed in order to survive in an often unkind world. Those who are self-rejecting need to learn to accept and love themselves as worthy and lovable beings, for it is said that self-deprecation can be as great an obstacle to realization as is ego inflation.

Also, many now realize that the diet needs adjustment, that harmful habits of excess of various kinds (such as addictions), unresolved conflicts, and other destructive patterns of behavior all need to be confronted.

For the latent issues will come up and demand to be dealt with, and emotions may run strong. It has often been noted that meditation itself can bring into consciousness painful past issues still awaiting attention, much to the surprise of those expecting to enter unbroken bliss in the new state. Likewise, Kundalini acts as a "teacher to the soul," pointing out in unmistakable ways those areas needing to be healed.

THE TRUE DARK NIGHT

Although the initial awakening may have been preceded by a time of grief and despair, Underhill asserts that the most trying dark night of the soul comes at a later stage. After the bliss, after the many convolutions and returns, there is, suddenly, a seeming withdrawal of divine favor. Bliss, which may have become a regular feature of one's life, suddenly departs, and one is left to ponder what has gone wrong. For the Christian disciple, the feeling is often one of profound despair, as if God has simply turned his face away from an unworthy subject. And, for those on the Kundalini path, the effect is much the same.

We feel that somehow, we did not measure up, or we failed the final test, and now we are left to dwell in the perpetual awareness of acute loss. According to Underhill, this grief is greater than any experienced earlier, because we have now "tasted God," known the deep splendor of divine acceptance.

The Christian saint thrown into this abyss of despair must make final surrender, acknowledge and repent all sins and weakness, and allow herself to be guided by divine authority into favor once more. The lesson is much the same for the Kundalini novice—we discover (again) that the journey is not under our control, that it is directed by some still-mysterious force seemingly both within and outside the self. We must release all attempts to guide or force a return to the earlier state, and simply stand still and wait in patience and humility for the renewal of connection.

Some ask why it is that once we have sampled "paradise" on this plane, it is then so often snatched away from us, and pain and forms of "dis-ease" ensue. Why can we not continue in this elevated state in which all was bathed in the bliss of limitless love and our bodies and souls seemed to exist (finally) in total accord?

To begin with, we have to remember that when Kundalini is awakened into consciousness, we are (if we are among the lucky ones) more or less removed from this world into an inner Eden. We exist and feel in ways we have never experienced before. We are like babes enjoying the total attention and devotion of mothers who dote on us and give us constant love and support.

And then, suddenly, our Edenic world fades, and we become aware of the pressures of the outside world. The mother-force vanishes (or diminishes radically), and we are on our own in a disturbed, sometimes uncaring, sometimes threatening world. We realize we have to do more than sit and sigh in rapture, that we have to earn a living, care for the urgent needs of friends and families (who may be facing major challenges in their own lives), and attend to our own health, which may appear to falter. Old psychological wounds may again surface and demand attention, and old physical scars may ache once more.

The first period is the honeymoon time of Kundalini. It can last for days or weeks or possibly even years, but at some point (at least for most of us) it will take a different turn. The honeymoon is now over, and we must deal with some very urgent issues before we are ready to go forward to the next stage. What we have experienced thus far is a massive leap into another level of existence. That part was easy. Now the real work begins.

So we must go back yet again, deal with all the remaining unfinished business in our lives, learn new ways of coping with the world and its stressors, and find new methods to maintain balance. This is our time of deep purification, of making ourselves ready to sustain these new energies and this new way of life in a more consistent way.

And then, in the midst of our struggle, the blissful energies return, and all is in harmony once more. We know we are on the right course. We are in alignment with source and so move ahead. Even now, though we make discernable progress, we suffer setbacks and returns, shifts and oscillations, as we continue our struggle on this uneven and unpredictable path. The rewards are many, but the cost may be extreme.

Now our responses may become more sensitive than ever, bringing alternately bliss and pain. Coming into the presence of a highly evolved spiritual teacher or group may evoke sensuous energies of delight. Sacred places, sacred objects, and works of art, literature, or music may serve as triggers for stirring the sweet vibrations within. Bowing before a representation of Buddha may send streams of ineffable delight into the head. A passing stranger may bring a sudden opening of the heart chakra. The possibilities seem endless, each encounter bringing a shift in tone and feeling.

Likewise, unpleasant encounters with disturbing persons, witnessing unexpected conflicts in the street, even harsh noises such as a car backfiring may send flashes of pain through the system.

As the process continues, our energies become ever more delicate, ever more refined. What once arrived as a great storm of thunder and lightning now comes quietly, resembling soft rain falling on the trees in the forest. At first, we may have practiced the strenuous asanas of yoga to send the exquisite energies streaming, but now a bit of music, a gentle turning of wrist or hand may be sufficient to stir the familiar bliss flows.

Each initiate undergoes a different experience, even a different sequence of events. Some may never experience the bliss despite years of devoted practice. Some may discover suffering rather than joy. What I am describing is the pattern I am most familiar with, and which resembles in certain ways that of some others. There are, indeed, many paths up the mountain, and Kundalini selects its own course.

AFTERMATH

Kundalini is at once the most personal and the most universal experience we can have. It strikes at the very heart of the self, touches and transforms it in every imaginable way, and leaves it in a state of unending change and adjustment. Although there are some common features, each person undergoes the initiation process in a unique way. The beginning circumstances, the unfolding, the mental and psychological responses are decidedly our own, unlike those of any other.

Often, the seeker's experience is framed in terms already familiar: Taoist alchemy, tantric yoga, Native American spirituality, goddess lore, Buddhism, Sufism, Christianity—whatever has captured the seeker's imagination in the past or is now thrust into consciousness may become the template for this overwhelming life event. And the discoveries (whether mental or emotional) that manifest during this critical juncture come as radically new insights, holy mysteries revealed for the first time.

These revelations are precious, for they carry the initiate into the heart of the sacred, a world one has longed for but never before clearly discerned. The initiation is unique, a gift to be treasured and revered.

At the same time, deep spiritual transformation is itself a universal human experience, one with a very long history across time and space. Whether it is the journey of the Christian mystic into divine union or the Sufi seeker yearning for the Beloved, the story of the soul's encounter with inner reality carries certain features common to a great many traditions and lineages. Kundalini operates as the basis for all such entries into transcendence, and it will emerge into consciousness for many on the path, whatever their orientation, for it is the vibration of the ultimate mystery that constantly calls us to awakening.

In addition to the traditional stages of the mystic path that Underhill and others have discussed, there are also certain recurrent motifs or themes that seem to run through many personal accounts of spontaneous inner transformation. Here are some that come readily to mind:

- The sense of loneliness before the moment of awakening. We know that something is missing in our lives, but we don't know exactly what. We may have lived in essential isolation from the world at large, with a sense that we are "not of this time, not of this place."
- The feeling that we are now a "new being" whose transformed state is not perceived by the world, including our closest associates. We appear to be the "old self," but are in fact a "new self" in disguise.
- The feeling that we have been granted a gift we have not earned. We ask, "How could this happen to me, of all people?"
- The difficulty of expressing such ineffable experience in words. How can we adequately articulate the indescribable?
- Questioning whether we are indeed undergoing authentic spiritual transformation or instead are victims of some abnormal biological or neural imbalance. (Am I awakened or deluded?)
- Deep hesitation over sharing such intimate and unfamiliar experience with others. How could anyone else possibly understand?
- Further, such revelation might seem to diminish the sacred nature of the encounter, or, worse, appear as some form of boasting or ego inflation.
- The sense that our own experience is part of a larger process of universal change, of planetary initiation, whose ends and ultimate purpose no one knows.

The goal of the mystical journey is, for the religious, permanent union with the higher being, total surrender of self—annihilation into God. St. Teresa of Avila and St. John of the Cross in the Western tradition are examples, as are the many holy men and women of the East who often abandon all involvement with the things of this world and retreat into remote caves or forests in order to maintain their state of connection with this ineffable reality.

But most of us do not commit our lives to such demanding paths. Rather, we continue on our course of balancing and discovery, moving always to new levels of stability as we learn to live "in the world and out of it." We are like the hero who, at the end of his journey, does not turn away from the world but seeks a way to "bring the treasure back home." We know that at this critical time the planet needs all the help it can get from whatever quarter. Some become healers; some share the wisdom they have gained through speaking or writing, music, or the visionary arts (becoming technicians of the sacred); some accept humble occupations of service. In the East, this is called the way of the bodhisattva, one who foregoes personal enlightenment to help others as they progress.

Kundalini is the goddess force, the ultimate creative energy, the dynamism that keeps the world alive. It is the power resting at the heart of every entity and being in the universe. It lies for most of us in quiescent form, a sleeping serpent ready to rise within and lift us to unimaginable levels of ecstatic union with ultimate reality. It is then that we know that It and we ourselves are One, that this inscrutable source not only defines but comprises who we are, for we in ourselves are nothing but pulsating atoms within this infinite consciousness.

In the midst of chaos, planetary awakening is occurring, at times arriving in unexpected places and manifesting in unlikely circumstances. Sometimes a result of laborious preparation and discipline, sometimes as pure gift, it is, I believe, the path to the new consciousness and the means of our survival as we transition into the next stage of species evolution.

You may think
that first lit flame
was the ultimate blaze,
the holy fire revealed.
What do you know
of furnaces?
This is a sun that returns
again and again, refining, igniting,
pouring your spirit
through a cloth of fine gold
until all dross is taken
and you are sweet as
clarified butter
in God/the Goddess' mouth.

Kundalini

The Role of Life-Force Energy in Self-Realization[1]

BONNIE GREENWELL, PHD

Bonnie Greenwell, author of Energies of Transformation: A Guide to the Kundalini Process, *personally experienced kundalini and has spent decades working with people who have had spiritual awakenings. In the essay that follows, she introduces us to the different ways in which kundalini can be awakened, as well as discussing the true function of kundalini. Greenwell also explores the relationship between kundalini and the illusion of a separate identity. She shares her findings on how many kundalini awakenings result in true enlightenment and how we may get closer to a genuine spiritual awakening by asking the simple question: "Who am I?"*

I HAD BEEN a meditator for fifteen years, intermittently practicing the teachings of Swami Muktananda, Paramahansa Yogananda, and Zen Buddhism, which I learned from teachers and books, when I first experienced the awakening of kundalini. It was 1984, and I was forty-three, married with three children, and a doctoral student at the Institute of Transpersonal Psychology.

At that time, I was beginning to do Radiance Breathwork with Gay Hendricks, longing to let go of any barriers to the realization of God. Radiance Breathwork is a combination of deep breathing and neo-Reichian bodywork, aimed at releasing contractions held in the cellular and muscular structures. This practice involves lying on a massage table and doing deep or rapid breathing practices while the therapist presses trigger points in the body.

I had gone to class one day after having had an energy session with Gay. While sitting in that somewhat dull classroom, ripples of pleasurable energy began rolling up my spine to the top of my head. Increasing in frequency and intensity, similar to the experience of labor pains, they became stronger and stronger until I soon felt intoxicated with bliss. I stumbled out of the classroom and found a quiet space to meditate, intuiting that bringing this bliss into stillness was the best thing to do.

This experience initiated weeks of emotional and psychological shifts, through which I felt intensely drawn to meditate, found great expansiveness in silence, and from time to time felt waves of spontaneous ecstasy. Self-consciousness fell away, my heart felt wide open and loving, and I experienced an inner happiness I had never known before. Sometimes waves of emotion would flush through me that I could not explain. Often my body would go into spontaneous shaking and releasing, especially when I was trying to relax, sleep, get bodywork, or meditate. Gradually the intensity subsided, but the energy events continued on a quieter level. It was always internal and felt like a sweet humming, an easy shift of consciousness that produced subtle blissful feelings.

I began to meet people who were personally familiar with the experience I was having—in spiritual circles, in training programs, and at the Esalen Institute—many of whom had difficult and dramatic stories to tell. I began to wonder why I was having mostly positive experiences, by contrast to others I was meeting. As I had to choose a dissertation topic that year, this question became the basis of my doctoral research. I set out to learn everything I could about both ancient and modern experiences of kundalini. This unfolded into many exciting years of meeting people from all walks of life who had known these experiences, and to exploring the commonalities and uniqueness of these awakenings.

This awakening was not the end of my spiritual realization, but rather the beginning of it—the beginning of the restructuring of the energy and quality of perception that self-realization demands. Such awakenings may occur gradually and gently, suddenly and violently, blissfully or with huge medical and emotional challenges. Over the years since this energy came alive in me, it has led me on a marvelous adventure, seeking truth, meeting others who have walked these paths, and pushing me to express my discoveries as simply and broadly as possible.

The term *kundalini* comes from the Sanskrit word *kunda*, meaning coiled. In the Indian perspective, the life energy (also the energy of consciousness) comes into the egg through the sperm during conception, stimulates the growth of the fetus, and coils at the base of the spine—where it rests in stasis throughout our lives. At the time of death it leaves the body, returning into the universal field. When this energy opens and moves up through the body before death, this event is called *kundalini awakening*.

When kundalini becomes awakened within us, it feels like the life force has amplified itself and has suddenly become even more alive. This is felt in its movement up the spine and sometimes as an electrical or radiating feeling in every cell. This sensation can be uncomfortable, pleasurable, terrifying, or ecstatic—or all of these at once. Our natural energy—which has quietly danced through our bodies up until this point, carrying the messages of the mind and senses through the nervous system—has slipped into a higher vibration, completely disrupting the status quo. Along with major energy shifts, the functioning of our consciousness and mind changes, and our ways of defining who we are begin to fall apart. Nothing in our education or previous experience prepares us for this eruption, for it is not spoken about in most spiritual circles, and Western spiritual concepts have succeeded in separating most people from appreciation of the role of the body in spiritual awakening—a role that was probably better understood in early pagan and ancient tribal practices, as well as in secret mystery schools. That is why those who have researched kundalini energy have found their best evidence for explaining it in systems that predate Christianity—such as Indian yoga, tantra, Chinese Qigong, Hawaiian Huna, and the rising of energy demonstrated in some ancient indigenous practices.

ACTIVITIES THAT AWAKEN KUNDALINI

Most advanced yoga practices, as well as other systems of energy practice, include activities that have the possibility of awakening kundalini energy. Such practices may include breathing, holding specific postures, focusing one's concentration, emptying the mind of thought, imagining complex visualizations, chanting, and taking part in specific movements. Some emphasize the transmission (known as *diksha* or *shaktipat*) through touch or eye contact or simply the presence of a teacher, while others emphasize devotion and service as a foundation for this awakening.

Because of the powerful upheaval the kundalini awakening may produce—and its capacity to destabilize the personality structure—these practices have traditionally been reserved for those practitioners who have spent many years in preparation. Apparently, the more one lives a healthy and stress-free lifestyle, with reliable teachers and simple daily routines, the more smoothly the process of living authentically with this energy can progress. Most classical ways of dealing with kundalini energy are based on this expectation, and many well-qualified kundalini guides or gurus are simply not available to those who have sudden and unpredictable awakenings, because such guides only work directly with people who are committed to the structure of the system they use.

Unfortunately, many teachers of meditation, yoga, and tantra are not prepared for a student's spontaneous and confusing awakening of energy, as they have never worked through the process themselves. Moreover, many students who seek spiritual awakening do not understand the dynamics involved and are not interested in making the major life changes that support the process. Many spiritual seekers are naive in their understanding of the major psychological and physical changes involved in spiritual awakening. This can lead to resistance, fear, and other reactions that make the awakening process more challenging.

This lack of understanding on the part of the teachers and lack of preparation on the part of the students leave many thousands of people floundering each year, having had awakenings that occurred spontaneously, were reactive to life circumstances, or were related to practices they did without adequate guidance. As a therapist and educator specializing in this issue, I have met people from dozens of countries, in many spiritual traditions, of all ages, who have had radical awakenings of energy and were unable to find people within their traditions who could offer them useful guidance. Among them have been Buddhist monks, Catholic nuns, kundalini yoga teachers, fundamentalist Christians, young college students, people doing tantric sexual practices, people who had read a book and tried the practices in it, those who did modern breathwork practices, those who had overextended themselves using biofeedback, and masters of martial arts. Aside from practices, this energy awakens for many reasons including devotion, meditation, intense love, shock, childbirth, drug use, sexual or physical abuse, automobile accidents, and being struck by lightning. Does this mean we should avoid all of these things? We can't, and we shouldn't. It only means we should understand that we as humans are energy fields, wired to wake up to our true nature, and thus may encounter an awakening at any given time—if our number comes up! We have the possibility to wake up whether we plan to or not.

The reason this experience is so closely tied to the yoga and tantric models is because the positive aspects of such awakenings were recognized in these traditions, and methodologies were developed several thousand years ago to facilitate them. However, the experience is beyond methodology, and beyond any form of spirituality. It is a human experience, a movement within our own energy body that triggers not only energetic changes but a major shift in human identity.

When correctly understood, the process of kundalini awakening can lead us into a profound cellular knowing of our true nature, which wakes itself up and puts us in touch with a wisdom that lies beneath personal identifications and the conditioned mind. This is the internal process through which the human race can evolve into a kinder, more wise, and more compassionate species. That is why this energy awakens not only in those who undertake kundalini yoga or other energy practices, but in many who do Buddhist meditation, Christian contemplation, intense psychological introspection—or nothing at all.

THE TRUE FUNCTION OF KUNDALINI

Some systems and individuals have thought of kundalini awakening as a way to gain powers, referred to as *siddhis* in the Indian traditions. Working with energy is also recognized as bringing personal power in the Chinese Qigong systems. As kundalini heightens and transforms the capacities of both the energy system and brain, it is not unusual for individuals to experience sudden psychic or healing abilities, a much deeper quality of presence, and intuitive responsiveness to formerly stressful situations. As presence increases, the senses become more alert, and the body feels more alive and harmonious. Gopi Krishna, an Indian sage who wrote extensively about his own awakening experiences, felt that kundalini was the energy responsible for genius, and encouraged scientific research to study it. I think it is more correct to say that as the life force heightens and clears away old patterns of thinking, making the mind more clear and open, a more direct form of intuitive wisdom becomes available when needed. There is a heightened perception of how things work on the collective level and an impersonal capacity to address issues or situations with an intention to support the common good. It is also possible that, in some individuals, formerly inactive energy patterns in the brain become activated that increase intelligence, or at least broaden the understanding of human experience.

It is important to understand, however, that the ultimate capacity of kundalini is not about creating powerful people. Rather, its power has to do with stripping away our illusions of separateness and our attachments to our own personal history. Kundalini leaves us with a sense of vastness within and a connection with the entire field of consciousness—both in its essential stillness and in its expression as form. Another way to say this is that it ends in a sense of being one with all, appreciative of all, unattached to any form or experience, and thus in great peace. Fully awakened people may fall into many roles but have no attachment to them, responding to circumstances from an authentic movement within that feels impersonal. They are unlikely to tell you they are awakened, because they know the form they appear to be is just a shadow or an illusion based on a conditioned mind, and that what is really awake, is this force of consciousness within that has always been awake and is the same force in everyone and everything. Those who think they are special and deserve special attention for their spiritual attainment have not honestly fulfilled the possibility of this process, but are caught in a cul-de-sac where their separate identity has usurped the natural unfolding into Self.

For most people kundalini awakening continues over many years and includes challenging experiences—both crushing and ecstatic, paradoxically—before there is a sense of completion. You can find evidence of this in the biographies of people like Gopi Krishna, Krishnamurti, Muktananda, Motoyama, and other individuals who have recorded their stories. During this process there may be a lingering attachment and a periodic return to a sense of a separate "me." As the kundalini energy unfolds itself throughout the energy system, there can also be a sense of doing battle inside. The ego may glimpse its own irrelevance and fight to preserve itself in both gross and subtle ways. As the life force intensifies through our subtle body field, we can have problems with old physical wounds, latent illnesses, appetite, and sexual urges, as well as the upheaval of emotions, heightened sensitivity, sudden memories of repressed history, or sudden waves of anger, grief, fear, or love that feel beyond the personal. Some bodies occasionally feel electrified, overheated, or chilled. The adrenal and hormonal systems may go haywire. Some people may not be able to tolerate crowds or negative energy in others. Psychic openings and other paranormal experiences can occur. Some feel at times that their heart has stopped. Startling images, lights, or symbols may appear in the twilight zones of consciousness, such as before falling asleep or when thoughts are drifting inattentively. Some report visions or internal music and sounds. It isn't surprising that many people feel they are physically ill or dying, and that often their doctors search vainly for evidence to support this and end up attributing their symptoms to a mental illness.

TYPES OF AWAKENING

In rare circumstances, kundalini energy may be present from birth. In these individuals, the energy system was always more open and receptive than the average—less in stasis, less focused. These people may be more prone to what we label "mystical" or "psychic" experiences. Such children may report or demonstrate unusual capacities, which might be labeled genius or mental instability, depending on the perspectives of their culture and families. Others simply grow up with a perception and openness that are far beyond the norm of their society.

In others, kundalini energy opens itself gently and over time. This type of gradual awakening seems to move slowly through the chakra system, which is a series of vortexes located in what is called the subtle energy field along the spine. Gradual movements of kundalini can almost be charted, depending on where the transformative energies are active at the moment. For example, there may be intense sexual activity, heat or vibration in the lower chakras for a while, and then stomach gurgling and jerking and eating issues, and later a great awareness of the heart contracting, followed by a release into expansiveness and love. The arising of old emotional

memories and even apparent past-life memories is usually corre-
lated with energy in the third chakra (solar plexus), which seems to
hold a cellular bundle of old hurts and injustices. It is also common
for people to have blockages around the throat, because most of us
have many contractions related to things we felt but never said, or
moments when we were silenced, slapped, or shut down by fear. If
this is the case, there may be a twisting of the neck, trouble swallowing, or just simply a sense that the body jerks and vibrates up
to the neck and no further. Great creative outpourings sometimes
occur when blockages are released in the neck, while kundalini is
flowing there but hasn't yet penetrated the chakras above it.[2]

Spiritual experiences occur in many ways, including an overwhelming feeling of loving or being held by love (heart chakra),
or visions of gods, goddesses, or other beings and also light phenomena (third eye). As the brain begins to respond to the heightened energy, we become opened to the possibly of merging into
a sense of being that is unbounded, with inexplicable vastness,
universal consciousness, or being one with everything and having
no separate self. Blissful vibrations and ecstatic sensations may
occur from time to time.

In her remarkable book, *My Stroke of Insight*, Harvard-trained
neuroanatomist Jill Bolte Taylor, PhD, describes a stroke she had at
age thirty-seven, in which her left brain shut down and she experienced clear awareness of dominant right-brain functioning. This
caused significant changes in her personality and world perspective.
Her descriptions of right-brain activity include many phenomena
described by mystics, such as having a realization of herself as one
with everything and as a consciousness that has eternal life. She tells
us her "right mind character is adventurous, celebrative of abundance, and socially adept." She also says it is empathic, accurately
identifies emotions, is open to the eternal flow, and is the seat of
"my divine mind, the knower, the wise woman, and the observer."[3]

In reading this, I was struck by the fact that almost all spiritual
practices are activities that would stimulate right-brain functioning

and discourage left-brain dominance. So it appears to me that kundalini awakening, among other things, activates the dormant potentials of the right brain, "lighting up" these capacities, which then makes it possible for consciousness to experience itself in a new and greatly expanded way. Once activated, the brain is no longer dominated by the divisive and separating intellectual tendencies of the left side. This is not to say that left-brain activity is not useful; it allows us to function in many practical ways in the world and understand how to interact with the details of existence. But in this narrowing of perspective, or excessive activity in the left brain, it is easy to fail to recognize the source from which we arise, and the joy and appreciation of the oneness we share with others.

Kundalini energy, or the life force, may expand gently and quietly in some people, or move steadily, like an overflowing river bouncing up the chakras in others, bringing shifts in consciousness along with physical and psychic eruptions. But in a few people it explodes like a geyser, and they feel like they are blowing apart.

Adyashanti, a modern nondual teacher, experienced such an event after five years of Zen meditation, a practice which he is inclined to say was a failure because the awakening occurred when he had a moment of completely giving up hope in his meditation practice. It is clear he experienced a shift of the ground of consciousness, for after this event he felt himself to be essentially the whole of life or source of all, not the separate self. In a personal interview we recorded in 2002, he described his experience this way:

> It happened after about five years of serious spiritual practice. It came while I was meditating—I was actually working on a koan—and I had been sitting for no more than a couple minutes when I achieved total and absolute and utter frustration. I had spent a lot of my practice and spiritual life being unable to penetrate. In the direct school you can spend a lot of time being utterly frustrated—you either get it or you don't.

You have no gradual cultivation to feel good about, at least if you have enlightenment on your mind, as I did. So I hit this point of utter frustration, and at that moment there was also a moment of utter letting go, almost a complete defeat. It was something that was sort of spontaneous: it wasn't a decision, just a complete letting go in the mind and the body and everything, and as soon as it was happening there was just an explosion of what people call kundalini.

For me, it was just that—an explosion—and I could see the energy inside my body with a sort of inner vision, and my heart was pounding, and I was breathing really heavily. So that was the awakening of the energy, and very, very quickly I was quite certain that the energy itself was going to kill me physically. It wasn't that I was afraid of this. I just had knowledge that it was going to happen if it kept up much longer. As soon as I realized this was going to kill me, the very next thought that ran through my mind was "If this is what it takes to be enlightened, then okay, just go ahead and die." This was a spontaneous thought, too, not a thought because I was in the middle of a catastrophe internally. As soon as that arose—"I'm willing to die now"—as soon as the decision was made, the energy stopped in the blink of an eye. The rest is very hard to describe, but I was in infinite space. I was the space and there was just complete emptiness and then there was just a download of information, almost like the deepest spiritual insights that were coming like a hundred to a thousand a second, way too fast for thought. It was an intuitive thing, but there were also utter stillness and utter silence.

This whole thing played itself out in a half hour. Afterward, I got up from my cushion and bowed to the Buddha figure, and all of a sudden the wisdom came, and I started to laugh hysterically. I realized I had been

chasing the Buddha for the past five years with great
intensity and that what I was chasing was what I am.
There was great laughter and relief, and the whole thing
just seemed to be such an amazing joke. And when I
went outside the world seemed to be sparkling and just
alive, and I could see intuitively the oneness of everything. But the kundalini energy, as soon as I was ready
and willing to die, it just imploded upon itself. So I
didn't take it out the door with me—it was almost as if
it just ran its course in fifteen minutes.

Adyashanti has described this experience as the beginning of a
series of awakenings; the others were more subtle and related to
shifts of identity and consciousness rather than kundalini. In his
teachings he does not emphasize kundalini, but rather the realization of true nature through stillness, sensing into the nature of
awareness, or inquiry. Few people have the kind of dramatic and
explosive energy awakening he describes.

THE NONDUAL ASPECT OF AWAKENING

The sense of losing the separate "me" and knowing oneself to be
essentially nothing, but recognizing a mysterious sense of existing
that continues nonetheless, is the equivalent of the words of Jesus,
"I am that I am," or of the Indian Master Nisardagatta's expression,
"I am That," or the Buddha's insight, "There is no self." Although
it cannot be described in a way that allows the unawakened mind
to understand it, this experience is pointed to by mystics of every
tradition. To know it beyond considering it as a concept—instead,
to know it as if consciousness has fallen out of all identification
with time, structure, and the body—is called awakening to our
true nature in the Buddhist tradition. Systems of nondual teachings such as Advaita Vedanta in Hinduism, or Zen and Dzogchen
in Buddhism, emphasize this aspect of awakening rather than the
kundalini energy aspect.

I have listened to the kundalini stories of more than a thousand people in the past twenty-five years, and it is clear that many have experienced sweeping life changes, but few have actually found themselves fully awakened. Many have had glimpses of their true nature along with all the other phenomena stimulated by this energy movement. Some spiritual systems recognize this "glimpse" as what they call *satori,* or identify it as an early stage of *samadhi.* In the Christian tradition it is perhaps known as union with God or Christ consciousness. It appears in near-death literature in descriptions of people who are dying, so it seems that most of us may have that moment of opportunity as the personal attachment to living begins to fall away in the dying experience. This is clearly implied in the various versions of the ancient *Book of the Dead* that chronicle the interior process of dying.[4]

I have noticed in many spiritual practitioners that when spiritual emergence happens, there is such delight—such joy in the phenomena of bliss, merging, and expansiveness that occur at certain points of a kundalini awakening—that the practitioners become attached to repeating these experiences, and despair arises when they pass (as all experiences do). Their minds then take on the task of finding the perfect experience, a moment of transcendence that will not pass, so they can stay in this vast sense of being more than life, or in a place that is so much better than life, forever.

It is a great moment when kundalini has moved through its passages and given us even a brief taste of transcendence. As humans we find these moments very seductive, for they are higher and more ecstatic than any other experience we have in our lives. But this is not the completion of the awakening process—a fact rarely discussed in spiritual circles. Becoming attached to these moments pulls us back into the separate sense of self, makes us vulnerable again to disappointment when the moments pass away, and can make us think we are special. This is because it feels like "I" am having an experience that "I" need to have, or want to have, often. But the natural fulfillment of this process is actually the recognition that there is no real "I" and that the term is only a subtle, felt sense that acts as a locater for a movement happening in apparent time.

I didn't notice until I moved deeply into the teachings of Advaita Vedanta and Zen Buddhism, long after my own kundalini awakening, that some wisdom teachers have emphasized the non-existence of a separate self. This is horrifying from an individual's point of view, especially in someone who has spent decades developing and individuating this separate self. Our minds hold numerous concepts that define who we are, and our emotions become very dramatic whenever we feel this conceptual "me" is threatened. Of course, there is a sense of a separate me, which I have called "the locater," that represents consciousness contained in an individual body. But if we really search inside to find the source of this "I" we think we are, instead of just taking it for granted, we open a true portal into the nature of life itself. As Adyashanti often says, what spiritual seekers need to question is "Who is the seeker? What is it that is looking for enlightenment?" If you do not go to thought for an answer, what is this "I"? Ramana Maharshi, the sage who inspired modern Advaita Vedanta or nondual teachings, had only one suggestion for practice—asking "Who am I?"[5]

In the kundalini process it is easy to miss this questioning because we are struggling so hard to deal with the deconstruction of personal self that kundalini creates, with its intense and relentless shaking of both body and consciousness. Whether we are trying to stop what is happening or are working hard to encourage it with practices, we are strengthening ourselves as someone who does something, and feeling ourselves to be a someone this is happening to. I feel like "I" must take action! Some people spend their lives struggling against all the challenges of kundalini, fearful that they are being invaded or destroyed by a relentless intruder that has overwhelmed them with an energy that will take away their life as they know it. And in many ways, they are right. This energy process is stripping away many of their identifications, and can make them feel physically uncomfortable or disoriented for a long time. But if even for a moment they can get a glimpse of what they truly are, a pure consciousness beyond the confines of the dreamed-up and conditioned separate self, they will know that it is this that wants to take them over: the real Self, the Self of openness and universal stillness that is beneath all existence and holds a possibility of unlimited love, wisdom, and compassion—because it knows it is the source of All.

The mind cannot hold this, cannot possibly accept this. So this falling into truth has been called surrender. How it feels and what it means cannot possibly be described from one mind to another, so teachers of nonduality can only offer pointers and encouragement. It is much more simple, comforting, and fulfilling to directly recognize what I am than to collect beautiful and dramatic spiritual experiences. And once this recognition occurs, the kundalini experience, along with the attachment to a personal life and the spiritual searching, are simply seen as aspects of the nature of human form and the mystery of existence. After this, kundalini usually settles down into a quiet hum.

A PEACEFUL OUTCOME

When we rest as consciousness without an attachment to "me," kundalini may unfold itself, and we are not troubled by its methods, just as the world unfolded its appearance and we are not troubled by that either. This is what has been called by mystics and teachers "the peace that passes understanding," or interior happiness without a reason, or mystery. We could make guesses about how this releasing of personal attachment occurs through specific energy movements or patterns in the physical or energetic bodies (either gradually or suddenly) as the person's karma or conditioning may dictate, and perhaps this would offer some comfort to the academic or scientifically structured left brain. But when kundalini has completed its journey and consciousness has been directly known, freed from its entanglements with our separate identity, there is such a sense of truth and of seeing existence as a joyous mystery that analytical approaches to it seem burdensome at best.

After the kundalini force has opened us into awakening, it may complete itself by settling back into the source (of energy and consciousness), which Ramana Maharshi described as being on the right side of the chest parallel to the heart, a few finger-widths from the sternum.[6] Some systems of yoga emphasize that after the transcendent knowledge of Oneness, kundalini energy needs to fall back into the heart, its source, so that one is reconnected to form, to life. Buddhism emphasizes awakening as a here-and-now realization of what is, not being lost in a transcendent space. In Qigong, the chi energy is said to be circulating and harmonizing when the process is complete. This is a time of returning into a full acceptance of the world as a play of the divine. In less spiritualized terms, we know that all the forms of life are no less beautiful or sacred than the experience of the formless, and our sense of needing to change anything about ourselves is gone. Instead, we feel we have access to wisdom when we need it and harbor a sense of quietness deep inside. It has been called living outside of time, or being in the flow of the moment, or being in the unknown, all of which suggest that we are no longer tied to past memories, personal agendas, or mental conditioning.

Clearly, most people do not dwell continually in this state of Being, not even those who have had lifelong kundalini activity and profound spiritual openings. Awakening can be clear and true, and is always real, even when it lasts for only a moment. But relaxing into the living of it can take many years of seeing through and abandoning our old patterns and concepts and structures, which will arise often or occasionally, following the realization of Self. Kundalini is the way the energetic body deconstructs these old patterns and brings them to awareness, so we can see how insubstantial they are. It also seems to activate new potentials in the brain, or *brain centers,* as the yogis say. For these purposes it accompanies our evolution into living from the truth of what we are.

We can call this kundalini activity spiritual awakening or simply the way the universe is playing itself into conscious recognition of its own roots.

Kundalini

Unfolding the Human Design

PENNY KELLY

━━━━━━━━━

Penny Kelly is the author of five books, including The Evolving Human *and* Consciousness and Energy *and a teacher of consciousness and personal development at Lily Hill Farm and Learning Center in Lawton, Michigan. After thirty years of experience with kundalini, she has a remarkable perspective on it and how it can affect one's life. Taking this opportunity to reflect upon all she has seen, she addresses such questions as: What are we left with when we are empty of everything physical, mental, emotional, and spiritual? How does the experience of kundalini transform our core self or core being? And how do truth and purpose fit into this milestone in one's life?*

I'D NEVER HEARD of kundalini or spiritual awakening back in 1978 when my first, seemingly innocuous experiences began. They were relatively mild then, resulting in a sudden loss of boundaries and an experience of oneness so profound that I could not find my body and for a moment thought that I was everything in the room. Unaware of what was really happening, I just thought these were odd instances of confusion.

In February of 1979, my kundalini experiences became markedly more dramatic. While making love I experienced spectacular orgasms in my head that exploded consciousness and rocketed me into a place where there was nothing but bliss and a simple but powerful awareness that amounted to *"I Am!"* Still ignorant of what was happening, I paid little attention. I just thought I was having great sex.

However, when the orgasms in my head began to occur in the middle of the day, while at work or in places such as the grocery store, with no lovemaking to prompt them, I began to be frightened. I tried to short-circuit these orgasmic waves, but the result was a misery of intense heat and pressure throughout my body and a heart that pounded away at a frightening rate.

If someone had told me, "You're undergoing a spiritual awakening," I would have been even more confused, because orgasms and spirituality did not go together in the small-town, Catholic reality I was raised in.

In addition to the problems caused by intense heat, pressure, and unexpected orgasms, my perception began going awry in the most perplexing ways, sliding into other times and places, seeing things before they happened, or hearing the thoughts of plants, animals, and other people. Suddenly I would find myself out of my body and moving through walls as if they didn't exist. I was unable to read or relax and was completely distracted by the glowing lights I saw around everyone and everything.

For someone who was young, working as a tool and process engineer at Chrysler Corporation, and totally ignorant about spiritual unfolding, there was precious little information available to help me understand what was happening to me. My inability to control or manage perception left me certain I was going insane at the ripe age of thirty-one. In the end, I quit my job, and over the next few years I watched my entire perception of reality crumble.

During that period of time, one of the most disturbing changes was my inability to fall asleep. Every night I went to bed hoping to drift into the relaxing blankness of sleep and wake in the morning as I had done my entire life, but when consciousness has awakened, you are *awake!* There is no such thing as sleep.

Night after night for two and a half years I put my body to bed only to discover all over again that my awareness could not be turned off.

Completely frustrated by this constant wakefulness, I frequently left my body and went up through the ceiling and attic to sit on the roof. From there I watched the goings-on that took place in the night: planes taking off or landing at Selfridge Air Force Base, an occasional car moving slowly along the street in the wee hours, deer in the empty lot across the highway, or raccoons and skunks scrounging around the dumpster at Mrs. Kraft's Grocery.

One night while up there, sitting quietly and looking out toward the western sky, I noticed something moving in the distance. It looked like three dots of light. I watched the dots without a great deal of curiosity simply because I assumed they were airplanes preparing to land at the air base.

However, as they drew closer, I thought the shapes didn't seem right for airplanes, nor could I hear the sound of engines. In fact, the dots of light looked more and more like people.

Then the lights flew directly toward me and began to descend toward the roof where I was sitting. They were three Beings made of light, and they approached my post on the roof with arms extended in greeting and invitation. They wanted me to go with them. Unable to put enough coherent thought together to refuse, and having nothing else to do, I agreed.

They took me by the hand and I immediately felt pulled upward and outward from the very core of my entire body-mind system. I had great difficulty focusing as I usually did. It was as if I was being forced to let go of everyday seeing and hearing, both of which were replaced by an intensely felt *knowing* and an exquisite feeling that came with its own vision and sound—and threatened to disintegrate me altogether.

In a slow-motion blur, we approached a place, a world, a universe made entirely of light. The shocking thing about this place was not the light; it was the fact that it looked exactly like earth, with all the same people, plants, animals, buildings, and landscapes—except there were no wars, no crime, no sickness, no accidents. Greed, fear, anger, and corruption did not exist. People were extraordinarily beautiful. No one was overweight, poor, unkempt, or disabled. Everyone was made of light, as were the flowers, rivers, trees, houses, schools, and buildings. Love seemed palpable and alive, and everything responded to our presence as if it were alive and conscious, even the stones.

I have a vague memory of having been taken on a tour. I also have the impression of being told things like, "This is your real home. . . . Everything you have made on earth has been an attempt to duplicate what is here—but you have done a really sorry job of copying. You can return here to your real home, but you will have to let go of the reality you've made for yourself on earth." I was told other things, some of them very important, but when I arrived back on the roof at dawn, I could not recall what they were.

Over the next few months the three Beings came to get me a couple more times, and then I didn't see them again. Perhaps they were disappointed with me. Maybe they knew I didn't understand what I had seen and experienced with them, and that I wasn't ready to deal with such things as people or cities made of light. I *was* struggling terribly to manage the flood of phenomena that had become my life—and I wasn't doing very well. Still, the overall impact of those journeys was indelible. The stunning beauty and flowing love that were part of everything in that world of light have remained with me like a gift that constantly renews itself.

BECAUSE IT *CAN*

It has now been almost thirty years since the awakening of kundalini and I cannot count the number of times over the years that people have asked me why I thought this experience happened to me. The answer is always the same: "Because it *can* happen! It is a potential that is built into us."

"But what triggers it?" is often the next question.

When I reply, "I accidentally moved into a moment of complete presence and unconditional love," their response is always the same—a blank, baffled look on their faces. Not only is the meaning of one's ability to be completely present in the moment beyond them, unconditional love is a mystery whose relevance is uncertain at best.

What is it about unconditional love that would trigger such a massive response in the human body-mind system? Unconditional love is love that is freely given without conditions attached. It doesn't say, "I will love you if you clean your room," or "I will make love to you if you say the right things to me tonight." It simply pours out of you without hesitation, evaluation, or thought of any kind.

Think of God as a huge ocean of love, light, and bliss all around you. Think of yourself as a delicate bubble submerged in that ocean the same way a submarine can be submerged in the Atlantic. The walls of your bubble are made of the ideas, beliefs, habits, and rules of reality you learned from parents, teachers, and society. These ideas keep you intact as an individual. They form the sandy soil of self-perception. They guide and direct your behavior. And they are fierce obstacles to the love you are immersed in. Poke even a small hole in the walls of your bubble, and God immediately squirts in. Step into unconditional love for the briefest second, and it's like momentarily dissolving the walls of the bubble. You are instantly engulfed in an ocean of God, bliss, and light. You are face to face with the Source of all life, and when you emerge, you know the Source of yourself in a whole new way. You are awake to your *real* self.

Imagine yourself on a solitary rocket ship leaving the earth with an explosive roar, a feeling of moving at the speed of light, and then:

There was total silence and stillness, and I was peacefully afloat in an endless, timeless place of completeness. My ordinary sense of myself and the everyday world disappeared, and whatever was left of that self was floating like a brilliant point of light in a sky filled with other points of light.

I was not just a star in that sky, I was a whole universe of sky filled with uncountable points of light spread out in every direction, flashing, twinkling, and intermingling as points of myself. These points of light seemed to be a living continuation of my whole self, or else I was an extension of them, seeing and feeling as one being and somehow knowing all there ever was to know.

This oneness of light, love, and self sparkled and flowed in perfect union, riding on long, slow, pulsing waves of color, and in this state, if someone had asked me to explain all there was to know, I could have said it all in two words—I am.[1]

Kundalini is the awakening of consciousness. It is the release of consciousness from the small, tight boundaries that comprise ordinary physical reality. It can happen once, or it can happen many times. It can be a little awakening—like a moment of oneness—or a massive, full-blown experience of the *I Am* at the core of each individual.

In ancient times, God was known as the *I Am*. Sometimes the old stories were accompanied by descriptions of a place called *The Void*. When kundalini carries you into the full experience of the Godhead, you end up in a place that is totally empty of everything physical, mental, emotional, and spiritual. There is no yesterday or tomorrow, no thought, no sense of being a physical body, no world of family or friends, no list of things to do. A full kundalini experience is a visit with God and the discovery that you are *It*.

God is *Life*. In a full awakening, immersed in total ecstasy and knowing only one thing—that you exist—you fully experience the life force that comprises your true self. Only later will it dawn on you that if the great power of the *I Am* is your core self, then you are made of life and will always exist! You have discovered your eternal self, your God-self.

Following this discovery, old habits and limits begin falling away. Even a "little" awakening can change your life radically because one single, tiny taste of God is transformative—and relentlessly so.

UNFOLDING HIDDEN POTENTIAL

After kundalini, *truth* and *purpose* become cornerstones in life. The problem with these is that if your awakening comes in your thirties, forties, or later, you will already have your life set up and working. You may have a spouse, children, a house, and a career. If the setup you have made doesn't match the truth and purpose that come from within, you will suffer. Marriages end, children are hurt, the house can be lost and the career dumped because something inside will not submit to a life that no longer holds meaning for you. You find that you must live your own truth and accomplish the purpose you were designed for. Society does not look kindly on this because we have never developed a spiritual tradition of understanding, valuing, and nurturing either spiritual awakening or those who are awakened and deeply spiritual. Nevertheless, fortified by a new inner strength, the spiritual neophyte often blunders through, learning to express the self in a whole new way.

Kundalini—the full, spontaneous awakening of consciousness in the human being—is a wake-up call to begin unfolding the hidden pattern of potential within each of us. That pattern contains the design of the God-self. In the West, it has long been known as the pattern of the Christ within us. In the East it may be called developing Buddha mind. In other places it may be called something else. But whatever you call it, it is the call to move past death and step into life.

Jesus got there. He figured out what was possible for himself and realized that if he could do it, anyone could do it. He then tried to teach it to the people of his time and place. After his death, churches organized to continue his teachings, but they quickly lost the thread of truth.

The truth is that deep inside each human being is a river of Life. That Life is an Intelligent Presence within you. It is like a seed that can grow and become something marvelous and beautiful.

When this Intelligent Presence is nurtured, developed, and brought to full maturity, you become a living Christ, able to maintain deep peace and joy, perfect health, access to immediate abundance, and eternal life. When you do, you bring about your own salvation, saving yourself from the need to come back again and again to the suffering and sorrow of the physical realm.

The secret to developing this Intelligent Presence, which is sometimes referred to as the inner teacher, is to stop everything, become silent, and listen for the "still, small voice within."

What will that voice say? It will be different every time you hear it because it will offer an insight, direction, or solution to something you are dealing with *at the moment*. Past and future do not exist for the Intelligent Presence that lives in the now and attends only to the present. By listening to its voice and following the advice given, no matter what it says, you deepen the relationship with this Presence. As it deepens, you will discover that it always moves you in a direction that nurtures and supports Life. Always choosing to nurture Life is how you transcend death to reach eternal life.

The Intelligent Presence within you is a powerful advocate for personal peace, love, patience, joy, forgiveness, health, integrity, gratitude, humility, and beauty. When you stop every thought that contains any hint of fear, anger, hurt, vengeance, or other negativity, you stop creating a world full of pain, sorrow, sickness, and suffering.

When you gracefully sidestep conversations about the past, the future, someone's sense of injustice, or gossip about your family, coworkers, or the world, you become more and more silent—and more able to hear that still, small voice within.

As you listen for that voice, you must let go of what your family thinks. You must forget what your neighbor does and concentrate on changing yourself. You must develop your own consciousness.

When you decide to make every action a thoughtful, compassionate, timely, humble, and loving action, you demonstrate a way of being that transforms yourself and others. Get enough people doing this and you end up creating a world of light and love like the one I visited with the three Beings who escorted me from the roof and back, a world I now realize was one of the heaven worlds.

One of the most destructive ideas in the world today is the idea that Jesus died to save you. Jesus died to demonstrate that he was beyond believing in death. The second most destructive idea is that he is going to come back and save you at the "end of the world" and that you can sit back and wait for this to happen. The third most destructive idea is that becoming a religious or spiritual person means becoming a clone of Jesus and acting just like you think he acted.

Each person is a unique and wonderful expression of human individuality. Likewise, Christ consciousness will be expressed in a way that is unique for you. If you are a painter, it will be expressed in your artwork. If you're a cook, it will show up in your food. If you're an architect, it will appear in your buildings. If you're a mother, it will unfold in the way you raise and care for your family.

Each of us has a set of gifts and skills that are perfect for the time, place, and relationships we find ourselves in. Imagine a world in which everyone did what they loved to do. Imagine there was an unlimited awareness in each of us for what those who are special to us need from us. Imagine that money was neither a priority nor a solution, and that the real priority in life was managing ourselves and our resources so that everyone is cared for. Imagine that instead of going to a corporate job each day, we simply met locally to find out what needed to be done that day, then did it.

What would it be like to meet all of our needs out of the same kind of knowing and abundance that healed the sick, raised the dead, fed multitudes with just a few loaves and fishes, appeared wherever help was needed, and taught love in every situation? What would your life be like if you unfolded the full potential of your human design?

When we look at the world today, we see perfect examples of hellish existence for millions of people who are caught in wars, hunger, or catastrophic illnesses. It is a far cry from the world of light I once visited where war, crime, sickness, fear, pain, sorrow, and corruption did not exist.

Perhaps we needed to sink to this level just to see how bad it could get. Yet the lower the conditions on earth sink, the more spirituality and an awakening of consciousness will arise as its polar opposite. The result will be a need to choose which direction to go.

Will you sit around waiting to be saved? Or unfold your potential, coming to know the God within and living your life in a whole new way? The awakening of kundalini starts the process of developing our human design to its fullest expression. Once it begins, the path to unending Life will open, and we will discover we have found the royal road to creating a whole new reality filled with peace, joy, health, abundance, and eternal living.

Life, Happiness, and Kundalini Yoga

STUART PERRIN

Stuart Perrin, author of five books, including A Deeper Surrender: Notes on a Spritiual Life *and* Leah: A Story of Meditation and Healing, *teaches spiritual work in the lineage of Albert Rudolph, known to many as Rudi. As he explains in the following essay, he did not actively seek the experience of kundalini; rather, he learned about kundalini through developing what he calls a "strong chakra system," studying meditation, and practicing kundalini yoga. In the following essay he reflects on his own experiences and shares advice, addressing questions such as: How do life, happiness, and kundalini relate to one another?*

THE FIRST TIME I heard the word *kundalini*, I was eighteen years old and working as a counterman at a coffee shop on 59th Street and Lexington Avenue in New York City. The manager of the shop was an elegant Latino man who practiced Buddhism, and during every work break, we'd discuss spiritual subjects. On one occasion, he lowered his voice and asked me in a mysterious way if I knew anything about kundalini yoga. I shrugged my shoulders and said no.

The next time I heard the word *kundalini*, I was twenty-five years old and living a Bohemian lifestyle on the Parisian Left Bank. It was three o'clock in the morning, and I was walking on a dark, narrow street behind Boulevard St. Germain with a drunken American friend of mine who got down on both his knees, lifted his hands in the air, and shouted, "Oh, sacred kundalini in the sky!"

The third time I heard the word *kundalini*, I had been studying with my spiritual teacher, Rudi, for about two years. One day he asked me if I knew the name of the kind of yoga we practiced. I said no. I told him I didn't care what it was called as long as it worked. He laughed and said we practice kundalini yoga. "It's okay," he said to me. "I was teaching this for ten years when someone asked me if I knew that the yoga I teach is called kundalini yoga."

I never read books on kundalini. I learned about it by developing a strong chakra system and a connection with Higher Energy in the universe. I also discovered that a gradual unfolding of my inner life enabled me to experience the force of kundalini and use it in everyday situations. When I listened to people express fear of the power of kundalini, when I listened to them analyze this unexplainable subject, I used to chuckle to myself, then tell them the word *kundalini* reminded me of Italian ice cream. It was a way of keeping the subject light, of never taking myself too seriously, of exploring my inner life through meditation without having to understand the results of the process.

I discovered that my experience of kundalini was the end result of chakra development. I also discovered that kundalini was just another word unless its force was integrated into everyday living. It made for interesting conversation, but talking about it didn't quiet my mind, open my heart, or get me an inch closer to my spiritual enlightenment.

Finally, when I discovered that enlightenment is the living experience of joy and love, of compassion and forgiveness, it became apparent to me that kundalini was essential to the spiritual evolution of a human being. When it is awakened from a deep slumber at the base of the spine, kundalini transforms fear, anxiety, and unhappiness into spiritual energy; it transforms the human into the divine. Kundalini is like an incinerator that burns people's inner garbage and purifies the soul.

THE AWAKENING OF KUNDALINI

There are seven basic chakras (or energy centers) in every human being, and each of these chakras is a direct link to Higher Energy or God. They are located in various areas of the body; for instance, there's a chakra at the center of the forehead, and there are others in the throat, heart, below the navel, the sexual area, the base of the spine, and the crown of the head. I often tell my students that the proper use of meditation will strengthen their chakra systems and help them to become masters of themselves.

The question always arises: what do we have to master? The answer is simple: a chaotic mind, emotions that are like quicksand, sexuality that transforms us into horny or repressed children who can't deal with an energy so intense it wreaks havoc in our daily lives. I tell them that meditation is not a religion or a cult—it's simply a technique we learn that helps us transform our tension into spiritual energy. First, we have to learn to master the energy of mind, emotion, and sexuality and put an end to the war that has run unabated within us from the time of our birth—a war that doesn't allow us to enjoy a single peaceful day.

If meditation is a craft, then like any other craft, it has tools, and in this case, they are the mind and the breath. When we learn to master these tools and use them to open and strengthen the chakra system, we take major steps in the process of activating kundalini. The first step is to build an inner foundation and balance, to strengthen what the Chinese, Koreans, and Japanese call *qi* or *chi,* to know that our center of balance is located in the chakra just below the navel. Then we must use the tools of meditation to gain inner balance, harmony, and a strong foundation.

The mind is like a surgical instrument. When it's focused on the third chakra, it cuts through thick layers of tension that often create serious physical, emotional, and mental blocks. It gets us in touch with our center of balance, opens it, and transforms the third chakra into a lotus-like base similar to the bases on which sculpted or painted Buddhas often sit.

Then we must learn to breathe into the third chakra; we must learn that the power of breath will expand and strengthen that area and make it possible for us to live consciously in the world. Enlightenment is not just a matter of releasing dormant kundalini energy, because, when kundalini awakens, it could easily tip sanity's balance. I've been told there are thousands of people living in mental institutions who have had strong kundalini awakenings. In fact, drugs like marijuana and LSD will activate kundalini in people who haven't enough inner strength to support the intensity of the experience. Enlightenment is a matter of building a chakra system capable of handling kundalini—a chakra system developed gradually over a long period of time—and an inner life that has a strong foundation and a quiet mind, an inner life that makes it possible for us to live every moment with an open heart.

In a world where a fast-food mentality creeps into and dominates spiritual practice, in a world where people haven't the patience to sustain a spiritual practice over a long period of time, there are thousands of teachers of thousands of different methods. Each teacher charges hefty fees to heal us emotionally, mentally, spiritually, and physically, and each path offers different guidelines for enlightenment. The problem isn't that there are so many paths; the problem is the promiscuous nature of the people who follow them. People skip from seminar to seminar, from lecture to lecture, from spiritual practice to spiritual practice, rarely, if ever, extracting the full benefits of any one path. They don't have the time and patience to use whatever practice they have chosen to follow to achieve mastery over self, instead all too often worshipping at the shrine of fast-food spirituality.

I meet many people who talk about the great kundalini experiences they had twenty or thirty years ago, but today they are often dried-out, aging, unhealthy people who live in the haze of memory instead of the creative and vital expression of the moment. Without a steady diet of inner work, without a step-by-step building of the chakra system—from a strong foundation to clarity of mind and an open heart—without joy and love and the ability to sustain the highest levels of our own humanity, without forgiveness and compassion, patience and wisdom, kundalini is nothing more than a powerful force that could turn the inner life of a human being to ash.

The awakening of kundalini can't be an isolated experience fed by a need for something cosmic. It is part of a healthy spiritual evolution of consciousness if it coincides with the awakening of the deepest elements of our own humanity. If it's the end result of an organic, day-by-day development of one's chakra system, kundalini becomes a vehicle for the human soul to connect with the divine.

LEARNING TO BE HUMAN

When we come into the world, our hearts are full of trust, love, innocence, and joy. Somewhere along the line, we lose these precious elements of life and have to relearn them. We go to therapists, yoga teachers, gurus, priests, imams, and rabbis in order to regain the exact state of being we were born with in the first place. The whole thing is absurd. It's also no different from Adam and Eve leaving the Garden of Eden. The rest of the Old and New Testament is a turbulent story on a road that leads to the Messiah.

As long as the mind limits the world to our own meager levels of understanding and creates a killing zone of nonstop conflict in a perpetual war of polar opposites, people will experience chaos, unhappiness, and a desperate need to find inner peace. As long as the mind tries to define the external world as something other than a mirror image of itself, the real battlefield of truth will always remain a mystery—and an ongoing war will rage between our misguided sense of what's right and the misguided rightness of six billion other people. But the moment we quiet the mind, the moment we allow ourselves to be guided by spiritual energy, we begin to see the difference between truth and illusion; we discover there is no right or wrong on earth other than each person's interpretation of truth. Whatever we see in the external world is a manifestation of spiritual energy interpreted by our own preconceived notion of what's right and what's wrong.

When we learn to live with a quiet mind, the universe will fill us with wisdom we can use in our day-to-day lives. But to attain this wisdom, we have to let go of everything we've learned from the time of our birth; we have to trust a logic that defies all earthly logic, a logic that transcends anything the rational human mind can understand, a logic that's connected to infinite energy in the universe, or God, or whatever one wants to call it. The moment we can keep our minds centered in the third chakra, the force of *qi* will expand and create balance and harmony inside us. The mind's throbbing, nonstop, chaotic presence will no longer drive us crazy.

It took me many years to learn that we're born on earth to develop qualities that make us fully human. It took me many years to realize that the only successful people on this strange and bewildering planet are happy people. And it took me years to realize that the reason I'm here is to develop traits within myself that enable me to live my life as a human being full of unconditional love and forgiveness, a human being who is nonjudgmental and able to sustain an open heart no matter what circumstances I have to deal with.

A quiet mind is a vital step on the path to spiritual enlightenment. It ends the twenty-four-hour-a-day war raging inside just about every living person.

The heart chakra is also a turbulent place where strong emotion weighs heavily on our creative energy. Fear, anxiety, jealousy, and a host of other emotions destroy our ability to see the world clearly. The work of meditation is to transform these negative emotions into love and build a strong third chakra so that when the heart opens, it can stay open—it has a foundation to rest upon. Without inner strength, it's almost impossible for love to survive the intense battle being fought in the human mind. It's almost impossible for innocence to thrive in a world full of greed. But love and innocence, joy and happiness are essential ingredients in spiritual evolution. They are what make us human. They are what we are born here to learn. They are the highest language of God on earth.

TRANSFORMING THE HUMAN INTO THE DIVINE

A combination of a quiet mind, an open heart, and a strong inner foundation is essential to spiritual awakening. When we've mastered the movement of energy from chakra to chakra, when we're able to distinguish between reality and illusion, when the mind, heart, and navel chakras work together to heighten consciousness, we are ready to transform the human into the divine. This transformation takes place in the sexual area (second chakra) where the mastery of tantric yoga is essential to the conscious awakening of kundalini.

As we learn to draw energy from the sexual area to the base of the spine, be it through lovemaking or through meditation, the male and female aspects of ourselves unite and give birth to a force that's strong enough to activate sleeping kundalini. Just as sexual energy gives birth to every living creature, when it's internalized, it also gives birth to one's higher self. In many ways it's like an alchemical process that transforms life's lower elements into a spiritual force. It frees us from the blocks that form a strange and difficult inner prison. The energy of kundalini then rises up the spine and accumulates in the crown chakra. After a long period of gestation, the crown chakra opens, and the soul of a spiritual seeker will ascend into the cosmos and enter the bosom of the universal soul. This marriage gives birth to a river of energy that flows down from the cosmos into the third eye, the throat, the heart, the third chakra, the sex, and the base of the spine. It brings with it all elements of a spiritual life.

The process is simple: The first cycle of energy flow through the chakra system develops our humanity. The second cycle begins a spiritual life. Meditation practitioners should be well rooted in the third chakra when a dormant kundalini awakens. This keeps them from being turned into cosmic ash by kundalini's powerful force. Then there's a slow dissolution of bloated ego, of lack of patience, of lack of compassion and forgiveness; there's a slow dissolution of our tendency to judge other people based on preconceived notions of what's right or wrong. We gradually get close to a state of nothingness that allows Higher Energy to guide our lives. The past and future disappear, and we joyously live in the moment. We enter God's inner playground: a world full of love and happiness, a world without fear, a world that exists fully and completely in the present. We have learned to let ourselves be. In doing this, we have also learned to let the outside world be. We finally realize that happy people are enlightened people, and that happiness is an inner state manifesting when kundalini energy has transformed the human into the divine.

Deep Light and the
Great Retruthing

WHITEHAWK

―――――――

Whitehawk's kundalini awakened despite the fact that she did nothing intentional to activate it. Her experience is one filled with out-of-body adventures, supersensory episodes, dream messages, and a roller-coaster ride of energy transmissions. Here, she shares her journey in detail, including how she became a human antenna for "tonal transmissions" and experienced spontaneous physical movements (called kriyas)*, as well as a variety of other extraordinary occurrences. She relates messages she received regarding shifts that are currently in progress on earth—including the dissolution of karma—and describes her visceral experience of the harmonic state of oneness. Whitehawk explores such questions as: What does the future hold for our species? Do we have the ability to overcome our destructive inclinations and step toward an enlightened destiny?*

WHEN I FIRST became acquainted with the exquisite, mystical poetry of Rumi, I was in the midst of a long and rigorous dance with the Divine in the form of awakened kundalini. Rumi's missives made my soul swoon; they reflected an octave of love I had not previously accessed before my turn with this amazing energy attuned me to its existence. Legend has it that in a Turkish village square some eight centuries ago, Rumi encountered a wandering dervish named Shams. Their meeting unleashed a mysterious something so powerful that Rumi was knocked off his mule by the impact. He and Shams then surrendered themselves into a furtive relationship of deep spiritual communion that ignited a copious flow of ecstatic poetry, which to this day moves millions.

One of my favorite Rumi poems ends with a refrain about being *opened* by the divinities, an experience I now relate to deeply. When I "met" kundalini, I was knocked off my high horse and opened inward to my cellular and soular depths, as well as outward to the infinite cosmos—and the trajectory of my life changed forever. I had been opened—by and also into—something infinitely greater, wiser, and more powerful than myself—and which demanded my ongoing participation.

This is a vast, vast tale I am attempting to relate in the space of a few pages. I feel almost apologetic in asking you to hang in with me as my experiential lens zooms in and out among the deeply personal, transpersonal, transdimensional, and even galactic levels and layers I wish to share. This has been the wildest of rides for me, yet I believe it represents mere baby steps compared to the quantum leap that's about to launch us full throttle into an entirely new model of existence: the prophesied "New Earth." That is what I believe it's *all* about now: kundalini "popping" in people across the planet, opening our species to new vistas beyond our current ability to even imagine. Also involved are earth changes, accelerating sociopolitical events, and the changing nature of our personal priorities and relationships—all pieces of the same multidimensional hologram. On one hand, I'm tempted to suggest you buckle up for the ride; but actually, don't bother, because there's really no way to brace for this journey. More useful would be to prepare for *opening,* as this is what's being asked of our minds, our hearts, our relationships with each other, ourselves, our values, and even our relationship with time, space, and the Creator who breathed it all into motion. Also opening are the gates of a kind of perverse prison we've been sequestered in for centuries. In matters such as these, kundalini provides passage to profound liberation. Our part is to relinquish our need for control (not easy for most) in favor of absolute trust and surrender to the strangeness that becomes part and parcel of life when kundalini takes the reins. All such experiences are unique; similar threads run through some of them, but overall they are as unique as the humans who have them.

Mine is the story of a fairly typical American woman; not a physicist or a practicing yogini. I am, however, free-spirited and mystically inclined, given to pondering the meanings and mysteries of that which lies beyond (or behind) the mundane. This atmosphere of consciousness tends to magnetize the extraordinary into its orbit. It is also reflective of the out-of-body experiences (OBEs) that have been integral to my life since the crib. I felt this detail worth mentioning up front, because some of the upcoming vignettes involve experiences in other realms, the nature of which have evolved since kundalini entered the picture. My approach to such things has essentially been to let events flow and to observe, consider, and respond to them as they come, under what can be quite unusual circumstances. I'm also given to consulting a nonphysical team of guides when necessary, for they consistently offer the most direct and helpful information regarding whatever situation might be at hand. Were it not for them (and the woman through whom they speak so eloquently), I would have fared far worse with my extremely erratic—and deeply dismantling— kundalini experiences. Some people have a relatively easy (i.e., brief, even blissful) ride with kundalini. I, for reasons I will be touching upon, have taken a more "scenic route."

My intention in sharing a few postcards from my journey is not to exploit metaphysical experiences for their wow factor, but rather to provide a few glimpses into a particularly strange and far-reaching phenomenon that is occurring increasingly often to expanding numbers of people. Perhaps doing so will assist others who find themselves encountering such things but lack awareness about a situation that could seem as though Pandora's box has erupted in their world. When I went through phases of being daunted beyond measure, I could not find enough "voices of experience" with whom I might compare notes, and the void added to an already stressful situation. I'd like to offer reassurance that, yes, "unbelievable" things *are* happening to ordinary people on an escalating basis, but it does *not* mean they are losing their minds and need to be put away or drugged into oblivion. Nor are they likely to be dying of a bizarre, undiagnosable illness. (Of course, one should consult medical experts if inclined to do so.) The weirdness that is happening around the world may well be intimately connected to "the energies of transformation": kundalini energies activating in humans, galactic energies now entering our solar system, and the astonishing connection (*collaboration,* even) between the two. Yes, kundalini is on a mission to *open* us far beyond our previous limits into entirely new octaves of existence.

During the earliest stages of my kundalini activation (which I dubbed *Special K*), I was unaware of the cause. Signals began appearing, though I remained oblivious to their significance for at least a year, maybe even two. One pronounced early phenomenon involved the appearance of symbols resembling petroglyphs, hieroglyphs, and Aramaic characters in my waking and sleeping consciousness. They seemed at once both ancient and futuristic. I felt *surrounded* by these glyphs, though unable to focus in on them enough to discern details or glean meaning. Walls, objects, even the air itself seemed alive with their energetic presence, albeit in a diffuse way. I had no conscious clue what they signified, but intuited that something major was going on. I wondered if I might be on a kind of "ethernet" with the ancients. I became enamored with cave and rock art, bringing likenesses of it into my home until it became a dominating theme.

Trends emerged in my dreams early in my kundalini awakening and evolved over the duration. One theme involved construction sites and rehab projects, scenes of demolition and reconstruction happening simultaneously. The color red often dominated the earlier "k-related" dreams: red clothes, red vehicles, red bridges, red décor. I understood these dreams to be about the root chakra and my foundations, or place, on earth—which seemed slated to be completely razed and rebuilt. Another recurring dream theme involved things launching skyward: trains leaving their tracks in a vertical ascent; a guy in a (red!) jet pack zooming upward; and my chair launching with me in it. Once, my entire house launched off its foundation into the sky. In one particularly exhilarating dream, I surfed up a river of sparkling white light. *Something* was on an assertive ascent; this much was clear. Snakes are also common characters in kundalini dreams. When I dreamed of a floor full of snakes circling me and starting to wind around my legs, I immediately related it to the rise of the "serpent" kundalini.

THE LION'S MESSAGE

A year or two into such dreams and experiences, something remarkable occurred, and in the aftermath things accelerated exponentially. A friend's father had an intriguing encounter the night before he was to have surgery on an abdominal tumor. He was in bed, pondering his situation, when a mountain lion—an actual lion, not a dream—came right up to his bedroom window, locked eyes with him for a few mesmerizing moments, then turned and disappeared into the night. He had never seen a lion before during the years he'd lived in his populated, upscale community; this was an absolute anomaly, and he wondered about its significance—particularly given the timing. I wondered as well. The mountain lion is my power animal—a messenger and ally— and for one to penetrate a crowded area to "meet" a man with an acute health condition seemed meaningful.

Reflecting on this matter, a sentence suddenly popped into my consciousness, though it was not *my* thought. "He is trying to retruth himself," the inner voice stated simply. *Retruth* himself? Even more curious than the phrase was my absolute knowing that there was something meant for *me* in this event. The lion captured my attention, and the phrase about retruthing felt important, as though I had been given a message by proxy. But why? I believed myself to be an honest person. What did "retruthing" have to do with me? The answer would be revealed in due time.

NIGHT MOVES

Soon after the lion incident, powerful energies started kicking up in my body, usually at night: *clearly* kundalini unleashing in fuller expression. In one common routine, an irrepressible thrashing began once I reached a certain state of relaxation—jerking me around, body and limb, incessantly for hours and hours, night after night, for months on end. This phenomenon of kundalini-catalyzed physical movements (called *kriyas* and believed to be how yoga postures originated) contorted me into positions that were most bizarre. I had no way of stopping this; it consumed hours of time I dearly wished to spend sleeping. An apparent explanation about one of these positions came in a lucid dream. I was shown a particular position (it resembled a symbol in human form), and told that arranging the body this way served to facilitate correspondence with the Pleiades! Next, a penetrating tone wailed through the atmosphere and woke me up—to find myself in that very position in bed with a sizable chunk of broken tooth lying on my tongue! Could an actual "tonal transmission" have beamed in from the Pleiades to my "human antenna," and shattered my molar? It was quite a concept to entertain, but then, my notions regarding possibilities *were* being stretched by the hour.

Nocturnal phenomena came in abundance; it was just one way in which my life seemed turned inside out. Most things happened in the quiet of night; days were often spent recovering from the activities of the night before. I found myself out-of-body regularly, although as time went on, it seemed to become more a matter of shifting the focus of my attention to other aspects of my totality, often located in places that I've come to accept as "off planet." As time went on, I caught on that this "me" with whom I identify so strongly is but a modicum of a much greater self; this body is like a small point at the end of a long, interdimensional sentence. I realize now that we are *great* configurations of consciousness, some portions of which are in physical bodies, others in energy bodies—quite possibly in other realms (i.e., higher dimensions, other worlds, or traveling craft). And still other aspects are sheer awareness possessing no form whatsoever. In the unified field of our holographic universe, myriad points of perception are available once we start unlocking the mystery—which is happening even as I write this.

One recurring "otherwhere" scenario seemed to be a campus, complete with dorms (I had a "studio," quite nice), cafeterias (with food geared to support one's current vibratory needs), and classrooms. In these environs, a ubiquitous glow emanated from everywhere, as though everything could be constructed *of* light. Returning to the earlier subject of those mysterious glyphs in the peripheries of my consciousness: in one learning setting, I found myself before screens of symbols, training in the language of codes. Occasionally my grandmother, who died when I was a teenager, stood behind me, observing my progress!

In another curious out-of-body experience, I had prayed to request help in expanding my ability to *hold* more of this *total self,* the existence of which had become obvious. I sought more conscious awareness and control over my evolutionary experience. That night I was "pulled out" and suspended directly over my body, *measured* in some way (I heard what seemed to be coordinates relayed up the "chain of command"), then given an infusion of energy that sounded like a combination of fax transmission and trickling water. I interpreted this as a transmission of codes (which have tonal counterparts), the significance of which still eludes my conscious mind to this day. I know on some level I'm storing knowledge to use eventually. Actually, I'm using it already during the "night moves" I experience; I just can't remember much detail in ordinary consciousness.

I've also been shown a symbol that represents me: my name, or more exactly, my signature *tone* in graphic representation. I understand these symbols and codes to be a galactic language (possessing energies and purposes just beyond the communication of concepts), preparing us to step up in our roles as players on the greater galactic stage. First, an impending, unfathomably sudden (dare I say "quantum") *shift* will occur en masse; then "*Homo luminous*" (the upgraded *Homo sapiens*) can join the Cosmic Collaboration.

One more "night theme" I'd like to relate involves healings I've received from other beings (or other aspects of my totality; a possibility I entertain). In one instance, I was pulled out of body and suspended vertically over my reclining form, while receiving pronounced thumps on either side of my lower back. I received the telepathic message that my kidneys were toxic and this would help flush them out. Turning around to see who was doing this work, I found a large (about seven feet tall) being of light with no discernible features suspended there behind me. Another time, I had an ongoing bout of terrible nerve pain in my right hand (related to pathcutting, I suspect; described further on). Again I was pulled out, given etheric surgery in a hospital setting, and returned to my body, where the energetic template of that surgery healed the physical condition; it was gone by morning.

The further I went down this rabbit hole, the curiouser it got, and the more expanded my sense of existence—and *myself*—became. Kundalini is the extraordinary fuel and guidance system for *human expansion* (a term I use interchangeably with enlightenment). Once you are accepted as its protégé, doors of reality begin flinging open in miraculous and mind-bending ways, and my inclination is to walk (or fly!) through them.

KARMIC CLEANSING AND PATHCUTTING

One preliminary symptom of active kundalini involved a pronounced sense of grief that dominated my emotions for months. This was puzzling, as it seemed connected to nothing in particular, just a continual, pressing, existential grief. I had no clue it was related to kundalini. Then the guides reported that I had a world of grief stashed in my second chakra (our energy bodies record virtually everything), which was being flushed up and out by kundalini. I hadn't mentioned my state of grief to them, nor was the notion of kundalini yet on my radar; they just always *knew* things. They went on to explain that any energies of low vibration (which include negative emotions, even repressed or forgotten ones) must come up to be healed for good, because soon, only energies of a clearer, higher octave will survive in the New Earth (and the new *us*). Earth, or Gaia, is ascending into a higher vibrational state, as are we, right along with her in one massive, unprecedented event. The hour has come to deal with any and all lower, darker, or denser issues, from anywhere in time, as they are now emerging from the deep freeze of denial to be acknowledged, addressed, permanently healed, and released. This all makes for *quite* a shakeout—personally and planetarily, as evidenced by the breakdown of so many systems in our society and the upheavals Gaia herself is experiencing in her land masses, oceans, and weather.

In my current understanding, karma can't simply float away or evaporate randomly of its own accord. One way it works itself out is to manifest corresponding physical symptoms: a proven effective attention-getting device! Because of the significant time period for the planet (the end of a great galactic cycle, when many souls are supposedly "graduating" from the karmic wheel of reincarnation), the energetic and psychic debris that kundalini is purging probably has roots spanning many lifetimes. So this undertaking has become quite interesting. Regarding the grief: eventually I focused it on the death of my mother years before and performed a ritual in her honor, which seemed to resolve the problem.

I was soon to discover that not only were my personal karmic issues imprinted throughout my body (in the nerves, organs, bones, and DNA) in need of healing and clearing, there was *more* work to be done *through* me, on behalf of my ancestors! This may sound extreme, but actually many of us have made agreements, or soul contracts, to do this for our ancestral lines. I view it as sweeping up after a long, multigenerational earth-plane bash (at least we had some fun, eh?). Karma created in the physical plane, it turns out, must be discharged here as well. This often occurs by proxy via someone who is willing to take it on in place of others—perhaps a biological ancestor, or a kindred acquaintance to whom the surrogate extends an act of generosity or karmic payback. The point is that a portion of any "light work" we do may well be on behalf of others. It took time for me to understand why I was having so many challenges, but when I understood that I was often processing various types of karma on behalf of others (in ways no mere mortal could conceivably orchestrate), the wisdom of the process was impressive. A person can withstand quite a lot if she understands the reasons behind it all.

An example of the emotional lineage work in which I was involved was depression karma, an insidious gift that gave of itself on both sides of my family. During sessions with my guides, I was led to understand how this emotional burden originated, perpetuated, and accumulated over generations. I clearly felt its sucking, dismal energy as it came up to be met, healed, and discharged. Eventually I came to regard genetic karma as an energetic entity that carries a family's burden as long as it takes for it to be resolved at its causative root, at which point it is freed from that "tour of duty." Viewing disease (or any karma) as a *partner in learning,* to my mind, is less antagonistic than the typical "illness as enemy" perception. It represents wounded psycho-spiritual aspects of ourselves, after all. Do we kick others when they're down? This holistic "partnership" invites grace to participate in the healing journey.

As my kundalini kept doing its job, quite a bit of time went into numerous physical familial issues. Diseases originate in consciousness (or subconsciousness), which then lowers in vibration (probably in response to difficult life experiences) until it reaches the density of physical matter and finally results in illness—which then becomes genetically stamped and passed down to descendants. During one particularly trying period, I manifested symptoms of diabetes, a disease prevalent on my father's side that caused his death after a long period of literal dismemberment. I worked on this family matter through my own biology and psychology for about a year. It wasn't too surprising to hear that diabetes is rooted in the lack of sweetness in life—possibly even the inability to *accept* life's sweetnesses. It's not a big jump from the presence of family depression to family diabetes, going back centuries, possibly, to times of physical and emotional hardships that were then written on the DNA and genetically transmitted. (DNA is highly responsive to consciousness; it's not a fixed blueprint, as was once believed.)

My unseen mentors explained what caused the symptoms plaguing me at the time (blacking out regularly from insulin shock) and advised in detail what to do about it. Their advice worked beautifully! This was quite a defining moment with my ascended team; my trust in them was sealed, and they continued to provide a loving lifeline for me through many difficult passages over the years. In a journey as long, harrowing, and daunting as mine was with kundalini, I could have incurred a fortune in medical bills trying to decipher so many strange and disparate symptoms. Thank heaven I understood the underlying commonality of these illnesses: it was *Special K* on a thorough deep-cleaning mission!

Beyond even the above-mentioned levels of cleansing, I (and many others—perhaps you as well) have apparently agreed to even *more* expansive service pertaining to what I think of as "batch karmic processing," but which is more widely referred to now as *pathcutting*. As this phase of earthly existence quickly winds down, we pathcutters are quite busy. Whether I'm involved in this service to make amends for a major mistake in an earlier lifetime, or I'm just a hardy enough old soul that I've felt I could take on more than my personal share of karmic clearing for the team, I'm not sure. What's quite clear, however, is that this *is* happening; I've been through a lot of it, as have many, many others who offer themselves as pathcutters for the transmutation of earthly karma.

The term *pathcutting* refers to completing (i.e., cutting) karmic bondage with the past, as well as forging ahead (bushwhacking) into the karma-free zone of the future. Pathcutters could be considered a transition team for the New Earth. The whole journey has assumed epic proportions, only the slightest fragments of which I am able to share in this space. One pathcutting project involves transmuting myriad viruses—a common issue because there are so many varieties presenting themselves at this time. This is due to all the acceleration of frequencies and raising of vibratory rates happening now: low-vibe, long-dormant viruses are getting agitated into action, to our collective discomfort, or worse. But they will not be an issue, nor will other parasitic life (or energy) forms, after the shift transpires.

At one point in my experience, I had severe abdominal pain on my left side that ebbed and flowed for weeks; I felt as though I had a gut full of broken glass. One night I crawled out of bed, flopped into my favorite chair, put my head back, and just *surrendered* the whole ordeal to God. The pain lifted immediately! Surrender isn't something that comes easily for me, and the same could probably be said for most human egos. More common is whining for relief! Surrender has a particular quality involving trust that you and the greatest force in the universe, God, are *not* separate from each other. This realization can truly accomplish anything if the ego just steps aside and allows it. The woes of the world could be resolved if everyone *got it*. I apparently hit on it that night, because the pain vanished once and for all. In my next session with my guides, they jumped right in without my mentioning this event to congratulate me on transmuting a particular virus through my system, adding that it was now gone not only from me but from the entire planet! They confirmed it was the act of surrender that had done the trick.

Along a different trajectory, pathcutters are working on energizing five new chakras currently becoming active. (They aren't actually *new*; they've just been largely dormant for eons.) Chakra activation—another service of our indefatigable kundalini—presents its own quirky experiences. For instance, when the chakra at the base of my skull, which functions like a receiving dish for telepathic communications, started sparking to life, I heard all kinds of loud "firing" going on in there, ranging from electrical sizzling to zipping to loud smacking—very similar to the sound of firecrackers going off—to the even louder, heart-stopping blast of what seemed like *explosions* detonating in my skull. Most anyone else would have hightailed it to a neurologist (if not the ER) with such symptoms, but I knew it was "just" kundalini putting that special chakra through its ignition sequence. And—in case you're wondering—I have had quite a few telepathic and clairvoyant experiences since. Also, for the sake of full disclosure, I've endured quite a few massive headaches in the process.

Another chakra coming into its own is the "high heart" center, located between the throat and the heart, which generally vibrates the color aqua. It is paired with the long-depleted thymus gland, and its awakening will regenerate the thymus (responsible for our immunity and longevity) as well as support us in expressing the truth of our hearts. When this chakra started engaging, I became covered with unbelievable rashes on my chest, neck, and jaw. These energies are recalibrating our biological vehicles, and there *is* a period of physical adjustment and adaptation when this happens—especially for the more mature among us who are dealing with kundalini. The older the vehicle, the greater the gap between its model's vintage features and the new hybrids coming down the pike—think of "indigos" and "crystal children," who are born with the upgrades as standard equipment. I admit to quipping on occasion that I felt I was being "nuked by God." This was not a thought I held with any seriousness, however; the energy behind the comment was of good humor, and humor can help you through some rough times.

The more this "transition team" works to create infrastruc-
tures for the New Earth and Homo luminous, the sooner we will
all be able to enjoy the benefits (and responsibilities) of ascendant
gifts such as telepathy, spontaneous healing, and eventually the
unified human chakra, which will be in synergy with the unified
field of the planet, functioning collaboratively in the blessed state
of integrated oneness.

THE AMPLIFICATION OF EVERYTHING

As my journey with kundalini progressed, I went through stages
during which my ordinary senses amped up to extraordinary heights.
For a time my olfactory sense was affected: I smelled everything so
acutely that it was sometimes difficult to discern where the odors
were coming from. Sometimes it was my hearing that was off the
charts—or my nervous system. Hearing everything hyperacutely
while simultaneously feeling one's nerves vibrating to the verge (it
seemed) of snapping makes for quite a stressful combination.

I might as well mention sex, as the subject tends to interest everyone. People who have heard of kundalini at all often
associate the exotic-sounding term either with a type of yoga or
incredible sex—and I'll leave yoga for others to address. Because
dormant kundalini sleeps at the base of the spine, once it awakens
it may well send "good vibrations" through the whole neigh-
borhood. Early on, around the time I was having the "red" and
"launching" dreams, I was also noticing an amplified sexual component. I finally had some sense of what teenage boys go through
when their testosterone starts raging! It was definitely distracting,
and it also initiated a striking and creative array of dreams. The
guides advised at the time that I enjoy as much sex as I liked while
my root chakra balanced out. I have to say, this isn't advice one
expects to receive in conversations with spiritual beings. But they
correctly assessed my situation, as usual, and my lower centers
were cleared and opened in a grand way. It was nice to balance
the earlier flood of grief with something quite the opposite![2]

A couple of years later, another go-round with this heightened sexual component came on, this time integrated with a previously unimaginable sense of divine love. The caliber of this experience was beyond anything I'd encountered before; I suddenly *got* the tantric idea of merging and flowing sacred masculine and feminine energies in a way through which a unified holy encounter can actually be achieved, and it involves understanding how to work with kundalini. I felt as though a thousand tumblers of some great lock had clicked into place, and an entirely new level of intimate experience opened up. This was also around the time I really "took in" Rumi, inhaling his poetry like it was my very breath. I met God through another person, and through myself as well, in this dynamic. I mean this literally, not figuratively; it was all light years beyond the typical interpersonal experience. My ego seemed to recede way into the background, and my spirit was experiencing the male/female dance in an entirely different way. It wasn't romance; it was exaltation! I once had no understanding of, or appreciation for, the whole tantric sex *thing;* I even suspected it might just be an excuse used by spiritual types to sanctify their carnal appetites. Now I can comprehend genuine sacred union, and I believe it to be the way all intimacy will be expressed in the awakened world to come. Our bodies are *wired* to merge with the divine, in a most intoxicating, blissful state of grace, *through each other!* This, my friend, is the ultimate Big O. Who *knew?*

DEEP LIGHT

After kundalini had been putting me through my paces for a few years, something truly amazing happened one night. It seemed to be an initiation or graduation ritual of Divine magnitude. I was once again pulled out of my body and escorted in my light-body state into a realm of light unlike anything I'd ever seen or experienced before. I found myself ascending through fields of white light; *strata* of light would actually convey a more exact representation. I rose through layers of light that seemed denser in some places, and louder in others—yes, louder, as this light was not just silent and luminous, it was vibrant and crackling loudly with energy and life. If you were to imagine going up past the floors of a building in a transparent elevator, and all the floors consisted of varying densities of whiteness that emitted complex electrical sounds, you'd have an approximation of what this was like. Moreover, I was aware that there were many others in this place going through the same experience as I. Crazy as it this may sound, when I reflect on this, it reminds me of a crowd of lightbodies being led through a "lightbody purification process," like a car wash!

At one point I dropped back into my body and sat up excitedly to take notes. But documentation would have to wait, because off again I went, back to the crackling light and the others who were there. I spent the better part of an entire night in these energies. In the morning, I was stunned by the experience: what on earth (or *off* earth) was that about? I took stock. I was still alive, I noticed—presumably a good thing. I hadn't graduated to "angel status" or some such during those hours in the deep, living light. It actually seemed an ordinary morning by all initial appearances; but how could everything be so *normal* after a night like that? What was the *point*?

As the day went on, it became apparent that something was different, something I could never have imagined until I was living it. My perceptions had expanded to the point at which I seemed to pop through a membrane of ordinary existence into the unified field, the great hologram, which I now realize is the true nature of this creation. This was a subtle perceptual alteration, and gentle—but radically different from the norm nonetheless. In this state, I clearly felt the oneness of *all of it*— this body I wear, the tree outside the window, the bird in the tree, the beauty in the world, the pain in it as well—all of it is an extension of me, as I am an extension of it. All is intimately connected; all is *one*.

If someone or something crossed my mind, I instantly felt a "runway of light" roll out between me and that person or thing; I came to understand that it was *that part* of my totality (or *the* totality of which I'm an aspect) which is John, or the rainforest, or Afghanistan, or the moon, or beings or events in parallel planes, or distant galaxies—*all of it*. It's as much a part of me as is the foot at the end of my leg. And amazingly, it's all beautiful. It is perfection, which seems ludicrous to say considering all the agony in the world. But there's a living, loving perfection in the essential fabric of everything. Actually, the fabric is primarily a screen upon which our reality is a collective fabricated projection. We perceive our physical world as "real," and our dreams, for instance, as unreal, insubstantial. In my current worldview, though, the dreamtime is closer to what's real (and enduring) than is the physical universe. In days to come, we will awaken en masse to this "unreasonable fairy tale," and life on earth will shift in an instant. Its false foundations are crumbling even as I tap away on my keyboard here, preparing the playing field for a very new game.

The screen that now holds us entranced by the projections *we produced ourselves* like movies and then allowed to become "life," will be transmuted in a way that will no longer hold these false projections of psychological bondage, physical limitation, uneven distribution of resources, disconnection from the God Source, and so on. Much like my lightbody being purged of so much karma and illusion about the nature of reality after a gradual, multilevel cleansing by kundalini over the years, so is the energy of our universe about to be cleansed in a cosmic "system reset."

Of course, this is all fodder for deep discourse, which is not possible in the context of this essay, but plenty of information is now available about quantum physics, the unified field, the holographic universe, and so on. One book that might be a suitable start along these lines is *The Disappearance of the Universe* by Gary Renard. It is a friendly and accessible read and points to what I have known to be true since the revelations of my deep light experience.

The beautiful sensation of oneness I had lasted for about six weeks following my night in the light. The best single word I can use to describe how oneness feels is *buoyant*. In the unified field, nothing is separate from anything else, no one is competing with anyone else, there are no "agendas," there are no duplicities, and nothing is to be gained by taking something away from someone else. It is truly like being a self-aware drop floating in a crystal clear ocean of bliss. Nothing bothered me; I loved it all. I was in the world but not of it, and feel that this is how it's meant to be; this is the elegance of a system that works, and this is what we are shifting toward: no competition or opposition, no estrangement, no egoic distortions and attachments, nothing to lose, fear, or feel threatened by. The difficulties will be in the interim between here and there, as our screen becomes cleansed of all the "burn-in" of our collective, dark trance.

As I was writing this essay, I had a lively recurrence of kundalini activation, complete with kriyas, major electrical disturbances (including blown circuits and a crashed computer), a few visions, and a couple of "downloaded messages." It's been quite a while since I've had such an energetic period as this; I have no doubt it came on in response to my focus on the subject! (It doesn't take much to charm the serpent from its basket; a little attention will often do it.) So in closing, I thought I'd share one concise message that came through in the process regarding kundalini's role in the imminent, spontaneous evolution of man:

> *You are being cleansed of*
> *everything you think you are, so*
> *you can finally become what you*
> *really are.*

may your journey be blessed.

Beyond Kundalini Awakening

JOHN SELBY

▬▬▬▬▬

John Selby has long been a voice in the kundalini community. Psychologist and author of Kundalini Awakening in Everyday Life; Seven Masters, One Path; Jesus for the Rest of Us; *and* Quiet Your Mind, *he shares his overall experience of merging a postChristian meditative sense of life with the Hindu kundalini tradition. He reveals his discoveries in this grand experiment, as he encountered LSD, mescaline, and* kriya yoga, *and many different forms of mind and spirit adventures. He asks the provocative questions: How helpful are manipulative approaches to spirituality versus participatory approaches? Does enjoying the essence and divinity of our lives require regular disciplined time or many hours of cultivated meditation or drug use? When do we cross the line into a spiritual masturbation of sorts? Do we need a kundalini boost to be satisfied with ordinary reality? And what are the emerging new approaches to meditation and spiritual awakening?*

IT's WITH PLEASURE and also a sense of perfect timing that I respond to the offer to write an essay for this book. Even after twenty years, I still regularly get e-mails from readers of my first meditation book, asking for special advice on kundalini meditation. This essay affords me the chance to state several rather startling insights that have come to me since writing my kundalini book, insights that have changed my approach to kundalini—and my approach to meditation and the spiritual path in general.

Since writing the original *Kundalini Awakening in Everyday Life* in the early eighties, I have experienced in my own meditations a clear shift in my understanding of how consciousness itself functions, and for myself, where the spiritual path truly leads. Even in the early days of that book's initial success, I was considered a bit outside the traditional fold of kundalini aspirants because I attempted to merge my culture's basic Christian meditative sense of life into the Hindu kundalini tradition. I now find myself almost completely outside both traditions.

I offer you these new insights into kundalini and meditation for what they are worth, while also honoring your perspective if you remain within traditional beliefs and practices.

SPIRITUAL PATHS CONSIDERED

As I type this, I notice that my new computer has underlined kundalini in red, indicating that the word doesn't even exist in its spell-check memory. And indeed, is kundalini a real force in contemporary life?

Obviously a great many people over the centuries have experienced something commonly called the kundalini phenomenon, a great inner flow of what feels like energy moving powerfully through certain channels in the body, roughly congruent with the major neurological systems of our biological organism. In kundalini meditation as I understand it, the aim is to manage that flow, control it, and encourage it. There exists a vast tradition about what this energy flow is, how to understand it symbolically, and how to steadily increase it through the seven chakras, or energy centers, of the body. I'm sure that other essays in this book will explain all of this to you.

I first encountered this inner experience of the kundalini flow as a child spontaneously during ecstatic moments in nature, as short moments of supercharged bodily presence. Perhaps you had similar experiences. They came and went as they chose to, and I considered them just a natural part of life. They seemed to fall away in my teen years. Then, during college in the sixties, I worked at one of the seven LSD research centers the government sponsored. There, I encountered the kundalini flow like crazy during a mescaline experience—and from that day forward knew that there was something peculiar that could happen in the body that was both a great thrill and quite scary.

I spent four years in graduate school getting a degree in spiritual psychology, during which I studied kriya yoga intensely with teachers such as Kriyananda, and then with my primary master in that tradition, Thakan Kung. And yes, I learned how to manipulate this energy experience quite successfully. There is no doubt that the experience itself can be generated at will, and many people are attracted to the challenge of spending considerable time in their lives doing so. I myself did: I sat daily for at least an hour, practicing the visualization methods for moving the energy properly through my body and increasing it as well.

But do I still practice this part of kundalini meditation? No, not at all. I definitely still do the basic chakra balancing process I wrote about in my book, but that's it.

When people write to me asking for inspiration regarding kundalini-energy meditation, I tell them the truth—that I have moved beyond a manipulative approach to meditation, preferring a participatory approach to my spiritual life. This question of participatory versus manipulative lies at the heart of my meditative practice these days, and I encourage you to take a close look at this theme as you advance on your own spiritual path. I am not judging in this regard, only looking carefully at the reality and allowing common horse sense to determine which path to follow.

HONEST EXAMINATION

I was lucky enough to grow up in Ojai, California, the same town where a truly great spiritual teacher named Krishnamurti spent his winters, and I was exposed to his voice teaching his particular path from the time I was two or three. One of his key teachings regarded how to look closely at something without judging it, to simply see it more and more clearly. Jesus, of course, taught the same practice, in his insistence that we "judge not."

So what do we see when we look closely at the actual practice of kundalini? At first, in my twenties, I saw a pragmatic process for boosting a sensation inside my own body that felt just tremendous. I really couldn't get enough of it. I'd sit there in my meditation closet with a beautiful wife upstairs awaiting me, and prefer the rush of kundalini to the rush of sexual pleasure (well, at least they were equal as pleasure thrills).

Kundalini energy meditation delivers pleasure. But as I grew older, I began to realize that, in my case at least, my addiction to my daily doses of kundalini pleasure was very much akin to what is called *spiritual masturbation.*

We live in an age when masturbation of a sexual nature is considered fine and healthy for people without a sexual partner. Giving ourselves pleasure and fulfillment is considered perfectly normal and is encouraged. There's of course nothing inherently wrong with masturbation, but it does expend considerable energy as a purely self-contained experience, rather than sharing that energy and experience with others.

I admit that I became a bit addicted to the kundalini rush. Meditation was a place I could go and totally escape from the crazy world of Vietnam and all the rest. In my youthful spiritual seekings, I learned a tremendous amount about my own consciousness. And I very much valued the sense of being in charge of my own spiritual body, master of my own infinite potential. But as time went by, I began to feel a growing emptiness in fixating on that experience and found myself seeking a new approach to the spiritual path beyond my own self-stimulation, no matter how gratifying and insightful it was.

So here's the first question in examining kundalini meditation: in the long run, is this the most effective way of working with and employing the life force within us, or is kundalini meditation akin to spiritual masturbation?

SEEKING THE CORE MEDITATION

My life's work as a "psychologist with a spiritual bent" has been to explore the phenomenon of meditation from both the inside-out (subjective internal) and scientific perspectives, and to identify the primary psychological process that underlies all the world's meditative traditions. I've experienced the Christian, Hindu, Buddhist, Taoist, and Native American approaches to quieting the mind and entering into communion with the spiritual power, wisdom, and love that permeate the universe. This has been a large study.

In my first kundalini book, I did my best to advance the ancient Hindu tradition so that it fit seamlessly into our Western culture. Specifically, I broke with the Hindu tradition that the goal of kundalini meditation focused on raising the kundalini energy higher and higher up through the top of the head into total final transformation and enlightenment. Instead, I encouraged a meditation on the chakras that held the heart most important, and balancing of the chakras rather than hyperstimulation as the primary goal. I also offered a meditative process that was pretty much free from preconceived beliefs about the kundalini experience, so that one could explore one's natural kundalini nature beyond all manipulation. (Manipulative techniques are those in which you are first taught a mental belief or concept, such as how energy flows through the kundalini paths, and then try to imagine this happening in your own body.)

I once worked for two years as a research hypnotist conducting National Institutes of Mental Health studies into the power of the human mind to convince itself that an imagined experience is real. People often hold beliefs that they cling to even though those beliefs fly in the face of reality itself. A great many religious beliefs are of this nature, as I'm sure you've noticed.

So the question naturally arises: how do we tell the difference between a real and an imagined experience of kundalini energy flow in our bodies? I can't answer this question for you, but in my case, I have come to realize that I was at least partly imagining my experience, even though there seemed to be a deeper energetic and spiritual reality that inspired my imaginations. I challenge you to look in this direction yourself.

REPEAT PERFORMANCE

One of the big ways in which we seem to lead ourselves astray in meditation is this: we have a great meditative experience once, and then we try to have it again and again. In the process we begin to manipulate our experience and fool ourselves with imagination, thus losing the real thing. Genuine spiritual experience is always a unique, spontaneous, present-moment happening.

So no matter how great an inner experience you might have, I strongly recommend that you never try to repeat that experience. Why? Because the reality of spiritual life, in fact of all life, is that reality never repeats itself. We can never have the same experience twice, except in our imaginations.

This is why I began to shift away from meditations in which I was trying to make a concept in my head turn into an experience in my body. Instead, more and more I explored the Taoist and Zen methodologies in which I simply did my best each new moment to be aware of the air flowing in and out of my nose, the movements in my chest and belly as I breathed, and my whole-body participation in the present moment.

I shifted from a mental fixation on beliefs and ideas, expectations and anticipations about an inner experience I wanted, to a simple sensory focus on reality itself and my spontaneous involvement in that unfolding reality.

What I discovered was that, indeed, the kingdom of heaven is at hand. And every present moment offers the opportunity for spirit to act through us in the world—that's where the real rush of life is found. This doesn't mean that I now ignore the chakra practice that I taught in my kundalini book; it just means that I do that meditation in the context of continual present-moment awareness.

NONSTOP MEDITATION

Another significant change that has come over my meditative practice has to do with how often I meditate and for how long. Often I'm asked this question: "How long do you meditate each day, John?" To which I answer, "Oh, three or four times a day, for three or four minutes. And also, all the time, nonstop, while I'm awake."

I know tradition dictates that you've got to sit yourself down for at least half an hour at a time for anything to "happen" in a meditation session. But once again, notice that you hold in your mind the belief that something should "happen" when you meditate. You want some sort of meditative payoff, right? You make yourself do something for a certain amount of time, you expend a certain amount of concentration and discipline, and you want dividends. That's how the meditation equation is set up: you pay the price, and you get the goodies.

There's an underlying one-liner in this core attitude of many meditation traditions that's questionable—the belief that plain old reality isn't good enough, that you need a spiritual boost to be satisfied with life.

But do you really? My experience has been that boredom comes from fixating overmuch on my inner thoughts and future expectations rather than focusing on the actual event of the emerging present moment. I come alive when I shift from past-future thoughts to present-moment participation. It's never boring, living on the edge of life!

QUIET YOUR MIND

In my psychological studies of the meditative experience, I found one theme running through all the world's great traditions: meditation means quieting the flow of chronic thoughts through your mind and focusing instead on the emerging moment. And where meditation techniques really work, they succeed in quieting the stream of consciousness that tends to dominate our awareness.

Patanjali taught ways to quiet the flow of thoughts through the mind and so did Buddha and countless other masters over the centuries. But as you know, none of them are easy, quick, or predictable. From my studies, it seems that the priestly cult throughout history has always made the meditative path difficult—otherwise, the priests have no power over the popu-lace—and all too often religion has ended up as a power game even when it's selling enlightenment.

I say this because, when I approached meditation techniques as a psychologist, it took me only a few years to crack the "quiet your mind" challenge. I began to watch my own thoughts flowing through my mind, and I took note when they temporarily stopped. I encourage you to do this yourself; it's a basic Buddhist meditation.

What I noticed was that certain perceptual experiences in and of themselves temporarily quieted my mind instantly, naturally, and with no effort at all. You've noticed this as well—viewing a sunset, for example, tends to quiet the mind and boost good feelings; so does gazing at the rippling of the surface of a lake or pond; so does tuning in to the breeze blowing on your face and the scent in the air; so does making love; so does a great meal or an engrossing con-cert; so, in fact, does any event that turns your attention toward two or more sensory experiences at the same time!

Wait a minute, I said to myself. I remember being on a team doing perceptual research way back in the early days of my career, when we found out that very same thing and noted it, not real-izing what we'd found. For years I'd been walking around with the answer without knowing it. We'd been studying three Hindu yogic masters who could actually stop their hearts from beating at will, get cut with a razor and stop the bleeding, lower their blood pressure at will, and so on and so forth. We wired them to EEG machines and watched their brain waves during all this. And we noted that when they did one of their meditations of focusing on two or more sensory events at the same time (moving a toe and turning the head, for instance) their EEG indicated a sudden shift into alpha. We noted it, but were more fascinated by the bigger feats these guys could perform—and missed the insight.

Looking back, I realized the "quiet mind" insight and began purposefully putting together a meditation that applied the insight. I drew as much as I could from existing Hindu and Buddhist methodologies: they'd known for thousands of years, for instance, that the primary tool of meditation is focused awareness—the mind's ability to consciously choose, in each new moment, where to aim its power of attention. That's always the initial step, to remember to use that tool effectively.

And where to aim that attention? Toward the most important constant sensory event of the human experience: the sensation of the air flowing in and out of the nose. That's basic Hindu and Buddhist meditation in a nutshell.

But here's where the perceptual research added its insight: not to stop with breath awareness per se, but to expand the awareness another crucial notch to include, at the same time, another sensory event. I had found, for instance, that quite naturally, consciousness expands from breath awareness in the nose to also include the movements in the chest and belly while inhaling and exhaling.

It's this second expansion of awareness that generates the inner shift in attention away from chronic thoughts to pure experience.

As I explored this utterly simple process, I found that something truly remarkable happens psychologically as the mind expands from being fixated on a point (thought after throught) to perceiving two or more sensations at the same time—awareness shifts from point-fixation into "seeing everything at once" mode. And it's this cognitive shift that quiets the mind. Thoughts are linear; they flow through the mind one after another, word after word, phrase after phrase. The mind looks from one to the next (that's how we think psychologically) through chronic point-fixation.

You can be aware of the air flowing in and out of your nose, and still think. That's why the Buddhist meditation that challenges you to stay aware of the air flowing in and out of your nose, but offers no further guidance, drives most people up the wall—thoughts keep returning to dominate your mind. You can play that game for years, half an hour a day in meditation, and still be plagued by a chattery mind. But as soon as you expand your awareness to include, at the same time, the sensations of your breathing in your chest and belly—kapow! I'll give you a dime if you can keep thinking.

Why does this work so effectively? Because of that cognitive shift from point-fixation to "seeing everything at once." When you let go of point-fixation and see the whole at once (two or more sensations at the same time), you shift into that blessed present-moment condition in which your mind is quiet, and you're tuned in to your deeper intuitive aesthetic brain function instead.

TRUE AWAKENING

In the Hindu and Buddhist traditions, much emphasis is placed on attaining enlightenment: awakening permanently into a totally conscious state of mind. Is this what you want from meditation? Most people do. It's a dandy idea.

Unfortunately though, this belief that the average person can meditate and somehow achieve total permanent enlightenment is simply not psychologically true— nor is it even really desired by most people deep down. I personally have thrown out the whole notion of enlightenment; it's a belief that doesn't quite fit reality. How many enlightened people do you know? Really?

And what do you get when you throw out that belief? You get the freedom to accept yourself just as you are, as perfect. Jesus said it: "Be ye therefore perfect, even as your Father in heaven is perfect." Wow. That's quite an order. And then he provided the same key to that perfection in everyday life that Buddha had centuries earlier—accept and love yourself just as you are.

Probably the most bothersome habit and indeed addiction of the New Age movement (an overcommercialized phase that is hopefully over and done with at this point) was the built-in one-liner that you're not okay just as you are. It was the same old priestly mantra—that if only you dig in and "improve" yourself by doing this and that and buying this and that, then (at some point in the future) all will be well in your life. In other words, being just the way you are is not good enough. You must strive toward perfection.

But deep in the true teachings of all religions is the core belief that you are perfectly fine, whole, and acceptable, just as you are. You don't need to improve yourself in order for God to love you.

Likewise with the emerging eternal moment. Sure, Barack is right, we need change in the world. We are an evolving society, and evolution is healthy because we steadily adapt our attitudes and behaviors to better match reality. But this moment right here and now, as the air comes flowing into your nose, just happens to be God's perfect creation, and who are we to judge it as less than perfect? And that goes for our own selves as well. We are perfectly okay right here, right now, with zero change required for total love and acceptance.

My understanding is that what most people really want when they meditate is to enter into this feeling of everything being perfect just as it is. Sure, it can be a radical rush to experience kundalini energy flowing throughout your body in perfect channels. But ultimately that's not going to bring that feeling of quiet peace and fulfillment, that sense of direct communion with God, that certainty of being one with your creator.

A SHORT ETERNAL PATH

What process can we do regularly, even constantly, to stay tuned in to our inner wellsprings of peace, insight, and contentment? Here's what works for me—just say the following focus phrases to yourself, often, every day:

1. "I feel the air flowing in and out of my nose."
2. "I also feel the movements in my chest and belly as
   I breathe."
3. "I'm aware of my whole body here in this present
   moment."
4. "I honor and love myself, just as I am right now."

If you pause for just one minute and say these focus phrases to yourself once an hour, you'll transform your life. And once a day, remember to move through a basic chakra-balancing kundalini meditation. And of course, sit quietly for however long you like. There are also a few other focus phrases I've generated from the merger of cognitive psychology and meditative traditions, which will add to your experience. (For more information, go to uplift.com.)

What especially concerns me these days is the quality of consciousness we maintain at work—and the spiritual connectedness we bring to important decisions. You probably spend at least eight hours a day at work, and I challenge you to remain aware of your breathing and your heart each moment of that day. Also, when you're with family and lover, apply the same effort. Make breath awareness primary, and all else unfolds as a spiritually inspired and empowered experience. That's what I consider good use of our kundalini charge!

PART II

Kundalini and Your Health

*Accounts from Health Experts, Therapists,
Scientists, Researchers, and
Clinical Surveys of Kundalini Experiences*

Kundalini Yoga as Therapy

A Research Perspective

SAT BIR SINGH KHALSA, PHD

Currently the director of research for the Kundalini Research Institute and an assistant professor of medicine at Harvard Medical School, Sat Bir Singh Khalsa has practiced a yoga lifestyle for more than thirty-five years and is a certified Kundalini Yoga instructor. In the following essay, he shares an analysis of the therapeutic aspects of the practice of Kundalini Yoga that Yogi Bhajan brought to the West. He reviews research on how kundalini yoga has been used to treat health problems, including obsessive-compulsive disorder and sleep disorders, among other health challenges. He raises the compelling likelihood that Kundalini Yoga can treat a variety of disorders, improve one's quality of life, and restore health—and that clinical research can validate this possibility.

THE WORD *Kundalini* and the much more specific term *Kundalini Yoga* have been used widely in the literature of yoga by a variety of different authors and yoga schools. In yogic philosophy and theory, Kundalini generally has referred to subtle, etheric energy that flows in the spinal column and has been associated with Kundalini awakenings or spiritual/mystical experiences. These are indicative of the states of consciousness that are the goal of yoga practice; in general, the goal of all yoga disciplines is to achieve a unitive state of consciousness, or *samadhi*. Therefore, it can be argued that if the Kundalini energy is at the root of this state, then all yoga practices are in some way aimed at activating the Kundalini energy, not just those practices that have been referred to as Kundalini Yoga.

Despite this argument, in modern practice, different styles and schools of yoga have adopted a variety of names. Most common is the generic term *Hatha Yoga*, which, depending upon the teacher and the school, incorporates yoga postures and may also include additional techniques associated with yoga including meditation, breathing, or mantra practices. There are also a number of yoga styles that are essentially Hatha Yoga associated with a particular school or yoga master and have adopted names that distinguish them (e.g., Iyengar, Ashtanga, Bikram, Kripalu, Integral, etc.). Fewer schools practice Kundalini Yoga, the most prominent of which incorporates the style taught by Yogi Bhajan. (This school is usually distinguished from other Kundalini Yoga schools by the phrase "Kundalini Yoga as taught by Yogi Bhajan.") In essence, all of the Kundalini Yoga–style practices overlap a good deal with the practices associated with Hatha Yoga and are similar in over-all goals and philosophy. Since Kundalini Yoga as taught by Yogi Bhajan incorporates many of the same postures and breathing exercises of generic hatha yoga, a casual inspection suggests it is indistinguishable from the typical hatha practices. A closer explo-ration reveals a significant difference in its use of *kriyas*, protocols for particular problems, and a seamless integration of profound meditation practices and a great variety of exercise sets. This makes it a rich source of techniques to study the comparative differences for therapeutic applications as well as the universal mechanisms underlying most meditations.

Yogi Bhajan began teaching Kundalini Yoga after his arrival in North America in the late 1960s, and although it has little pres-ence in India, it is now one of the major yoga schools in the West and is practiced widely here. There are now very active formal teacher training programs. These are developed and regulated by the Kundalini Research Institute, a nonprofit established by Yogi

Bhajan in 1972. They assure authenticity and quality of teaching and promote research and application. There is also a Kundalini Yoga teacher's association as part of the 3HO Foundation. Yogi Bhajan's Kundalini Yoga is decidedly focused on inner psychological and spiritual growth and development, and it is therefore consistent with the deepest goals of yoga and yogic philosophy. Accordingly, this style of yoga has somewhat less relative emphasis on the physical asanas than on the incorporation of specific mantra and meditation practices.

Although yoga in general originally targeted inner development, its capability to engender positive psychological and physiological changes has naturally led to its use as a therapeutic intervention. This relatively recent application of yoga began formally in India in the early twentieth century. However, "yoga therapy" is now widespread in both India and the West as a preventive and therapeutic practice for the general public. The International Association of Yoga Therapists holds annual meetings and sponsors a peer-reviewed research journal and a professional newsletter.

It is likely that much of the therapeutic benefit of yoga practice may be general in nature through positive effects on mood, fitness, stress, and lifestyle. However, it is also certain that some yoga practices are particularly active upon specific physical and psychological processes, and therefore may be especially effective as adjunctive therapeutic practices for specific medical and psychological disorders. Many effects have been ascribed to the variety of different yoga practices, and the nature of these purported effects can vary depending upon the yoga master, instructor, or yoga school making the claim. But from a scientific perspective, there has been very little research conducted to support these assertions: this question represents an area of future interest in yoga research.

Kundalini Yoga as taught by Yogi Bhajan incorporates a wide array of practices, and Yogi Bhajan attributed specific effects for most of them on both normal, healthy psychophysiology and on medical and psychological abnormalities. Kundalini Yoga practitioners and instructors are endowed with a wide menu of practices to choose from, targeting specific areas of physical and psychological development as desired or needed; thus it may be well suited as a therapeutic intervention.

Yogi Bhajan formally expanded and elaborated on the therapeutic use of Kundalini Yoga by developing an associated set of teachings and body of knowledge he called *Humanology*. Furthermore, he inspired the formation of the Guru Ram Das Center for Medicine and Humanology, an institute devoted to the practical medical application of his teachings; it provides instruction in Kundalini Yoga and meditation for people with chronic or life-threatening illnesses and their family members, offers continuing education and professional training to health care providers, and conducts outcome studies on the health benefits of Kundalini Yoga practice. There are now training programs for the therapeutic application of Kundalini Yoga techniques offered in New Mexico by the Guru Ram Das Center and in other venues, including a program in Sweden.

Yogi Bhajan's rationale for yoga as a therapeutic intervention shares many of the common principles used in the modern application of yoga therapy. In addition to serving as a fundamental practice for reducing arousal and improving stress tolerance and resilience, yoga practices are also claimed to be capable of restoring imbalances within the body and mind; such imbalances are believed to be the underlying cause of many medical and psychological conditions. Yogi Bhajan was particularly and perhaps uniquely specific on the exact mechanisms through which the yoga practices had their effects. He frequently referred to the subtle energy centers and processes within the mind-body complex that are often discussed in yogic theory, including Kundalini, prana, chakras, subtle energy fields, and auras. He would often add to these a description of other subtle energy systems such as acupuncture, pressure points, and meridians. In his practice as a therapist and counselor, he often diagnosed a condition and then prescribed for it a meditation, a set of exercises or postures, or even dietary recommendations that were to be practiced over specific periods of time—often forty days or longer.

Given this history, it is not surprising that Kundalini Yoga practices have been considered effective for a number of different disorders and for special populations. Numerous books and manuals on Kundalini Yoga have been published containing yoga exercises and meditations recommended for a variety of physical and mental states. Authors and researchers Mukta Kaur Khalsa,[1] David Shannahoff-Khalsa,[2] and Dharma Singh Khalsa[3] have all published books that provide Kundalini Yoga techniques that target a number of psychological/psychiatric conditions. Publications in scientific and alternative medicine journals and chapters of books have discussed the medical utility of Kundalini Yoga practices as either adjunct or primary treatments for a number of medical conditions including heart disease, gastrointestinal disorders, infertility, depression, and anxiety.[4]

A growing body of scientific biomedical research has addressed the utility of a number of Kundalini Yoga practices, both in normal subjects and in patient populations. However, in this essay, I review only the Kundalini Yoga research that has been conducted in patient populations. My hope is that this will provide a sense of the broad potential application and utility of these practices. This research is particularly important as the vehicle by which such practices can be validated and, therefore, ultimately accepted as valuable adjunct medical mind-body interventions, not only for the treatment of existing disease, but also for disease prevention.

Perhaps the earliest effort in the application of Kundalini Yoga for special or clinical populations was what has been called the 3HO Foundation SuperHealth program. This was an addiction recovery program started in the 1970s in Tucson, Arizona; it was a comprehensive residential intervention that incorporated not only intensive Kundalini Yoga practices but also dietary and lifestyle changes Yogi Bhajan prescribed as being helpful for treating addictive behavior and for substance abuse recovery. Although the program did not undergo published research evaluation in Tucson, it was largely successful, and it received continuing grant support from the state. In one unpublished evaluation, it was shown that the program had strong outcomes for both alcohol (76 percent recovery) and drug abuse (73 percent recovery). Furthermore, its collateral effects, such as improvements in overall job performance and peace of mind, were also notable.

A recent SuperHealth addiction program conducted in the Indian city of Amritsar also underwent a research evaluation, and results were ultimately published in a substance abuse research journal.[5] In that program, ten patients with a variety of substance abuse profiles underwent a comprehensive ninety-day 3HO Foundation SuperHealth lifestyle and residential treatment program. Substantial and statistically significant improvements were found in a number of key outcome measures important in substance abuse, including impulsive and addictive behavior, depression and anxiety, daily living and role functioning, and quality of recovery. There is a continuing active interest in, and application of, Kundalini Yoga practices for addiction recovery among a number of Kundalini Yoga instructors, and it is likely these programs will continue to be conducted and researched.

With support from the National Center for Complementary and Alternative Medicine of the National Institutes of Health, David Shannahoff-Khalsa researched the efficacy of a Kundalini Yoga protocol for the treatment of obsessive-compulsive disorder in a clinical case study of five patients who completed a one-year treatment protocol.[6] The patients experienced statistically significant reductions in a number of psychological characteristics, and some patients were able to reduce their medication doses. This study was followed by a more formal and comprehensive randomized controlled trial conducted at Children's Hospital in San Diego.[7] Results of this study confirmed those of the previous preliminary study and showed significant improvements over a three-month period on a number of clinical measures for this disorder, including the Yale-Brown Obsessive Compulsive Scale and the Symptom Checklist-90-Revised Obsessive Compulsive Scale. Shannahoff-Khalsa was able to conclude that the Kundalini Yoga protocol was an effective treatment for obsessive-compulsive disorder. Furthermore, Kundalini Yoga treatment was without negative side effects. Importantly, it demonstrated an efficacy that compares well with that of standard pharmacotherapy for this disorder. Given that obsessive-compulsive disorder is a subclass of the anxiety disorders, it is likely that Kundalini Yoga may also prove useful in treating other anxiety disorders such as generalized anxiety disorder, panic attacks, and phobias.

My own research has been evaluating the efficacy of a Kundalini Yoga breathing meditation called *Shabad Kriya* that was taught by Yogi Bhajan as a technique to help with sleep. Although he provided a number of yogic practices for sleep, this particular meditation was especially suitable in that it was simple to learn and could be practiced by chronic insomnia patients who did not have the strength or flexibility to practice vigorous physical postures. In a preliminary trial of twenty patients with chronic insomnia, an eight-week treatment including up to thirty-one minutes of Shabad Kriya was evaluated with daily sleep diaries. This was delivered in a self-care format; subjects were given a one-hour instruction session with a brief in-person follow-up one week later and were provided detailed written instructions. They then practiced the prescribed technique on their own, daily, just before bedtime. The outcome of this preliminary trial indicated that subjects on average showed statistically significant improvements over the eight weeks in a number of key sleep measures including sleep efficiency, total sleep time, and total wake time,[8] with no reported negative side effects. Subsequently, a randomized controlled trial has now been completed with the same intervention. The outcomes from that trial have indicated that the results were as good as or better than those from the preliminary trial.[9] These results suggest that Kundalini Yoga may prove to be a valuable adjunct to existing conventional behavioral treatments for insomnia as well as for other disorders that, like insomnia, are characterized by high levels of physiological arousal.

Another technique Yogi Bhajan taught for therapeutic purposes is called Breathwalk. This technique incorporates Kundalini Yoga meditation, mantra, and breathing into a variety of walking techniques, and has been promoted by Gurucharan Singh Khalsa, one of Yogi Bhajan's senior teachers, the director of training for Kundalini Yoga, and principal author with Yogi Bhajan of a book on Breathwalk.[10] It is a particularly practical therapeutic approach for Westerners who have difficulty with the practice of specific yoga techniques and may be drawn to the fact that this technique is already socially familiar and can be practiced under ordinary life circumstances. Recently, a Breathwalk intervention was used in a clinical trial in chronic hepatitis C patients with insulin resistance syndrome at the University of Guadalajara. The results of that study revealed significant improvements in fitness, body composition, lipid profile, liver enzymes, and metabolic and mood state.[11] The authors concluded that "Breathwalk is an innovative exercise technique that is easy to perform which could be implemented as a tool for patients with chronic liver diseases, especially at early stages of disease and in other chronic pathological conditions such as obesity, metabolic syndrome and type 2 diabetes." New research is continuing at University of Utah Pain Center to study the effects of Breathwalk on alleviating pain in fibromyalgia and continuing pain syndromes.

A recent study has suggested that Kundalini Yoga may also have utility in stroke rehabilitation through improvement in aphasia as well as in fine motor coordination. A small pilot study on three stroke patients was conducted using a twice weekly, twelve-week Kundalini Yoga intervention at the Continuum Center for Health and Healing in New York City.[12] Using standard methods for evaluation of dexterity and aphasia, the authors found that all three patients showed substantial improvement in both outcomes. The authors concluded that "this study illustrates the potential benefits of Kundalini yoga on speech impairment and demonstrates the need for further studies of the effects of Kundalini not only on stroke-induced aphasia but also on other speech disorders such as stuttering and speech impediments. The combined positive effects of Kundalini yoga on both the cognitive and physical conditions examined in this study suggest that many other medical problems could be benefited as well."

In addition to the published studies described above, there are also a number of unpublished clinical Kundalini Yoga studies. In addition to my research in insomnia, two other studies have been conducted to evaluate improvements in sleep. An unpublished Swedish study by Goran Bol found improvements in sleep through a vigorous set of Kundalini Yoga exercises recommended for "conquering sleep." This particular set of exercises makes extensive use of a posture referred to as "bridge pose" in Kundalini Yoga but known as "table pose" in Hatha Yoga, a posture that Yogi Bhajan taught specifically as a useful practice for sleep improvement. In a recent thesis dissertation of a controlled study conducted at Alliant International University in San Diego, participants with sleep disturbances practicing Kundalini Yoga were found to have significant improvements in wake time after sleep onset and quality of life, compared to control subjects.[13] Ongoing studies by Dharma Singh Khalsa through his Alzheimer's Research and Prevention Foundation, in association with University of Pennsylvania researchers, are demonstrating the efficacy of a Kundalini Yoga meditation called *Kirtan Kriya* in treating mild cognitive impairment (or early Alzheimer's disease). This work is aimed at providing a potentially useful adjunct treatment for prevention or treatment of Alzheimer's. Other unpublished research work conducted by researchers at the Guru Ram Das Center for Medicine and Humanology has evaluated the benefits of Kundalini Yoga for patients with diabetes. These studies showed improvements in a number of important mood and psychological outcomes in this patient population. These studies represent a small sampling of the Kundalini Yoga treatment initiatives currently under way. The Kundalini Research Institute is dedicated to facilitating these programs and providing support for proper and thorough research evaluations of these programs to document their effectiveness.

In summary, it is clear that Kundalini Yoga has potential utility as a therapeutic treatment for a wide variety of medical and psychological conditions. Whether its efficacy can be attributed to the general ability of mind-body practices to induce the relaxation response, and thereby reduce arousal and promote stress tolerance and resilience, or to specific physical and psychological effects of these practices remains to be determined by future research. Another scientific question of interest that may need to wait for future studies is the role played by subtle energy processes, including the Kundalini energy itself, in the health and healing process.

See the following Websites for additional information:

3HO Foundation: 3ho.org

Kundalini Research Institute: kriteachings.org

International Kundalini Yoga Teachers Association: kundaliniyoga.com

Guru Ram Das Center for Medicine and Humanology: grdcenter.org

Breathwalk: breathwalk.com

Alzheimer's Research and Prevention Foundation: alzheimersprevention.org

Kundalini and Health

Living Well with Spiritual Awakening

OLGA LOUCHAKOVA

Olga Louchakova is a professor of transpersonal psychology and director of the Neurophenomenology Center at the Institute of Transpersonal Psychology. She is a master teacher of the Hridayam® School of Kundalini Yoga. In this essay she shares her experience with kundalini awakenings—how kundalini interfaces with physical and mental health. Having worked as a neuroscientist at the Pavlov Institute of Physiology in St. Petersburg, Russia, she combines this knowledge of the biology of the brain with her experience of kundalini to detail the different possibilities of energy openings in chakras, meridians, and "knots," otherwise known as thresholds where kundalini energy can become stuck and cause sickness, disease, or emotional turmoil. She also advises those who experience these challenging kundalini awakenings that there are ways to work through them and experience their spiritual power in a positive way. She answers such questions as: Are certain chakras or areas of the body associated with particular autoimmune diseases or nervous systems malfunctions? Can we better prepare for kundalini through expanding our awareness of ourselves on all levels, including psychological and spiritual?

KUNDALINI HAS A dual nature. According to Indian metaphysics, "she" is Shakti, the manifesting power of the universe, flowing from spirit into matter. In her reverse flow, which is one's spiritual awakening, she flows back to her source in spirit. Through her flow, matter and spirit manifest as the opposite ends of a single continuum. This living energy in the human body connects the dual realities that our mind-born philosophies have sentenced to forever exist in different ontological orders: the realms of the "real" and the realms of the "ideal." Mystics of all traditions have always seen these realities as connected, as a continuum from corporeal "earth" to spiritual "heaven." Through the spectrum of subtle energies, the solids of the material body flow into intangible creations of the mind. This "mind-stuff" continues into a domain that is completely transcendent to any materiality, into that which is transcendent to thought itself and to any meaning or form, and which possesses only the suchness of existence, sentiency, and eternal fullness in the "now." This is the path of the return to the self, the path of kundalini. It always contains a paradox of the immortal spirit, unveiling itself moment by moment in the density and darkness of the perishable, finite, limited human body. Thus, the body becomes a participant in spiritual awakening and a conduit to energies of a high spiritual nature, which bring to light whatever obstacles and latent conditions were dormant in the body.

Traditional kundalini yoga dealt with the paradox of embodied awakening by introducing preliminary spiritual practices that prepared the body for a current of high spiritual energies. The practices of ethical purification, of awareness directed to bodily sensations, and of physical postures and breath control were intended to precede the activation of kundalini energy. Body, psyche, and behavior, thus brought into alignment and harmony, created the perfect container for the awakening of kundalini. Ideally, like a river flowing through a clean and welcoming riverbed, the transformational energies penetrated and informed the perfected body without causing any problems for the health of the body or mind.

By contrast, the spontaneous awakening of kundalini amid the ongoing stresses of life is by no means an event that adds to the harmony of our being. On one side, spiritual awakening leads to the attainment of self-knowledge and hence happiness. On the other side, the uncalled-for transformation inherent in awakening creates conflicts with the feeble homeostasis of our existence. How does the body respond to spiritual awakening? What does such awakening do to our physical health? An embodied kundalini awakening contains the *promise* of full physical health, but may well bring out or activate dormant diseases that manifest until the body "clears up" or resolves these potential blockages and then restores the flow of energy. Because of the way spiritual awakening unfolds, fields such as psychosomatic medicine, psychoneuroimmunology, and other areas of medicine that take into consideration the connections between the mind and the body can be of special use in troublesome kundalini awakenings.

THE IMMENSITY OF SPIRIT AND FINALITY OF THE BODY

Consider the relationship between the immensity of spirit and the finality of the body. Here is the story of Sherry, a woman in her mid-forties. One night, she felt strong anxiety and a pain in the left side of her body, culminating in the chest. She wondered if she was having a heart attack. She decided to put off calling the ambulance, hoping the pain would subside. Indeed, after several hours of turmoil, her state shifted. The pain was gone, and she passed into a new state of being in which she was simultaneously herself and every living being there is. She was insects and animals, whales and angels, her children and her ancestors, saints and killers, extraterrestrials and beings yet to be born. She/they experienced delight, pain, insights, terror, love, perils and paradise, births and deaths, and everything else imaginable. This continued for some time, and then subsided. If one's own life can be hard to cope with, how much harder it is to be present in the life experience of all beings! The sentience that lives in the heart of everyone and everything and contains the whole universe revealed itself through Sherry's experience of heart pain.

Sherry managed to surrender to the experience of what she later discovered was kundalini opening her heart center. She was also able to integrate this experience with the experience of mundane consciousness, which returned after the opening had passed. But one may imagine a less benign situation. For example, French Benedictine monk Henri le Saux, also known as Swami Abhishiktananda, experienced a full-blown heart attack that was evidently a spiritual awakening within his heart center.

The juxtaposition of the spiritual expansion of an opening heart center and the limitations and "normalcy" of everyday ego-based consciousness creates a significant conflict for the mind. As one of my meditation students, an eight-year-old girl, rightly noticed, "Inside we are much larger than on the outside." If one's mind is too attached to the trivial, is closed to the perception of the nonordinary, or is simply afraid to lose control over the habitual dimensions of time and space and one's habitual power relationships with others, the state of consciousness associated with the heart center's opening will be threatening to one's psychological status quo. Thus, spiritual energies that need to be channeled toward the spirit—the nonmaterial level of the body-mind-spirit spectrum—will be trapped in the corporeal domain. Like lava, which is safe, vital, and useful when abiding at the core of the earth, such energies are safe, vital, and useful when they are allowed to follow their natural flow into the spirit. But just as released lava burns the surface of the earth, these spiritual energies cause physical afflictions when they become trapped amid our psychological inability to surrender, to be authentic and honest with our inner experiences, or simply to face the painful contents of emotional experiences, shameful memories, or insufficiencies of the self. Then, the intermediary of the mind between the physical body and the spirit becomes contracted or closed, the flow of energies opening the spiritual dimension is blocked, and the physical body takes the brunt of this energy that does not belong to it. This is why heart attacks or strokes may be associated with spiritual awakening—a price the physical body pays for being the conduit of spirit while living an unbalanced, so-called normal life.

I first recognized that the kundalini process can include physical problems in the late 1980s. I had been working as a medical doctor and neuroscientist while also teaching intense kundalini-raising practices in the Russian spiritual underground community during the years of Soviet power. At times, my participants developed exacerbations of chronic conditions such as gastritis, angina pectoris, or migraines. But as meditation deepened, awareness of the body brought the psychological conflicts associated with pathology to consciousness and allowed them to be resolved: the symptoms disappeared, and then all practitioners reported a subjective improvement in their health.

As my observations cumulated over the years, it became clear to me that health problems can develop in people who do not practice kundalini techniques but are the subjects of spontaneous kundalini awakening. However, health conditions *associated with kundalini awakening* tended to self-heal or present few complications or residual symptoms, while regular "unspiritual" health problems—even those with the same diagnosis—commonly worsened and demanded medical treatment.

KUNDALINI-RELATED PATHOLOGY

Gradually, it became possible to differentiate between several kinds of disease that were obviously related to kundalini awakening. Cardiovascular problems associated with kundalini, such as strokes and heart attacks, differed from regular strokes and heart attacks because they healed better, faster, and with fewer complications and were accompanied by profound personal transformation bordering on character change. In contrast to personal changes in response to the disease—such as might occur as a result of the life-transforming influence of hardship—it was as if these conditions were wrapped around a particular neurotic conflict. Positive personality or character dynamics occurred when the conflict was resolved, and this in turn caused the disappearance of the bodily projection of the conflict: the disease.

Both strokes and heart attacks are related to the areas of the body where, according to the kundalini process model, there are important centers associated with the principal structures of the psyche and transcendent spiritual experiences of a higher order. Spiritual experiences in these areas are related to psychological experiences. In a sense, both can be seen as residing along a continuum of meaning that begins in personal realms (within the domain of the ego) and resolves into spiritual realms (beyond the ego). Those kinds of polarities in meaning associated with our inner structure are described in Jungian literature, and in my studies of the phenomenology of the self this kind of organization of meaning becomes especially prominent.

Recently in psychological literature, there has appeared a plethora of works, including those by Eugene Genlin and psychologist Steven Rosin, that place meaning upon the spatial organization of the body. Mind dwells in the body, whereas body-mind-spirit inhabit a continuum; they are not separate, watertight compartments. These and other concepts addressing the continuity between the body and our internal worlds are becoming increasingly present in public awareness. They relate well to the kundalini process, as they describe the realities of inner experience and the dynamics of the process as it emerges.

In the case of kundalini-related strokes or heart attacks, the neurotic conflict on the level of the mind blocks the resolution of awareness into spirit, which the energy and vector of the process of spiritual awakening require. But when the obstacle is resolved, the process becomes harmonized with its internal tendencies, and instead of causing affliction to the physical body, it causes an experiential unveiling of the spirit connected with the area of the body where the affliction existed. In other words, gateways to spirit open at the location in the physical body where the disease used to be, in the affected areas of the brain or heart. The same holds true for other areas of the body that correspond to spiritual centers.

The next group of physical afflictions relates to those areas of the body where there is less possibility of an associated neurotic conflict due to the specific meanings associated with these areas, because such meanings are multilevel and present a very complex structure. In the Indian psychology of kundalini yoga, at least two levels of mind are differentiated: mind without certainty of knowledge (*manas* in Sanskrit), and mind—intellect—that has certainty (*buddhi* in Sanskrit). In Western science and philosophy, the levels of the mind and the types of cognition form a complicated, frequently self-contradictory map. What is important to the understanding of kundalini-related pathology is to differentiate between the thinking that relates to solving mundane problems and the frequently preverbal set of deep existential beliefs that govern our behavior and relationship with life. These thoughts or beliefs concern what is real and unreal, what it means to die and to exist, what is moral and what is not. There is a group of centers in the body that are specifically associated with these mental processes. While none of these processes are better than others, some of them are truer to the reality of spirit, to the "enlightened" state of mind that accepts the primacy of the ideal, of spirit. Others are mostly true to the reality of the unenlightened mind: the premises associated with a purely materialist orientation. These mental domains are associated with structures of the subtle body that are called "knots" in the psychology of kundalini.

In contrast to other structures of the subtle body such as chakras or meridians, knots are thresholds, places where the current of kundalini energy, or the process of spiritual awakening, tends to become stuck in a specific way. If kundalini leads one to the unveiling of one's essential self—to a recognition of the

realness of the ideal world (spirit as the essence of the self)—
the self is mostly veiled in the zones of the subtle body knots.
Thus the obstructions or conflicts in those areas are related to the
dynamics of a deep understanding of one's nature, as opposed to
the dynamics of simple neurotic conflicts. While delusions about
one's enlightened nature are not neurotic conflicts per se, they
are in a sense afflictions associated with the kundalini process
itself. When energy gets stuck in one of these zones, it develops a
physical pathology specific to that zone. As the kundalini process
progresses, this "stuckness" clears; we become more aligned with
the truth of our nature, and the symptoms disappear.

The first knot is located in the area below the navel. In Indian
kundalini-related metaphysics, it is known as the knot of Brahma,
the Creator. The essence of this knot is the understanding of the
subtle realms underlying the perceptions of the material world. It is
also the understanding of the different degrees of materiality, from
gross to subtle. Clearing obstructions in this area can be associated
with the development of prostate cancer in men or fibromatosis
and various pathological conditions of the uterus in women.

Next is the knot of Vishnu (*Vishnu-granthi* in Sanskrit). It is
located right above the center of the diaphragm. Transitioning
through this knot involves important transformations in one's
perception of self and others and in one's relationships with other
people. While kundalini energy dwells below the knot of Vishnu,
we perceive and relate to others as "objects" without consciousness. When kundalini rises above Vishnu-granthi, our relationships
with other people deepen and become more complex, and we
are capable of perceiving other people as filled with the same
depth and intensity of life and consciousness as ourselves. In psychological terms, this is a transition from object relations to real
relations: the perception of consciousness in the other. Thus, this
threshold of kundalini is connected with the veiling of the universal nature of consciousness: the sameness of self at the heart
of all beings. I have observed that in the kundalini process, the

opening of this center is frequently associated with diabetes, which doesn't go away afterward but does become controllable as the knot is passed.

The third granthi, the knot of Rudra, coincides with the location of the vestibular area in the brain stem. Obstacles or conflicts at this threshold are psychologically connected with the negation of the self, from the most primitive and mundane manifestations of self-hatred to intricate and sophisticated forms of negation of one's own existence. When energy gets stuck at this center, people can develop vertigo, which goes away as the process progresses and self-hate and self-negation are resolved.

The two other groups of health conditions I have observed involve cancer and mental health. As much as I would like to present a coherent theory of cancer in relation to kundalini, I consider the area too complex and the etymology of cancer too diverse to present such a theory at this stage of our evolving knowledge. Even in the case of diseases more evidently connected to the process of spiritual awakening, such as the strokes and heart attacks previously mentioned, conclusions about their relationship to spiritual awakening are based on my intuitive understanding and my many observations of both the symptoms and spiritual advancement, taken together.

It is necessary to keep in mind that no scientific research has yet been conducted to evaluate the stages of the extremely complex process of spiritual awakening, to prove the existence of kundalini itself, or to suggest the measurable validity of her connections with particular diseases. The only proof supporting this intuitive knowledge is clinical practice: working with people who are in the process of psychosomatic kundalini-related disease correlating to the kundalini process model, and observing the subsequent improvement of health and the predictability of the developmental stages that follow.

When we consider a process of such duration and depth, one rooted in realities of a metaphysical nature, perhaps we must look toward scientific research yet to come. The modern scientific paradigm is materialistic, and medicine does not yet have much knowledge about systemic, multimodal developmental processes in the psyche or psychosomatic conflict that could affect the physical body. Having said this, however, I should also note that numerous clinical observations, as well as successful work in managing and healing psychosomatic disorders that emerge in the process of spiritual awakening, argue for further research in the field. With cancer, however, studies can become especially complicated, as the anomalous growth of cells in cancer may be related to numerous psychological conditions, conflicts, deficiencies, and extremes.

PROBLEMS ASSOCIATED WITH THE SPIRITUAL HEART

The last condition I will address in this essay is bipolar disorder, one of the most "popular" diagnoses in modern industrial culture. From the standpoint of kundalini, bipolar disorder may be rooted in the spiritual awakening associated with the complex of centers of the spiritual heart. While the chakra system is generally thought of as originating from a Hindu analysis of spiritual awakening, this system of centers, known as *lataif* in Arabic, is less familiar and is rooted in a different spiritual "technology." The centers of the heart are, in fact, found in all traditions that postulate the ultimate reality as the Self, and that describe the manifestations of the Self in the human body in the construction of the human, experientially perceived self. This includes Hesychasm (the body-based system in Christian mysticism), Sufism, and the Shakta-Vedanta teachings of Hinduism. Centers of the self in the chest are also known in other spiritual systems and wisdom traditions such as the shamanic cultures of Latin America and the Hellenistic cultures of the Mediterranean. My research has mainly involved Hesychasm, Sufism, and Shakta-Vedanta, so the following description of the centers is related primarily to these three traditions.

The complex of the centers of the heart includes five domains, each associated with a set of psychological functions and spiritual experiences. It appears, however, that the bipolar disorder-like condition is associated with only three of these centers, so I will restrict my discussion to those three.

It is commonly known that all types of bipolar disorder include fluctuations between depression and mania. There are specific locations in the complex of the heart where depression and mania are normal, expected experiences. In a sense, one can say that in the kundalini process associated with the opening of the heart, depression and mania conditions are predictable states of the purification and transformation of the subtle body.

The center on the right side of the chest is associated with the experience of depression. This center is described in the teachings of the Indian saint Sri Ramana Maharshi; however, he does not address the psychological aspects of it, only the associated spiritual experiences. People who have spontaneous spiritual awakening going through the right side of the chest, however, may experience spiritual conditions as entirely secondary to the mood swings of early emotions, experienced most often as depressive episodes and a clouded mind. Physically, this center is located above the third rib on the right, near the right edge of the chest bone. Psychologically, it is associated with the individual's history, especially the early experiences that helped shape what in self-psychology (an American psychoanalytic school created by the analyst Hanz Kohut) is known as "false" self versus the so-called "true" self. Consequently, the developmental tasks of kundalini in this center are those of deconstruction of the false self and explication of the true self. According to my observations, this deconstruction process, as a stage of spiritual development, can last for up to several years if the kundalini energy continues its motion upward. In the case of a stuck process, deconstruction turns into depression, which can stay for life.

This center can be experienced as a condensed sense of somatic personhood, which expands into the inner awareness of the body. Its meaning and contents are related to one's individual history and packed with memories of early childhood interactions, including old painful emotions. When we become aware of the constructs of the self through this center, empty or depleted areas of the early self can surface, and typical results are fatigue and deep emotional pain. While therapeutic intuition is not the best research tool, I can say that on many occasions when my clients reported symptoms reminiscent of chronic fatigue, such symptoms were associated with a tangible sensation centering on the right side, which I perceived energetically as the opening of the right-side center. When the process was completed, primarily through self-psychology techniques—which could take as much as a couple of years—the symptoms of fatigue disappeared.

This center of awareness on the right side of the chest is emphasized in the writings of Maharshi as the seat of the "I" sense: the somatic sense of individual personhood that leads into the interior quality of the Heart. The nondual experience, however, emerges not in this right-side center but in the core of the chest, in the center known as spiritual heart (or *qalb* in Sufism), which is connected with the right-side center by a small, internal subtle meridian. In spiritual seekers with an interest in nonduality, and especially those exposed to the environment of New Age neo-Vedanta satsangs, frequent fluctuation of awareness between the core and the right-side center create a typical dynamic of fluctuation between the "nondual" state of mind and the state of mind resulting from the right center's process of deconstruction: fatigue, depression, or early memories. These fluctuations are especially active for people who enter relationships with their partners during this time in their development. Then, the seeker finds herself in the position of being "enlightened" one day and immersed in mundane and emotional pain the next, and then enlightened again, and on it goes. This is a condition of the developmental of the heart.

On the left side, corresponding to the anatomical heart, sits another center, which can be associated with the maniacal state.

In the heart, everything acquires cosmic proportions. Sherry's experience, described at the beginning of this essay, involved the opening of the left side of the heart. This center is associated with the physical heart. It has the pure emotion of love at its depths, and God as love is known here at a depth beyond the thickness of the muscle.

The dreams and impressions associated with the center on the left side of the chest—which is located approximately below the third rib and into the thick of the heart muscle toward the center of the chest—are generally characterized by their cosmological, transegoic character. An example of perceptions associated with this center is found in the Bhagavad Gita, where the hero, Arjuna, asks his friend Krishna, a divine being, to show his true form. The cosmic form of Krishna contains all possible opposites as well as images of cosmic birth and destruction, all of which overwhelm Arjuna. Another example of this kind of perception is found in the legend where Krishna's mother looks into the mouth of her child, trying to figure out if he is the one who stole the butter. She sees innumerable universes within the body of the child, and these are the universes of the heart. In Greek mythology, a similar situation takes place in the myth of Zeus showing his true form to Semela. The cosmic heart of Inanna and the cosmic heart of Sufism also refer to this phenomenon.

It is necessary to "purify" this center because its content varies from cosmological visions to expressions of the meaning of what is called in esotericism the Divine Names: the aspects of the mind condensed in relatively homogenous fields of meaning such as Beauty, Mercy, Power, Betrayal, Violence, and the like. Sometimes, when this material that is usually hidden from daily awareness breaks through, it can create mania—or even psychosis. The metaphysics of the Divine Names is quite complex, but in practice, the Names manifest those psychological overtones that give the experience of them a certain quality of interpretation. They serve as lenses to one's perception of the world by giving the perception a specific ambiance: the overarching meaning that seems to interpret one's whole life. For example, if the lens that is the Divine Name Betrayal is stationed in the heart, many experiences will be interpreted as related to betrayal. At first, I will see myself as a betrayer; then I will see others—in fact, the world—as betraying me. The experience of a Name and the stories connected with its meaning can obscure normal perception, and in combination with the magnitude of scenes that play out in the cosmic perception in the heart, make everything appear manic.

The first stages of the opening of the heart may be associated with fear "leaking" from the left side of the chest, a sense of immensity opening within, and a sense of insanity rising from the anatomical heart. Generally, it is an episode that lasts for several hours. In one of my dreams, Ramana Maharshi, who for me is the personification of the deepest heart-Self, was breaking into my spiritual heart from the left side. My students have reported similar dreams, and if, contrary to my experience, the emerging archetype is experienced as alien—that is, not friendly—these dreams can be quite frightening.

When the kundalini process proceeds normally, the centers develop in the context of normal life, and the awareness of unusual, depressive, or manic conditions of the left- and right-side hearts become integrated with the contents of normal awareness.

The processes connected with opening and healing the heart centers on the right side of the body can take several decades. In my own case, the process of bringing somatic awareness of the "I" sense to the right side started in the early 1990s; in the mid-nineties I discovered the passage connecting the right side with the core of the chest. The development of the center on the right included all the stages of the deconstruction of the false self and lasted until early 2000. Meanwhile, that process was accompanied by opening on the left side and fluctuations of mood that gradually became more and more integrated with the material from the right. On the left, I experienced three major episodes of opening, including very intense emotions associated with Divine Names and the core of love in the heart's center. In 2000, the sensations and images on the right became more differentiated from one another, and there was the sense of archetypal "others," with whom relationships gradually developed; their images became less and less frightening. I actualized the feminine (as myself) and integrated the feelings coming from the right side, and eventually my analyst identified my dreams as related to family wounds and paternal narcissism. This in turn led to the opening of a pattern of deep psychological definitions of the self related to my family constitution.

I have seen the fragments of this process in others, but because it is so longitudinal, it has been hard to observe its entire development in a single case. It is, however, possible to predict forthcoming developments in the process, and I have found them supported in my clinical experience.

Contrary to the process of relatively benign integration I experienced, if the opening is very deep, the energy is unstable, and the integration suffers for any of a variety of reasons, the stations of the heart become disconnected from normal awareness and are experienced as psychotic episodes. If energy begins fluctuating between the left and right sides of the spiritual heart center, it fosters a bipolar disorder, including mood swings, deep depression, and manic episodes.

MAINTAINING A BALANCED AND HEALTHY LIFE

The conditions I have described so far represent only part of the broad canvas of the possible conditions related to physical and mental health that are associated with spiritual awakening. The questions arise: How might one manage the physical aspect of awakening? What would be the work that would allow one to cut through the rising obstacles and challenges, and to enjoy communion with the spirit illumined by the goodness of the Divine

Presence? All the usual recommendations for monitoring the kundalini process, including a healthy lifestyle, meditation, and reading literature associated with the rise of self-knowledge, can help. But in the case of somatized awakening, these things may not be enough to maintain a balanced and positive quality of life while the process unfolds.

I believe that in-depth personal work—involving focused awareness and raising to the surface of consciousness matters connected with an understanding of the self on all levels—is of the uttermost importance. This includes awareness of the whole map of the psyche, of all possible psychologies. The maps Ken Wilber has developed are helpful here, as they list the psychological perspectives pertinent to different levels of consciousness. All of these psychological perspectives work at certain stages of development during the awakening process and can serve as tools for self-knowledge. Direct intuition of the contents of one's mind, awareness of one's inner life, and introspection are the most important skills to cultivate. In a sense, one becomes a navigator of the internal universes of the mind, learning to unlock the puzzles that the developing, ever-deepening process of awakening presents.

The physical body, then, becomes a barometer that gauges the weather of the awakening process: disease is an indicator of the work to be done on both psychological and spiritual levels. For many people, disease becomes a blessing in disguise, as without this "call" they would never choose a path of disciplined self-knowledge. I remember, for example, the situation of a man who resisted the opening of his spiritual nature because he didn't want to get distracted from building his life and family by spiritual issues. Being a person of strong will, he directed his entire awareness to external matters, fully succeeding until, in his midfifties, his internal universe opened within a period of three days. Every spiritual experience that would have happen during the previous twenty years was condensed into that period, and it was beyond overwhelming. Still, the person managed to integrate the information this opening afforded, even though it required a wholesale reorientation of his picture of himself, the world, and God.

To illustrate how spiritual awakening may be intertwined with health issues, and how one can cope with the challenge and live a balanced and healthy life, I will share a story of a friend of mine whose spiritual awakening was accompanied by diabetes, leukemia, and prostate and kidney cancers. I am choosing to share this extreme situation because my friend's health and well-being at the completion of the process serve as empowering examples of courage and hope when dealing with a very tumultuous awakening.

This story is especially interesting because the organs targeted in the sequence of diseases my friend went through were not "aligned" according to the stages of ascending kundalini. However, every disease was resolved after he had attained significant and specific spiritual and psychological shifts, which, from my perspective, allowed the flow of the kundalini process through the area of the body to be freed from affliction. The only disease that happened "in sync" with the succession of stages in the process was diabetes, corresponding with the transition from a lower chakra "object relations"–based contact with the world to a real relationship with the other as the conscious self.

The next step in his process was the recognition of the self in the heart: the nondual experience of himself as "not the body," which happens in the silent mind. While it is difficult to understand the full scale of thinking and conflicts that underlie a systemic cancer such as leukemia, it was evident that the problems were related to the whole functioning of the mind. At this juncture, he was reviewing his whole life and finding it meaningless and failed. The key event during leukemia, which I believe was instrumental to my friend's recovery, was that he managed to stop his mind—he attained the condition of "no-mind" while reading Eckhart Tolle's *The Power of Now*. It cut through the maze of negative thoughts that were, in fact, existential obscurations of the nature of his own being. After reality emerged from this obscurity, my friend experienced a potent episode of kundalini: energy rushed through his entire body, and he became telepathic and able to perceive subtle energies.

After this event, he began to clear the latencies left in the subtle body. He developed prostate cancer, I think, in the process of clearing his relationship with the feminine—major relations with the unconscious and with the mother, the primary care-giver. The task at this stage was rooted in looking at his deepest convictions and regulating his relationship with certain parts of himself. The latter took several years and culminated in bringing to consciousness and reeducating the earliest parts of self. While he matured to a greater understanding of himself, he was not able to let go of his efforts to control many areas of his life, which contradicted his spiritual insight. Kidney cancer was next, and hopefully was the last disease my friend will have to "beat" in the process of his spiritual awakening. He has been enlightened, he is largely through with his psychological difficulties, and at sixty-four years old he is enjoying the first truly successfully conscious relationship of his life.

So, if spiritual awakening can have as a component the mani-festation of various physical problems, what would be the way to avoid this, or at least reduce the cost to the physical body of awakening? This area requires careful medical research, which would allow us to distinguish the diseases connected with spiri-tual awakening—the group of somatoform diseases, when the symptoms present a coherent picture but show no pathology in laboratory findings—from regular diseases with the same diagnosis. Preliminary observations indicate that the "spiritual component" in the etiology of the disease affects recovery, providing for a fast and uncomplicated healing. Because of the profound per-sonality changes involved, it seems at times that the disease goes away together with the old character structure; the new structure that comes in is devoid of the disease and healthy. Living well with spiritual awakening means opening to this fluidity of the personal self, opening to transformation, which takes one beyond oneself and changes one's relationship with the world and others. Sometimes I think that the Indian expression "twice born" relates not so much to those who have experienced the true self, or nondual consciousness, as it does to those who, as a result of this experience, have changed so profoundly that it feels like the birth of a new person. This can happen at any age, defeating our beliefs in the stability of personality traits.

Understanding the process, its inner logic, its rootedness in one's own beliefs and conflicts, its stretch through the continuum of body–mind–spirit, and its general spiritual nature seems to me crucial for navigating diseases toward a successful healing. It puts the sickness into a larger perspective, creates more intention toward healing, brings meaning into areas of seeming meaning-lessness, and in general creates momentum toward attaining the highest objectives of spiritual realization. Diseases related to spiritual awakening are indeed a blessing in disguise. It is a challenging blessing, however, where the tasks of surrender, understanding, and patience are at their zenith.

The Yogic Brain

ANDREW B. NEWBERG, MD

Neuroscience and kundalini yoga come together in the following essay as scientist Andrew Newberg, author of several books, including Born to Believe: God, Science, and the Origin of Ordinary and Extraordinary Beliefs, *probes the far reaches of what is known about the "yogic brain." Drawing upon research that has been done with the most cutting-edge brain imaging equipment, Newberg discusses recent discoveries that a network of brain structures, including the hypothalamus, are activated when people engage in spiritual activities, including kundalini yoga. Detailing both the positive and negative effects of kundalini yoga, Newberg presents a critical look at current research and explores the questions: Can we find scientific proof that kundalini yoga affects the brain in a positive, life-changing way?*

Is THERE SUCH a thing as a yogic brain? In other words, can we find the neural correlates of various practices and experiences related to kundalini yoga? There has been very little direct research exploring the effects of kundalini yoga and the experiences of the energy rising through various chakras of the body, but there is a substantial amount of evidence regarding related practices that might be useful in helping us better understand what happens within the brain and body when an individual practices or experiences kundalini yoga.

The relationship between kundalini yoga and the brain can be explored by considering the various feelings, experiences, emotions, and thoughts that arise when somebody practices kundalini yoga or experiences a kundalini awakening. As with all research of this nature, it must be stressed at the beginning that simply finding a brain response to kundalini yoga by no means reduces kundalini yoga to "nothing more" than brain function. More specifically, if an individual's brain is studied during a kundalini awakening and it is found that certain parts of it are activated during this experience, this would not necessarily imply that the awakening was created by the functioning of the brain. While that is certainly one interpretation, it may be equally valid to say that the brain was *responding* to the kundalini awakening experience. In this way, the brain is "going along for the ride" rather than actually producing the experience itself.

The notion of whether a kundalini awakening experience is generated by the brain or experienced by it is critical when trying to determine the reality of the experience. For individuals who deeply believe in kundalini yoga and the awakening experience, there is no question as to the reality of those experiences. For them, the kundalini awakening experience represents the true manifestation of the energy coiled within the body as it rises through the various chakras until it reaches its ultimate expression. For the individual who does not believe in the notion of an energy that is separate from the biological functions of the body, a kundalini awakening experience is nothing more than various neurons firing in specific areas of the brain that enable a person to have that experience. For this individual, there are no chakras, no energy, and no true awakening of consciousness. All of these subjective experiences are merely the production of the human brain's complex functioning.

On a grander scale, such issues lie at the heart of much research on the relationship between spirituality and the mind. The sense of realness of these experiences presents a great challenge to both our philosophy and our science. After all, if consciousness and energy are something fundamentally different from the biological processes of the body, then current science itself is in for a great paradigm shift. But let us take a look at what some of the possible biological underpinnings of kundalini yoga practices and experiences may actually be before returning to a final evaluation of the true reality of those experiences.

NEUROPHYSIOLOGICAL FINDINGS ASSOCIATED WITH SPIRITUAL PRACTICES

One of the best ways to study spiritual phenomena is by using high-tech brain imaging equipment. Brain imaging studies of spiritual practices in general have used such techniques as magnetic resonance imaging (MRI), positron-emission tomography (PET), single photon emission computed tomography (SPECT), electroencephalography (EEG), and a number of other physiological measures throughout the body. Researchers have also begun to explore the relationship between these biological changes and the subjective nature of the experiences an individual actually perceives. In general, there seems to be an extended network of brain structures that get into the act when people engage in spiritual practices, and kundalini yoga should be no exception. Several studies have shown that when people perform a practice in which they actively focus their minds on something such as a mantra or an image of a sacred object, they activate their frontal lobes. In fact, the frontal lobes activate whenever we focus our minds on anything, so focusing on a spiritual object should also result in increased frontal-lobe activity. In a similar manner, when focusing on the various chakras of the body and the energy flowing through them, one might expect there to be an initial increase in the areas of the brain that are associated with paying attention. Several specific studies of yoga-type practices have revealed increased activity in these brain regions.

Once the frontal lobes are activated, they interact with a number of other important structures in the brain. The thalamus, which has complete neuronal connections with the frontal lobes, is a key relay that enables different parts of the brain to interact with each other as well as for the brain to interact with the rest of the body. As the frontal lobes and thalamus are activated, another part of the brain, the parietal lobe, also becomes involved. The parietal lobe typically takes our sensory information, creates for us a sense of our self, and orients that self in the world. As one deepens the focus on a sacred object, the brain increasingly prevents irrelevant sensory information from reaching the parietal lobe until, and even though this part of the brain is trying to create a sense of self, it no longer has the information with which to do so. It has been suggested that this is associated with the experiences of losing the sense of self and a sense of space and time that are commonly reported during spiritual practices. Brain imaging studies of practices such as meditation and prayer have typically shown a decreased activity in the parietal lobes. Such an experience is also a part of the kundalini yoga tradition. Thus, one might expect to see such changes occurring in people who practice kundalini yoga and have strong awakening experiences, especially if they lose their sense of self.

A very small but crucial structure called the hypothalamus is probably also associated with spiritual practices. This structure controls many body functions including heart rate, blood pressure, and respiration. It also regulates most of our body's hormone systems. Finally, it helps control the autonomic nervous system that regulates our arousal (or sympathetic) and quiescent (or parasympathetic) functions in the body. Since a number of studies exploring spiritual experiences have shown changes in hormone function as well as in autonomic activity, it makes sense that the hypothalamus would play a key role during spiritual experiences. The autonomic nervous system in particular seems to be involved because people typically report intense feelings either of arousal or of bliss during such experiences. In fact, an intriguing aspect of certain mystical experiences is the simultaneous sense of arousal and quiescence. This might be described as an active bliss.

And it is easy to speculate about the importance of this autonomic nervous system in the kundalini awakening experience. Whenever one considers a strong sense of a surge of energy in the body, it would seem likely that the part of the nervous system that turns on the body's energy systems would be strongly activated. A powerful sense of energy and alertness is likely to be experienced when the arousal part of the autonomic nervous system is activated. Since this system is connected to virtually every organ in the body, it may also help to explain how the energy can actually be perceived in different parts of the body at specific times. Therefore, activation of this arousal system may make one experience a substantial energy in the heart at one point and in the abdomen at another point. And while no one has ever drawn a clear correlation between the various chakras and specific organs in the body, a study of this type is certainly within the realm of possibility.

In addition to the body's response, we would also expect there to be a strong surge of the energy-producing chemicals in the brain. For example, one brain scan study showed a release of dopamine during yoga meditation practice, a neurotransmitter that is involved with positive emotions, including the reward system of the brain and even intense feelings of euphoria. Dopamine is the primary mediator for the effects of cocaine, for example. The release of dopamine during meditation practice may certainly explain frequently described intense positive feelings. Other studies have shown changes in the body's hormone systems, notably to cortisol, the body's main stress hormone, which is typically found to be decreased during meditation practices. This reflects a lower stress state of the individual. Since cortisol also suppresses the immune system, lower levels of cortisol during meditation may help enhance immune system function, and this in turn might ultimately have a beneficial effect on how the body handles disease. This leads us to a broader discussion of the overall relationship between kundalini, spirituality, and health. After all, if there are physiological effects, there should be health effects.

THE POSITIVE EFFECTS OF KUNDALINI YOGA

The positive effects of kundalini yoga may be divided into two broad categories. The first category pertains to the actual practice of kundalini yoga. Yoga practices in general have been associated with a number of beneficial effects on the mind and body; they have been reported to help in a variety of different disorders including high blood pressure, heart disease, asthma, arthritis, and many others. For the most part, many of these changes are mediated through the brain changes described previously. For example, if a practice helped augment the function of the autonomic nervous system, we would expect to see changes in blood pressure and heart rate that may have a beneficial effect on the cardiovascular system. Meditation and yoga practices have also been shown to benefit mental health; in particular, such practices appear to lessen anxiety and depression. From a physiological perspective, such an impact may make sense, since these practices may be able to affect the serotonin and dopamine systems, which are vitally important to symptoms of anxiety and depression. Spiritual practices also are important coping mechanisms for dealing with a variety of health and other life-related issues. In fact, spirituality is frequently reported as the most widely used coping mechanism. All of the present research studies taken together suggest that practices such as kundalini yoga should result in a variety of potentially beneficial effects.

The second broad category of effects related to kundalini yoga would pertain to the more transformational aspects that might be associated with kundalini awakenings. A growing number of studies have explored how spiritual transformation affects the mind and body. Transformational experiences are frequently reported to be associated with many positive benefits. For example, those individuals who have a spiritual transformation experience typically report a greater sense of meaning and purpose in life, better interpersonal relationships, and improved perspective on their jobs and life goals. These individuals also report less fear of death. From a physiological perspective, what is unclear about transformational experiences is how they can occur so rapidly: there are no known mechanisms at the present time that would allow for a vast array of neural connections to suddenly shift in a matter of moments, thereby altering a person's entire perspective and approach toward life. While the notion of a tremendous release of energy arising through the body may make sense from a kundalini yoga perspective, a clear biological correlate remains to be fully elucidated. The problem is that one never knows when such transformational experiences are going to occur, and this makes studying them directly almost impossible. In spite of this, it is clear that transformational experiences, including those associated with kundalini awakenings, are powerful, life-changing events. Furthermore, these events must be associated with substantial changes in the brain and body's physiology.

THE NEGATIVE EFFECTS OF KUNDALINI YOGA

Although most studies have shown positive effects, kundalini awakening and other strong spiritual experiences may also negatively affect health. It is relatively unlikely for kundalini yoga practice to result in negative health effects. There are always anecdotal reports of individuals who become more depressed, or even psychotic, when doing various meditative or spiritual practices. The more likely cause of a negative effect related to kundalini yoga would be associated with awakening experiences the individual is not fully prepared for—a well-described problem in the kundalini yoga literature. When individuals are not adequately prepared for a kundalini awakening, the tremendous energy and power associated with this experience are believed to cause substantial harm, mentally and physically. Some of the problems reported include mental confusion, memory problems, emotional mood swings, sleep disturbances, gastrointestinal problems, muscular and sensory problems, changes in sexual desire, and changes in pain perception. No studies have documented the physiological correlates of these problems; however, one might speculate that such a negative experience would be associated with a substantial disruption of normal brain circuitry. There may also be related abnormal activity in specific neurotransmitter systems such as the dopamine and serotonin systems that are also involved in anxiety, depression, and even psychosis. It might also be the case that a negative kundalini awakening experience may be very difficult for an individual to recover from because of the potentially long-term effects on the brain itself.

And there could be another potentially negative aspect of kundalini awakening experiences, something that has also been reported in other powerful spiritual experiences, including mystical states, near-death experiences, and spiritual visions. The problem I am referring to here is that sometimes even a profoundly positive experience can be so markedly different from the individual's usual worldview that they have trouble incorporating the experience into their prevailing belief system. For example, an individual who had been raised Catholic and was a practicing Catholic up to the time of their spiritual awakening might feel great guilt, anxiety, and depression if their experience cannot be easily accepted into the Catholic paradigm. Individuals may even feel reluctant to discuss their problems with members of their family or clergy because they fear they may be labeled as crazy or heretical. Perceived religious transgressions can cause emotional and psychological anguish, manifesting as physical discomfort. This "religious" and "spiritual pain" can be difficult to distinguish from pure physical pain.

CONCLUSION: ARE WE HEADING TOWARD A PARADIGM SHIFT?

While the biological and health evaluation of religious and spiritual phenomena has advanced considerably since some of the initial studies were performed over thirty years ago, this field of research is still in its early stages. This is particularly true in the context of kundalini yoga and its associated experiences. There are many unique methodological issues that face this field—in addition to the potentially more problematic barriers of funding and academic stature. However, pursuit of such projects may ultimately pay large dividends both for science and spiritual perspectives. From the spiritual perspective, the results of such studies may lead toward a better understanding of the human experience of spiritual practices such as kundalini yoga. These studies enhance human knowledge of how spiritual pursuits affect the mind, brain, body, and behavior. From the scientific perspective, such research may shed new light on the complex workings of the human brain, as well as the relationship between brain states and body physiology.

All of this information leads to a potentially fascinating and powerful possibility. Do we need to change our most fundamental way of understanding the human being? For the past century, the biomedical world has focused almost exclusively on the biological models of the brain and body. However, today we are revolutionizing the way in which we think about the entire person. We have come to realize that people possess biological, psychological, social, and spiritual domains. The research further suggests a very complex linkage between spirituality and health. And if there is energy, spirit, or some other aspect of the human person that is responsible in some way for making us who we are, this could dramatically change the existing paradigms of both science and spirituality.

Kundalini Awakening

DAVID LUKOFF, PHD

David Lukoff, a licensed psychologist and a specialist in "spiritual emergency," coauthored the new diagnostic category "Religious or Spiritual Problem" in the Diagnostic and Statistical Manual of Mental Disorders, Fourth Edition, *a widely used psychiatric manual for diagnosis and treatment. He defines mystical experiences like kundalini this way: "The mystical experience is a transient, extraordinary experience marked by feelings of being in unity, harmonious relationship to the divine and everything in existence, as well as euphoric feelings, noesis, loss of ego functioning, alterations in time and space perception, and the sense of lacking control over the event." In the following essay, he shares his own introduction to kundalini, as well as the most recent research on the phenomenon, which often becomes a spiritual emergency. He shares data from the Spiritual Emergency Network, and the Kundalini Research Network, common symptoms of kundalini experiences, and how kundalini functions in relation to* Qigong, *or chi kung, and other meditation practices. The research he presents brings this question to mind: Are the medical and kundalini support communities equipped to handle the increasing occurrences of spiritual awakenings?*

To set a context for this essay, it is useful to know that I went through kundalini awakening myself. Back in 1971, I spent two months convinced that I was a reincarnation of Buddha and Christ, and wrote a forty-seven-page holy book to unite the world around a new universal religion that I would create. (Seemed like a good idea at the time.) Fortunately, I was not hospitalized or medicated. My friends provided food and shelter and spent time just talking to me.

I really feel quite grateful that I was allowed to go through the full experience. It was a touchstone experience in my life that set me on a spiritual journey. I needed to understand what had happened to me, and this has led me to the work I do today. It is baffling: how could this Jewish boy (I was twenty-three at the time) have believed himself to be Buddha and Christ, about whom he really knew very little? With this question in mind, I entered Jungian analysis, read Joseph Campbell, and went to many of Campbell's workshops. I also worked with shamans and Native American medicine chiefs who helped me integrate this experience and taught me how to control entry and exit from such ecstatic states. I later became a psychologist, and I have worked to help other mental health professionals understand how to recognize and work with kundalini and other potentially transformative experiences that can be misdiagnosed as psychotic disorders.

Since the 1960s, there has been a significant increase in people adopting a wide array of spiritual practices, including yoga, meditation, Qigong, *tai chi*, chanting, and others. There has also been an explosion of interest in mystical, esoteric, shamanic, and pagan traditions that involve participation in sweat lodges, goddess circles, and "New Age" Groups.[1] These activities have triggered many mystical experiences and spiritual emergencies among people who were not prepared and were not working with knowledgeable teachers:

> When novices who don't have the proper education or
> guidance begin to naively and carelessly engage mys-
> tical experiences, they are playing with fire. Danger
> exists on the physical and psychological levels, as well
> as on the level of one's continued spiritual development.
> Whereas spiritual masters have been warning their

disciples for thousands of years about the dangers of
playing with mystical states, the contemporary spiritual
scene is like a candy store where any casual spiritual
"tourist" can sample the "goodies" that promise a variety
of mystical highs.[2]

The connection between spiritual practices and psychological
problems was first noted by Roberto Assagioli, who described
how persons may become inflated and grandiose as a result of
intense spiritual experiences: "Instances of such confusion are not
uncommon among people who become dazzled by contact with
truths too great or energies too powerful for their mental capacities to grasp and their personality to assimilate."[3] Dr. Lee Sannella's
book *Kundalini: Psychosis or Transcendence?* published in 1976, was
the first to link yoga with problematic kundalini awakening.[4]

Stanislav and Christina Grof coined the term *spiritual emergency* and founded the Spiritual Emergency Network (SEN, later
the name was changed to the Spiritual Emergence Network) in
1980 to support individuals experiencing psychological difficulties associated with spiritual practices and spontaneous spiritual
experiences. SEN provides information and makes referrals to
therapists for such problems. When interviewed in 1995, Stanislav
Grof noted this from his experience with SEN:

There exist spontaneous non-ordinary states that would
in the west be seen and treated as psychosis, treated
mostly by suppressive medication. But if we use the
observations from the study of non-ordinary states, and
also from other spiritual traditions, they should really
be treated as crises of transformation, or crises
of spiritual opening. Something that should really be
supported rather than suppressed. If properly understood and properly supported, they are actually
conducive to healing and transformation.[5]

The term *spiritual emergence* is used to describe the whole range of phenomena associated with spiritual experiences and development, ranging from those that are not problematic, do not disrupt psychological/ social/occupational functioning, and do not involve psychotherapy or any contact with the mental health system (probably the vast majority), to spiritual experiences that are full-blown crises requiring twenty-four-hour care. The Grofs note that "episodes of this kind have been described in sacred literature of all ages as a result of meditative practices and as signposts of the mystical path."[6] Such literature has described the more common presentations as including: mystical experiences, kundalini awakening, shamanistic initiatory crisis (a rite of passage for shamans-to-be in indigenous cultures, commonly involving physical illness and/or psychological crisis),[7] possession states,[8] and psychic opening (the sudden occurrence of paranormal experiences). A distinguishing characteristic of spiritual emergencies is that despite the distress, they can have very beneficial transformative effects on the individuals who experience them.

YOGA AND KUNDALINI AWAKENING

In the Hindu tradition, kundalini is spiritual energy presumed to reside at the base of the spine. When it is awakened by practices such as yoga, it rises like a serpent up the spine and opens the chakras' psychic centers, which are situated along the spine from the tailbone to the top of the head. Dr. Brant Cortright describes the kundalini awakening process as follows: "As each chakra opens, new levels of consciousness are revealed. Since the consciousness of most people is fairly restricted, the opening of the chakras is accompanied by consciousness expansion and purification of the limitations or impurities that correspond to each chakra."[9]

As kundalini rises, it is associated with physical symptoms including:

- Sensations of heat
- Tremors

- Involuntary laughing or crying
- Talking in tongues
- Nausea, diarrhea, or constipation
- Rigidity or limpness
- Animal-like movements and sounds

Kundalini awakening is probably the most common type of spiritual emergency. The Spiritual Emergence Network Newsletter reported in 1988 that 24 percent of its hotline calls concerned kundalini awakening experiences. In kundalini awakening, there is typically a surge of energies along the spine and throughout the body that can overwhelm and incapacitate the ego and leave the person adrift in a sea of profound consciousness changes at every level—physical, emotional, and mental. Kundalini awakening most commonly occurs as an unintentional side effect of yoga, meditation, Qigong, or other intensive spiritual practices. Some also consider psychotherapy, giving birth, unrequited love, celibacy, deep sorrow, high fever, and drug intoxication to be triggers. Others believe kundalini awakening can occur spontaneously without apparent cause.

However, Bonnie Greenwell, PhD, a transpersonal therapist whose work focuses on kundalini awakening problems, believes that the term *kundalini* is most applicable to problems specifically associated with spiritual practices. When Dr. Greenwell was asked online about a case that included symptoms such as shaking at night, which can occur in kundalini awakening, she responded: "If the person had presented me with a description of an awakening experience, if he did exercises such as meditation, yoga, or a martial art regularly, or if he experienced strong meditative states where he went beyond concentration into stillness or a sense of unity, then I would be more likely to consider it Kundalini."[10]

Greenwell did her dissertation study on individuals who had experienced a kundalini awakening, and she summarizes the clinical issues she observed in her book, *Energies of Transformation:*

A Guide to the Kundalini Process.[11] In it she describes a number of key features of kundalini awakening that were experienced by people in her study:

Pranic Movements or Kriyas

Prana is the Hindu word for vital energy. As intense energy moves through the body and clears out physiological blocks, some people experience intense, involuntary, jerking movements of the body, including shaking, vibration, spasm, and contraction.

Yogic Phenomena

Some people find themselves performing yogic postures or hand *mudra* gestures they have never learned or could not do in a normal state of consciousness. Unusual breathing patterns may appear, with either very rapid or slow, shallow breathing.

Physiological Symptoms

Kundalini awakening often generates unusual physiological activity, which can present as heart, spinal, gastrointestinal, or neurological problems. Internal sensations of burning, hypersensitivity to sensory input, hyperactivity or lethargy, great variations in sexual desire, and even spontaneous orgasm have been reported.

Psychological Upheaval

Emotions can swing from feelings of anxiety, guilt, and depression (with bouts of uncontrollable weeping) to compassion, love, and joy.

Extrasensory Experiences

Some people experience visions of lights, symbols, or spiritual entities. Auditory sensations may include hearing voices, music, inner sounds, or mantras. There may also be disruption of the proprioceptive system, with loss of a sense of self as a body, or an out-of-body experience.

Psychic Phenomena

A person may experience precognition, telepathy, psychokinesis, awareness of auras, and healing abilities.

Mystical States of Consciousness

Some people may shift into altered states of consciousness in which they directly perceive the unity underlying the world of separation and experience a deep peace and serenity.

The sudden onset of these experiences led many in Greenwell's study to become confused and disoriented. Unlike those suffering from psychosis, individuals experiencing kundalini are typically much more objective about their condition, communicate and cooperate well, show interest in sharing their experiences with open-minded people, and seldom act out. An example of such a case follows.

> Terry's experience of kundalini awakening was triggered by an intensive weekend workshop involving emotional release work. Several days later she experienced an explosion of energy throughout her body that signaled the awakening of kundalini. It moved throughout her body, up her spine, and through her limbs. Accompanying this energetic flow were profound changes in consciousness in which she felt opened up and expanded, yet which at times left her terrified and unable to function. Although she knew about the kundalini phenomenon, this knowledge did not prevent her ego from being overpowered by the intensity of consciousness changes within her. She was able to take a leave from work for several months and work with a therapist on an outpatient basis, and after three months she was able to begin working again part-time. Diet, energy work, modifying her meditation practice, grounding exercises, deep therapeutic work on the

emotional issues activated by the rising kundalini energies, journal writing, and mobilizing her support system
were some of the things that helped in her process. After
nine months, almost all of the experiences had faded,
but she had radically reoriented her life during this time
to be more fully aligned with her spiritual path. [12]

Kundalini awakening can resemble many disorders, medical as
well as psychiatric. The symptoms can mimic conversion disorder, epilepsy, lower back problems, multiple sclerosis, heart attack,
or pelvic inflammatory syndrome. The emotional reaction to the
awakening of kundalini can be confused with disorders involving
anxiety, depression, aggression, and organic syndromes. While in
some cases the psychological upheaval is so acute that it resembles
a psychotic episode, medication can further complicate the process. Dr. Greenwell suggests that it would be therapeutic for the
individual to study some of the Eastern theories and descriptions
of kundalini. Her other recommendations include:

Look for ways to discharge this energy by running,
exercising, gardening, or working with something
solid, like wood or clay. I would suggest doing a regular
meditation practice, and letting the process develop and
teach him. . . . The best support is a balanced lifestyle
and a commitment to live one's life in alignment with
the vision it brings—that is, if you have a heart-opening
or a visionary experience, instead of being attached to
holding on to it, ask yourself what you can bring into
the world as service to it. . . . Think of it as if the amps
have been raised in your electrical system. This is why
balance, taking care of ourselves, being in nature, and
regular physical exercise all help. We may have to change
old patterns to meet the invitation to a new kind of
energy flow and engagement with spirit in our lives. [13]

She also suggests creative activities such as art, music, or writing as ways to express the energy. Since this kind of spiritual problem is related to a type of practice, consultation with a teacher of the practice who also has mental health training would be advisable. Dr. Greenwell indicates that learning some basic yogic breathing practices, under the supervision of a knowledgeable yoga teacher, can help guide this energy as well.

KUNDALINI AWAKENING AND QIGONG

The Diagnostic and Statistical Manual of Mental Disorders (DSM-IV)[14] includes in Appendix I: Culture Bound Syndromes "Qigong psychotic reaction," which is similar to kundalini awakening. (Qigong, or chi kung, is an ancient Chinese moving-meditation practice.) *DSM-IV* describes this syndrome as "an acute, time-limited episode characterized by dissociative, paranoid, or other psychotic or non-psychotic symptoms" and says that "especially vulnerable are individuals who become overly involved" in Qigong. Researchers R. Lim and K. Lin reported in 1996 that the "Chinese psychiatric literature describes a syndrome called 'Qigong Induced Psychosis' characterized by the appearance of auditory hallucinations and delusions after the initiation of Qigong in a practitioner who has never experienced these symptoms before and in whom these symptoms remit soon after the cessation of Qigong practice."[15] It seems, though, that this disorder is only caused by extreme types of Qigong, which place practitioners in a trance and have them attempt to communicate with other beings.

> Mr. A is a 44-year-old married male painter. He taught himself He Xiang Zhuang (a popular Qigong method since 1984 for the treatment of disease of the cervical vertebra). He had no previous psychiatric history or any family history of psychosis. Several days after Qigong practice, he suddenly became agitated and dysthymic. He claimed that he knew something special

about the world including "the sea is associated with water." He talked to the sea and had American ideas in his head. He was subsequently diagnosed as having a schizophreniform disorder and was admitted to a local psychiatric hospital. One month later, he had a relapse while practicing the "long men five flow," which is a Qigong method. On the third morning after the practice, he suddenly cried aloud and danced around. He thought that his deceased mother had come back to life but that he would become a ghost. He said that he could see the images of Buddha and other gods and he smelt a special smell. He intermittently maintained a special Qigong posture. He was thus readmitted into the psychiatric hospital. He was given chlorpromazine 100 mg intramuscularly twice daily. A week later, he was completely recovered and had resumed work.[16]

As with yoga, Qigong, especially when practiced alone and unsupervised and to extremes, can trigger a kundalini awakening crisis. And most of these crises resolve after the practice is terminated.

KUNDALINI AWAKENING AND MEDITATION

The *DSM-IV* emphasizes the need to distinguish between psychopathology and meditation-related experiences: "Voluntarily induced experiences of depersonalization or derealization form part of meditative and trance practices that are prevalent in many religions and cultures and should not be confused with Depersonalization Disorder."[17]

Depersonalization disorder is a mental disorder, so it is important to distinguish such problems from episodes related to spiritual practice. Intensive meditation practices can involve spending many hours each day in meditation for weeks or months at a time. Asian traditions recognize a number of pitfalls associated with intensive meditation practice, such as altered perceptions that can be frightening, and "false enlightenment," associated with delightful or terrifying visions. Mark Epstein describes a "specific mental disorder that the Tibetans call 'sokrlung'"as "a disorder of the 'life-bearing wind that supports the mind' that can arise as a consequence . . . of strain[ing] too tightly in an obsessive way to achieve moment-to-moment awareness."[18]

When Asian meditative practices are transplanted into Western contexts, the same problems can occur. Anxiety, dissociation, depersonalization, altered perceptions, agitation, and muscular tension have been observed in Western meditation practitioners as in the case described below. Yet R. Walsh and L. Roche point out that "such changes are not necessarily pathologic and may reflect in part a heightened sensitivity."[19]

Treatment involves discontinuation of the spiritual practice, at least temporarily, and engaging in alternative "grounding" activities. Jack Kornfield, a psychologist and experienced meditation teacher, described what he termed a spiritual emergency that took place at an intensive meditation retreat he was leading:

> An "overzealous young karate student" decided to meditate and not move for a full day and night. When he got up, he was filled with explosive energy. He strode into the middle of the dining hall filled with a hundred silent retreatants and began to yell and practice his karate maneuvers at triple speed. Then he screamed, "When I look at each of you, I see behind you a whole trail of bodies showing your past lives." As an experienced meditation teacher, Kornfield recognized that the symptoms were related to the meditation practice rather than signs of a manic episode (for which they also meet all the diagnostic criteria except duration). The meditation community handled the situation by stopping his meditation practice and starting him jogging, ten miles in the morning and afternoon. His diet was changed to

include red meat, which is thought to have a grounding effect. They got him to take frequent hot baths and
showers, and to dig in the garden. One person was with
him all the time. After three days, he was able to sleep
again and was allowed to start meditating again, slowly
and carefully. [20]

Meditation has been reported to trigger psychotic episodes in
schizophrenic patients with active psychotic symptoms. [21] However,
I developed a multimodal holistic health program for schizophrenic patients at a state psychiatric hospital that incorporated
meditation, and none of the patients experienced adverse effects.
Meditation was also used with schizophrenic patients at the San
Francisco VA Day Treatment Center for fourteen years. [22]

KUNDALINI AWAKENING AS
A SPIRITUAL PROBLEM

In the *DSM-IV*, spiritual problems are defined as distressing experiences that involve a person's relationship with a transcendent
being or force, but that are not necessarily related to an organized
church or religious institution. Sometimes such experiences
result from intensive involvement with spiritual practices such
as yoga. The impetus for proposing this new diagnostic category
came from transpersonal clinicians whose initial focus was on
crises triggered by spiritual practices and psychedelic drugs, as
well as spontaneous spiritual crises. In 1990, to redress the lack of
sensitivity to religious and spiritual problems, the author, along
with two psychiatrists on the faculty at University of California,
San Francisco, Department of Psychiatry (Francis Lu, MD, and
Robert Turner, MD), proposed a new diagnostic category for the
fourth edition of the *Diagnostic and Statistical Manual*. We viewed
such an addition to the *DSM-IV* nomenclature as the most effective way to increase the sensitivity of mental health professionals
to spiritual crises and issues in therapy. The proposal involved a

three-year process of working with various subcommittees (for a more detailed history of this diagnostic category, see the 1988 journal article, "From Spiritual Emergence to Spiritual Problem: The Transpersonal Roots of the New *DSM-IV* Category"),[23] and resulted in the acceptance of a new diagnosis entitled Religious or Spiritual Problem, defined as follows:

> This category can be used when the focus of clinical attention is a religious or spiritual problem. Examples include distressing experiences that involve loss or questioning of faith, problems associated with conversion to a new faith, or questioning of other spiritual values which may not necessarily be related to an organized church or religious institution.[24]

Articles on this new category have appeared in the *New York Times, San Francisco Chronicle, Psychiatric News,* and the *APA Monitor* where it was described as indicating an important shift in the mental health profession's stance toward religion and spirituality. What did not receive attention in the media is that this new diagnostic category has its roots in the transpersonal movement's attention to spiritual emergencies such as kundalini awakening.

CONCLUSION

The spiritual journey has risks and perils. The self can become disorganized and overwhelmed by an infusion of spiritual energies or by new realms of experience that it is not able to integrate. David Steindl-Rast, a Benedictine monk who teaches spiritual practices, has noted that spiritual emergence can be disruptive: "Spiritual emergence is a kind of birth pang in which you yourself go through to a fuller life, a deeper life, in which some areas in your life that were not yet encompassed by this fullness of life are now integrated. . . . Breakthroughs are often very painful, often acute and dramatic."[25] Yet it seems that more and more people are exploring spiritual practices such as yoga and meditation, reading books on spiritual topics (many are bestsellers), and attending retreats, workshops, and conferences on spiritual topics. While this can certainly be seen as a hopeful sign for the survival of the planet, since spiritual traditions share many values such as peace and harmony, on the individual level there will likely be an increase in the number of people who experience kundalini awakening and other spiritual problems related to the spiritual practices and exploration they undertake on their journey.

Mental and Emotional Health in the Kundalini Process

BARBARA HARRIS WHITFIELD

Barbara Whitfield, author of five books including Spiritual Awakenings: Insights of the Near-Death Experience and Other Doorways to Our Soul, The Power of Humility: Choosing Peace over Conflict in Relationships *and* The Natural Soul, *has worked with the kundalini experience and spiritual emergencies throughout her career. In the following essay, she describes her experience with kundalini and near-death experiences (NDEs) and what she has learned about difficulties during spiritual awakenings. She discusses what she calls a "spiritual bypass," or what happens when we try to ignore the lower levels of consciousness to get to the higher levels. Whitfield also outlines the differences between the voice of the ego and the voice of the soul, asking us to consider this question: Are we able to use the power of humility and compassion to find our True Self during spiritual awakening?*

> "The Journey to God . . . is a journey without distance
> to a goal that has never changed."
>
> —*A Course in Miracles*

THIS ESSAY IS a guide to assist those who are opening up and experiencing, or who want to experience, the mystical or heart side of their nature and the nature of the Universe. This awakening is not something to be understood logically, but through experience, perception, and intuition. It is a *heartfelt* experience. Your head will have a hard time sorting through some of this material, so it will help to read it with your heart as well as with your eyes and mind.

Near-death experiences (NDEs)—transcendental experiences on the threshold of death—have been hypothesized to be related to the awakening of a biological process known as Kundalini.[1] Some who are new to this process can get caught in believing that any attendant psychic abilities that manifest are the end result. They may become ego inflated, leading to a "spiritual bypass," which I will explain further on. Practicing humility is a way to avoid or release these impediments, which leads to better mental and emotional health. That, in turn, allows us to safely extend compassion to others and gives us a peaceful sense of gratitude and a joyful sense of mission. In this essay, I will talk about my own experience in dealing with these phenomena of transcendence.

MY PERSONAL STORY

Like many Western writers and researchers on and in the Kundalini process, my entry point was deeply personal—a near-death experience. This triggered in me what I can now identify as a process we call Kundalini. Like so many other Westerners, I didn't know about it and didn't ask for it. Even so, it started me on a lifelong exploration that continues to this day, thirty-four years later.

In 1975, I was suspended in a Stryker frame circle bed after having had five and a half hours of spinal surgery. Postoperative complications set in, and I started to die. After various traumatic medical interventions, I found myself out in the hall, up near the ceiling. I came back into the room and actually saw my body lying in the bed. The next thing I knew, I was being embraced by my grandmother, who had died fourteen years earlier. We relived all of our memories of each other. I could experience her memories of me as well as my own. I knew she was seeing and feeling all of them from both of our perspectives.

Then I was back in my body and confused. I had been an atheist and only believed in physical existence—until this NDE. About five days later, still in the circle bed, I again left my body. This time I reexperienced my whole life of thirty-two years, and again I saw it from everyone else's perspective as well as my own, just as I had with my grandmother. Only this time there was a third perspective involved: God. It would take me many years as a recovering atheist to use that word.

God's Energy and mine merged so that we were one energy field. Together we watched thirty-two years of my life. In every scene, each person's energy field and mine overlapped and sometimes merged. It was as though we were this churning mass of consciousness that became the "dance of life." Every time I witnessed something that was painful for me, being held and infused by this Energy became the bigger focus. My relationship with It neutralized my judgments against myself and evoked Love throughout my being in a way that can't be explained in words.[2]

Even as I was merged with God, I still had an individual point of perception. I had few relationships where I could be my True Self or Soul. Most of my relationships were ego-based because most of us were projecting outward our wants and needs and feeling resentful if they weren't met. I felt no real connections with others, only an awful swinging between feeling needy and numb.

This Life Review showed me a dance that pulls us back and forth between light and dark, good and evil, neediness and extension. It's this dance that leads us to waking up so that we have choices in all our relationships: with ourselves, with others (including our community and this planet), and with the God of our understanding. As we wake up, we seem to move along a healing continuum toward Unity consciousness.[3]

Then the Life Review ended, and I was back in this reality, still in the circle bed. I tried to tell a few of the medical staff what had happened. They told me I was hallucinating.

After a month in the circle bed, I was then in a full body cast for six months. During that time I went to see a psychiatrist. The near-death experience was deeply personal and like many other near-death experiencers, I couldn't share it with my family or anyone else for the first several years. I have since learned it takes most of us a long time to feel safe enough to share what we went through. It took me six sessions with the psychiatrist to finally trust him enough to tell him about my experience. He listened carefully and then said that what I might do is come back after I recovered and start in analysis with him. He believed that I was depressed and wrote a prescription for an antidepressant. I didn't feel "depressed." I felt confused and overwhelmed, not depressed. I often felt a mystical awe.

After the cast came off, I went through six more months of physical therapy to get my strength back. I knew I couldn't go back to my old life, my old way of being. I was still a mom and loved being one, but my three children were in school all day, so I filled my days with volunteering in the emergency room of the hospital in which I had stayed. That led me back to school, where I eventually became a respiratory therapist. Some of my patients in intensive care and the emergency room told me about their near-death and out-of-body experiences, and I started writing about some of my observations. I was eventually published in respiratory therapy journals while still a student, calling this new topic in health care "The Emotional Needs of Critical Care Patients."

In 1982 I met Kenneth Ring and told him my story. In 1984 his book *Heading toward Omega: In Search of the Meaning of the Near-Death Experience*[4] was published and my story, including most of the subsequent aftereffects, was in it. I now had a framework for the part of my journey that didn't resemble anything I knew of before, and it was called *Kundalini*.

In 1985 I began to work with Bruce Greyson at the University of Connecticut Medical School, studying the aftereffects of NDEs, especially what we called "The Physio-Kundalini Syndrome." I also studied massage therapy and energy work. Finally, I combined my knowledge of respiratory therapy with hands-on energy work to create the kind of healing aid I intuited was possible with Kundalini emergencies.

In working with those who are in the Kundalini process, I start with a respiratory evaluation. Many times they need to take deeper and slower breaths or be reminded to breathe more often. This in turn helps their body to relax. It seems that those who are new to this process take shallow breaths because of anxiety until they are helped to "reframe" some of their fears into a sense of "This is all right; this is natural." Then they can go deeper into their breathing and watch their bodies let go of unnecessary stress.

Sometimes, all my client and I need to do is just sit and meditate facing each other. I talk them through what meditation feels like. They mirror my breathing, and I help them to do a body scan to release stress. Then I explain how our ego chatters, and we let go of that, focusing on the middle of our brains where we sit with feelings instead of the upper part of our brains, which thinks in words. I ask my client to focus on a positive or joyful feeling such as awe, love, trust/faith, compassion, gratitude, forgiveness, joy, or hope. To help clients understand what I'm asking for, I sometimes give them an example of a time with my eight-year-old grandson. I had been showered with wonderful homemade gifts from my other grandchildren at my birthday party, including a homemade cake with lots of candles. He walked up to me, made strong eye contact, and told me he had one more present for me. He took his hand out of his pocket and pretended he was sprinkling something over my head as he told me the present was his love. My heart melted. There were no words. When I bring up this memory of his eyes gazing into mine, I can still feel his hand sprinkling love on top of my head. Then my limbic system (in the middle of my brain) gets activated because that is where these positive feelings reside. The limbic system is at least one place that doesn't think in words; it is a feeling place. (The neocortex uses words, and it is automatically shut down at this point.) As I sit there bathed in this joyful feeling, my parasympathetic nervous system is activated, and that sends out messages to make my body relax and at the same time nourishes my immune system. Explaining this helps my clients understand how meditation can help us heal.

When working with my clients' painful energy, I start with EFT—Emotional Freedom Technique [5]—to help them release fears and phobias. EFT uses energy points on the face and trunk to move stuck or blocked energy. Clients learn to do this for themselves in one session. (See more at emofree.com.) If there are painful "blocks," they lie down on my massage table, and I place my hands where their pain is (felt as burning or other pain). They breathe into the block as we visualize energy coming through me and moving through the block. There is usually relief when these blocks release. Occasionally clients will later report a dream, or while still on the table, a memory comes up that has an emotional charge. I help them to metabolize or process and grieve the blocked feelings, rather than probe for buried memories.

For those clients who want to go deeper, we have individual and group psychotherapy. When you read Charles Whitfield's essay in this book (page 161), you'll see that he refers to the Stages of Recovery. Many who are in the Kundalini process may decide to enter a Stage Two or Stage Three psychotherapy group. [6]

SPONTANEOUS TRIGGERS

Phenomena associated with the Kundalini process are occurring with increasing frequency among Westerners who have never heard of it before, and, like those who have near-death experiences, they have done nothing intentionally to arouse it. Felt as vast rushes of energy through the body, Kundalini rising can create profound changes in the structure of people's physical, mental, emotional, and spiritual lives. (A few research subjects never experienced the rushes of energy but still reported the signs and symptoms of the Kundalini process. [7])

Over the years, as a public speaker addressing hospices, hospital staffs, universities, churches, support groups, and media interviews, I have heard of other spontaneous triggers of Kundalini rising besides the NDE. Audience participants have told me about their experiences in childbirth, meditation, intense prayer, experiencing the death of a loved one, withdrawal from chemical dependence, bottoming out from an overwhelming loss, alien encounters—including angels or other beings—intense, transcendent sexual experiences, being in nature, reading spiritual literature or hearing a spiritual talk, in a "big dream" that is remembered for life, and during breath and body work.[8] Recently I was the keynote speaker at the 2007 Annual Convention for Adult Children of Alcoholics. There I heard from multiple participants about Kundalini phenomena occurring in their advanced recovery while working a Twelve-Step program. Note that Step Twelve starts off with: "Having had a spiritual awakening as the result of these Steps . . ."[9]

PSYCHIC PHENOMENA AS A BY-PRODUCT OF THE KUNDALINI PROCESS

Psychic abilities may appear as part of the Kundalini process. Such abilities have been an accepted part of the world's traditional spiritual teachings over the millennia. This is consistent with Kenneth Ring's and my view that the near-death experience serves principally as a catalyst for spiritual awakening and development and that psychic abilities usually manifest as a by-product, and other independent researchers support our observations. Ring says that the ancient literature of the great spiritual psychologies links psychic phenomena to the unfolding of higher consciousness.[10] These gifts are specifically identified with the awakening of Kundalini energy in some Indian scriptures and are described in many cases of modern people who have experienced a Kundalini awakening.[11]

When psychic phenomena are discussed in spiritual literature, there is usually a warning included about the dangers of becoming attached to them. From the Buddhist perspective, attaining such psychic powers is only a minor advantage. It has no value in itself for psychospiritual growth. In one who has not yet attained the state of nirvana,[12] these psychic abilities are even seen as an impediment and may endanger progress by enhancing and strengthening one's attachment to one's false self. We can, however, appreciate or celebrate—but not be attached to—these new abilities, since they serve as a reminder that we are connected with others and that our subtle energy fields overlap and act upon one another, sometimes even across great distances.

As the masters of the ancient spiritual psychologies warned, focusing on the talent of psychic ability will create attachments that distract us. Many people get caught in this trap. Having these psychic phenomena seems to be so provocative that it becomes a kind of stopping-off point. Then, after a while, the person tends to incorporate it into normal reality. As our transformational journey continues, we realize that these abilities are useful when used with humility and in the act of selfless service. They parallel the Buddhist idea of the bodhisattva: an enlightened being who, out of compassion, forgoes nirvana in order to help save others.

Those who develop psychic abilities who are still centered in their false self or negative ego may believe they are using their abilities for selfless service, but they actually can be projecting their own wishes or other issues onto others instead. Even a sense of compassion can become confusing for those experiencing rapid spiritual growth. They can believe that they are suddenly needed by another, and this may become "ego inflation." Many hear about, read, or study Eastern spiritual literature and identify strongly with the authors, teachers, or gurus. But being Westerners with different cultural roots, it may be hard to translate some Eastern metaphors and principles.

SPIRITUAL BYPASS

Some with awakening Kundalini experience a small degree of ego inflation. Others become grandiose and may get stuck. A way out is to work on ourselves over time, psychologically, emotionally, and spiritually. To believe we can be instantly healed through a religious or spiritual experience alone is to attempt what we call a "spiritual bypass." We try to bypass or ignore the lower levels of consciousness to get to the higher levels. Eventually, however, our false self will usually pull us back until we work through our particular unfinished business.

Other names for spiritual bypass are *high-level denial* and *premature transcendence.* It is seen in any number of situations, such as being prematurely "born again," having a spiritual awakening and focusing only on the "Light," focusing on psychic ability as a major part of our identity, or becoming a guru or teacher who exploits his or her students. [13]

The consequences of taking a spiritual bypass are often active codependence or conflict, including: denial of the richness of our inner life; trying to control ourselves or others; all-or-nothing thinking and behaving; feelings of fear, shame, and confusion; high tolerance for inappropriate behavior; frustration; addiction, compulsion, and relapse; and unnecessary pain and suffering. [14]

If we live from our ego or false self, we may find it impossible to quiet down our inner life during meditation or when attempting to center. We can only experientially quiet down and connect with God, each other, and ourselves by developing our True Selves—living as our natural souls. Ego inflation and spiritual bypass are instead cognitive intellectual experiences, or "head trips." Being our True Selves and connecting spiritually with God are instead deeply emotional "heart" experiences. [15]

DEFINING HUMILITY

Our reward for working through ego inflation and spiritual bypass is recognizing and using the power of *humility:* the solid foundation of an authentically spiritual, healthy, and whole human being. We can begin to define humility as *having openness and willingness to learn more about our relationship with ourselves, others, and God.*

Humility is not about groveling or being a doormat. Instead, it is a powerful attitude and state of mind that, when we are in the pain of conflict, opens us to more choices and peaceful resolutions. Humility helps move our ordinary ego-centered unawareness toward a more expansive, alive, and conscious awareness in which we can live in and as our natural souls. Having humility levels the occasional bumps in the Kundalini process.[16]

With humility, we are willing to continue learning throughout our lives. In its openness, we are free not only to avoid any of the pitfalls of ego inflation, but also to experience a connection with our Higher Selves and Higher Power. In this state of humility, a kind of "second innocence," we can more easily witness our lives as "heartfelt" experiences.[17]

THE CONTRIBUTION OF NEUROSCIENCE

Recently, scientists have found that the anatomical location of these "heart" or mystical experiences is the limbic system of the brain, which I mentioned earlier in discussing my work with clients. Neuroscientist Andrew Newberg from the University of Pennsylvania School of Medicine used functional magnetic resonance imaging (fMRI), positron-emission tomography (PET scans), and single photon emission computed tomography (SPECT) to show that experiential spirituality lies in the limbic system of the brain. The limbic system is where we *feel* positive emotions and our positive relationships with others.

Newberg studied Tibetan Buddhists who practiced Kundalini yoga meditation and had been meditating for many years. They were advanced in their practice. Newberg showed that when these meditators achieve a state of mystical union, followed by a profound sense of calm, the activities of the neocortical brain were functionally cut off from the rest of the brain. At the same time, both the limbic hippocampus and amygdala were more active.[18] Newberg's subjects meditated on a spiritual symbol or a positive emotion, some focusing on the feeling of forgiveness.

He found that the area these positive feelings activated increased their parasympathetic activity, producing relaxation followed by a profound sense of serenity. There are no words used in this experience; there is only a sense of positive or joyful feelings.

Newberg suggests that experiential spirituality reflects "limbic questions" about love, community, positive emotions, and the feeling of "being one with the universe." He also reports that, for meditating nuns, "while in prayer, their sense of God becomes physiologically real," and the meditating Buddhists catch a glimpse of what for them is "an absolute reality."[19]

Religious and "New Age" theology usually activate the brain's neocortex, where we *think* in words. If we are *thinking* about our spiritual process, we can become confused and even create closed-loop thinking by trying to analyze what is happening to us. When a similar Kundalini process becomes overwhelming and perhaps interferes with our normal life, which sometimes happens, I have personally found that not reading any spiritual literature for a while and not trying to analyze where I am in my current state helps to calm the uncomfortable or overwhelming aspects of the process.

I almost never recommend prescription medication for my clients who are undergoing a Kundalini awakening, even though many physicians believe it will help. Some psychiatrists and neurologists wrongly diagnose an upheaval in this process as psychosis, depression, mania, or "bipolar." They commonly misprescribe psychiatric drugs such as neuroleptics, antianxiety agents, and antidepressants, which are toxic and hard to quit.[20]

Any upheavals along the Kundalini journey should be treated using nondrug modalities first. Try increasing or decreasing meditation, or increasing or decreasing energy-type massages. Acupuncture and psychotherapy focusing on the release of painful emotions may be all that is needed. Spending time in nature may also help. Eliminate television viewing or reading anything with highly emotional content. Nutrition should be of primary concern because we are what we eat. Fast food and processed food should be eliminated.

COMPASSION AND EMPATHY

Psychic abilities and compassion can be confusing for those experiencing sudden openings and rapid spiritual growth. Our abilities to sense others' (or our own) pain can overwhelm us. When we sense others' pain, we can practice giving them compassion without taking on or absorbing their pain. The more aware and connected we feel to spiritual energy, the better we tend to know that feeling of compassion. Having compassion for others may become easier once our heart chakra is opened, but problems with it will probably continue if we haven't finished our own emotional release. Our hearts—our attention, sympathy, empathy, compassion and the like—can be open to others but still carry our own wounds. Then our thinking brain (neocortex) can trick us into projecting our own need for love onto others, while simultaneously rationalizing that we are being compassionate. If we feel exhausted, agitated, or needy after an encounter in which we believed we were giving compassion, we may have instead been projecting our own needs.[21]

The word *empathy,* in part, means feeling for the *other.* The pain or distress they are feeling is now registering in us, but it originated in them. With compassion, in contrast, we are stepping aside selflessly and allowing energy from a higher source to flow through us. We can do this without feeling what the other is feeling.

Compassion registers in our metaphoric heart. (As Newberg has demonstrated, it may also reside anatomically in our limbic brain.) It opens us so we can actually feel ourselves in a new way. In order to experience this opening, everyone must develop a method that works for them. In my case, I state my intention in a prayer and ask for help in getting my ego out of the way. At this point, the chatter in my inner life quiets down and stops for a little while. The connection to Spirit and to the healee is then a subtle yet sometimes profound felt sense that can even be experienced with the healee at a distance.

HEALTHY BOUNDARIES

It takes a kind of balancing act to actually know for sure when we are helping someone else as opposed to helping ourselves by *thinking* we are helping someone else. Somewhere in the middle of this we have the choice of proceeding or backing off, remembering and activating our own healthy boundaries. We can benefit from learning ways to set these boundaries that will give us another choice: allowing the other person the freedom of working through their own painful predicament while we avoid becoming enmeshed in it with them.

A boundary or limit is how far we can comfortably go in a relationship and how far someone else can comfortably go with us. A boundary is not just a mental construct: Our boundaries are real. Other people's boundaries are real. [22]

Boundaries and limits serve a useful purpose: they protect the well-being and integrity of our True Selves. Our awareness of boundaries and limits first helps us discover who we are. Until we know who we are, it will be difficult for us to have healthy relationships of any sort. Without an awareness of boundaries, it is difficult to sort out who is unsafe to be around, including people who are toxic and people who may mistreat or abuse us. Becoming more sensitive to our environment is part of the evolving Kundalini process, which also includes a greater sensitivity to toxic people.

OUR SENSE OF MISSION

When I practiced as a respiratory therapist, I wrote about the emotional needs of critical care patients because I could see and sense how much my patients needed to talk about what was happening in their inner life. We, the health care team, were focused on their *physical* needs because every second was critical. But at the same time we were ignoring their *emotional* needs. That was what had happened to me while I was suspended in the circle bed. Because of this experience, I found a way to help others a few years later in the way I had not been helped; I eventually published my work and taught it to others.

I often tell people our Kundalini process works this way: there is an invisible intelligence that seems to gently pull us along. We may not be able to see what of a higher order is actually happening at the time. But looking back over our process helps to show us the richness and beauty of our path. Keeping a journal helps to identify this blessed guidance, including in it any dreams that stand out as possibly being spiritual in nature.

Early in the Kundalini process we may feel frustrated because we do not know what our mission might be. As we relax into the journey, though, our answers will appear over time, and then we can realize that wanting to know the future is a source of agitation. Peacefully surrendering to the process makes the journey easier and more pleasurable. Our faith and trust settle in.

Assisting in Bruce Greyson's research revealed that I was certainly not alone in my search for expression of my newfound spiritual quest. The sense of mission can be profound, and we may need to find ways to express it helpfully in the present moment.

In Twelve-Step programs, this sense of mission is spelled out in the Twelfth Step, which reads: "Having had a spiritual awakening as the result of these Steps, we tried to carry this message to others who still suffer, and to practice these principles in all our affairs."[23]

HELPING PROFESSIONS

Those of us who work in the healing arts are fortunate to have an appropriate setting in which to open ourselves to others and help them. It is clear in a healer/healee relationship whose feelings are going to be focused on, and in which direction the healing energy is going to go.

In my private practice, I work in individual and group psychotherapy with adults who have been repeatedly traumatized
and abused as children. When I am in a session with a client, I
sometimes feel awareness of heat, pain, or pressure in the same
physical area the client is feeling pain, although not with the
same intensity. This is a kind of empathy I referred to earlier:
understanding or actually feeling what the other person is physically and emotionally feeling without identifying personally
with the feelings. It is observation and a kind of understanding
without taking on another's pain. This is a complex area: I am
feeling what my client feels, but I do not identify those feelings as my own. To make sure I don't so identify, after a session
I use a ritual of shaking my hands and washing them in cold
water to break the connection and reactivate my own healthy
boundaries. "Boundaries" in this context means distinguishing
and keeping out what does not belong to me, and maintaining
in place what does. [24]

For anyone working on emotional and psychological levels
with patients, it is important to educate ourselves on the psychological definition of transference and countertransference and
then, when needed, seek supervision from another therapist who
can be objective. This is a safe way to stay clear and make appropriate responses. [25]

THE POWER OF HUMILITY

In *The Power of Humility*, we list twelve key characteristics of humility. These include openness, an attitude of "don't know," curiosity,
innocence, a childlike nature, spontaneity, spirituality, tolerance,
patience, integrity, detachment, and letting go—all of which lead
to inner peace. After describing these twelve characteristics, we
address two more related aspects: gratitude and "being nobody
special." [26] I find gratitude to be my internal mantra. It keeps me
focused in my soul. Being nobody special is more difficult, and I
didn't understand it as clearly until we wrote this book.

We spend the first half of our life becoming "special." That's part of the journey, part of our development. But in the second half of life, or when our journey of spiritual growth becomes apparent, being nobody special allows us to become all that we can be. It's the ingredient and paradox that gets our sense of self, alone and in relationship with others, out of the way so our True Self can emerge. And it is a relief in every present moment to give up roles of who we think we are and instead just be.[27]

Here is a table to help us know whether we are in our egos or being our True Selves.

VOICE OF THE EGO AND VOICE OF THE SOUL

EGO TRAITS	SOUL TRAITS
Flatters	Informs
Commands	Suggests
Demands	Guides
Tests	Nudges
Chooses for you	Leaves choice to you
Imprisons	Empowers
Promotes dependence	Promotes independence
Intrudes	Respects
Pushes	Supports
Excludes	Includes
Instills fear	Promotes well-being
Becomes bored easily; not at peace	Realizes peace when doing nothing
Is status oriented	Is free and open
Judges	Accepts individuality
Demands obedience	Encourages growth and development
Implies having ultimate authority	Recognizes a Higher Power

EGO TRAITS	SOUL TRAITS
Offers shortcuts	Offers integration
Seeks personal gratification	Extends unconditional love

HEALTHY BOUNDARIES BALANCING HEALTHY COMPASSION

As we continue our own healing and grow spiritually with Kundalini energy, we will know when the time is right to focus on our psychic abilities because we will be able to trust our own judgment. We can open in deep trust to this process. While these signals, these moments of empathy for another, can be in our awareness, we have the choice to act on and use them or ignore them, and we have the confidence to recognize what is ours and what isn't. If it is appropriate to act, I then answer in honesty, all the while being in a clear, expanded state of consciousness. I start with the same prayer each time: asking to be an instrument of a Higher Power and asking for help to get my ego out of the way. I set aside my sense of separateness and join for a time with the other. I open myself to feel what he or she is feeling. In turn, my heart opens with a sense of compassion that becomes an instrument of the Energy coming *through* me. I become a connection, a conduit between the healee and the Energy of Spirit (God's loving Energy, Kundalini, Holy Spirit, Ruach ha Kadosh, etc.) doing the healing.

A few times I have been naïve enough to use my psychic abilities with my family, and it has backfired. I quickly found out that I was invading their boundaries, their privacy. I then realized that my false self, or ego, can't always be out of the way when I am personally involved. Now, occasionally, someone close to me will ask for my help. I am careful to stay objective, keeping my own agenda out, or I say I can't do it. Then I offer them the opportunity to hear my opinion. The water gets murky when working

on a psychic level with family members, and I don't recommend
it. I try to be respectful of others' boundaries, but this is a hard
lesson to learn. It requires psychic maturity as well as trusting and
learning when to speak (seldom) and when to be silent (mostly).
When in doubt, if you choose to proceed, a helpful way to begin
is by saying a prayer *with* the family member.

STUDENTS OF OUR INNER LIFE

Once we have a spiritual awakening and move into the Kundalini
process, our unconscious material from our inner life tends to
come into our conscious awareness in powerful ways. We can now
actually recognize when we are stuffing—repressing or suppress-
ing—our own hurts or traumas. With this new awareness come
new choices. These include being able to choose whom we care to
be around. Before awakening to this process, we might have been
able to numb out when in the company of toxic people. Now
the signs of another's toxicity are collecting, and part of becoming psychologically and emotionally healthy is to learn to protect
ourselves instead of numbing out. We can welcome this material
from our unconscious for our own personal growth and well-
being. We can identify ourselves as awakening spiritual beings in
human physical bodies. And we can ask Spirit to help us cocreate
better ways, such as practicing compassion for ourselves. [28]

Being aware of our inner life with compassion for ourselves
and without blaming others requires a delicate balance. This takes
patience and practice.

I have been a student of my own inner life since my awakening almost thirty-four years ago. I had no choice. I was suddenly
awakened not only to my spiritual connection, but to the emotional connection of my True Self, and it was letting me know it
needed protection. After years of experiencing personal growth,
it is fun to observe all of this going on in my inner life. I trust
my abilities to negotiate when to stay open and when to protect
my innocent True Self. Occasionally, I can still hear my negative

ego/false self doing a good imitation of loving friendship as it tries to take back control. This may translate into some humor that keeps me chuckling at times. My inner life is always busy. I have to stay on my toes and stay aware of who's "running the show." And in meditation, during play, or when doing any conscious centering, I can relax, letting my inner life quiet down and allowing the Light of God's unconditional love and compassion to wash through me.

The bonus for the hard inner work of healing is the realization that being truly spiritual means the wordless feelings of awe, love, trust/faith, compassion, gratitude, forgiveness, joy, and hope. Like Andrew Newberg, Harvard psychiatrist George Vaillant suggests that these feelings appear to reside anatomically in my limbic system. When I am focused on them, they engage my parasympathetic nervous system, which relaxes me and helps generate nourishment for my immune system. At the same time, this mechanism gives me an experiential connection with God/Goddess/All-That-Is. These two realizations—the positive feelings that I just listed and a connection to something greater than ourselves—is what Vaillant proposes as true spirituality. In his book *Spiritual Evolution: A Scientific Defense of Faith,* he writes: "Spirituality is virtually indistinguishable from these positive emotions and is, thus, rooted in our evolutionary biology."[29] He goes on to say that spirituality is not about ideas, sacred texts, and theology. Rather, he sees spirituality as being about positive emotion and social connection. These are the very emotions that Newberg's meditators focused on for the research that demonstrated that this is all going on in our limbic system. It appears that in this sense we actually have spirituality built into our biology!

As we heal and proceed along our spiritual journey, which may be directed by what has been named Kundalini in the East, we can release our past emotional and psychological wounds and replace them with positive feelings and a clear mind. As we work through our Kundalini process and find balance, so much more comes with it than we could ever have predicted. Gratitude and humility give us constant renewal that allows us to feel the over-flowing abundance of the Universe. As our physical beings and our souls become one, our journey and destination become one, demonstrating the truth about dark and light, positive and nega-tive, Yin and Yang: it was all an illusion, a dance to help us to wake up spiritually. Separation collapses. All our striving to become who God meant us to be comes to fruition. We realize that we are One. Even the belief in heaven *after* this lifetime recedes as we experience creating heaven here. We remember who we are, and we are Home. [30]

God has a dream—
And, the dream comes true
Each time one of us
Awakens.

Spiritual Energy

Perspectives from a Map of the Psyche and the Kundalini Recovery Process

CHARLES L. WHITFIELD, MD

The author of ten best-selling books, Charles Whitfield has worked for decades with people who have had spiritual awakenings and emergencies, using a comprehensive understanding of the psyche, the recovery process, and how they relate to our True Self, Higher Self, and ego. In this essay, Whitfield outlines this understanding of the many pitfalls or "traps" that those who experience a kundalini awakening may encounter and the stages of recovery they can expect to undergo. He also explores these questions: How can we overcome past traumas brought up by spiritual awakenings? How do we cope with post-traumatic stress or denial when kundalini energy causes these kinds of unconscious issues to resurface?

HAVE YOU HAD a spiritual awakening? Or do you wonder if you might have had one? A spiritual awakening is an experiential opening to a power greater than ourselves. As a result, we become more aware of and open to our self, others, and the God of our understanding.

Based on informal surveys I have done of people attending my workshops over the years, I estimate that at least one in three people have had a spiritual awakening of some sort. Perhaps 25 percent of these were triggered by near-death experiences. The remaining 75 percent are triggered by numerous other experiences, from meditation to childbirth to "hitting bottom" in a critical or desperate life situation. Some of these events have opened people to experiencing the painful yet often liberating Kundalini process.

Who or what is it that actually does the awakening? Is there a part of us that becomes more aware and opens to ourself, others, God? My sense is that it is a spiritual energy that starts to awaken us to our Real or True Self, and helps us learn about our ego or false self.

WHO AM I? A MAP OF THE MIND

Throughout the struggle of the human condition, many people have asked some important questions: Who am I? What am I doing here? Where am I going? How can I get any peace? While the answers to these questions remain a Divine Mystery, I have found it useful to construct a map of the mind or psyche. And while the map is not the territory, maps can be useful.

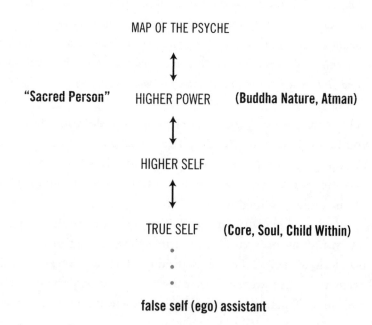

MAP OF THE PSYCHE

$\updownarrow$

"Sacred Person"   HIGHER POWER   (Buddha Nature, Atman)

$\updownarrow$

HIGHER SELF

$\updownarrow$

TRUE SELF   (Core, Soul, Child Within)

.
.
.

false self (ego) assistant

Other names for, or dimensions of, the True Self—who I really am—include the real or existential self, the human heart, the soul, chakras four and five, and the Child Within. They are all the same because they are our True Identity. I also have within me a Divine Nature, sometimes called a guardian angel, Atman, Buddha Nature, Christ Consciousness, chakras six and seven, Higher Self, or simply Self. And both of these—my True Self and my Higher Self—are intimately connected to my Higher Power, God/Goddess/All-That-Is, a part of which is also within me.

I see this relationship—True Self, Higher Self, and Higher Power—as being so important that I can also view it as being one person, which I call the Sacred Person. In a loving, supporting, and teaching way, pervading throughout the Sacred Person is the Holy Spirit (Kundalini, Chi, Ki, Ruach ha Kadosh, and Divine Energy).

As a part of the Mystery, my True Self makes or constructs an assistant to help me in limited ways as I live out this human experience. We can call this assistant or sidekick the ego, also known as the false self or codependent self. When this ego is helpful to us, such as in screening, sorting, and handling many aspects of our internal and external realities, we can call it positive ego. But when it brings us unnecessary emotional pain or tries to take over and run our life, it becomes negative ego.

This map of the psyche is more evolved than the maps of Freud, Jung, and their colleagues of up to a hundred years ago, when they used the term *ego* to mean both True Self *and* false self. Since the 1930s, the self-psychologists and the object-relations psychologists have begun to make this more precise differentiation between True Self and false self, and today we use *ego* synonymously with false self. (This understanding is in contrast with many writers who still lump the True Self and false self together and call it the "ego.")

A contemporary holy book called *A Course in Miracles* says in its introduction:

What is real cannot be threatened.
What is unreal does not exist.
Herein lies the peace of God.[1]

What is real is God and God's world, that of the Sacred Person. The ego and its world are not real, and therefore in the grand scheme of the Mystery, do not exist. Herein, when we make this differentiation, lies our peace and serenity.

But growing up in a dysfunctional family and a dysfunctional society, we may have become wounded. That wounding made our Child Within, or True Self, go into hiding, and the only one left to run the show of our life was our ego (false self). And since it is not competent to run our life successfully, we often end up feeling confused and hurt.

The way out is to begin to differentiate between identifying with my True Self and my false self, and to heal my wounds around all the past traumas that hurt and confused me. That is what I have described in my books.[2] While all of this information is useful to know on a cognitive level, it is ultimately *healing* only on an experiential level. To heal, I have to experience working through my pain, as well as living and enjoying my life. If we can identify with having a Kundalini arousal, its spiritual energy can assist us as we heal.

SPIRITUAL AWAKENINGS AND THE RECOVERY MOVEMENT

Over the decades of the 1980s and the 1990s, and into the twenty-first century, an increasing number of people have begun to awaken to many of their traumatic experiences and are starting to heal themselves. This phenomenon, called the *recovery movement,* with its free and effective Twelve-Step Fellowships, is part of a new paradigm, a new and expanded understanding and belief about the human condition and how to heal it. This approach is effective and has developed momentum for two reasons: it is *grass roots*—its energy comes from the recovering people themselves—and it employs the most accurate and healing of all the accumulated knowledge about the human condition. But what is different about this knowledge is that it is now *simplified* and *demystified* while at the same time *spiritual*.

TRAPS IN SPIRITUAL AWAKENINGS

There are some traps in spiritual awakenings. After we have had our particular spiritual experience and possible Kundalini arousal, one trap is being misled by other people who may try to steer us off our personal spiritual path. They may be therapists, counselors, clergy, gurus, family, or friends, who may not understand and may even have distorted boundaries. And so they may label our awakening and subsequent signs and symptoms as being psychotic, the "work of the devil," hallucinations, or flaky, or they may try to invalidate our experience in some other way. This can lead to the second trap: they may try to prescribe or even force us to take toxic psychiatric drugs, from sedatives to antidepressants to major tranquilizers to "mood stabilizers." In the most extreme cases, they might lock us up in a psychiatric unit or a jail, or shame and guilt us in other ways. But the fact remains that we have had a spiritual awakening, and something has been aroused in us; we are looking for validation and support based on what is actually happening, now and on the rest of our journey.

When we allow our kundalini process to evolve naturally, the result is usually psychological and spiritual growth over time. A problem is that many of the associated symptoms and experiences mimic what psychiatry and psychology call "mental disorders" or "mental illness." Today, most psychiatrists and some psychologists, social workers, and counselors are unable to recognize Kundalini and instead prescribe or recommend one or more psychiatric drugs in an attempt to lessen the patient's symptoms. In Kundalini awakenings we become progressively more connected with self, others, and God, but these psychiatric drugs are toxic to the brain and body and tend to shut down or aggravate the normal flow of the kundalini process. The drugs slam shut the door to our psychospiritual growth.[3]

Psychiatrist Peter Breggin writes, "It is difficult, if not impossible, to determine accurately the psychological condition of a person who is taking psychiatric drugs. There are too many complicating factors, including the drug's brain-disabling effect, the brain's compensatory reactions and the patient's psychological responses to taking the drug. I have evaluated many cases in which patients have deteriorated under the onslaught of multiple psychiatric drugs without the prescribing physicians attributing the patient's decline to drug toxicity, including drug withdrawal. Instead, physicians typically attribute their patients' worsening condition to 'mental illness' when in reality the patient is suffering from adverse drug reactions."[4]

Breggins's work has reflected the sometimes missing conscience of psychiatry. If you accept help in the form of psychiatric drugs, realize that you are entering an area that you may regret or be unable to stop. Each drug has toxic effects that turn out to be at least as bad as the original complaint, and such drugs often lead to more drugs to counter these toxic effects, which include drug withdrawal. Breggin spells this out in his comprehensive textbook.[4]

In his groundbreaking book *Kundalini: Psychosis or Transcendence?* Lee Sannella, MD, writes, "There are many undergoing this process who at times feel quite insane. When they behave well and keep silent they may avoid being called schizophrenic, or being hospitalized, or sedated. Nevertheless their isolation and sense of separation from others may cause them such suffering. We must reach such people, their families, and society, with information to help them recognize their condition as a blessing, not a curse. Certainly we must no longer subject people, who might be in the midst of this rebirth process, to drugs or shock therapies, approaches which are at opposite poles to creative self-development."[5]

A third trap is the frustration that usually comes with trying to do what is called a *spiritual bypass*. A spiritual bypass happens when we try to avoid working through the pain of our prior traumas and instead try to jump from an early stage of healing directly into the most advanced stage. Because this concept is crucial to making sense of and handling spiritual awakenings and the movement of spiritual energy (also called Kundalini, Ki, Chi, and the like), I will briefly describe the generic stages of the healing or recovery process.

STAGES OF RECOVERY

A spiritual awakening and movement of spiritual energy may happen during any of the following stages of recovery.

Stage Zero

Stage Zero is manifested by the presence of an active illness or disorder such as an addiction, compulsion, or physical illness. This active illness may be acute, recurring, or chronic. Without recovery, it may continue *indefinitely*. At Stage Zero, recovery has not yet started. It may be at this stage that the spiritual awakening happens: stimulated by a near-death experience, bottoming out from an illness, or the like.

The actual trigger for the awakening could cause what we call "retraumatization." First we carry traumas from our past, commonly from our childhood, that may not have been "metabolized," and now we are traumatized by the trigger for the spiritual awakening. This retraumatization brings back the past experiences we may have suppressed or repressed. If these traumas and their effects are validated immediately, we can avoid a more painful acute stress disorder. If they are not validated, we may eventually experience acute and/or post-traumatic stress disorder (PTSD). This trauma and its effects commonly underlie Stages Zero through Three wounding and recovery work.

RECOVERY AND DURATION ACCORDING TO STAGES, WITH EASE OF UNDERSTANDING AND USING SPIRITUAL ENERGY

RECOVERY STAGE	CONDITION	FOCUS OF RECOVERY	APPROXIMATE DURATION	UNDERSTANDING AND USING SPIRITUAL ENERGY
3	Human/ Spiritual	Spirituality	Ongoing	Easier
2	Past trauma	Trauma-specific	Three to five-plus years	Some difficulty
1	Stage 0 disorder	Basic-illness full recovery program	One-half to three years	Difficult
0	Active illness	Usually none	Indefinite	Most difficult

Stage One

At Stage One, recovery begins. It involves participating in a full recovery program to assist in healing the Stage Zero condition(s). People who have a spiritual awakening while in Stage Zero may try to bypass doing Stage One recovery work.

During Stages Zero and One, clinicians who don't understand or are not educated about Kundalini arousal may want to prescribe psychoactive drugs (antidepressants, antipsychotics, "mood stabilizers," or sedatives). This will usually have a detrimental effect that has the potential to abort the transformational process. These drugs may give some relief for a short time but will soon numb the person out and "dumb them down," like a chemical straitjacket.[6] Even worse, they can cause anxiety, depression, or psychotic symptoms for those who are in a delicate phase of their process.

The label of depression creates a frozen diagnosis: there is no movement. But we can reframe depression as unresolved grief, and when we allow our grief from past traumas to surface in Stage One or Stage Two, we may experience a bittersweet emotional release and even sense the movement of energy.

Once the Stage Zero condition is resolved in a Stage One program, Stage Two therapy groups are safe, productive places in which to identify and release grief coming from our past.

Stage Two

Stage Two is one that many people may also try to bypass. It involves healing the effects of past traumas, sometimes called adult child or codependence issues. Once a person has a stable and solid Stage One recovery—one that has lasted for at least a year or longer—it may be time to consider looking into these issues. *Adult child* is a term that has been used to refer to anyone who grew up in an unhealthy, troubled, or dysfunctional family. Many adult children may still be in a similarly unhealthy environment, whether at home, in one or more relationships, or at work. Because a Kundalini arousal often brings up our unconscious material, working a Stage Two recovery will likely help us heal, and authentic humility assists us with this and in our spiritual growth. Humility is facilitated by having the courage to make the choice, moment by moment, to let go of ego-centered thinking and behaving.[7]

Spiritual practices and awakenings can revive and exacerbate unresolved conflicts. This is not necessarily bad, however, since the process can bring to the surface issues and difficulties requiring attention and can result in considerable healing and personality integration.[8] If treating therapists can respect these spiritual awakenings as possible Kundalini arousal, they will be able to support trusting relationships in which their patients feel cared for and safe. This will create a positive attitude so patients expect that the process will prove valuable and healing. Thus, opening to and talking about the experience can be helpful and can be facilitated by psychotherapy.[9]

Stage Three

Stage Three recovery is the stage into which we may be compelled prematurely by having a spiritual awakening. It includes the experience of spirituality and its incorporation into our daily life. It is an ongoing process. In this stage we *make meaning* of our past. We are now more aware of being free of old beliefs and can work through conflicts faster as we create more stability in our lives. We make use of several spiritual practices, including meditation and prayer, as we access the powers of gratitude and humility.[10]

CONCLUSION

If we try to go around or bypass the darkness to get to the Light, that is, if we try to ignore the lower to get to the higher levels of our consciousness, some dynamic or force—we can call it our shadow (Jung) or repetition compulsion (Freud)—will usually pull us back until we work through our particular unfinished business. Trying to avoid this work of Stages One and Two recovery can also be called *premature transcendence* or *high-level denial*. This experience is seen in any number of situations, such as being prematurely born again, having a spiritual awakening and focusing only on the Light, or becoming attached to a religion or way that is the "only" way. As previously discussed in Barbara Harris Whitfield's essay "Mental and Emotional Health in the Kundalini Process," the consequences of taking a spiritual bypass are often active codependence: denial of the richness of our inner life; trying to control ourselves or others; all-or-nothing thinking and behaving; feelings of fear, shame, and confusion; high tolerance for inappropriate behavior; frustration, addiction, compulsion, relapse, and unnecessary pain and suffering.

A way out of this trap is to develop humility (i.e., openness to learning more about self, others, and God) and work through the pain of wherever we may be, or just enjoy the joyous feelings.[11] Those who are actively addicted or disordered can work through a Stage One full recovery program. Those who are adult children of troubled or dysfunctional families can also soon work through Stage Two recovery. We need to stay mindful of these truths: We cannot let go of something if we do not know experientially what it is that we are letting go. We cannot usually transcend the unhealed, and we cannot connect experientially to the God of our understanding until we know our True Self, our human Heart.

When we have progressed in our Kundalini process, we can consider joining a Stage Two therapy group or a Twelve-Step fellowship program to help support ourselves in our new experience of co–creating our life with our Higher Power. Our new expansive and creative abilities may not fit into our prior life relationships. Being in such a weekly recovery or therapy group gives us a place to talk about and work through our emotional pain and other life issues.

If we can expand our beliefs and bring our higher nature into our everyday life, we can experience true humility. Kundalini energy invites us to stretch beyond the limits of who we thought we were and become all that we are. This process allows us to experience a healing unity with ourselves, others, and our Higher Power.

Near-Death Experiences and the Physio-Kundalini Syndrome

BRUCE GREYSON, MD

Bruce Greyson, MD, is the Chester F. Carlson Professor of Psychiatry and Neurobehavioral Sciences and director of the Division of Perceptual Studies at the University of Virginia. He is also coauthor and editor of several books on near-death experiences (NDEs) and has devoted much of his career to studying them. In the following essay, he shares clinical studies that correlate NDEs with kundalini arousal. Examining the various symptoms for NDEs and how these relate to kundalini experiences, Greyson looks for answers to the questions: Can an NDE serve as a catalyst for human evolution? Can having an NDE propel people to awaken to a higher consciousness?

NEAR-DEATH EXPERIENCES

Near-death experiences (NDEs) are profound spiritual or mystical experiences that many people report as they approach or start to cross the threshold of death.[1] The contents and aftereffects of NDEs suggest that they are more than just hallucinations.[2] The contents do not appear to be influenced by past religious beliefs, but after the experience they do have a profound effect on religious or spiritual beliefs.[3] Near-death experiencers (NDErs) also report a consistent positive change in attitude toward the transition from life to death.[4]

There is still no accepted scientific cause of NDEs. Such a complex phenomenon does not lend itself to a simplistic mechanistic

explanation. Despite the psychological or physiological interpretations of the NDE that some authors propose,[5] the experience is
almost universally regarded by those who report it as spiritually
authentic. This is not necessarily paradoxical, as the measure of an
experience's authenticity is not the nature of its trigger, but rather
its ability to promote authentic spiritual growth.[6] One of the most
consistently documented features of the near-death experience is
its profound range of aftereffects, including decreased fear of death,
decreased competitiveness, decreased interest in personal gain, and
increased joy of life, altruism, and interest in spirituality.[7]

Some investigators in the field of consciousness and near-death
studies have suggested that the significance of the near-death experience may be its role as a catalyst for human evolution.[8] They view
the reported mental, physical, and spiritual aftereffects of NDEs as
indications of an accelerated development of intuitive functioning
on a different order, and as similar to changes traditionally reported
by people awakening to a higher-order state of consciousness. But
if evolution of consciousness implies the continuing biological
evolution of humanity, then personality transformations should be
accompanied by signs of biological transformation.

KUNDALINI

In Eastern spiritual traditions, the biological mechanism of both
individual enlightenment and evolution of the species toward
higher consciousness is called *kundalini,* a potential force that,
once awakened, can produce a variety of mental, emotional,
physical, and spiritual effects. The ancient yogic texts describe
a life energy present in all living beings called *prana;* corollary
energies have been identified in many other cultures, such as *huo*
and *chi* of Tibetan yogis, *quaumaneq* of Eskimo shamans, *incendium
amoris* and *photismos* of Christian mystics, Henri Bergson's *élan
vital,* and the more recent terms *bioenergy, bioplasma,* and *orgone
energy.* Kundalini was described as a normally dormant mechanism, or organizing principle, that could be activated or aroused

under certain conditions to strengthen or purify an individual's prana, transforming its effects upon the individual. Comparable potential forces or organizing principles have also been described in other traditions: examples are *shakti,* the Odic force, the Holy Spirit, the Pearl of Great Price, the Serpent Power, the Rod of Aaron, the Sacred Fire, Osiris, and the Sun Behind the Sun.[9]

Kundalini has been held responsible for life itself,[10] the sexual drive, creativity, genius, longevity, and vigor,[11] and our evolution toward an ultimate, magnificent state of consciousness.[12] The dormant kundalini is said to be situated at the base of the spine, and when aroused can travel upward along the spinal cord to the brain, where it can stimulate a dormant chamber of the brain (the *brahma randhra*), leading to biological transformation and immensely expanded perception.[13]

KUNDALINI AND NEAR-DEATH EXPERIENCES

Eastern traditions have developed elaborate lifelong practices and lifestyles with the intent of awakening kundalini; this is, in fact, the implicit purpose of yoga.[14] However, the same ancient Eastern traditions have also recognized that when the brain is deprived of oxygen, kundalini as the life force in rare circumstances may actually rush to the brain in an effort to sustain life. In fact, one unorthodox yoga sect practices suffocation by tongue-swallowing in the hope that kundalini will rush to their brains and produce enlightenment,[15] a practice that may have a Western counterpart in *la petite mort,* in which a considerable number of adolescents die each year seeking orgasmic initiation by asphyxiation.[16]

This theoretical arousal of kundalini by life-threatening crisis has traditionally been regarded by most Eastern philosophers as dangerous.[17] In Eastern traditions, kundalini would ideally be activated at the appropriate time by a guru who can properly guide the development of that energy. If awakened without proper guidance, as social psychologist Kenneth Ring believes happens in near-death experiences,[18] kundalini can be raw, destructive power loosed on the individual's body and psyche.

Though the vocabulary of the kundalini hypothesis is foreign to Westerners, the process bears some resemblance to the Christian concept of the Holy Spirit. The process of kundalini awakening is essentially a spiritual one, outside the domain of science. However, its traditional roles as the vehicle of evolution, if guided, or of psychosomatic havoc, if spontaneous, should be accompanied by observable physical and psychological effects.

THE PHYSIO-KUNDALINI SYNDROME

Because Western medicine does not acknowledge the Eastern concept of kundalini or even the westernized physio-kundalini model, symptoms of kundalini arousal are often diagnosed as physical and/or psychological problems that fit within Western allopathic diagnostic categories. For example, the shaking, twisting, and vibrating so well known to experiencers could be diagnosed as a neurological disorder. It is also hard to recognize the energy's presence because it manifests itself in so many different patterns. Because its symptoms mimic so many disorders of the mind and body, even people familiar with the kundalini concept are unsure whether they are witnessing rising kundalini energy or disorders of the mind and body. However, taking psychotropic medications to alleviate symptoms, on the assumption that these represent a psychiatric disorder, may disrupt the natural healing mechanism of kundalini activation.[19]

Three decades ago, biomedical engineer Itzhak Bentov formulated a scientifically verifiable version of the kundalini concept, which he called the physio-kundalini hypothesis; psychiatrist and ophthalmologist Lee Sannella developed the physio-kundalini model further, collecting cases, experimenting with ways to help channel it, and outlining research strategies.[20] While both scientists acknowledged that the physio-kundalini concept is less comprehensive than the classical kundalini model, they argued that its simplified, mechanistic description made it more accessible to scientific study.

THE STUDY

Following up on Kenneth Ring's suggestion that NDEs can arouse kundalini, I measured features of NDEs and features of kundalini arousal in people who had had near-death experiences and in two comparison groups. The participants in this research included 153 people who had had NDEs, 55 who had come close to death but did not have NDEs, and 113 people who had never come close to death.

I gave all 321 participants the NDE scale to identify the presence of a near-death experience and quantify its depth. With a range of 0 to 32, the scale has high internal consistency and correlation with other measures of NDE, reliably differentiates near-death experiences from other reactions to a brush with death, and produces scores that do not change over decades.[21] The 153 participants identified as NDErs had a mean score of 16.7 on the NDE scale, whereas the 55 participants classified as not having an NDE had a mean score of 2 on the NDE scale. The third group of 113 participants had never come close to death.

I analyzed responses of NDErs and control subjects on a nineteen-item questionnaire I based on the Bentov-Sannella physio-kundalini model.[22] This questionnaire includes motor "symptoms," such as spontaneous body movements, strange posturing, breath changes, and the body getting locked into certain positions; somatosensory symptoms, such as spontaneous tingling or vibrations, orgasmic sensations, progression of physical sensations up the legs and back and over the head, extreme heat or cold, and pain that comes and goes abruptly; audiovisual symptoms, such as internal lights or colors that light up the body, internal voices, and internal whistling, hissing, or roaring noises; and psychological symptoms, such as sudden bliss or ecstasy for no reason,

speeding or slowing of thoughts, and expanding beyond the body
and watching the body from a distance.

As a group, NDErs reported experiencing almost twice as
many physio-kundalini items as did either people who had had
close brushes with death but no NDEs or people who had never
come close to death. As a check on whether the physio-kundalini
questionnaire might be measuring nonspecific unusual experiences, I also analyzed the responses of a group of hospitalized
psychiatric patients; they reported the same number of physio-
kundalini items as did the non-NDE comparison groups.

There were two additional unexpected comparison groups
in my studies, as shown below: people who claimed to have
had NDEs but described experiences with virtually no typical
NDE features, and people who denied having had NDEs but
then went on to describe prototypical near-death experiences. In
their responses to the physio-kundalini questionnaire, the group
that made unsupported claims of NDEs were comparable to the
non-NDE comparison group, while the group that undeservedly
denied having NDEs were comparable to the group of NDErs. In
regard to kundalini arousal, then, *having* a near-death experience
mattered, but *thinking* you had one didn't.

PHYSIO-KUNDALINI SYNDROME INDEX

GROUP	PHYSIO-KUNDALINI SYNDROME ITEMS REPORTED
Near-death experiencers	7.6
Those who denied NDEs but reported NDE features	7.7
Those close to death without NDEs	4.6
Those never close to death	4.6
Those who claimed NDEs but reported no NDE features	4.5
Hospitalized psychiatric patients	4.9

PHYSIO-KUNDALINI SYNDROME INDEX: MOTOR SYMPTOMS

	NDErs	CLOSE TO DEATH WITHOUT NDE	NEVER CLOSE TO DEATH
Body assuming and maintaining strange positions	17%	2%	2%
Body becoming frozen or locked in strange position	20%	7%	5%
Breathing spontaneously stopping or becoming rapid, shallow, or deep	39%	18%	21%
Spontaneous involuntary movements	43%	40%	36%

Here is a breakdown of all the items on the Physio-Kundalini Syndrome Index in four categories: motor symptoms, somatosensory symptoms, audiovisual symptoms, and psychological symptoms. Three of the four *motor* physio-kundalini symptoms were acknowledged significantly more often by NDErs than by the two comparison groups.

While some *somatosensory* physio-kundalini symptoms, such as spontaneous orgasmic sensations, ascending anatomic progression of sensations, and unexplained isolated temperature changes, are more commonly reported by NDErs than by the comparison groups, the differences were not statistically significant, possibly because they are either too infrequent in any group, as with temperature changes so extreme as to burn other people, or too common in all groups, as with spontaneous unexplained pains and tingling or vibratory sensations.

PHYSIO-KUNDALINI SYNDROME INDEX: SOMATOSENSORY SYMPTOMS

	NDERS	CLOSE TO DEATH WITHOUY NDE	NEVER CLOSE TO DEATH
Ecstatic tickle or orgasmic feeling	37%	13%	17%
Sensations starting in the feet and moving to the top of the head	37%	16%	20%
Extreme heat or cold	54%	27%	19%
Heat or cold affecting someone else	10%	2%	2%
Abrupt pains that end abruptly for no reason	59%	45%	53%
Tingling, vibration, itching, or tickling on the skin	58%	51%	53%

With the exception of unexplained internal noises, which were reported significantly more often by NDErs than participants in the comparison groups, *audiovisual* physio-kundalini symptoms were acknowledged either so commonly by all groups, as with internal voices, or so rarely, as with internal lights or colors, that differences between groups were not significant.

PHYSIO-KUNDALINI SYNDROME INDEX: AUDIOVISUAL SYMPTOMS

	NDERS	CLOSE TO DEATH WITHOUT NDE	NEVER CLOSE TO DEATH
Internal noises: whistling, hissing, chirping, roaring, flutelike sounds	41%	21%	21%
Internal voices	46%	35%	27%
Internal lights or colors	19%	5%	7%
Internal lights or colors illuminating parts of the body	19%	5%	7%
Lights bright enough to illuminate room	7%	5%	1%

PHYSIO-KUNDALINI SYNDROME INDEX: PSYCHOLOGICAL SYMPTOMS

	NDERS	CLOSE TO DEATH WITHOUT NDE	NEVER CLOSE TO DEATH
Sudden intense ecstasy, bliss, peace, love, devotion, joy, or cosmic unity for no apparent reason	76%	51%	50%
Watching what is happening, including one's thoughts, from a distance, or "witness consciousness"	55%	31%	35%
Thoughts speeding up, slowing down, or stopping for no apparent reason	61%	38%	41%
Sudden intense fear, anxiety, depression, hatred, or confusion for no apparent reason	52%	27%	38%
Experiencing oneself as physically larger that the body, as expanding beyond the material body boundary	31%	18%	19%

Finally, with regard to *psychological* physio-kundalini symptoms, sudden unexplained positive emotions, changes in thought processes for no apparent reason, and watching oneself from a distance or "witness consciousness" were reported significantly more often by NDErs than by either comparison group, whereas sudden unexplained negative emotions and the "greater body" experience were not reported with significantly different frequency by the different groups.

In summary, ten of the nineteen symptoms on the physio-kundalini syndrome index, most notably the motor and mental symptoms, were significantly more common among the NDErs than among the comparison groups: assuming strange positions, becoming locked into position, changes in breathing, spontaneous orgasmic sensations, ascending progression of sensations, unexplained heat or cold moving through the body, internal noises, sudden positive emotions for no reason, watching oneself as if from a distance, and unexplained changes in thought

processes. These ten items then may be useful indicators of kundalini arousal.

Also of note, among the 153 near-death experiencers, there
was a significant positive correlation between NDE scale score and
number of physio-kundalini symptoms reported. That is, those
with deeper NDEs reported more physio-kundalini symptoms.

Kenneth Ring and his student Christopher Rosing reported
almost identical results in their Omega Project: NDErs reported
experiencing almost twice as many physio-kundalini items as
did people who had close brushes with death but no NDE, and
people who had never come close to death.[23]

Here then we have NDErs reporting precisely the kind of
physiological changes that are associated in Eastern traditions
with the bioenergy that drives evolution. From verbal reports of
such evidence as patterns of physiological functioning and disease
history, as well as physio-kundalini manifestations, we can identify
which items best differentiate NDErs from comparison groups.

IMPLICATIONS

The data from this study demonstrate that a number of physio-
kundalini symptoms derived from classical descriptions of
kundalini arousal are reported more often by NDErs than by
comparison populations.[24] This finding corroborates the anecdotal evidence of previous investigators that NDEs are associated
with kundalini. It must be borne in mind that the physio-kundalini
syndrome—this consistent pattern of physiological and psychological symptoms—is connected with the classical kundalini
arousal of Eastern spiritual traditions only by theory and circum-
stantial evidence. A true measure of kundalini awakening, such as
an enduring state of higher consciousness, is beyond our current
ability to measure.

Although in theory the physio-kundalini syndrome may imply
spiritual evolution, in practice it often denotes a crisis requiring adjustment. While there has been little scientific literature on

kundalini, there has been even less from a clinical perspective. What has been written by physicians and therapists suggests that common physio-kundalini symptoms and individuals' responses to those symptoms are often mistaken for physical and mental illnesses, with tragic results.[25] Given that the increasing frequency of near-death experiencers was estimated by a Gallup poll more than a quarter century ago to be 5 percent of the adult American population,[26] this study suggests that the physio-kundalini syndrome may be far more common in Western society than previously imagined.

This documentation of the frequency of kundalini arousal and of its association with events such as the near-death experience may foster greater awareness of kundalini among the scientific and medical professions. Studies of kundalini phenomena should be enlarged to encompass other populations at risk, such as combat veterans, heart transplant patients and those with terminal illnesses, and individuals following spiritual paths. Further research and dialogue among scientists and clinicians may help individuals experiencing kundalini arousal to cope with the psychophysiological crises and fulfill the promise of spiritual growth.

Finally, based on such findings, it is possible that future work in this area could lead to vital new insights into the evolution of humanity toward a different order of consciousness, echoing a major theme in many books written about the near-death experience—that the importance of the near-death experience is not its association with death, but its implications for life.[27]

Healing Through the Three Channels

SHANTI SHANTI KAUR KHALSA, PHD

Shanti Shanti Kaur Khalsa, PhD, is founder and director of the Guru Ram Das Center for Medicine and Humanology. A yoga instructor since 1971, she began to specialize in teaching kundalini yoga and meditation to people with chronic or life-threatening illnesses and their family members in 1986, under the direction of Yogi Bhajan. At the Guru Ram Das Center she works with people who have diabetes, cancer, heart disease, chronic fatigue, fibromyalgia, HIV, anxiety, depression, and major life transitions. In the following essay, she shares the results of that work as well as answering such questions as: Does kundalini yoga have the potential to improve quality of life for those with chronic illnesses? If so, how does it heal?

"I HAVE ALREADY passed the cross in the road, haven't I?" Sarah asked.[1] It wasn't really a question. "And I made a choice, a decision which direction to go. And I acted on that."

Sarah had spent the past two years exhausted and in pain. She had seen a series of physicians, including many specialists, who could not give her a clear diagnosis. No one knew: Did she have chronic fatigue syndrome? Fibromyalgia? Something else? Desperate, she turned to the practice of kundalini yoga to help support her while she grappled with a chronic condition that could not be named.

At first, Sarah practiced simple breathing techniques to raise her vitality and build endurance. She chanted mantras accompanied by rhythmic movement to relieve pain and emotional distress. She particularly benefited from a sound current that is basic to the practice of kundalini yoga: *sat nam*. This mantra means "truth is my identity" and has the effect of bringing forward one's clear self. As she grew stronger, she began to practice *kriyas*—predetermined sequences that combine breath, posture, movement, and mantra—that her teacher matched to her ability and needs.

Shortly after she started practicing these kriyas, Sarah noticed the benefits. She slept better, she was less anxious and depressed, and the intensity and duration of pain were reduced. She was more hopeful about the future, she had more energy, and her energy lasted longer—she had more "better days" than not.

The "cross in the road" came when Sarah realized she could use these techniques to get well, and that she had the tools she needed to do so. She made a decision to improve her condition and acted on it. She continued to seek and receive medical treatment when she needed it, and to practice kundalini yoga a little longer each day. Over time, she fully recovered her health.

"The year I was diagnosed with breast cancer was the most transformational of my life," Leigh recalls. She was just thirty-six, and the mother of three young children. "I had been mildly depressed for some time, dissatisfied with my life, but not enough to do anything about it. I knew I was not myself, that I wasn't authentic, really, to myself—not that I knew what to do about it. There was nothing wrong with my life—I was simply getting by."

After her diagnosis, Leigh joined a kundalini yoga class for women with breast cancer and discovered that raising her energy allowed her to tap into her hidden gifts and make new decisions in her life. She enrolled in an art class and began creating award-winning pieces. "This is what I had been missing. I learned that in illness and in health, it is important to stay receptive to what is unseen and the possibility of change. I am awake now, and I find joy in most of what I do each day. No longer do I drag through and take my blessed life for granted."

A graphic artist, Martin had lived and worked in San Francisco for twenty-eight years before he was diagnosed with a serious viral condition. "When I tested positive for hepatitis C, it was so far along and my liver so damaged I thought my life was over. The help I received through the practice of kundalini yoga gave me an experience of myself and made me aware that I can have a future, that I *do* have a future. I learned what I need to do in order to stay well, to live my life in a way that reminds me all life is sacred. I believe I would not be alive today if I had not started to practice kundalini yoga and make the life changes it helped me to make."

After practicing kundalini yoga regularly, Martin recognized that recovering from illness and then maintaining health through conscious flow of the kundalini energy are a result of a total way of living, not just practicing exercises to raise the kundalini.

KUNDALINI YOGA AND LIFE-THREATENING ILLNESS

In October 1986, it was my blessing to teach the first kundalini yoga class especially designed for people living with HIV. This was the same year that azidothymidine (AZT [2]; now called zidovudine and manufactured as Retrovir) went into clinical trials, and many of the students in the class found themselves sicker from the side effects of the medication than from any opportunistic infection. The kinks had not yet been worked out in the dosing.

The purpose of kundalini yoga practice is to enable healthy people to experience their excellence. It is not inherently a therapeutic practice. When we train to teach this form of yoga, we prepare to teach it to healthy people, not people with life-threatening health conditions. Yet I learned firsthand that it has therapeutic value.

In 1986, there was no curriculum or protocol for teaching people who were as ill as those who came to class. Over the next few months, under Yogi Bhajan's guidance, an approach was formed to meet the wide range of needs of people in all stages of HIV disease, and thus our service to people with this illness began.

For many centuries kundalini yoga practices were kept secret, and because of this, myths have surrounded the term *kundalini* to fill in the gap created by lack of knowledge. Other teachers in the yoga community cautioned me, "You can't teach kundalini yoga to ill people; it is too vigorous, too strenuous." These words, though well intended, showed a misunderstanding of the practice of kundalini yoga and how it can be applied in recovering health.

Although the people who came to our HIV classes wanted to get well, most were in a tough position because they believed that to improve their condition meant to return to the state they had been in before they were diagnosed. But as they became more aware of what was possible with kundalini yoga, they realized they did not want to go back to how they had been living. They wanted to be well *and* more aware, conscious, and open to kundalini energy.

What became apparent to me through teaching people with chronic or life-threatening illness was that a healthful recovery and living well are based on uncovering and discovering hidden talents, meaning, and purpose within each individual. It is important to identify this divine purpose or highest state of being and form it into a concept, or an image, of the future for which we want to be well.

Any conflict about the past that one might have can be resolved in directing one's energy toward a more compelling vision of the future. In this way, we all might live up to a higher state of being. This is the "cross in the road" that the person recovering her health must face. When this happens, she is then free to get well and become open to her most genuine essence, as Sarah did. Raising kundalini energy is essential to this process. It brings awareness and vitality, and we need both of these qualities to get and stay well.

THE ANATOMY AND PRACTICE
OF KUNDALINI YOGA

Contrary to one popular myth, kundalini is not some exotic energy that shoots up your spine without warning. It is a natural flow of energy inherent in each person, part of the subtle structure of each human being. It is at home and flowing through your nervous system right now, even as you read this.

There's more concentrated kundalini energy untapped beneath the fourth vertebra, also called the seat of the soul. This is the dormant energy that is awakened through the practice of kriyas. Once it is awakened, it moves through the chakras to unfold and integrate one's gifts, creativity, and capacity. Kundalini energy is a tool we can use to break through the silence of the self and experience what is possible, to give us the foundation and endurance to achieve our unique purpose.

We have all seen the caduceus, the ancient symbol used to represent the modern Western medical profession. Through Eastern eyes, the two serpents intertwined on a staff represent the rise of kundalini energy through the two nerve channels, the *ida* and the *pingala*. The central channel, the staff, is the *sushumna*. It raises the question: was it known or intended that the symbol of modern medicine signifies these three channels of ancient healing?

These three channels are called *nadis*. The ida channel is experienced via the breath through the left nostril. Breathing through the left nostril relates to the parasympathetic nervous system; it is calming, cooling, and restorative and assists with elimination. The pingala channel is experienced by breathing through the right nostril. This relates to the sympathetic nervous system; it is energizing and warming and allows assimilation. These two channels cover the distance from both nostrils to the base of the spine, the seat of the kundalini. The sushumna, the central channel, originates at the base of the spine where the three nadis meet and carries energy to the top of the head.

The practice of kundalini yoga balances the prana through the use of breathing methods and allows the self-healing potential that is already present to flow. In ancient times, healers invoked prana through the three channels as their medicine and mode of treatment. Yogis used specific breath techniques through the nadis to create the necessary effect. They included different *bhandas,* or locks, each relating to a specific area of the body. In the neck lock, for example, the neck is lengthened, and the chin is positioned in toward the spine. Because the process of kriya invokes kundalini, the application of the bhandas is necessary to establish the integration of energy through the three channels.

The three major nadis of yogic anatomy, the sushumna, ida, and pingala, are each employed naturally in the structure of kriya incorporating breath, movement, posture, and mantra. Through the ida nadi, healing involves the whole being in relationship to the sacred using sound, which regulates the breath, image, and thought or belief. Through the pingala nadi, we heal through movement and the application of the bhandas, guiding prana from one area of the body to another. Through the sushumna, we invoke healing through neutral awareness or stillness. *Mudra* (the position of fingers and hands) and *dhrist* (eye focus) are part of the kriyas and also function to direct the flow of prana.

Though the methods are sophisticated and often subtle, there is a simple formula for healing through the three channels: when we access energy through breath, strengthen through rhythmic, targeted movement, and integrate these changes through sound, this brings us to stillness, where the healing force of kundalini energy is most effective.

Breathing consciously is a basic yogic technique, common to all traditions. To breathe at a rhythmic, focused pace is to put the key into the ignition and get the energy started. Long, deep breathing opens the lungs, balances the nervous and endocrine systems, improves lymphatic and cardio circulation, and brings alertness.

Rhythmic movement in relation to yogic posture strengthens weaker areas of the body, opens and clears energy blocks, and builds vitality and endurance. The application of bhandas and mudras directs the flow of prana and builds natural immunity.

In Native American tradition, there are songs that are specifically intended to cure illness. Similarly, when yogic mantra is included in the practice, it can relieve pain, alleviate depression and anxiety, improve lung capacity and lymphatic circulation, raise vitality, and build self-efficacy.

Sound is essential to healing through kundalini energy. Mantras regulate the breath and flow of prana, stimulate meridian points in the tongue, mouth, and lips to activate and balance brain function, and create distinct frequencies to integrate the effects of the kundalini energy.

Yogi Bhajan explained: "As long as you practice a total discipline or a complete and balanced kriya, there is no difficulty. In kundalini yoga, you will notice that every meditation and kriya has some form of mantra in it. This ensures the channelization of the energy."[3]

Once kundalini energy is activated, engaged, integrated, flowing, and creating healing effects, it needs to be maintained. Daily habits of living, including diet, personal hygiene, one's manner of speaking and thinking, and service to others are part of maintaining this flow of energy

A SIMPLE KUNDALINI YOGA BREATH TECHNIQUE

I encourage you, regardless of your state of health, to experience the same type of energy in your life. Right now, right where you are, let's practice a simple, effective breath meditation as taught by Yogi Bhajan. Put the book down and place your hands on your knees, palms facing upward, the back of the hand resting on the knee. On each hand, the tip of your index finger touches the tip of the thumb, forming a circle. The other fingers remain extended. Close your eyes and gently focus them at the point between your eyebrows. Inhale deeply. As you exhale, open your jaw and let the sound of a long "saat" come from your navel out your mouth. As your breath comes to completion, end with a short "nam." Inhale and begin again. Continue for three to eleven minutes. When you are done, inhale deeply through your nose. Exhale and relax. Notice how you feel.

WHAT KUNDALINI OFFERS

What can raising kundalini energy do for people with a chronic or life-threatening illness? In their own words, they say it offers:

> "Hope for a return to health."

> "A sense of what is possible; I can explore what is available to me."

> "Connection, support. I know and feel that I am not alone in this."

> "Peacefulness, freedom from worry or uncertainty about the future."

> "Joy in being alive right now."

> "Calm, to just be in the present moment."

> "Clarity to make decisions and confidence to carry them out."

> "Energy to enjoy life."

> "Ability to take action. I believe in myself now."

> "Self-trust to be comfortable in the face of uncertainty."

> "Inner guidance to know what is my path."

> "Sacredness to meet life and death with joy and peace."

> "An awareness of my future."

May you live with joy, peace, and good health, in a life rich with discovery and adventure, service and community, creativity and fulfillment. Sat nam.

PART III

Kundalini at Large

*Kundalini in a Historical, Philosophical,
and Cultural Context*

Are the Chakras Real?

KEN WILBER

▬▬▬▬▬▬

Ken Wilber is the author of The Integral Vision: A Very Short Introduction to the Revolutionary Integral Approach to Life, God, the Universe, and Everything, *among other books. In this essay, first published in John Warren White's* Kundalini, Evolution, and Enlightenment, *he asks the intriguing question: Are the chakras real? Approaching this subject through Freudian theory and the question of true self-realization, he defines chakras as "knots." Wilber questions the experience of transcendental bliss, identity, and the Oedipal project. He then answers the question: How does kundalini yoga seek to "untie" these knots or chakras?*

> When all the knots of the heart are unloosened, then
> even here, in this human birth, the mortal
> becomes immortal.
> This is the whole teaching of the Scriptures.
>
> —*Katha Upanishad*

THE ORDINARY HUMAN body, as Freud has extensively documented, is under sway of a well-organized tyranny—a tyranny imposed by a separate-self sense in flight from death and in flight from loving unity with the world of phenomena. Under these circumstances, the self does not consciously participate in the light and life of the Adi-Buddha, the Godhead, the Brahman, and is forced to retreat instead to the pale substitute of mental and symbolic forms, with a corresponding de-forma-tion of the body. Hence, the being-consciousness-bliss of one's formless self is distorted and constricted, and under this tyranny appears in the restricted forms known as the chakras.

It is for this reason that the chakras are properly referred to by the terms *granthi* (knots) and *sankhocha* (contraction). In the *Chandogya Upanishad* we read, "In acquiring the traditional doctrine there is release from all knots." And in the *Mundaka Upanishad*, "He, verily, who knows that Supreme Brahman, becomes very Brahman. Liberated from the knots of the heart, he becomes immortal." Likewise, according to the *Surangama Sutra*, Sakyamuni Buddha explains liberation as the final dissolution of the "knots we have tied in the essential unity of our own Mind."

And yet, strictly speaking, final liberation, being the time-less and therefore eternal condition of all worlds and selves, is not so much the *result* of the *action* of untying these knots, but rather the tacit acknowledgment that these knots do not, and cannot, obstruct ultimate consciousness. Liberation, in short, is not the actual untying of these knots, but the silent admission that they are already untied. Herein lies the key to the paradox of the chakras: they are ultimately dissolved in the realization that they need not be dissolved.

Finally, therefore, the chakras are not real—in the sense that they do not pose a barrier to self-realization, nor do they constitute mandatory stages in an upward climb to liberation. In the last anal-ysis, there are no stages in eternity—nor any ladder *to* the infinite that does not begin *with* the infinite. That the chakras in themselves are not real is the conclusion of most of the great sages, siddhas, mystics, and masters, such as Krishnamurti, Sri Ramana Maharshi, Shankara, Bubba Free John, and virtually all Ch'an and Zen masters. To quote but one, the illustrious Sri Ramana Maharshi: "Do not waste time meditating on chakras, nadis, padmas, or mantras of dei-ties, or anything else of the kind. The six subtle centers (chakras) are merely mental pictures and are meant for beginners in yoga."

And yet—and this is the point to which much of our discussion must be directed—the chakras do *appear* real to the separate self who constructs these knots in his flight both from death and from a prior unity with all manifestation. The flight from death generates time, while the flight from unity generates space. Now, the self-created world of time-and-space is, by all accounts, the world of *samsara*, the ropes of our own bondage and suffering, and the chakras are but the knots in these binding ropes of misery. There are an enormous number of descriptions and explanations for the genesis of these knots in awareness, given, from several different angles, by the major metaphysical traditions. There are, to name some, the sefiroth of the Kabbalah, the vijnanas of the Yogacara, the kosas of the Vedanta, the hierarchies of the neo-Confucians, the kuei–hou intervals of the Taoists, the transmutation series of the Alchemists, and the energetics of the tantras. All of these deal, in one way or another, with the apparent hierarchy of knots man has tied in his consciousness. But there is secreted in the works of Freud (and eloquently explained by the likes of Brown, Marcuse, and Lacan) an explanation—in the most rudimentary form—of the evolution of the chakra knots, an explanation that might be better suited to a Western readership, and therefore one I will briefly outline.

The infant, according to psychoanalytic observations, is under sway of "polymorphous perversity" and moved solely by the Pleasure Principle, which means that the child lives in a noncorrupted, blissful, and erotic unity with all of nature. For all practical purposes, its awareness is transpersonal, timeless, and spaceless. Very simply, its world is one of transcendent bliss, and for this reason alone Freud was quite right in announcing, much to the horror of his contemporaries, that children have a richer, more extensive, and more satisfying sex life than adults; for the infant takes equal erotic and blissful delight in all organs, surfaces, and activities of the body, and thus his entire cosmos is one of bliss, while the normal adult finds exuberance and bliss, if at all, in only one specific and narrowed region of the body—the genitals. Genital bliss can thus only be viewed, in comparison with the body's natural possibilities, as a constriction, a restriction, a cramp, a knot. Now it is not so much genital sexuality that comprises this knot, but rather the *restriction of bliss to only one specific region* of the body, excluding all others. This restriction of transcendent bliss is thus normal, but not natural. It is but one peculiar arrangement, out of infinite possibilities.

How, then, comes this unnatural restriction of man's potential participation in transcendent bliss? According to the last formulations of Freud—which, alas, are carefully scrubbed out of all modern psychiatric texts—this restriction is engineered by a separate-self sense in flight from death and from loving unity with all objects; for the infant's earliest "identity" is literally with the cosmos itself—a type of immature "cosmic consciousness." He cannot distinguish his world from his actions upon it; nor differentiate self from other, subject from object, inside from outside. He knows nothing of the illusions of space nor of time, and thus, as Jung constantly emphasized, lives in a transpersonal and supra-individual world.

But as the infant learns to construct an irreducible barrier between self and other, between inside and outside, he forfeits his loving and blissful at-one-ness with the cosmos and centers his identity instead on his *personal organism*. He shifts from a Supreme Identity with the All to a personal identity confined to the boundaries of his skin. Thus Freud's famous dictum: "The ego-feeling we are aware of now is thus only a shrunken vestige of a far more extensive feeling—a feeling that embraced the universe and expressed an inseparable connection of the ego with the external world."

This shift in identity carries with it a host of unforeseen ramifications, for, identified almost exclusively with the personal organism, the infant is faced, for the first time, with the imminent fear of death. He suffers anxiety, and "anxiety is the ego's incapacity to accept death." Since he has identified his once transcendent self exclusively with his organism, the death of that organism seems to be an utter annihilation of his very self, a total subtraction that he cannot bear.

The infant, therefore, arrives at a fantasy solution to this illusory problem of death—a solution that eventually culminates in what is known as the Oedipal project. Now the Oedipal project is only secondarily the wish to sexually possess the mother and kill the father, for the infant's primary aim in the Oedipal situation is to abolish death by becoming the father of himself. He imagines, in his infantile fantasy, that he can gain a type of immortality by conceiving himself. As strange as this sounds, remember that even a typical adult will feel he can in some ways cheat death by leaving behind progeny, something of himself that will "survive death." Conceiving a child thus seems at least to touch immortality, and even more so to the infant's untutored fantasy.

The infant, therefore, attempts in fantasy to conceive himself, to become his own parent and thus assuage the anxiety that death presents to him. And by the time of the Oedipal project, the child's fantasies have centered around the genital area, as common sense and the analysis of children as well as adults disclose. But more significantly, the libido of the infant has also concentrated in the genital area, by and large to the exclusion of all other bodily regions. Now libido does not mean sexual, genital pleasure. Libido, in its undiluted form, is simply that capacity for overall bodily pleasure, for transcendent bliss, and in the earliest years of infancy it is distributed equally throughout all bodily organs, surfaces, and activities. The infant participates in transcendent bliss through any area or activity of his body.

But under the Oedipal project, this libido is concentrated in the genital region alone, driven there by the fantasies of overcoming death by uniting bodily with the mother. The libido is no longer democratically available to the entire body, but is now tyrannized by a single region. And the fate of this tyranny is sealed by what is known as the castration complex, for this complex—whose intricacies we need not detail here—smashes to pieces the Oedipal project, *but leaves the genital organization of the libido intact.* The Oedipal project continues its aims in other forms of fantasy, but the body itself remains deformed, with its libido, its transcendent bliss, diluted and restricted to only one particular area of the body. The body, in short, is left crippled with the constrictions and knots of infantile wishes. The ego becomes the dominant element in consciousness, and the genital the dominant element of the body and world.

And so it comes about that the normal adult's only access to transcendent bliss and ecstasy is through genital sexual release, a drastic and morbid reduction of the delight he enjoyed as a child. As Norman O. Brown put it, in infancy a person tastes the fruit of the tree of life, and he knows that it is good . . . and he never forgets. This is why Freud ultimately, unlike Ferenczi, Fenichel, Reich, and others, did *not* see full genital release as a cure for neuroses, because even the genital act itself is a necessary source of conflict, since full and unobstructed bliss is frustrated by its unnecessary restriction to a single, tyrannizing region of the body. But again I must emphasize that the "tyranny of genital organization" results not so much from genitality itself, but from the restriction of bliss to this region alone.

Now notice that with this restriction of transcendent bliss to the genital area, we arrive at . . . the first *major* chakra![1] And notice also the path that original consciousness-bliss has taken in order to arrive at this first major knot: from a blissful, transcendent, timeless, and therefore eternal unity with all of manifestation, to a partial, fragmented, and abysmally restricted ego awareness stealing what bliss it can from a genital tyranny. From a cosmic body to a personal body—indeed, only a region of a personal body! This is the normal, but not natural, state of affairs for the ordinary person, and this is the state of affairs that kundalini yoga seeks to reverse.

It should be obvious, even from our brief and popularized Freudian discussion, that the processes that culminate in egoic awareness and exclusive genitality do not constitute a *single* event or a single step from a cosmic body to a deformed personal one. There are numerous intermediate stages, levels of identification, and bands of awareness that range in gradients from the Supreme Identity to egoic fantasy, forming what amounts to an *apparent* hierarchy of knots or chakras, each progressively "lower" knot being more restrictive and exclusive than its predecessor, with the entire process finally culminating in egoic-genital tyranny.

Kundalini yoga therefore wisely proceeds to reverse this tyranny of awareness and bliss step by careful step, untying the knots in what it sees as roughly the reverse of the order in which they were tied, until finally the chakras themselves lie dissolved—that is, fully "opened"—and transcendent bliss is returned to its prior and unobstructed condition, a condition essentially similar to the polymorphous freedom of the infant but now transmitted through a matured and fully developed personality. So we must emphatically point out that this process is not one of regression but of *involution*, a return to the Source and not to childhood. On the contrary, it is normal adult genital organization that is supported by regressive fantasies of an Oedipal nature that attempt to avoid death and secure an ersatz immortality. On the other hand, to live in transcendent bliss, timeless and eternal, is to yank every conceivable support from under the Oedipal complex, because it means tasting again, in a mature and developed form, the fruit of the Tree of Life.

The aim of kundalini yoga, therefore, is to free transcendent bliss (ananda) from its dilutions and restrictions, and to recognize it as boundless, oceanic, without limits in time or space. Each dissolving of a knot, each "opening" of a chakra, represents—and actually *feels* like—a return of transcendent bliss to a more oceanic and unobstructed state. And this fact leads to what first seems the most puzzling aspect of the chakras: their apparent *localization* in specific areas of the body. Even Ramana Maharshi—who otherwise discounted the reality of the chakras as far as spiritual sadhana was concerned—acknowledged that specific areas of the body seem best to *contain* the different degrees of "freed up" bliss. That certain feelings are best *contained* in specific areas of the body does not seem a fantastic proposal. For example, the genitals of a normal adult *contain* sexual bliss better than the feet, and in like manner, other types or degrees of feelings, vibrations, and energies seem to be best contained in other regions of the body, localizing around specific organs, surfaces, nerve ganglia, or muscle groups. Thus the "gut region" seems to contain "vital" or life-force bliss, and actually *feels* so to one who works through that chakra. So also, the heart-chest region seems best to contain and even radiate loving bliss; the head region, intellectual bliss; and the sahasrara, final ascending and transcendent bliss.

As we shall presently see, it is not *necessary* for liberation that consciousness-bliss travels through these particular centers outlined by kundalini theory. It is just that it might, especially if someone concentrates on the appropriate areas and in the appropriate sequence prescribed by kundalini yoga. In this connection, I don't think we need be confused by the reported fact that concentrating on a specific region-chakra, along with certain visualizations, can *evoke* the appropriate feeling and energy best contained by that specific region. Close your eyes, concentrate on the genital region, visualize two people making sensuous love, and see if an appropriate feeling and energy isn't evoked! Thus, at the other end of the pole, Ramana could say, "If one concentrates on the sahasrara there is no doubt that the ecstasy of samadhi ensues." The localization of the chakras, in general, seems to be one of their more self-evident features.

In this regard, it is not surprising that bioenergetics, the school of psychotherapy most alive to bodily feelings and energies, even in just their personal and nontranscendent forms, maintains that different feelings and cognitions are "located," or best contained in, certain well-defined segments of the body: one feels stability and groundedness in the legs and feet (and not, for instance, in the chin!); orgasmic ecstasy in the genitals; joy-vitality-laughter in the gut; openness-affirmation-love in the chest; intellection-insight in the eyes and head; and spirituality at the crown—a formulation essentially identical to that of the kundalini model, but without, of course, the latter's eye to the degrees of progressive transcendence accompanying these energies, nor their increasingly "subtle" character.

So I don't think there is anything mysterious about the location of the chakras. They are "there;" they are "real," because (1) you can *feel* certain states or modifications of bliss and awareness at each major chakra, and (2) these feelings or energies just aren't appropriate to other areas of the body, as, for example, you cannot ordinarily feel an orgasm in your knee.

This, then, is the basis of the chakra system as presented in terms of feelings, vibrations, or *energetics* (prana, chi, ruh, ki). These energetics exist, they are "real," or rather, they are as real as any other feelings of joy or terror or excitement, and they take as their terminals specific centers, organs, muscle groups, nerve ganglia, or, as some maintain, endocrine glands. The most significant point, however, is not the localization of the chakras, but the modes of consciousness that take these regions as an appropriate outlet.

The chakras are *located* at specific areas or organs, but they are not *identical* to those areas. It is for this reason that kundalini yoga maintains that these centers deal primarily with the "subtle body," which is to say, with states of awareness and bliss that no longer recognize the conventional and illusory boundaries between the organism and the environment, and thus could hardly be localized *finally* in one or the other. It is just that, in the period of transition from a personal body to a cosmic one, the individual carries for some time the old and exclusive references to his isolated and personal body, and thus his insights might tend to take, as their *physical correlates*, certain terminals in the body. And as for the enlightened sages, even they walk on their feet, eat with their mouths, love with their hearts, and procreate with their genitals. These "localizations" hardly seem a mysterious affair. In other words, for the sage these localized centers remain, not as knots, but as appropriate and functional nodes of energy.

Thus far we have seen that the chakras represent both certain stages in a type of spiritual growth (steps in the freeing up of transcendent bliss) as well as certain locations of energies in the body. The usual controversy over the existence of the chakras—"Are they real?"—seems based on nothing other than an attempt to pit one of these characteristics of the chakras against the other. Thus, those who maintain that the chakras are purely metaphorical deny they have any "physical correlates" in the body, since this seems to drag spirit into the dirty realm of matter. This is an unnecessary concern, however, for spirit and matter have never been separated. On the other hand, those who claim that the chakras are purely physical—that is, *identical* to nerve plexes instead of *associated* with them—fall instantly into the Fallacy of Simple Location, a favorite pastime of physiologists, and thus have the utmost difficulty in theoretically extracting a transcendent state of consciousness out of an endocrine gland.

I have tried to suggest that these two views are complementary. The fact that the chakras are symbolic does not prevent their association with particular regions of the body, and the fact that they may be more appropriately experienced in certain regions of the body does not rob them of their transcendent symbolism.

The chakras, as we have seen, are predominantly concerned with the apparent hierarchy of *energetics*—with vibrations, feelings, vital force, and bliss. Naturally, not all spiritual systems or disciplines emphasize this aspect of higher states of consciousness, preferring instead to emphasize, and work through, the *equivalent* hierarchies of insight, or absorption, or ontological world view, or cosmology, or awareness—all of which are perfectly valid. The Hindu points out that saguna Brahman is "characterized" by absolute being, consciousness, and bliss, and some spiritual systems and practices simply emphasize, and thus develop, one of these equivalent characteristics and its manifestations over the others. Thus the tantras deal with the samsaric hierarchy of knots in predominantly energetic terms and states; the Kabbalah works with the cosmological and ontological aspects; the Buddhists emphasize awareness and insight. These are all roughly equivalent expressions of a central truth: In the apparent world, "existence is graded, and with it, cognition," and, we would add, energetics and vibratory bliss. As far as spiritual practice is concerned, all of these honorable traditions point to a progressive dissolution of the constricting knots we have tied in our own consciousness.

To return to kundalini specifically: Many investigators, having some familiarity with Freud's work on sublimation, assume that kundalini yoga consists in the progressive sublimation or "forcing upward" of genital sexual energy. Further, some have proposed that laboratory studies would confirm this hypothesis, and that here we would finally have the pulling of the religious rabbit out of the laboratory hat. Being a biochemist by training, I am wholly in sympathy with any experimental thrust in this direction, even though we will then be faced with an extremely difficult dilemma should physiological tests show that certain neurological or hormonal changes do in fact occur as meditation proceeds through the chakras to higher states of consciousness. The dilemma: Is the higher consciousness the *result* of chemical changes or the *cause* of them? If the latter, then physiological changes are totally irrelevant to spiritual pursuits.

But this physiological line of reasoning has led some people to conclude that the energy of higher consciousness can be explained in terms of sublimated, genital sexual energy. Aside from the fact that genital sexuality cannot in theory be sublimated (the pregenital organizations alone provide the reservoir of libido that drives sublimations), I think the conclusion is precisely reversed. As I have tried to explain, genital sexuality is a constriction and a restriction of higher consciousness, and this is the state of affairs that kundalini yoga seeks to reverse. It thus *appears*, to an ordinary onlooker or researcher, that sexual energy is transmuting into higher states of consciousness—but it's really just the opposite. The higher consciousness is being freed from its chronic constrictions in "lower"—that is, limited and bounded—modes of awareness and energetics. God-consciousness is not sublimated sexuality; sexuality is repressed God-consciousness.

All in all, I think we can fairly conclude that each chakra represents both an appropriate center in the body and a particular stage in a type of spiritual growth. I say "type of spiritual growth" because there is much evidence in the orthodox traditions themselves (especially Tibetan Buddhism) that suggests that kundalini yoga is a valid but partial approach to even the energetics of higher consciousness, tending to ignore—with its exclusive emphasis on the ascending kundalini current—the equally important "descending" currents. Further, even the Hindu generally concedes that, except at its very summit, kundalini shakti is a phenomenon of the subtle body only. Hatha yoga addresses the gross body, and kundalini the subtle body, but it is jnana yoga that deals with the underlying reality of the causal body. Jnana yoga of Vedanta, Dzogchen and mahamudra of Vajrayana, chih-kuan and shikantaza of Zen—these simply investigate, through present awareness, any knot that arises in consciousness, and, finding void of self-nature, are relieved of the burden of untying it.

Thus we return to the paradox with which we began this article—the chakras *do* appear to exist, and the chakras *are* knots. But the knots are illusory. Nothing binds us from the very start, but until we understand this, everything appears to. Nevertheless, kundalini theory, with its penetrating understanding of these shadowy knots themselves, offers sound, wise, and powerful advice on how to see through them, so that one may finally awaken, as if from a dream, to discover that the cosmos is one's body, and the sun one's solar self.

Kundalini

Sex, Evolution, and Higher Consciousness

JOHN WHITE

John White, author of fifteen books, including The Meeting of Science and Spirit *and* What Is Enlightenment?, *has long studied the kundalini phenomena. In the following essay he examines the relationship between sex, consciousness, and kundalini, journeying to the heart of erotic mysticism. Touching on the modern challenges psychology and philosophy face in the context of kundalini experiences, he focuses on Gopi Krishna's influence and his thoughts on the evolution of consciousness. Exploring Gopi Krishna's writings and legacy, he probes the ultimate question: Is kundalini the biological basis of both religion and genius?*

SEXUALITY AND SPIRITUAL experience have traditionally been linked in the literature of mysticism. Religious ecstasy seems strikingly similar to erotic excitement in the accounts of saints and holy people who have spoken of enlightenment—knowing ultimate reality or, in their usual term, God—in language that resorts to sexual imagery. Such images, they said, were the best they could find to describe an otherwise indescribable experience. Such terms as *rapture, passion, union,* and *ravish* occur frequently. St. Teresa recorded that she felt stabbed through and through by Christ's spear. Madame Guyon wrote that "the soul . . . expires at last in the arms of love." St. Francis de Sales spoke of sucking heavenly milk from the breast of God. Likewise, the poetry of Sufi and Hindu mystics is highly erotic.

Orthodox psychology tends to smugly dismiss such language as the products of aberrated minds whose main trouble was repressed sex, causing a regression to infantile behavior. But conventional psychological interpretations could be wrong. Why? Because in an ironic turn of events, a physical linkage between sexual and spiritual experience is emerging, and it promises a major upheaval in Western psychology. From this emerging view, *sexuality is really unexpressed or unfulfilled religious experience.*

Notice that term *religious experience.* The common element between it and sexual experience is consciousness. The states of consciousness experienced by lovers in union and mystics in God-intoxication are states in which the usual sense of self as a separate, isolated, lonely individual is dissolved. The individuals are no longer locked in the prison of ego, no longer in conflict with the world because of a socially conditioned image of who they are. Lovers sometimes attain this momentarily during orgasm, and afterward universally regard it as one of their most cherished experiences. It has a sacred quality, as if they had contacted something greater than themselves, something at the wellspring of life itself, something that transcends the merely human and takes them into a higher state of existence.

Mystics, of course, experience this with greater frequency, intensity, and duration. Some of the greatest have declared they are constantly in that state of mind, although to outward appearances they are simply performing their daily activities.

Try to imagine that: working, eating meals, driving the car, and doing everything else with the same sense of cosmic well-being you've felt at the peak of lovemaking. It's not just exquisite pleasure or intense passion. It's actually beyond emotion. It's tranquil, peaceful, serene, without any worries or cares, without attachments to status, fame, or wealth, without fear of failure or even death. None of our usual hang-ups and concerns. No anxiety. No past or future. Just pure being, pure consciousness, here and now. And all the while, everything necessary for living goes on. Nothing has changed, yet everything has changed because you no longer relate to reality in the same way. It is a new state of consciousness—not fleeting as in orgasm, but permanent—erotic mysticism.

That would be foreign to our range of experience—even to our whole culture—and we lack the language to describe it well. But we have hints and glimpses of it given to us in the sacred writings of various religious traditions and revered spiritual teachers. Moreover, they tell us there are techniques and disciplines that can be systematically employed to alter consciousness toward that state. Meditation is an example of such a discipline. Yoga is another. So is tantra, which, in some traditions, uses *maithuna* or ritual sexual intercourse for developing the psychosexual experience to religious heights.

In view of these facts, orthodox psychology ought to drop its illusion of knowing more than those poor, mixed-up mystics—whom it labels as cases of infantile regression—and recognize that there are realms of experience about which it is pathetically ignorant.

This, in fact, is happening. Because of rapidly increasing interest in consciousness research, psychology is being challenged in many directions. What transpersonal psychologist Abraham Maslow called "the farther ranges of human nature" is being considered more thoughtfully. Psychic phenomena, meditation, altered states of consciousness—the data from studying these are causing psychology to seriously examine ancient concepts and traditions of what Robert Ornstein, in *The Psychology of Consciousness,* calls "the esoteric psychologies."

The essence of the esoteric psychologies that so challenges Western psychology is precisely what lovers and mystics have discovered to varying degrees for millennia: humans have a potential for expanded awareness that can radically change their lives and transform them to the roots of their being. We may taste a small measure of that in moments of sexual ecstasy, but there is so much beyond the experience that, compared to it, orgasm is just a pale show.

So we find ourselves in the fascinating position of discovering new dimensions of the psyche—dimensions that could bring a tremendous evolutionary advance to humanity. If the nature of higher consciousness could be widely understood and experienced, there would undoubtedly follow a societal transformation around the globe.

That is why research in this area is so important. That is why I offer this essay summarizing the viewpoint of the Indian yogi-philosopher-scientist Gopi Krishna, who maintains that the language of sexual mysticism is to be understood literally and that it holds fundamental significance for psychology. There is, Gopi Krishna maintains, a direct physical linkage between sexual and spiritual experience. Ram Dass expressed the idea in the original title of *Be Here Now,* which was *From Bindu to Ojas.* As he explained it: "Bindu is sexual energy and [ojas] is spiritual energy, and it's the transformation of energy within the body through the conversion of a form of energy . . . it's called the raising of kundalini . . ."

This ancient yogic concept, recorded in literature and oral tradition, is becoming widely known in the West as people such as Ram Dass and Shirley MacLaine speak and write about it. But the most important voice among them is Pandit Gopi Krishna, who died in 1984 at the age of eighty-one. He brought a marked degree of good sense and insight to the field of esoteric/New Age studies. I knew him personally, having interviewed him in Zurich for four days in 1976 and on several later occasions when he came to America from his home in Srinagar, India. I also read with deepest interest his dozen-plus books on the subject of kundalini, beginning shortly after his first—an autobiography entitled *Kundalini, the Evolutionary Energy in Man*—was published in the United States in 1970. I was deeply impressed by the man, not only for his obvious erudition and clear thinking about this most profound human experience, but also by his character—his honesty, kindness, and humility. All these marked him in my judgment as a sage.

"Pandit" is an honorific term meaning "learned man," so Gopi Krishna should not be thought of as a guru. He said clearly that he sought no followers, accepted no disciples, and made no demands for asceticism. Rather, his mission was to arouse interest in the nature of evolution and enlightenment, and to do that he wanted coworkers in scientific and scholarly research, not devotees. Most important, he said that the truth of his observations about a potent biological link between sex and higher consciousness—which he claims is the motive force behind evolution and all spiritual and supernormal phenomena—should be tested using the principles, methodology, and (insofar as possible) technology of science.

The essence of his claims is threefold: first, he has discovered that the reproductive system is also the mechanism by which evolution proceeds; second, religion is based on inherent evolutionary impulses in the psyche; and, third, there is a predetermined target for human evolution toward which the entire race is being irresistibly drawn. Whether humanity will arrive there or extinguish itself is another matter—one that Gopi Krishna says is the fundamental motive behind his efforts to demonstrate our "divine destiny."

A NEW SPECIES OF HUMANITY

Kundalini is the key term in Gopi Krishna's theory of evolution. Coming from ancient Sanskrit, it means "coiled up" like a snake or spring, and it implies latent energy or potential to expand. Gopi Krishna often translates it as "latent power-reservoir of energy" or "psychosomatic power center." Kundalini, he claims, is the fundamental bioenergy of life, stored primarily in the sex organs but present throughout the entire body. This potent psychic radiation is normally associated with the genitals for simple continuance of the species by providing a sex drive. This is what Freud called *libido* (although the Freudian conception is strictly psychological and lacks the energy tie-in to physics and biology Gopi Krishna is pointing out).

However, Gopi Krishna says, kundalini is also the basis for the attainment of a higher state of consciousness. The kundalini energy can be concentrated in the brain to produce enlightenment and genius—higher mental perception. Its potency is our potential. Such a state, if widely attained, would mean a new species of humanity, a higher race. Thus, kundalini, the bridge between mind and matter, can be the evolutionary cause of creation as well as procreation. It is, Gopi Krishna says, the evolutionary energy and mechanism operating in the human race.

Kundalini is traditionally symbolized in Hindu, Vedic, and tantric texts as a sleeping serpent coiled around the base of the human spine, indicating its close relationship with the sex organs. The concept is not limited to Indian literature, however. It has been described in the ancient records of Tibet, Egypt, Sumer, China, Greece, and other cultures and traditions, including early Judaism and Christianity. The Pharaoh's headdress, the feathered serpent of Mexico and South America, the dragon of oriental mythology, the serpent in the Garden of Eden—all are indicative of kundalini, Gopi Krishna maintains.

The source of the "serpent power" is *prana,* a primal cosmic energy outside the electromagnetic spectrum and other forces known to official Western science. However, many prescientific and unorthodox scientific traditions have identified a life force from which other energies and paranormal phenomena are derived. Acupuncture calls it *chi,* the Greeks wrote of *ether,* Christianity terms it the *Holy Spirit,* Wilhelm Reich named it *orgone,* and Soviet psychic researchers have their *"bioplasma."* Carl

Jung said there are more than fifty synonyms for prana or *prima materia* in alchemical literature. (Dozens of other terms can be given, as I show in my 1977 book *Future Science.*) Apparently these are different labels for the same basic energy—or aspects of it—that permeates living organisms and is the source of all vital activity, including thought, feeling, perception, and movement. It especially focuses itself in the sexual organs, where the kundalini process begins.

Gene Kieffer, president of the Kundalini Research Foundation, has elaborated on the notion of prana as life energy. In a personal conversation, he told me: "The most powerful motivating force of life, as Freud has shown, is sex and the pleasure drawn from the sexual act. Similarly, the most powerful motivating force to draw humanity onto the evolutionary path, according to the traditional concept of kundalini, is *ananda,* a Sanskrit word meaning 'bliss.' This highly extended state of consciousness, permeated with an extreme form of rapture, is said to be possible only when the consumption of prana by the brain is greatly enhanced."

How can it be enhanced? As I mentioned, spiritual disciplines are the key. In a *New York Times* article, Gopi Krishna pointed out that sublimation—raising up—of sex energy is the basic lever of all spiritual disciplines. But, he said, "the all-inclusive nature of sex energy has not yet been correctly understood by psychologists. In fact, the very term *reproductive,* or sex, *energy* is a misnomer. Reproduction is but one of the aspects of the life energy, of which the other theater of activity is the brain."[1]

Surrounding and permeating the gross tissues of the body, Gopi Krishna writes in *The Dawn of a New Science,* "a living electricity, acting intelligently and purposefully, controls the activity of every molecule of living matter. It carries the life principle from one place to the other, energizes, overhauls and purifies the neurons and maintains the life-giving subtle area of the body much in the same way as the blood plasma maintains the grosser part."[2]

That vital essence is extracted by the nervous system from surrounding tissue in the form of an extremely fine biochemical essence of a highly delicate and volatile nature. In humans, this essence, existing at the molecular or submolecular level, especially focuses itself in the sexual organs, where the kundalini process begins.

FROM SEXUALITY TO SPIRITUALITY

There is a subtle but direct connection between the brain and the organs of generation via the spine, Gopi Krishna maintains. The spinal cord and the canal through which it runs serve as the avenue for transforming sexuality to spirituality. Through certain techniques known and practiced since ancient times, the kundalini energy can be aroused and guided up the center of the spinal cord (*sushumna,* in yogic terminology) to a dormant center, called the Cave of Brahma (*Brahmarandhra*), in the brain's ventricular cavity, the site of the entryway to the seventh *chakra.* (I'll explain that term in a moment.)

This "living electricity" or "superintelligent energy," as Gopi Krishna sometimes calls it, is an ultrapotent, high-grade form of bioplasma—concentrated prana. But the techniques for controlling it are extremely dangerous. They are equivalent, figuratively speaking, to letting a child play with a nuclear reactor, and should be undertaken only under the guidance of a proven master of the spiritual tradition being followed.

The nature of the chakras in yogic physiology is not clearly agreed upon by modern interpreters—so be careful of accepting dogmatic pronouncements by spiritual teachers and New Age commentators. For example, author Sam Keen and psychologist Robert Ornstein feel that the chakras are strictly metaphoric, lacking in any physical reality. Scholar Joseph Campbell likewise regards them as merely psychological teaching devices—merely concepts. Others such as M. P. Pandit, an exponent of Sri Aurobindo, and William Tiller, professor of materials science at Stanford University, maintain that chakras exist in the "subtle body" of man, sometimes called the astral or etheric body, and influence the physical body through the endocrine system, with which they correlate at a nonphysical level of existence. Swami Agehananda Bharati, chairman of the anthropology department at Syracuse University, declares kundalini to be a lot of "claptrap" and "latter-day nonsense." Gopi Krishna, however, says that chakras are nerve plexes—major ganglia along the spine, observed directly in the body through clairvoyance by ancient yogis.

There are said to be six major chakras along the cerebrospinal column, but the location of the seventh chakra (termed *sahasrara*) is disputed. It has been identified by various authorities as the pineal gland, the pituitary gland, and the anterior fontanelle. Gopi Krishna, however, says it is the entire brain itself. In a letter to me, he wrote, "The seventh centre in the brain is not actually designated as a 'chakra' but as 'sahasrara' in the Tantric books and 'Usha-Nisha-Kamala' in the Buddhist texts. It is often shown surrounding the head in the statues of Buddha, more or less like a cap. In this sense, 'sahasrara' refers to the cerebral cortex and, in fact, the whole of the brain. This is obvious from the fact that once Kundalini enters into the Brahmarandhra . . . the whole of the cranium is illuminated and a new pattern of consciousness is born."

From its repository in the reproductive organs, a fine stream of living energy filters into the brain as fuel for the evolutionary process. As the energy moves upward, it passes through various chakras along the central channel of the spinal cord into the topmost, the brain. This does not happen in every case. In fact, it is quite rare for the kundalini process to be carried to completion. But the genetically ripe person to whom it happens experiences a golden-white light within his or her head. Apparently this is the same light that is visibly seen by people as the aura or halo around saints and highly evolved sages.

The flow of kundalini into the brain has been described by mystics as "ambrosia" and "nectar," giving rise to exquisite sensations similar to those of orgasm but surpassing them by many orders of magnitude. The sensations are felt most intensely above the palate in the midbrain and in the hindbrain in a descending arc parallel to the curve of the palate. This is known in yoga physiology as the *sankini,* the curved duct through which the bioplasma passes into the brain.

Kundalini is at work all the time in everyone, and is present from birth in mystics and seers, but in most people there is only a "dripping" rather than a "streaming." This upward streaming, which is a biological restatement of what Freud apparently meant by the term "sublimation of the libido," explains the source of an artist's or an intellectual's mental creativity. Beyond that are those rare people whom Gopi Krishna calls "finished specimens of the perfect man of the future," such as Buddha, Jesus, and Vyasa. In them we see "an incredible combination of factors, both favorable heredity and cultural readiness, which produced those who, endowed with a superior type of consciousness and in possession of paranormal gifts, amazed their contemporaries with their extraordinary psychical and intellectual talents which [ordinary people] ignorant of the Law [of evolution] ascribed to special prerogative from God."[3]

Variations in the size of the energy stream determine the intellectual and aesthetic development of an individual, with geniuses having a comparatively larger volume of bioplasma streaming into the brain. The wide variation in types of genius depends on the particular region of the brain that is irrigated and developed. Thus, through certain occult techniques and spiritual disciplines, an individual of normal intelligence can accelerate the evolutionary process to attain the stature of an intellectual prodigy and beyond, to genius. This concept directly challenges current notions that intelligence is basically determined at birth by one's genes.

THE SECRET BEHIND YOGA

Prana, the fine biological essence, is not in itself consciousness. It is only the means of nourishing our consciousness-receiving equipment, the nervous system—the body's link with universal consciousness. During the kundalini process, the entire nervous system undergoes a microbiological change and is transformed, especially the brain. The result of a fully awakened and developed kundalini is both perceptible changes in the organism and a new state of consciousness, the cosmic consciousness of mystics and enlightened seers. This vital awareness of unity with God, Gopi Krishna says, is the core experience behind all the world's major religions, and is the goal of all true spiritual and occult practices. Humanity has an innate hunger for this state of paranormal perception. Moreover, bountiful nature has provided the means of achieving it: kundalini, the biological basis of religion and genius.

This is the "secret" behind yoga and all other spiritual disciplines, esoteric psychologies, hermetic philosophies, and genuine occult mysteries. It is also the key to genius, psychic power, artistic talents, scientific and intellectual creativity, and extreme longevity with good health. (An age of 120 with unimpaired mental faculties was commonly achieved among the ancient illuminati, Gopi Krishna says, and an age of 150 is quite probable in the kundalini-altered future.) But if improperly aroused, without right guidance and preparation, kundalini can be horribly painful and destructive, even fatal. Unsustained by a sensible, healthy manner of living—meaning regulated and balanced, not ascetic or orgiastic—kundalini can turn malignant and become the source of deteriorating health, terrible bodily heat and pain, many forms of mental illness, and even sudden death. In physiological terms, the pranic stream has gone astray into one of the two side channels of the spinal cord (the left side being called *ida* and the right side *pingala* in yogic physiology).

The pranic stream, Gopi Krishna says, is affected by "every shade of passion and emotion, by food and drink, by environment and mode of life." It is altered by desire and ambition, by conduct and behavior and, in fact, by all the thousands of influences, from the most powerful to the slightest, that act on and shape life from birth to death. Thus the need for balanced, moral living is based on biological imperative.

There is another condition, too, even worse for humanity. Kundalini-gone-astray has been the cause of evil geniuses in history, such as Hitler. However, in such cases the kundalini energy has been active since birth, as with all geniuses. Their lives are usually so filled with difficulties that the kundalini energy can become malignant if the finer qualities necessary for psychological stability have not been made a part of their upbringing. Lack of these finer traits constitutes a built-in safeguard of nature that bars the unstable individual from access to higher levels of consciousness. This moral dimension is what distinguishes seers and sages from psychics and gifted intellectuals who are otherwise quite ordinary.

Knowledge of kundalini, Gopi Krishna says, is the only real means of preventing further Hitlers. It is also the best means of preventing history from ending in either the bang of nuclear holocaust or the whimpering slow death of an overpopulated, starving, resourceless planet. "The only way to safety and survival lies in determining the evolutionary needs and in erecting our social and political systems in conformity with those needs," he maintains. His writings envisage a new structure of human society, a new social and political order to enable the entire race to devote itself to the development of the powers and possibilities latent within.

All reality is governed by one mighty law that is simultaneously biological and spiritual: *Thou shalt evolve to a higher state of consciousness via the kundalini process.* This law of evolution, Gopi Krishna says, can be objectively demonstrated in people with unquestionable proof using the techniques and technology of science: "The awakening of kundalini is the greatest enterprise and most wonderful achievement in front of man."

That is a vast claim, and most neurophysiologists and psychologists will probably regard it as simplistic, if not crackpot. After all, others from both East and West have talked and written about kundalini since earliest times. But Gopi Krishna, who makes clear that he has only rediscovered an ancient tradition, was also a man of science. In that regard, he says something that has not been said before: kundalini can be scientifically verified in the laboratory to prove the essential truth of religious tradition. We can get objective evidence that will show what has been the major claim of religious and spiritual teachers throughout history—namely, that man was born to attain a higher state, a state of union with the divine. Until such proof is available, Gopi Krishna says, don't believe what I say—just do the research.

How did Gopi Krishna come to have such a radical message? What are the sources of knowledge for this man who flunked out of college, lived a simple life as husband and father, and worked most of his career as a minor civil servant in the Indian government? The answer is: personal experience and scholarly research.

A WHITE SERPENT IN RAPID FLIGHT

In 1937, after seventeen years of steadfast meditation (he got up faithfully at 4:00 a.m. to meditate, even after his wedding night!), on Christmas morning, Gopi Krishna awakened the kundalini force. In his autobiography, he writes, "There was a sound like a nerve thread snapping and instantaneously a silvery streak passed through the spinal cord, exactly like the sinuous movement of a white serpent in rapid flight, pouring an effulgent, cascading shower of brilliant vital energy into my brain, filling my head with a blissful luster. . . ."

What began during meditation was the development of a higher state of consciousness in Gopi Krishna. But the process was far from complete. What followed were years of hell, periods of severe ordeal when the changes being made in his nervous system caused enormous pain, prolonged sickness, near-death, bewilderment, and self-doubts about his sanity.

Slowly, carefully, he began to conduct experiments in the laboratory of his own body, observing the sometimes terrifying effects as he encountered the mysterious bioenergy. He notes in his auto-biography, "I was destined to witness my own transformation . . . attended all along by great physical and mental suffering. But what I witnessed . . . is so contrary to many accepted notions of science . . . that when what I have experienced is proved empirically there must occur a far-reaching, revolutionary change in every sphere of human activity and conduct." The transformation included the spontaneous appearance of psychic, intellectual, and literary powers.

Local gurus and holy men were unable to give Gopi Krishna any relief or understanding, so he undertook a reading program through the literature of religion, psychology, and occultism. He found that kundalini was recognized at least five thousand years ago but was always a closely guarded secret recorded in veiled lan-guage and allusion that made little sense to someone who had no personal experience of it. Like acupuncture, which was also known that long ago, this knowledge had been lost to modern man. But, Gopi Krishna says, it can be recovered and grounded in scientific concepts and terminology through laboratory research and schol-arly studies of the thousands of still-untranslated old texts dealing with kundalini. Thus, what has been recorded until now in occult terms will be demystified and explained in simple language.

How might the reality of kundalini be shown? First, a person in whom it is fully developed will clearly be a genius. *New* knowl-edge will come from him or her, knowledge such as Gopi Krishna himself offers that elegantly unites the entire psychic/occult/spiritual scene with evolutionary theory and the transpersonal psychology arising from Freud, Maslow, and Jung.

Next, as the kundalini process transforms a person, the ner-vous system and brain undergo changes that will be observable (although the necessary instruments for observing them may still be only on the drawing boards).

Third, the "food" the body uses to nourish the nervous system during transformation comes from the sex organs—the "essence" of seminal fluid in men and what Gopi Krishna calls "the erotic fluids" in women. Thus, the reproductive organs increase their activity dramatically, producing much more copiously than usual. This, incidentally, explains why ancient statuary and paintings show men, even a Pharaoh and an Egyptian god, in meditation with an erect phallus. This is not meant by the artist to be erotic at all, Gopi Krishna says, but rather is a frank and literal depiction of a biological fact about kundalini.

This fluid sexual essence, existing at the molecular or submolecular level, streams from the reproductive organs into the spinal canal and then upward into the brain. This can be verified by a spinal tap at the time the phenomenon is occurring.

The bloodstream also carries nerve food during this organic transformation. Hence, the composition of the blood changes due to the awakening of kundalini and ought to be examined in any research program. Heart activity (pulse rate) and other internal organs undergo radical changes. Likewise, perception, digestion, and elimination change dramatically—still more clues to look for in the full spectrum of physical-mental-behavioral transmutations that necessarily must occur as nature prepares the organism through a total cellular reorganization for a higher state of being. These are matters that can be objectively determined by neurophysiologists and medical researchers.

In addition, the person will have high moral character and other traits typically associated with spiritual masters, such as psychic and literary talents. (Gopi Krishna says he was amazed to find himself at age fifty spontaneously writing poetry in nine languages, four of which were unknown to him. He had never taken any interest in poetry nor attempted any literary performance, he claims, yet long narrative poems in rhymed metrical verse would impress themselves on his awareness so quickly that he could scarcely write them down.)

WHAT ABOUT CELIBACY?

What about celibacy? In growing to higher consciousness, is it necessary, as some claim, to abstain from sex and to "mortify the flesh"?

From Gopi Krishna's point of view, the answer is a firm no-with one condition. Since he himself was married and had three children, he strongly disagrees with those who regard sexual contact as detrimental to spiritual evolution. Moreover, he points out that during the Vedic Age thousands of years ago, when many of the great yogic scriptures were first written, several hundred inspired sages were recognized as enlightened men, and in almost every case they were married and had children.

Gopi Krishna feels that an enlightened person can enjoy an active sex life up to an age of 100—and even beyond! But he emphasizes the need—arising from the biological laws of spiritual evolution—of basing sexual activity on love and respect, while avoiding immoderate or promiscuous behavior.

Generally speaking, he says, celibacy is contrary to nature, since enlightenment is an evolutionary process, with heredity playing an important role by stamping the genes of the enlightened so that their biological gains through spiritual disciplines can be passed to their progeny. Suppression of sexuality out of contempt or hatred of our "lower nature" is an act of ignorance leading only to atrophy of the sexual system. The biological fact that only the primates, especially humans, are perennially ready for sex is a clue to linkage between our animal origins and our higher destiny. But there is a critical period during the kundalini process—lasting possibly as long as a year or two—when celibacy is important. During that time, the fluid essence is needed for remolding the nervous system and brain. Otherwise, the kundalini awakening may be "aborted" through misuse. That is the only condition Gopi Krishna recognizes as demanding celibacy.

BREAKING NEW GROUND

The "sage of Srinagar" has broken new ground and—is it proper to say?—sown seed. He has written about his discovery of the mighty law linking biology, physics, and psychology in a dozen books and numerous articles. The scope and depth of Gopi

Krishna's thought is awe-inspiring. In unraveling the kundalini experience, he has apparently discovered the key to understanding practically every mystery and paranormal phenomenon that now puzzles science. The matters he raises relate to everyone on planet earth. They challenge the entire scientific community, a community that so far has been unable either to explain humanity or tame it. As Albert Einstein observed, nuclear energy and the atomic bomb changed everything except our thinking. And the renowned neurosurgeon Wilder Penfield admitted in *The Mystery of the Mind* that all his experience in trying to understand mental experience—the mind—on the basis of brain studies came to almost nothing. "The mind is peculiar," he wrote. "It has energy. The form of that energy is different from [the electrochemical energy in the nerve pathways]." Gopi Krishna feels we can identify the mysterious mind energy that eluded Penfield. He also feels that it can do what Einstein hoped—change human thinking. That is because kundalini, as Gopi Krishna presents it, is the first testable field theory of psychophysical linkages among body, mind, and cosmos, covering the entire spectrum of psychological, psychical, and spiritual phenomena. With it comes the possibility of objectively studying higher consciousness, thus answering questions presently beyond science and ending philosophical speculation about the condition.

This is a daring stance—daring, yet rationally and plausibly presented. It is a sober and serious call for science to become involved in demonstrating the high spiritual destiny of the human race. Nothing since the 1925 Scopes "Monkey Trial" so vigorously calls attention to the controversial cause of evolution. But whereas the Scopes trial flamed antagonism between science and religion, Gopi Krishna is making a breathtaking attempt to heal the split. And it is humorously ironic that Western science and technology—often called the product of a godless, materialist approach to life—might be the means by which this is demonstrated to the world. Let Gopi Krishna, therefore, have the last word:

The aim of the evolutionary impulse is to make man
aware of himself, and with this sublime awareness, to
make him regulate his life as a rational human being,
free from egotism, violence, excessive greed and ambition and immoderate lust and desire, to lead to a state
of unbroken peace and happiness on the earth . . .
Enlightenment, therefore, is a natural process ruled by
biological laws as strict in their operation as the laws
governing the continuance of the race . . . This is the
purpose for which you and I are here—to realize ourselves . . . to bring the soul to a clear realization of its
own divine nature.[4]

Kundalini

Her Symbols of Transformation and Freedom

LAWRENCE EDWARDS, PHD

Lawrence Edwards, president of Kundalini Research Network and author of The Soul's Journey: Guidance from the Divine Within, *has long been involved with the study of kundalini in a variety of ways—from exploring its beginnings in ancient texts to tracing it in our culture and art. In the following essay he takes a close look at how Kundalini can be used to understand the energy that makes up both the smallest aspects of our lives and the vast expanse of the universe. He introduces readers to the two significant ways in which we can understand Kundalini—one of them as our mind, body, and spirit and the other as the Divine, or Consciousness. He examines both of these as they pertain to "involution," evolution and the chakras. Edwards also shares his profound experience with Kundalini, during which he encountered Maha Kali. Examining a number of sources including ancient yogic texts, Carl Jung, and his own encounter, he probes the significant question: How can we pursue the same Kundalini described in the ancient texts, and in doing so, discover our own true divinity?*

> "It would not be too much to say that myth is the secret opening through which the inexhaustible energies of the cosmos pour into human cultural manifestation."
>
> —Joseph Campbell

KUNDALINI PROVIDES ONE of the most extraordinary maps of the inexhaustible energies within the body and in the highest consciousness. One may directly experience the enormous power of Kundalini through yoga, awakened Kundalini, and the system of chakras. In this context, a myth isn't something that is untrue; instead, it is the only vehicle capable of bringing truths that lie beyond language and beyond the mind into the realm of words. The language of symbols and myths has a rare capacity for pointing to the ineffable beyond itself. Great meditation masters have used mythic maps for thousands of years to direct those earnest and qualified seekers who desire to push far beyond the limits of the ordinary mind, conditioned as the mind is to suffer the bondage put on it by family, religion, and society. Westerners on their quest for true freedom, both inner and outer, have long looked to Eastern and esoteric traditions for ways to deeply engage in their search, ways that a materialistic culture doesn't provide. Joseph Campbell, the brilliant mythologist who worked with George Lucas on the first *Star Wars* trilogy, wrote about the symbolic quest in his book *The Hero with a Thousand Faces*:

> It has always been the prime function of mythology
> and rite to supply the symbols that carry the human
> spirit forward, in counteraction to those other constant
> human fantasies that tend to tie it back. In fact, it may
> well be that the very high incidence of neuroticism
> among ourselves follows from the decline among us
> of such effective spiritual aid. We remain fixated to the
> unexorcised images of our infancy, and hence disin-
> clined to the necessary passages of our adulthood.[1]

If we examine our life as a mythic journey, we may discover the deeper symbolic meanings of our struggles, our heroic battles—whether they are at work or at home, with our spouse, parents, or children, or addictions or disease. Connecting with the deeper symbolism of what we are doing allows us to know the significance of our lives regardless of whether the cultural markers of money and fame are present. Discovering the deeper personal symbolism of our journey, just as it is, also allows us to know and feel that our lives are deeply meaningful, or to make adjustments so they become more so. In this way, we progress on our personal quest. In the popular movie *National Treasure* and its sequel, Nicolas Cage's character has the unique ability to decode the symbols and find the treasure. Understanding the symbolic meanings of the clues, the experiences we have along our journey, is the key to finding the greatest of all treasures: the source of unbounded love, compassion, and wisdom.

To use the ancient treasure map requires the development of *viveka*—fine discrimination—and the cultivation of one's capability for reading mysterious symbols that one will encounter along the way. Some of these symbols will be archetypal, like those that can be partially depicted by chakras, *nadis* (subtle channels of energy), and the like, and some will have their archetypal nature clothed in more personal symbols. There are no quick and easy manuals for deciphering all that you will encounter on your path. For this reason, all ancient classic texts make it clear that this is a journey one can only undertake with the guidance and grace of a master. Still, many people find themselves thrust on this path by circumstances not of their choosing. Almost daily I hear from people all over the world who are having spontaneous awakenings or experiences that are transcendent, transpersonal, and powerfully transformative. That transformation can be extremely disruptive at times, and I work with people to help them regain their balance and functioning as they deal with the volcanic eruption of the Divine into their lives.

In the Bhagavad Gita there is an exchange between Arjuna, who among other things symbolizes the perfect disciple, and Lord Krishna, the archetypal guru, the guiding presence of the Divine operating through an individual form. Arjuna finally recognizes that Krishna, who has been his charioteer, friend, and teacher for many years, is much more than he seems to be. He asks Lord Krishna to reveal his true nature, and Krishna bestows upon Arjuna the grace needed to clear his ordinary mind and vision so he can directly perceive Krishna as God. The vision is so overwhelming that Arjuna, a great and strong warrior, begs Krishna to stop and come back to his ordinary form.

Greek myths told us that to see a god as it was would kill you. The ordinary mind and body have to be trained and transformed to withstand that vision and influx of Divine power. All the yogas and tantric training disciplines done with the guidance of a master teacher aim at such preparation. However, when the Divine suddenly penetrates people's lives as a result of trauma, near-death experiences, or the innocent use of powerful practices done with inadequate guidance or with none at all, people need help to integrate the experiences and move on with their quests. Kundalini and the system of chakras of the subtle body provide an ancient and richly detailed symbolic map of the spiritual journey to ultimate meaning, freedom, wisdom, and love.

THE POWER OF CONSCIOUSNESS

The power of Consciousness that propels us along our inner journey of discovery is given different names in various spiritual traditions: grace, the Holy Spirit, the soul's yearning, *mumukshtva* (Sanskrit for "longing for liberation"), the bond between the lover and the Divine Beloved, the fire of yoga, and divine discontent are just some of those names. That power of all-encompassing Divine Consciousness, what we in the West call God, which seeks to reveal our own true nature and unite us with itself, is called Kundalini in the yogic tradition. She is spoken of as a Goddess. Though this may make her seem alien or separate from us, She is not. In fact, She is more fundamentally "you" than you can imagine, and if you follow her with reverence and devotion She will reveal the mysteries of the universe to you. In essence, She is formless, not a goddess at all, but pure Divine Consciousness. She's the very power of grace, of revelation, residing within you even now.

It is Kundalini who creates the universe and knows itself as Creator. Kundalini has been called "the face of God." And just as we recognize a person by his or her face, we recognize the Divine by its power of Consciousness: Kundalini. It is Kundalini that clothes the formless in form, that gives the absolute a face to adore, a presence to inspire, traditions to revere, and a body of wisdom to serve and guide. She is the esoteric goal of all yogas, the awakened mind of the *thatagatas* (the Buddhas who have "gone beyond"), and the source of the transcendent vision of saints and sages of every tradition. By knowing Her, all is known. By knowing Her, life becomes suffused with *ananda:* sublime, eternal joy. The wellspring of that joy is our very own self, forever present, nearer than our breath, waiting in stillness to be revealed. Drown the ordinary ego-mind in stillness if you truly want to know the Knower—the Self of All.

The Eastern traditions revere Kundalini as the Great Mother, the one who gives birth to all that is. She is seen as taking on limitations, contracting and condensing to form the material world. She is the essential energy, Shakti, more fundamental than nuclear power, that is the basis of who we are and all that we experience. When our limited mind is infused with Her transcendent power of Consciousness, we know *directly* the truth of our unity with the Divine and all its creation. Every spiritual tradition has its name for Kundalini—Holy Spirit, grace, *Shekhinah,* anima, *chi, bodhicitta* among them—and every saint and mystic has known Her blessing. Seekers on all paths need Her grace to succeed on their journeys. For this reason, shamans, yogis, monks, priests, nuns, and aspirants of all types approach Her as suppliants. Being the Great Mother, the Great Lover, She's willing to take whatever shape and bear whatever name Her children wish to use as they bow to Her.

Kundalini is classically viewed as having two aspects. One maintains the entire existence of our body, mind, and spirit. The other aspect, considered dormant, is the power of Consciousness to know the Divine in its infinitude as Self. This potential power, innate to all of us, can propel our awareness from the paltry limitations of individual existence, with all its wants and needs and deficiencies, to Unity Consciousness—the sublime awareness of our Divine Self, infinite and all-encompassing.

THE FIVE POWERS OF GOD

In the monistic tradition of Kashmir Shaivism, one of India's ancient and most sublime expressions of the mystical vision of God and the Universe, the Lord is said to have five powers. Everything else in the universe is a manifestation of these five: the power of creation, the power of sustenance, the power of destruction, the power of concealment, and the power of grace, or revelation. When the Divine goes to create the universe, there's nothing to create it out of other than God. He or She (it doesn't matter which, since God is neither *and* both) can't run down to the nearest building supply center for stuff to create it with, so she uses herself. What is God? The Divine is Pure Consciousness, infinite power or energy that has the quality of all-encompassing Consciousness. That's what the universe is made of. Everything is united with God because everything is made of God. God has the power to create all the forms of the universe, the power to sustain the continued existence of those forms, and the power to dissolve them back into the formless Divine. Now, in order for God's play of creating, sustaining, and destroying to really work, all the forms in the universe—which are in union with God because they are made of God—have to forget they are one with the Divine. For their individual existence and the world drama to fully evolve, their union with God must be concealed from them. That's where the power of concealment comes in. Our truly unbreakable union with God is concealed, hidden from us by God. It's as if a part of God hides from another part of God in order to allow the drama of God's creation to unfold. That drama is the seemingly disconnected part of God evolving and beginning to yearn for reunion with God once again. This is a symbolic, mythic understanding of the unfolding of Creator: creature and creation in constant union while the illusions of separation, suffering, and reunion are played out.

Imagine a vast, deep ocean, calm and still, as the infinite Consciousness of God. God begins to create, and a wave forms on the ocean, a form that seems to have its individual existence yet is still one with the ocean. Now imagine that the wave's oneness with the ocean is concealed from it, and the wave is given permission to play at taking on all different kinds of forms. The wave is conscious and experiences itself as a huge wave, then a small wave, a ripple, a tall wave, a fat wave, and on and on. But, as with all activities, this gets boring after a while. The wave has learned all it can from taking on different shapes, and now it's no longer creative or meaningful to continue doing that. The wave has a vague memory of having been a part of something greater and begins to long for something greater. It wants to reunite with the ocean, with God. This is where the fifth power of God comes in, the power of grace, the power of revelation. By an act of grace, God undoes the work of the power of concealment and reveals our true unity with God. The wave delights in being a projection of the ocean. The illusion of separation is dissolved, and once again we enjoy the ecstasy of oneness with our Creator.

The 13th century poet saint Kabir wrote:

> *Rising,*
> *water's still water, falling back,*
> *it is water, will you give me a hint*
> *how to tell them apart?* [2]

With the bestowal of grace, *shaktipat,* a Sanskrit term for the awakening of Kundalini, we awaken to the Truth, the truth of our union of God, the direct experience of the union of the wave and the ocean.

When we wake up in the morning, we begin to experience a different reality from the one we were in just moments before while we were asleep. The power of consciousness that begins to operate with our awakening each morning allows us to experience the reality of the waking world around us. Kundalini is the power of Consciousness that allows us to know we are one with God, to know that all others are one with God, and to know that all of creation is one with God. Until that power of Consciousness is awakened within us, we can't know the truth directly for ourselves. But when it does awaken, transformation of the highest order ensues.

AWAKENING THE DIVINE WITHIN

Kundalini is often depicted in yogic texts as a coiled serpent lying dormant within us, a serpent whose mighty powers become manifest as it awakens. Many people have visions and experiences of this archetypal form of Kundalini in meditation and dreams as the process of Kundalini awakening and unfolding occurs. Given what we know about a microscopic bit of coiled, bound energy containing all the information necessary to make a human being—otherwise known as DNA—perhaps we shouldn't be too skeptical about a form of bound consciousness lying dormant within, symbolized as a coiled serpent, waiting to propel your awareness back to union with the Creator.

Shankaracharya, the eighth-century sage of Advaita Vedanta, wrote an ecstatic prayer, *Saundaryalahari*, which proclaimed the supreme power of Kundalini.[3] In it, he states that all knowledge, all wisdom, all inspiration, and all creativity—musical, poetic, literary, artistic, as well as union with the Divine—come through the power of Kundalini *alone*. For this reason, the awakening of Kundalini is the esoteric goal of all yogas. The ancient Kashmir Shaivite text the *Kularnava Tantra* states that without shaktipat there is no liberation or Self-realization.[4] The descent of grace may happen spontaneously and unexpectedly or through the power of a master of genuine attainment. In some cases shaktipat is received through contact with a mystic guide who appears in one's dreams or meditation. Often, it is awakened through an empowered mantra or the practices learned from an accomplished spiritual teacher. It may also have been awakened in a past life and is continuing to unfold in this life. No one person, practice, or tradition is the sole means of receiving the descent of grace, the awakening of the Kundalini. The Divine is too generous to put such limitations on its accessibility.

C. G. Jung wrote that "when you succeed in the awakening of kundalini, so that she starts to move out of her mere potentiality, you necessarily start a world which is totally different from our world: it is a world of eternity."[5]

Into that mystical world our quest leads us.

> *Mother of Ultimacy,*
> *unspeakable and unthinkable,*
> *who can comprehend your countless revelations?*

> *Sometimes you remove every veil*
> *to be known by enlightened sages*
> *as the formless Mother of the Universe,*
> *the transparent presence who dwells secretly*
> *within every atom, every perception, every event.*
> *Other times you manifest as Mother Kundalini,*
> *the evolutionary potency*
> *coiled at the root of the subtle body.*
> —Ramprasad, eighteenth-century Bengali saint[6]

EXPERIENCING THE SUBTLE BODY

The yogic system gives a fascinating description of what is called the *subtle body.* It is in the subtle body that the energy form of universal consciousness known as Kundalini resides. Once activated from her resting place within it, the awakened Kundalini begins her work of transforming and purifying the subtle and physical bodies. The ensuing experiences and shifts in consciousness constitute the seeker's unfolding spiritual journey, and the evolutionary potential becomes realized.

The subtle body is an energy body that interpenetrates our physical body. You may have heard of it without knowing it has this name. Acupuncture, for example, is a respected form of medical treatment that works on the energy flowing through the subtle body—subtle in comparison with the gross body that we experience very concretely through all the physical sensations our sense organs make available to us. The subtle body is the "body" of our mind, thoughts, feelings, emotions, intuitions, and other less commonly identified forms of energy, known as *prana* in the yogic system. It's a subtle realm that is very real to us, even though science can't verify the existence of any specific thought or feeling we might be having in this realm.

Science deals with the gross physical domain and can only detect physical correlates to thoughts and feelings such as brainwave patterns, respiratory rates, or galvanic skin response. A researcher using the most refined instruments attached to your skull may be able to give you data about neuronal activity, but only you know that at that instant you are recalling a tender moment of being held in the arms of a loved one. That kind of memory is not at all subtle, yet the rich content of it goes far beyond the ability of the most sensitive scientific instrument of measurement to detect. You, in contrast, already possess the most subtle and powerful instrument capable of apprehending such memories and even subtler phenomenon: that instrument is consciousness. Your conscious attention is your power of apprehension, and it can be developed and refined through meditation and the awakened Kundalini.

During ordinary waking-state awareness, our consciousness is almost entirely identified with the physical body. In waking-state consciousness, our experience is dominated by body awareness and things related to it. We're aware of various sensations, feelings, and thoughts about ourselves that are rooted in the gender of our bodies, the shape they are in, and the functions or roles they perform in our families or in society; we think of ourselves as man or woman, fat or thin, husband or wife, boss or employee. Waking-state awareness is primarily physical-body consciousness. Even the subtle-body activities of our minds and emotions are primarily related to the physical realm and what is happening there. Sadly, for most of us this comprises all of what we will give our attention to for our entire lives. But there's infinitely more to who we are and what we have available to experience and learn from.

The subtle body is another realm entirely.[7] We experience it most exclusively when we are in the dream state of consciousness and in some meditative states. In the dream state, which is the experience of the subtle body that people are most familiar with, we are outside the physical realm. The laws of physics no longer apply; we leave behind the constraints of ordinary time and space. We experience consciousness relatively free of the fetters of the physical body, but consciousness is still bound in certain ways. We're still identified with a limited sense of self, with the thoughts, feelings, and reflections of our body identity, but these can change dramatically and easily in this shape-shifting state. At the same time, we can move about through time and space in ways the physical body never can. In our dreams, we fly, and we move back to the past, ahead to the future, or to some alternate present. Because we are so identified with the body and waking-state consciousness, the subtle body and the subtle realms of dreams, thoughts, feelings, imagination, and intuition are often disorienting. These realms may seem alien, unknown, perhaps even incomprehensible to our waking-state sense of self. Usually our waking-state "I" dismisses or devalues our dreams and any other unusual subtle body experiences. But through meditation, we can enter and explore the subtle realms quite consciously. The great yogic sages have done this and reported on the physiology of the subtle body.[8]

Just as our physical body has conduits for vital fluids and nerve impulses, the subtle body has conduits for the energy of consciousness. They are the nadis, and they carry the living

conscious energy, prana. In meditation the nadis may appear like
the filaments of light in fiber optics. Where several nadis join
together, the conduit is larger, like a bigger fiber-optic cable. In
the physical body, the main nerve conduit running from the brain
down to the base of the spine is the spinal cord, a great bundle of
nerve fibers that connects the highest centers in the brain to the
entire body. In roughly the same location in the subtle body there
is the main conduit of Kundalini, called the *sushumna* nadi, which
runs from the head down to the base of the spine.

The sushumna nadi is seen as not only the major channel the
creative energy of consciousness flows through as it manifests the
universe of personal experience; it is also the repository for all the
past impressions left by our actions, both mental and physical. The
sushumna contains the impressions, called *samskaras*, of all our
many lifetimes. In this way, it is the storehouse of all our karmas,
all the consequences of our past actions that we have yet to experience. Everyone's familiar with CDs and DVDs. On a CD, millions
of subtle impressions are stored. When the laser light of the CD
player mechanism passes over the CD, it reflects those impressions and converts them into music, pictures, video, or whatever
it was that was stored on it. In a similar way, the sushumna nadi
stores within a subtle energy field the countless impressions of all
our various actions. When the light of one's individual consciousness passes through them, it picks up those patterns and manifests
them. In this way, patterns of thinking, feeling, acting, relating,
and creating are built up over lifetimes and reproduced again and
again. It is these samskaras, the patterns and consequences of our
own past actions, that bind consciousness to the forms of identity
we normally experience as ourselves each day.

To become liberated or enlightened requires becoming free
of those samskaras and the limited "I" awareness that creates them.
This is the work of the awakened Kundalini. She does this in
two ways. First, the Kundalini moves through the sushumna nadi
"erasing," if you will, the impressions stored there and releasing

the energy bound up in them. This extraordinary purification process then releases us from the patterns in our lives created by those impressions. Second, she opens up states of consciousness that give us access to unbounded awareness, awareness of the transcendent self, what some call God-consciousness, Buddha mind, or Christ-consciousness, totally free of ego-mind. These are the altered states of consciousness, the experiences of mystical union and profound meditation that allow us to perceive directly, perhaps for the first time, that we are much more than we think we are. They lead to the *mahavakya* proclamations of the ancient Vedas of "I am Brahman," "I am the Absolute," or in the words of the Christian mystic St. Catherine of Genoa, "My Me is God, nor do I recognize any other Me except my God himself." [9]

In order for that state of unity consciousness to become stable and fully manifest in the individual's mind, body, and actions, the sushumna nadi and all the lesser nadis must be purified: cleansed of impressions and blocks that contract or restrict consciousness to the confines of ordinary human experience. Though we are discussing the subtle body, nadis, samskaras, chakras, and the like, as if they are concrete things, we must always be mindful of the fact that this is the result of our language and not their subtle, symbolic true nature. No matter how beautiful or seemingly complete a description you may find in any ancient or modern text, it will always be incomplete. This keeps what needs to be hidden inaccessible to the uninitiated, for their own protection. However, it also means that people can spend years or lifetimes lost in delusions of their own incomplete knowing. The dharma of true teachers is to protect their students from that prolonged route of suffering. Concrete thinking—taking the symbolic for concrete, literal descriptions—always leads to fundamentalism in spiritual traditions, whether yogic, Christian, Buddhist, Jewish, Muslim, or others. The seeker must always maintain the finest levels of discrimination to properly understand the boundaries between domains.

SYMBOLISM OF THE CHAKRAS

Along the sushumna nadi, there are energy centers where numerous lesser nadis intersect the sushumna, similar to the nerve centers along the spinal cord (Figure 1). These energy centers along the sushumna are called *chakras* in Sanskrit, meaning "wheel." They may appear to the inner eye during meditation as wheels of energy or light. Chakras are also described as lotus flowers with various numbers of petals. The energy channels intersecting at a chakra form what appear to be the petals of a flower. The highest center, technically not a chakra though it is commonly referred to as one, is the thousand-petaled lotus of the sahasrara. Because the energy in the subtle body is conscious energy, these energy centers are actually operating centers of consciousness. The descent of Consciousness from the energy center at the top of the sushumna, called the sahasrara, to the energy center at the base, called the *muladhara,* marks the process of Consciousness going from the highest transcendent Unity Consciousness to the limitations of embodied consciousness you and I normally experience as we live out our existence on earth. The muladhara chakra represents the element of earth and is the final destination of Divine Consciousness, the Kundalini Shakti, through the process of descent and manifestation of the world. It is in this chakra that the Kundalini lies dormant after creating the world and embodied existence. It is here that she awaits the great awakening that will reverse this process, removing the limitations Consciousness has taken on, and allowing us to once again be aware of our transcendent, unbounded, divine nature; the wave merges back into the sea.

The process of *involution* is that of Consciousness descending from the formless transcendent Godhead, condensing, contracting, and taking on more and more limitations until it manifests the earthly realm of human existence, "involving" itself in all of creation in the process. *Evolution* reverses this, with Consciousness as awakened Kundalini ascending back up through the chakras, becoming ever freer of limitations, restrictions, and the illusion

FIGURE 1: THE PRINCIPLE CHAKRAS OF THE SUBTLE BODY

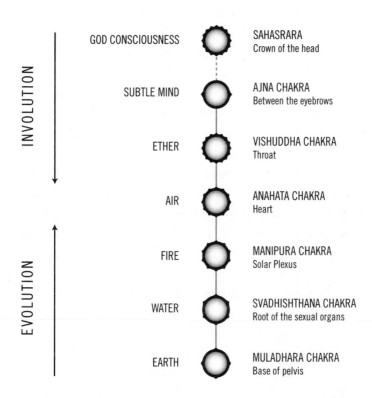

of being bound and separate from its source: God/dess. Between the sahasrara and the muladhara, between Divine Consciousness and earth-bound awareness, there are five other energy centers or chakras, representing the intermediate stages of Consciousness in the processes of involution and evolution.

In descending order (see Figure 1) the energy centers are: the sahasrara at the crown of the head, the *ajna* chakra between the eyes, the *vishuddha* chakra in the throat, the *anahata* chakra near the heart, the *manipura* chakra at about the level of the solar plexus, the *svadhishthana* chakra at the root of the sexual organs, and the muladhara chakra at the base of the pelvis. The involution of Consciousness from the transcendent realm of the sahasrara on down to the muladhara is in part symbolized in the progressive order of the elements that each chakra represents. Involution is a process symbolizing Consciousness coalescing, becoming grosser, denser, and more limited. (This is as seen from the pinnacle of understanding that this is all an illusion and completely non-existent, but since we're enjoying the play of this illusion, we'll continue to describe how it seems to come into existence!)

Just below the sahasrara is the ajna chakra, the "third eye" between and above our physical eyes, and this is the realm of pure individualized mind. Consciousness at this level has lost its formless, all-encompassing universality but hasn't yet coalesced into the physical realm. Here, Consciousness may be experienced simply as a limited sense of "I-ness" that doesn't yet have all the qualities we normally experience as ourselves, such as our gender, body shape, and role.

The subsequent five chakras represent the manifestation of the five elements comprising the physical realm. In descending order, there is a progression from the subtlest to the grossest of the elements. The next chakra, the vishuddha, at the level of the throat, represents the element of ether or space, the sub-tlest of the physical elements. After this we descend to the anahata chakra, the heart chakra, and the element of air, symbolizing con-sciousness becoming a bit denser and grosser than it was at the level symbolized by space. Next is the manipura chakra and the element of fire. Fire is still subtle, but it has more definition and is grosser than air. Then comes the svadhishthana chakra, which represents the element of water. Water is denser and more substantial than fire but not as gross and dense as earth, the last element, which is asso-ciated with the muladhara chakra at the base of the sushumna nadi. At this level we've come to the densest, grossest, most limited and bound form of Consciousness, the earthly physical realm.

Thus everything, from the most subtle sense of "I" awareness to the physical domain of earthly matter, is made of conscious-ness in varying levels of contraction. Even within the most bound forms of the physical realm, the full power and presence of God, of Divine consciousness, are present. The release of that bound energy is like the release of the potential energy bound in matter that suddenly results in the extraordinary power and light of nuclear reactions. The awakening of Kundalini is the release of the bound power and light of God present within the human form.

When Kundalini awakens—in other words, when our innate power of Consciousness to move our awareness beyond the limitations of body and mind comes to life—then the energy of Consciousness, also called Shakti, moves up the sushumna nadi and pierces the chakras in ascending order. Consciousness moves from the constrictions of the earth realm, ever expanding, shedding limitations along the way until it finally reaches the unbounded realm of the sahasrara once again. The wave once again knows its union with the ocean, and we experience reunion with God, the Self of All.

Now this is the briefest possible look at the chakras and what they represent. There's much, much more to them and what they symbolize. Each is a level of consciousness, and the yogic sages have explored and given detailed accounts of them. Each chakra has associated with it certain powers and characteristic feelings that affect how we create our individual realities—our relationships, our worldview, our sense of self, and our ways of interacting with the world—when we are acting from the level of that chakra. If you read Sir John Woodroffe's *Serpent Power*,[10] which includes translations of the yogic texts dealing with all the chakras and the Kundalini, you'll be awed by the rich symbolism and the extraordinary map of Consciousness they provide.

THE GIFTS OF MAHA KALI

Once a renowned author who had written about Kundalini came to meet my guru, Swami Muktananda. Baba, as my guru was known, was revered for his exalted visions of the Kundalini and his rare ability to give shaktipat. The author, too, had visions of Kundalini, but to him she appeared quite unimpressive, looking like an ordinary woman, not like a Goddess at all. As he waited outside the room where Baba was receiving visitors, he was astonished to have a vision of the Goddess Kundalini herself entering the room where Baba was—only this time she appeared in her most regal and resplendent form, magnificent and awe inspiring. The author was shocked. When he finally went in to speak with Baba, he asked why it was that she appeared so ordinary to him, while for Baba she came as the Goddess of the Universe. Baba replied simply, "Because I worship her."

After I first heard that story, I began contemplating what it means for an accomplished yogi to worship Kundalini. I kept wondering how a yogic master would worship Kundalini and why. After a year, my mind finally gave up its vain attempts at piercing the mystery on its own, and I prayed to the inner guru, the Shakti, for an answer. In a profound series of meditations, Kundalini, this great power of revelation, showed me how worship, actively honoring and revering the Divine power of grace within, is the key to receiving all the wisdom she wishes to impart. This is the path of *bhakti* yoga, the yoga of devotion, where the worshipper and the worshipped merge, where duality surrenders with love to nonduality. This ancient Kundalini Yoga (not the contemporary one that goes by that name, which has positive attributes of its own), the yoga that unfolds solely by the grace of awakened Kundalini, includes all yogas: bhakti, mantra, hatha, raja, laya. On this path, Shakti delights in the play of shifting back and forth between the sublime joy of dualistic worship and the ecstatic consummation of the union of Herself as lover and Beloved.

The intense practices I began doing culminated in a series of meditation experiences in Baba's ashram meditation hall during a weekend retreat in 1982. Various forms of the Goddess began appearing fully and spontaneously in meditation, as real as any person standing in front of me. I worshipped each in turn, trembling and awestruck as I did and only able to do so because of the strength the Shakti gave me in the moment to withstand Her

Divine presence. Goddess after Goddess appeared until finally Maha Kali was present there before me. I prayed with all my heart to be able to stay conscious. Her skin was blacker than black, like deep black velvet in a darkened room. Yet in some miraculous way Her form was radiant, revealing Her own richly magnificent blackness. A thought appeared in my mind: "My God, this is Kali! She's the Great Mother, Goddess of the Universe, creator and destroyer of all that is!" But She was in the most exquisite, beautiful, loving form, not the fearsome presence She is usually depicted as having. This was Her hidden form. I did the only thing I knew to do: I did puja to Her, an ancient Indian form of worship, while shaking with a mixture of fear, awe, and overwhelming love. Tears flowed down my cheeks. Then the Goddess came forward and embraced me, wrapping Herself around me. Everything slowed down. I could feel myself gradually merging into Her, and I could hear Her laughing the wildest, most ecstatic laugh! We disappeared from the ordinary world. My awareness shifted, and I could see the whole solar system with all its planets, and then stars and galaxies being withdrawn into Her. The entire universe was merging into Her, and all the while it was merging, the infinitude of the cosmos reverberated with Her ecstatic laughter. Finally, I disappeared into Her as I dissolved into infinite Light and Love, and then into a nothingness beyond even that, beyond the mind, beyond any duality of experience. There simply was no "me" left; I was gone, gone, gone beyond.

The next things I was aware of were the Light and Her laughter once again. Maha Kali's magnificent black form reappeared, and I began seeing galaxies, stars, and planets reemerging from Her womb. I, too, began to emerge and take on a subtle form of "I-ness," still without a body. I felt sad and pained taking on a form separate from Her and was startled to hear Her laughter continuing unabated. She then reversed the process and everything, myself included, began dissolving back into Her. Once again, waves of ecstasy washed through me, feeling Her laughter as my own. She continued alternating back and forth between creation and dissolution. Each time it was the same for me, ecstasy on the dissolution and pain during the taking on of form. Clearly for Her, both were equally ecstatic. I tried to rest in the ecstasy of taking on form and limitation, but at the time I just couldn't do it. Finally, She let me take on my complete set of limitations and form for this life—physical body and all.

I returned to my awareness of being seated on the floor in the meditation hall, my body trembling. She also returned my clarity of mind. The experience ended; feeling profoundly grateful, I bowed to my inner guru, my Goddess Kundalini. This had all unfolded as a result of shaktipat from my Siddha master, Muktananda Baba, years earlier, and my prayer to know the highest form of worship of Kundalini. Complete worship merges you with the one you worship. Through worship and prayer, the Goddess reveals the mysteries of Her creation to Her creature: the seeker—you! She doesn't want or need to be approached with force, prodded along like some servant, as degrading yogic perspectives still polluted by outdated patriarchal attitudes continue to maintain. Avoid such deluded paths or She'll let you roam the labyrinth of your own mental creation until you finally understand that love and surrender are the keys to Her realm. Reverence and devotion draw Her grace without reserve.

No words can describe how overwhelmed and truly awestruck I was by the appearance of the Goddesses classically depicted in the chakras, followed by Maha Kali Herself. These were the Goddesses that Kundalini manifests, as well as Her primal form as Maha Shakti, the great power, that takes the form of Maha Kali, the Black Goddess. It is this highest power that dissolves the universe as She merges into the sahasrara, creating it once again as She descends from that transcendent realm. Each and every one of us has the innate capacity to know this spontaneously and directly by the grace of Kundalini. No artificial visualizations can compare with this direct knowing.

Just as the aspects of Divine Consciousness were being presented to my awareness symbolically in the forms of the Goddesses, in the same way the union with those Divine forms was symbolized by sexual union. Readers familiar with the experiences of mystics of many spiritual traditions will recognize that this is a common way for union with the Divine to express itself. Very often the Tantric traditions, both yogic and Buddhist, that deal with the Divine Feminine depict union in this way. Sexual symbolism and the experience of that form of symbolic merger in meditation are often confusing for people, especially Westerners, who take it literally. That type of misinterpretation has led people to either conclude that Kundalini is just a form of psychosexual energy or to uselessly pursue "tantric sex" in an effort to enter a domain of knowing to which Her grace alone gives access.

The mysteriously radiant blackness of Kali arrests my mind every time I recall Her divine form. In an extraordinary book, *Mother of the Universe*, the ecstatic hymns to Maha Kali by the eighteenth-century Bengali saint Ramprasad Sen, the translator, Dr. Lex Hixon, writes:

> The mystery of Kali, impenetrable to conventional, dualistic thinking, is her blackness, her beautiful midnight blackness. The Goddess tradition, along with many other authentic spiritual transmissions during planetary history, fundamentally emphasizes divine inconceivability, the indefinability of Reality. The rich darkness within what Christian mystics call the Cloud of Unknowing is the radiant blackness of Mother's womb. Ramprasad is a consummate poet of this dazzling divine darkness:

> *Why is Mother Kali so radiantly black?*
> *Because she is so powerful,*
> *that even mentioning her name destroys delusion.*
> *Because she is so beautiful,*

Lord Shiva, Conqueror of Death,
lies blissfully vanquished
beneath her red-soled feet.
There are subtle hues of blackness,
but her bright complexion
is the mystery that is utterly black,
overwhelmingly black, wonderfully black.
When she awakens in the lotus shrine
within the heart's secret cave,
her blackness becomes the mystic illumination
that causes the twelve-petal blossom there
to glow more intensely than golden embers.
Whoever gazes upon this radiant blackness
falls eternally in love.

This black light expresses the highest teaching of the Goddess. It is the radiance beyond whatever we know as light, yet at the same time it constitutes all physical, intellectual, and spiritual light.[11]

The mystic vision the Goddess Kundalini gave me in that meditation in 1982 continued to unfold in subsequent meditations and has led to Her greatest gifts. I've heard so many stories of visions and other transformative and healing experiences people have had after sincerely praying to the Goddess that I'm sure She is as available to seekers today as ever. She demands that people do the necessary practices and disciplines in order to prepare themselves as vessels capable of holding Her gifts. Too often, people receive so many graces, so many treasures, but their minds are so full of holes, these blessings all leak out in no time. Meditate, follow the eight limbs of yoga or Buddha's eightfold path, and you'll be able to see Her treasures falling in your lap all the time!

On Being Moved

Kundalini and the Complete Maturation of the Spiritual Body

STUART SOVATSKY, PHD

Stuart Sovatsky, copresident of the Association for Transpersonal Psychology and trustee for the California Institute of Integral Studies (CIIS), has studied kundalini and psychotherapy for three decades. In the following essay, he illustrates the evolution of kundalini throughout a typical lifespan. Detailing the specific stages of kundalini unfolding, he explores its relationship to our life cycle before we are born, in our embryonic stage, and through childhood and adulthood. He also introduces practices for activating kundalini. Sovatsky answers these questions: Does kundalini exist before we are born? How do sexuality and celibacy affect the yogic pursuit of kundalini? And do we all have the potential to experience kundalini?

A coil of lightning, a flame of fire folded (224)

She cleans the skin down to the skeleton (233)

Old age gets reversed (260)

She . . . dissolves the five [bodily] elements (291)

. . . [then] the yogi is known as Khecar [tumescent tongued]

Attaining this state is a miracle (296)

Shakti [feminine power] and Shiva [masculine power]
become one
and in their union, everything . . . gets dissolved (306)
Further, there is nothing more to experience beyond [this]
Hence, let me stop speaking of it
For it is useless to talk (318)

> —Numbered lines related to kundalini,
> from *Dnyaneshwari (Jnaneshvari)* [1]

VIBRANT WELL-BEING, overwhelming ecstasy, effulgently enlightened consciousness, the summit of human evolution, pathway to
an endless eroticism, the Great Procreatrix, the deification, regen-
eration, and immortalization of the body, the somaticizing of
spiritual aspirations, the teleological freeing of soul from flesh via
the literal unwinding of the mortal coil into its constituent elements, the lost wisdom of the serpent of Genesis and the fuel of
all human genius, the energy of the Dionysian revelry, the spiritual side of DNA, Christ's fiery baptism and that of His followers
ever since, the seething cobra sheltering Lord Buddha—such are
the ancient and modern claimed manifestations of kundalini, literally, "the mother of all creation and of all yogas."

The practice can be traced back at least five thousand years
to the archeological relic known as the Pashupati seal. It depicts
an antler-crowned demigod, sitting cross-legged with one heel
pressing his androgynous perineum and the other the root of
his erect penis. He is mildly breasted, with a *phalam* fruit in one
hand and a phallic staff in the other. This is assumed to be the
ultimate attainer himself, Shiva, reincarnated some twenty-eight
times, most recently as Lakulisha, the staff-bearing Gujarati saint
(ca. 100 CE). He in turn was the inspiration of the legendary
yogic saints Goraksha-nath and Matsyendra-nath, from whom all
modern forms of hatha yoga have emerged.

Indeed, kundalini has ancient Vedic references in terms of an
inner sunlight, an inner *soma* (nectar of immortality), divine *vayu*

(circulating wind), *kunamnama* (a "crookedly shaped," serpentine) potential that the bodily vayu of the ancient *keshin* ("long-haired" ascetic) churns into serving his spiritual goals to know ultimate reality and its inherent bliss. And, as paths to the ultimate multiplied over the millennia of Indian history, those that were more inclusive of a positive role for the body (rather than on consciousness itself and meditative and ascetic modes of transcending the body) could be discerned.

Whether Buddhist or Hindu, they became known as *tantra*, the "expanded teachings" on the "interwovenness" of the ever more subtle vibrational dimensions of reality. While *advaita* (nondual) paths simplified their focus toward a singular oneness of consciousness, tantric traditions tended to broaden their scope to include the cultivation of the mind's spiritual powers, the material world, and, most significantly, the body. Extreme longevity and even physical immortality were attempted via rituals, sexo-yogic and celibate transmutations, and the herbal-mineral preparations of *rasayana*.[2] Important texts include *Kula-Arnava, Mahanirvana, Tantra-Tattva-Tantra, Panca-Tantra, Shiva-Sutra, Tripuropanishad,* the great Abhinava-gupta's *Tantraloka, Vamakeshvara-tantra, Kama-Kala-Vilasa, Saktavijnana* by Somananda, the *Amaurghasasana* by the legendary Goraksanatha, *Jnaneshvar-gita, Shiva-Samhita, Gherand Samhita, Hathayogapradipika,* and *Thirumandiram.*

The interwovenness of tantra typically resolved to the reverberations between masculine and feminine qualities, deified as Shiva and Shakti (or Durga, Kali, and other goddesses): the primordial couple. Their interactions create not only endlessly reproductive and evolving lineages, but also the entire manifest universe. Between all males and females and within each individual reverberated Shiva's tendency toward absolute and unwavering consciousness with Shakti's wide-ranging dynamic powers, from the most nurturing to the wildly purifying and even antinomian or "transgressive" (of orthodox or conventional) practices.

David Kinsley's *Tantric Visions of the Divine Feminine: The Ten Mahavidyas* and Gudrun Buhnemann's *The Iconography of Hindu Tantric Deities* (Volume I) describe the polar qualities of tantric goddesses, conveying both the benign and nearly unbearable purificatory powers of the awakened Mother Kundalini.

Unwavering auditory meditation upon mantric vibrations revealed deeper beauties and empowering intricacies within the mantras while also adding brilliance and clarity to the unwavering consciousness. Important mantras include *Om Namo Bhagavate Vasudevaya, Om Namo Shivaya, So-Ham,* and *Om Bhur Bhuva Swaha Tat Savitur Varenyam Bhargo Devasya Dhimahe Dhyo Yonah Prachodayat.* Likewise, visual meditation upon *sri yantra's* interpenetrating triangles would blossom into an infinity of vibrations as the meditator approached the radiant, inner source of his or her own consciousness—and perhaps of the subatomic structure of the manifest universe itself.

Of central importance, and dating back to the *Taittiriya-Upanishad,* are descriptions of a subtle energetic anatomy (*sukshma-sharira*) revealed via body-scanning meditations. This subtle body was seen to pervade the fleshy "food-eating" body (*anna-maya kosha*), consisting of some 72,000 *nadis* (subtle channels) and spinally aligned *chakras* (function-based ascending centers). Within these subtle structures, *prana,* the generic life energy, was seen flowing in various circuits (*prana-pran,* inhalation functions; *apana-pran,* exhaling and eliminative functions; *vya-pran,* circulating function; *samana-pran,* digestive function; and *udan-pran,* throat and speaking functions).

The primordial kundalini energy itself was seen glowing and seething at the perineum in the *muladhara* chakra, the "root generator" center that governs the earth element. The locus of sexual passion was discerned in the lower abdomen in the *svadhishthana* chakra that governs the water element. Willfulness was identified with the navel-level *manipura* chakra that governs the fire element. *Anahata* chakra was associated with the heart and its surges and moods of devotion, longing, courage, and love.

While the first three chakras govern the fleshy body (anna-maya kosha), anahata governs the air element and is associated with the nonphysical energy body, the *prana-maya kosha*. The *vishudhha* chakra, located at the throat and associated with speech, governs the subtle etheric element, including the *mano-maya kosha*, the thinking-emotional body. *Ajna* chakra is located in the head behind the midpoint of the forehead. It functions as the ever more refined capacity for reflective discernment and subtle judgement in the *vijnana-maya kosha*, the body of subtlest discriminations.

The reflective capacity of ajna chakra hovers around a central point of advaita nonduality or, more precisely from tantric perspectives, *dvaita-advaita,* "oscillating duality-nonduality." It is capable of the most refined discernment, extending into psychic powers. *Sahasrara* chakra within the *ananda-maya kosha* (causal bliss body) is the "thousand-petalled lotus" of endlessly effulgent light and bliss that is beyond all concepts and intellectualizations, where male and female live in ecstatically commingled union.

AWAKENING KUNDALINI

All the practices of hatha yoga—*asanas, mudras, bandhas* (visceral contractions), and *pranayama*—help to awaken the dormant kundalini in the muladhara chakra. Likewise, the vibrational practices of mantra yoga—*japa* (rosary-like mantra repetition), *kirtan* (group chanting with an awakened leader via an energetic transmission known as *shaktipat*), and personal mantric prayers over the course of many years—can awaken kundalini.[3] Still-sitting meditative practices tend to minimize the complete awakening of this energy, but instead focus upon inner peace, undifferentiated consciousness, compassion, insights into impermanence, and the limitations of egoic identifications.

Below is a regime of twenty asanas with chakra meditations and breathing prescriptions that are sequenced to awaken the chakras in preparation for kundalini arousal.[4]

ASANA	CHAKRA	HOLD BREATH IN AND/OR OUT
Yoga mudra (kneeling foldover)	muladhara	In and Out
Paschchimottana-asana (sitting legs extended foldover)	muladhara	In and Out
Ardha-matsyendra-asana (sitting spinal twist)	svadhistana	Normal Breathing
Buddha-padma-asana (lotus/crossed leg /sitting)	svadhistana	Out
Lola-asana (uplifted lotus balance pose)	manipura	In
Dola-asana (lotus v-balance, chin-lock)	manipura	In and Out
Ardha-supta-padma-asana (lotus lying on back)	manipura	In and Out
Matsyendra-asana ("fish" pose)	anahata	In and Out
Viparita karani-padma-asana ("reverse" pose in lotus)	anahata	Normal Breathing
Hala-asana ("plough" pose)	vishuddha	Normal Breathing
Karani pida-asana ("plough" knee-ear pose)	vishuddha	Normal Breathing
Sarvanga-asana (shoulder stand)	vishuddha	Normal Breathing
Viparita karani ("reverse" pose)	vishuddha	In and Out
Mukta pavana-asana (back-lying knees-to-chest pose)	vishuddha	In
Setu-asana (bridge pose)	ajna	In
Bhujanga-asana ("cobra" pose)	ajna	In
Salabha-asana ("locust" pose)	anja	In
Dhanura-asana ("bow/boat" pose)	anja	In and Out
Sirsa-asana (headstand)	sahasrara	Normal Breathing
Sava-asana (corpse pose)	vishuddha	Normal Breathing

Once kundalini awakens (or its far more common precursor, *pranotthana*, pranic awakening, occurs), many of these initially intentional practices can emerge spontaneously. Given the requisite level of pranotthana and meditative relaxation, one's body just starts moving into various yoga postures, mood-enhanced dance movements, intensified breathing patterns, and spontaneous utterances. At that point, many of the yoga "practices" reveal themselves to be innate or endogenous (though typically dormant) in all humans, with cognate phenomena visible in numerous charismatic or "inspired" religious and spiritual traditions worldwide.

Thus, we might distinguish two forms of kundalini yoga: the preparatory and willfully practiced form and the awakened and spontaneously emergent form. To further understand the latter, we must situate this "ultimate mothering energy" within the context of gestation and infant developmental behavior, as well as animating maternal labor contractions. For these are times when kundalini is temporarily and spontaneously active in the course of ordinary life.

EMBRYONIC BEGINNINGS

Kundalini's motherly creativity is first visible microscopically in the nucleus of the fertilized ovum as, literally, the immortalizing chromosomal process of cellular meiosis. The spiraled, bifurcating genetic strands quiver animistically like enthralled lovers, separating and realigning themselves within the nucleus of the fertilized ovum that divides again and again, recreating this same fibril ritual within the nuclear sanctum of each newly reproducing cell. What guides this primordial origination of all bodily life? Kundalini, the "coiled serpentine wisdom-energy." Thus, in contemporary terms, kundalini might be renamed "meta-DNA."

As the zygotic cells divide and ball up, kundalini quickens embrylogical development toward a recognizable human form. An elongating groove folds into itself and creates the dorsal protospinal cord whose subtle channel, *sushumna*, will be the favored pathway for adult Kundalini activity, while below, a ventral alimentary pouch and protoorgans manifest inside the emergent gut. This is the first step in separating the body's "heaven realm" of neural consciousness functions from the earth, air, water, and fire realms of digestion, circulation, elimination, and so on; thus kundalini creates a bodily home for the *jiva*, the "one who lives"—the "soul."

Continuing on, sweet-tasting mucopolysaccharides will secrete into the developing oral cavity as it divides from the heavenly cranial vault, causing the tongue to lick itself away from the heavenly hypophysis (protohypothalamus, pituitary, pineal) and into the earthy and watery realms of the just-forming mouth.[5]

The anterior end of the protospine blossoms into the protobrain, altogether forming the anatomical armature of Darwinian evolutionary history from invertebrate to vertebrate to *Homo erectus* and the uniquely neocortexted *Homo sapiens*. Simultaneously, kundalini will manifest a gill-slitted fishlike stage and tail-bearing and other lower-mammal stages in a mysterious process that biologists call *ontogeny phylogeny recapitulation*—a replaying of billions of years of evolution within the gestation of every human being who has ever lived.

Equally mysterious, kundalini manifests a urogenitally androgynous perineum stage that, for the advanced yogi, will later "fertilize" him with the bioconcentrated powers of the entire polarized universe. Thus, the supreme importance given by yogis (and seen in the Pashupati seal) to the heel-to-perineum *Siddhaasana,* "sitting pose that unleashes supernatural powers."

All the while, fetal movements perform their own profound asana dance, coaxing and vibrating arm buds and leg buds into tiny arms, legs, and fingers while also articulating joints, organs, heartbeats, and even pouting and smiling into existence. When the fetus is fully formed, kundalini sequesters herself at the posterior node of the spine (the muladhara chakra or "root center") and becomes quiescent.

When the fetus attains individual viability, this same kundalini dimension within the mother's body engenders the throbs of labor contractions and the ensuing downward pushing and birth of the child. Thereupon, spontaneous protolinguistic developmental sound-making emerges in the newborn as protomantric (*bija*) emotion- and larynx-developing utterances. Likewise, neonatal developmental stretching movements continue to more fully incarnate the neonate via protoasanas of hatha yoga. The baby's common spellbound staring into space or at some object emerges as one of the earliest of spontaneous meditative concentrations, whose adult version has been aptly called, "beginner's," "pure" or "unconditioned" mind.

As enculturation proceeds, the child's mouth- and tongue-shaped sounds will be molded into a native language and her movements and musculature into producing the skills and actions expected within the home culture. Although the primordial "pure consciousness" and its capacity to "rest in itself" will remain, her operative "ego mind" will be slowly filled with concepts, memories of delight or terror, moods, desire, and so forth, that ever more individualize her.

The power of Sanskrit (and other sacred languages) is based upon its salutary sonic or *mantric* effects on all dimensions of the maturing body, far beyond the semantic utility of conceptual meaning—thus, the emphasis upon nuanced pronunciation in all sacred language instruction. For the mesh of words, concepts, and "forms" inevitably reifies a secondary "ego" mind that can become self-obsessed with worded thinking and grow out of touch with the primordial consciousness of "pure feeling-awareness." Thus, mantra and silent meditation become ever more important practices in "remembering" the unconditioned consciousness itself.

As the individuating process continues, the child's glands will grow in congruence with common emotional states—anger, sorrow, joy, love, desire, shame. Likewise, via the events of her life, she comes to feel ever more unique (*too* unique and *overly* embedded in her historical conditioning, according to spiritual psychology). The primordial kundalini will remain dormant and, quite likely, grow ever more unknown within more "worldly," "ego-based," or "materialistic" cultures (such warnings can be found in many ancient texts).

Thereafter, the more general life energy of prana will guide physiology and empower thought processes, willful movements, and maintenance-level growth. But when growth intensifies during puberty or pregnancy, prana reenters a heightened condition of pranotthana, as is visible in the glow of infants, pregnant women, new fathers, and pubescent teenagers and the purported glow of saints. Lesser modes of pranotthana include the glow of superathletes, charismatic musicians and leaders, and those in certain psychedelic drug states. A miraculous pranotthana manifests in ordinary people in heroic moments, such as a mother lifting a car to save her child or a father enduring life-threatening situations to save his family.

Under special conditions, as introduced above and to be discussed in greater detail below, pranotthana vibratorily goes so far as to foment the reactivation of the dormant kundalini that was so very active during gestation. In this process—whether gradual or sudden—spontaneous sounding (anahata-nad), movements, and yoga positions (sahaja yoga) will emerge, breaking through the enculturated habits of body and mind, even breaking through learned, static hatha yoga postures. As sahaja (spontaneously arising) yoga, this takes on a surreal, that is, super-real, quality. As one of the most advanced of all kundalini yogis, Jnaneshvar, wrote,

> That is called [kundalini yogic developmental kriya]
> action of the body in which reason takes no part
> and which does not originate as an idea springing in
> the mind.
> To speak simply, yogis perform actions [asanas, mudras,
> kriyas] with their bodies, like the [innocent] movements
> of children. [6]

Likewise, under the influence of escalating pranotthana, viscera, musculature, and various moods of longing (*bhakti*, yoga of devotional moods) vibrate the larynx in characteristic overwhelming, trilling fashion as heard in operatic, Sufi *qwaali*, Judaic *nigune*, yogic anahata-nad, and shamanic and indigenous trance singing. These moods also gyrate and twist the body into ecstatic dance and, most mysteriously, into various time-honored yoga asanas— as well as others unnamed or unknown to the yogi—in the same innately emergent way that neonatal movements occur or, more vigorously, as birth contractions taking hold of a laboring mother's body. Thus, the mystical significance of *hatha*, "forceful," yoga asserts itself far beyond any egoic modes of agency.

Indeed, the passion of these longings is as compelling as any romantic love affair, revealing another mystical significance of hatha, the union of sun (masculinity) and moon (femininity) within a singular body. While seated, the heel magnetically draws itself into the once-androgynous perineum (siddha-asana) of the so-awakened one, like a flower unfolding in time-lapse photography. The spine becomes tumescently erect (*uju kaya*), similar to how the genitals can arouse at the thought of one's beloved. The diaphragm lifts into the chest (*uddiyana-bandha*), and the anal sphincter throbs and draws upward (*mula-bandha*).

Yoga as the union of Shakti and Shiva seems no mere symbolic metaphor to the kundalini yogi whose whole life becomes enthralled by these energies. Five to ten hours per day, for decades unto death, are consumed by the inner yogic pregnancy. Indeed, the *ardha-nari* manifestion of the ascetic Shiva as half male and half female could not be clearer as to the primordial, inwardly erotic and outwardly chaste powers unleashed by kundalini.

Breathing will become heavy or racy (*bhastrika* or *kapalabhati* pranayama) to animate the passionate stretching and longing. Altogether, we see why *Ishvara*, "the Mover," is the deity named in *ashtangha* yoga's second step of salutary prescriptions (*yamas*), while in the *hathayogaprapika*, bodily prana is also deified. Thus, the yogi gradually becomes ("gestates" into) the deity whom she has long been devoutly worshipping. In other words, a naturalistic quickening of the entire human being unfolds, *sui generis*. This is Kundalini, the Mother of all Yogas.

Likewise, we can understand common passive verb usage in ancient yoga texts, where one "gets" (manifests) some asana or bandha or mudra. Since it does not feel like the ego is involved in these "actions" any more than in embryonic body manifestation, one cannot discern any personal agency in their occurrence. Charismatic Christian's plainly call such phenomena, "manifestations" of the "Holy Ghost."

Other cross-tradition cognates include spontaneous Judaic and Islamic spinal-rocking *davvening* and *zikr*, Tibetan *tumo* heat, inspired Taoist *tai chi,* Bushman *thxiasi num*, shamanic and *voudoo* trance-dance, yogically derived Andalusian flamenco and inspired, stomach-undulating belly dance, the charismatic quaking and shaking in Quakerism, Shakerism, and Pentacostal "Holy Ghost" dancing, and Orthodox Hesychasm's quivering.

Raja yoga and Buddhism's still-sitting, long meditation periods seek the same awakening, but restrain the body in hopes of channeling all energies directly into the erect spine, thus bypassing the cultivation of numerous expressive and emotional potentials within the mobility of the body. Mortifications, severe vigils, and flagellation are the most desperate of the unnatural methods. Even Elvis Presley's charismatic gyrations and his teenaged fans' pubescent screams can be located at the beginning of this far more profound continuum.

Indeed, kundalini phenomena are not only cross-culturally ubiquitous, taken altogether they arguably indicate an innate somatic dimension to all manifestations of spirituality and religious aspirations. Within our still-dominant Freudian/Darwinian theories of development, I will make the case that altogether, these and other kundalini yoga spontaneous phenomena constitute as-yet-unmapped "post-Freudian," "post-Darwinian" stages of adult maturation.

That is, they are beyond Freud's "final" stage of genital primacy and Darwin's stage of mature fertility (thus, the perennial rub between sexuality and spirituality in many traditions). Likewise, they are beyond the egoic developmental stages of conventional Western psychology, as Michel Foucault notes with his concept of *ars erotica* and Ken Wilber, Jorge Ferrer, and Michael Washburn note with their notions of transpersonal development.

Just as Freud chose to name the fundamental developmental force "libido" or "yearning," so, too, does chapter 7, volume 11 of the Bhagavat Gita, as personified in the words of Krishna: *"Dharmaviruddho bhutesu kamo 'smi bharatasbha."* ("I am the *passion* [*kamo*, desire, yearning] in beings that will manifest the greatest maturation, truth, and goodness.")

According to Freud, this yearning is experienced foremost as sexual desire based in genital puberty, the hallmark of biological adulthood. Kundalini yoga merely reopens the matter of human development whereby the spine, hypothalamus, hypoglossus, and pineal and cerebral lobes are seen as capable of undergoing "puberties" with all the alterations in physiology, identity, and existential life purpose and even mortality itself that were attendant to genital puberty, but now with a more spiritual emphasis. Indeed, one of the oldest terms for yoga is *shamanica medhra*, "releasement beyond the genital thrall."

Yet, in their exportation of yoga to the West, early teachers such as B. K. S. Iyengar, Krishnamacharya, and their successors were not prepared to convey these endogenous depths, but modeled their instruction of the ancient asanas (and others invented at the turn of the century[7] upon the pedagogy and aesthetics of European ballet and gymnastics (complete with hardwood floors and mirrored walls); thus the perfection of held positions became the disciplined practice. These "positions" tap the outer edges of the Kundalini dimension and thus their singular therapeutic efficacy, but rarely so far as to enter inspired movement or transfixed stillness. Indeed, the concentrated willfulness of the practices quite effectively suppresses the *sahaja* path for the vast majority of practitioners.

Furthermore, to fit modern values, the inwardly "erotic" celibacy known as *brahmacharya,* held for thousands of years to be essential to kundalini yoga, has been largely dispensed with. So we barely ever see a modern practitioner who has fallen in love and married her yoga, with eight to ten hours of its spinal mysteries unfolding per day, decade after decade unto death, infused with the romance of a challenging, yet deepening love. As noted in the Bhagavad Gita (11:14), "He is my true devotee, whose voice is choked with emotion of love for me, whose heart is moved with tears rolling down from the eyes."

Indeed, Sri Aurobindo has called brahmacharya the "foundation" of all Indic wisdom traditions and cultural sophistication:

> The secret of that gigantic intellectuality, spirituality, and
> superhuman moral force which we see pulsating in . . .
> the ancient philosophy, in the supreme poetry, art, sculp-
> ture, and architecture [of India] . . . was the all-important
> discipline of *Brahmacharya*. [8]

It is also reflected in its role as the first of the four *Ashramas,* quartenary stages of the idealized, hundred-year lifetime (and reincarnating series of such lifetimes).

Yet the vast majority do not remain celibate yogis after age twenty-five, but enter a second stage, called *Grihasthya Ashrama* (sacred householder life), of marriage and familial creation into one's fifties, whereupon one's own children begin to marry and reproduce. Kundalini takes the form of apparently eternal lineage propagation and the mysterious phenomena of sahaja yoga rarely manifest.

A subsidiary householder's brahmacharya of one sexual union per month is considered within dharmic rhythms suitable for a moderated practice of kundalini yoga. If the tongue-hypothalamus-pineal puberty of *khechari mudra* should awaken, the couple might engage in the *coitus reservatus* of *pariyanga,* erotic yoga. According to the South Indian master, Thirumoolar,

> 825. Pleasure of Sex Union Is Endless When Breath Savoring Is the Only Way. Anointing her body with unguents diverse—Bedecking her tresses with flowers fragrant—Do you enjoy the damsel in passion's union:—If your desire becomes devotion—Prana will shoot up through the Spinal Pathway—Then your enjoyment will be endless.

> 826. Only Those Have Practiced (attained) *Khecari* Can Resort to *Pariyanga.*[9]

From the age of fifty to seventy-five, *vanaprasthya ashrama,* retiring grandparent stage (literally, "forest-dwellers"), emerges, whereupon one's grandchildren begin to bear children. The sense of the eternality of lineage spreads forth visibly in both directions as the embodied truth of human life. Thus, Kundalini matures these individuals to being equal to lifelong, creative marriage. Here, the powers of interpersonal devotion, forgiveness, apology, fidelity, honesty, and love mature between the spouses as Shakti and Shiva, the creative partnership of the human version of the primordial forces that manifest the entire universe. In this sense, the devotional worship of Krishna and Radhe as the divine couple is considered by some to be a form of kundalini yoga.

Beginning at seventy-five years, the "world shedding" *sannyasa ashrama* begins, whereafter great-great-grandparenthood can emerge. During sannyasa, prana and its most revered aspect, *citta* ("consciousness stuff"), are ever more released from adaptation to "worldly ways" of life, and one returns to the unconditioned or pure mind. A deepening spiritual wisdom of eternal rather than merely contemporary truths regarding the deeper purposes and possibilities of human life is discerned. Consciousness and body recognize their very different fates, the former as eternally aware and the latter as destined to wither upon death into the primordial elements of earth, air, water, and fire. Regarding consciousness, death is understood as an ultimately positive experience of *maha-samadhi*, the great knowing of the originating source of all, ever-awake consciousness, compassion, discernment.

Five generations of happy, creative marriages comprise the ideal social manifestation of Mother Kundalini as a wholly enlightened culture, via the *grihasthya* householder path. Each family member matures to the point of being equal to the requirements of marriage and family life, with grand, great-grand- and great-great-grand-children and parents all flourishing. A world of such lineages fulfills the greatest possibility of the central maxim of *Sanatana Dharma* (the indigenous name for all Indian wisdom traditions): *Vasudhaiva kutumbakam*, "The world is, indeed, one [unbroken] family."

The joint-family system that incorporates newlyweds and in-law families is a structural manifestation of this hoped-for ideal and the extremely low (5 to 8 percent) contemporary Indian divorce rate are testaments to and remnants of this increasingly forgotten sociological ideal of a fully dharmic, highly enlight-ened society. The energetic foundation of such a social order is kundalini, from the quivering chromosomes of meiosis, to the blush of adolescent puberty and new parenthood, through great-great-grandparenthood, and the esoteric *khecari* mudra puberty whereby the pineal orgasm secretes the mystic soma or *amritas* (nectar of immortality).

Yet, there is an alternative to the four-staged path of ashramas wherein the power of the developmental trajectory begun in the womb predominates over sociological adaptation and family creation. This second and far rarer *marga,* or life path, manifests as the variety of monasticisms throughout world history. In the yogic model, it is known as *nivritti dharma,* "naturalistic, without intentions way" or lifelong *sannyas*. Instead of joining in the family *jati* or trade or by leaving one's "worldly" occupation and bypassing the romance of mating (or via some tantric form of brahmacharya within marriage), those on this path become yogis in the original sense of the term. Indeed, to this day, modern Indian civil law grants "renouncing the world" to follow the spiritual aspirations of yoga, meditation, and religious practices as honorable grounds for divorce.

KUNDALINI THROUGHOUT THE LIFE CYCLE

The following schema situates numerous manifestations of kundalini and trace the complete maturation of all potentials, physical and spiritual, of *Homo sapiens*.

Beginning
Sperm-ovum fertilization: zygote, blastula, and gastrula stages develop.

First Months
Starting at the embryonic spinal base, kundalini energy-intelligence guides the formation of the neural groove, the evolutionary fundament of all ever more complex vertebrate bodies, from amphioxus on; gill-slits, tail, and other "ontogeny phylogeny recapitulation" vestigial phenomena emerge and vanish; organs form; heart beats as anandamaya kosha (causal body), vijnana-maya kosha (reflective-mind body), mano-maya kosha (neuroendocrine-based mind/emotion body), prana-maya kosha (mitochondrial-meridian vital energy body), and anna-maya kosha (food-eating or "ordinary" fleshy body) develop.

Middle Months
Jiva ("the one who lives") enters the causal body.

Late Months
Continued gestation of the fetal body toward fragile sufficiency by the sixth or seventh month as kundalini completes its formation of the body and recedes into dormancy at the spinal base; the more

generic "life energy" or prana of the prana-maya kosha (udana, samana, apana, prana, vyana circuits of head, gut, elimination, respiration, and circulation, respectively) continues as the flesh body's (anna-maya kosha's) sustaining force, as nourished with earthly foods and oxygen via the umbilical connection to mother.

Birth
First breath, umbilicus cut, eye contact, reaching, *anahata-nada* (polysignificant neuroendocrinal developmental utterances that are related to the yogic developmental breathing of pranayama—a "crying" that can be overassociated with adult anguish); psychomotor developmental movements akin to sahaja yoga asanas and hand and finger mudras emerge; nursing.

First Decade
Teething, walking, play; glandular secretions underlying character-building sentiments of yamas and niyamas (specific character-trait cultivations and moral observances) begin to fructify within the child's social and family context; language appropriates mind and tongue, and psychosomatic enculturation occurs; prepubescent pranotthana sustains the child's growth, visible as "the glow of childhood."

Second Decade
Childhood pranotthana intensifies, fomenting genital puberty/ fertility as the embodiment of infinite future incarnations; hormonal-temporal urgencies quicken as gender-oriented desires; intermediate puberty of yama and niyama neuroendocrine secretions emerge, with emphasis upon developmentally sublimative brahmacharya ashrama; basic prepubescent asana and pranayama emerge in willful and minimal sahaja or "spontaneous" forms.

Third Decade
Karma yoga, the life of responsible action and character maturation; the mind matures beyond childhood's scattered vitality

toward *pratyahara*, the capacity for sustained perceptions and careful attention; second ashrama of householder family creation of *pravritti* path or the solitary mystic *nivritti* path is entered; diverse worldly involvements are varyingly dharmic or aligned with the endogenous maturational process; the maturations known as the "good neighbor" or "well-balanced person" emerge; if pranotthana continues to intensify via dharmic life, the postgenital puberties of *urdhva-retas* quicken.

Fourth Decade

Dharana begins: the dawning of awesome awareness of/as endless impermanence and soteriological radiance-secretions of *tejas* ("brilliance-radiance" of spiritual zeal) and *virya* ("virtue-secretion/ radiance") emerge; advanced asanas, mudras, bandhas (inner yearning-contractions), and shaking mature the body for more intensified energies; *dhyana* begins: devout and unwavering appreciation of the flow of endless impermanence and the poignant grace of life; the puberties of the linguistic anatomy (tongue, larynx, brain centers) underlying further meditative/ mental maturation begin: *simha-asana* (tongue-extended "lion pose" seen in certain goddess images) and *nabho* mudra (inward-turned tongue, "heaven-delight gesture") precursors of khecari mudra (tongue curls back in delight above the soft palate), initiating the puberties of the hypoglossal larnyx, hypothalamus, pituitary and pineal glands; anahata-nada, known rudimentarily as "speaking in tongues" and resounding in the sacred chantings of numerous cultures, emerge.

Fifth Decade

The desire-self identity matures toward the immortal soul-self identity; auras (auric glow of spiritual maturity) emerge; continuation of khecari mudra, culminating in the subtle pineal secretion-radiance of soma or amrita ("immortal-time essence," revitalizing melatonin-like, endorphin-like hormone).

Kundalini awakens, initiating the puberties of the six chakras and the inner heat; *shambhavi mudra*, the puberty of the eyes and the pineal leading to inner vision of the soul's (melatonin-like) radiances and the matter-time-space-scent-taste-light-bliss continuum emerges; *unmani* mudra, the "delight-gesture of free consciousness" cerebral puberty emerges; internal or breathless respiration in the *akashic* ethers emerges; grandchildren emerge for householders, and then the third ashrama of retirement and the fourth ashrama of worldly renunciation; great-grandchildren emerge for householders.

Sabija-Samadhi **and** *Nirbija-Samadhi*
Fully matured origin-consciousness with, and then without, future waverings emerges.

Repeat Twenty-Five to Fifty Incarnations
Divya sharira: exceedingly rare full maturation of the ensouled body as an immortal "divine light body" of extraordinary longevity and *moksha*, complete maturation of all soul-body potentials.

LINEAGE OF RECENT EXEMPLARS
I will close this essay with a brief look at the lineages of some of those who have achieved the ultimate spiritual evolution of Mother Kundalini. The most recent appearances of a saint of this maturity (at the turn of the century and in the early 1950s) I have come across were documented in the book *Hariakhan Baba: Known, Unknown* by Baba Hari Dass [10], a lifelong Indian yogi residing in Santa Cruz, California. Other references to this Babaji, or perhaps to his guru, appear in Marshall Govindan's *Babaji* [11] and Satyeswarananda's *Babaji*. [12]

Known by various names, Satyeswarananda and Baba Hari Dass maintain that Hariakhan Baba is the several thousand year old "Babaji" who initiated Neem Karoli Baba, known as Richard Alpert's (Ram Dass's) guru, and the lineage of Paramahansa Yogananda, one of the first yogis to come to the West at the turn of the century.

Yogananda attained additional esteem after his death in 1952 when his corpse showed no signs of decomposition, even after some twenty days. According to Los Angeles Mortuary director H. T. Rowe's notarized statement:

> The absence of any visual signs of decay in the dead body of Paramahansa Yogananda offers the most extraordinary case in our experience. . . . No physical disintegration was visible in his body even twenty days after death. . . . No indication of mold was visible on his skin, and no visible desiccation (drying up) took place in the bodily tissues. This state of perfect preservation of a body is, so far as we know from mortuary annals, an unparalleled one. . . . No odor of decay emanated from his body at any time. . . . There is no reason to say that his body had suffered any visible physical disintegration at all. [13]

According to the late Vinit-muni of Pransali, India, Hariakhan Baba/Babaji is also Lakulisha (150 CE, born in Kayavarohan, India; organizer of the Pashupata sect), who initiated Swami Kripalvand (whose corpse showed no signs of rigor mortis during the first two days before his burial) [14] in the early 1950s, (and perhaps Babaji initiated many other unknown yogis). His image remains embossed in the Elephanta Island carvings (dated 500–600 CE) near Bombay, which purport the "practicing [of Kundalini] Yoga as the origin and culmination of all life." [15]

To help Westerners grasp the significance of these carvings, Indologist James Forbes ranks them with the pyramids of Egypt; I would also include the mound at Golgotha and Darwin's Galapagos Islands research. The *Vayu Purana*, the *Kurma Purana,* and the *Linga Purana* discern Lakulisha (or "Nakulisha") as the twenty-eighth incarnation of this immortal embodiment, known first as Shiva, Lord of Yoga.

An Illuminated Channel from the Ocean of Consciousness

GENE KIEFFER

Gopi Krishna (1903–1984) was one of the most formative figures in the kundalini landscape of the West. He authored eighteen books, including The Secret of Yoga *and* The Biological Basis of Religion and Genius. *Here, Gene Kieffer, founder of the Kundalini Research Foundation, provides a foreword to an interview with Gopi Krishna, discussing Krishna's unique understanding of academia and science through his kundalini consciousness. Having worked with Gopi Krishna for fourteen years, Kieffer provides insight into Krishna's background, his kundalini experience, and how his new wisdom relates to the scientific endeavors of the modern era. This essay serves as an introduction to a never-before-published interview with Gopi Krishna (which follows), in which he expands on his own experience of transcendental consciousness, his candid opinion of modern psychology and science, and his belief about the predetermined destination of the human brain and consciousness.*

KUNDALINI IS THE most mysterious force in the universe, bar none. Compared with the behavior of infinitely small particles such as quarks and neutrinos, or with astronomical objects such as black holes and quasars, all of which mystify scientists to no end, kundalini tops them all by many light years.

Gopi Krishna, who attributed his kundalini awakening at the age of thirty-four to a practice of single-minded concentration, a disciplined moral code, favorable heredity, and most especially grace, said nearly fifty years later, "The Mystery surrounding Kundalini is so deep that the human intellect can never hope to fathom it. It is, in other words, the profound Mystery behind the universe."[1]

Stephen Hawking, the world's most respected theoretical physicist for more than thirty years, once thought that if science pushed just a little further and a little harder, it would be possible to "know the mind of God." But a couple of other theoreticians convinced him he had been wrong—not about everything, but about one of his most fundamental theories: what happens when "information" crosses the "event horizon" of a black hole. He said it would disappear forever, but now he admits he was wrong.

When the Large Hadron Collider goes into operation at CERN in Switzerland, sometime in 2009, launching what is being called the "God particle" hunt, scientists hope to solve one or two longstanding puzzles about the nature of the universe and how it came into being. No doubt they will discover some extraordinary new facts, but I believe they will come away more baffled than ever. Does this mean that we may never discover all of the great mysteries?

Never say never. For as long as our sun continues to shine forth as it does now, the human race will continue to steadily climb up the ladder of evolution. We may colonize other planets similar to earth, and the path of evolution will still be beckoning us to keep on climbing. There is no end. For us humans, evolution has hardly begun.

After he had awakened kundalini, Gopi Krishna hovered between life and death for nearly a dozen years, with no help available to show him what to do to lessen his agony. His story, a classic tale of survival, has been published in many languages all over the world. Although he lived in India, where just about every yogi has some knowledge of the phenomenon, no one came forward to help him in any way.

In 1975, a three-day seminar on yoga, science, and man was held in New Delhi, sponsored by the government and several leading institutions of science, education, and yoga. On the final day, participants and observers were invited to ask questions of the principal speakers and panelists. A gentleman in the audience held up his hand and asked, "Would one of you please describe what it is like to be illuminated?" All eyes turned to Gopi Krishna for the answer. Nobody, including the yogis on stage, doubted that he was illuminated. Anyone who has read one of his more than twenty books on kundalini will agree that there is no other modern writer on kundalini with his command of knowledge on the subject of mystical ecstasy.

A person such as Gopi Krishna doesn't come on the world's stage by an accident of nature. His physical and mental torment for more than a decade after his awakening wasn't without purpose. He had to learn everything possible about the phenomenon so that he could pass it on to future generations.

His first book, *Kundalini: The Evolutionary Energy in Man,* was published in 1967, and it still stands as the primary source for all other writers on the subject. It may well be that nothing new will be added to the world's store of knowledge on kundalini for another two or three centuries, until the next specimen of illuminated consciousness appears on the stage.

We've all heard about autistic savants. Up until a few years ago, they were called idiot savants. There may be between fifty and a hundred of these extraordinary people in the world today. Many have appeared on television shows such as *60 Minutes.* And despite a growing number of institutes solely concerned with understanding the cause behind the phenomenon, very little is really known about it.

Take the case of Daniel Tammet in England. He can reel off the number for pi to 22,500 decimal places. When challenged by scientists to learn Icelandic, one of the most difficult languages in the world, he did just that in one week! Born January 31, 1979, he is known as a high-functioning autistic savant gifted with a facility for mathematical and language learning. In his memoir, *Born on a Blue Day*, he describes how having epilepsy, synesthesia, and Asperger's syndrome all deeply affected his childhood. Scientists will one day confirm that autistic savants have an active kundalini but that the cosmic *prana* is confined to a very small section of the brain. When they do, they will have proved that the epilepsy and Asperger's syndrome in Daniel Tammet's childhood were also caused by kundalini.

A "regular" genius, like Mozart, Michelangelo, or Shakespeare, is also born with kundalini active, but in his or her case the cosmic prana floods a much larger section of the brain. Some are great musicians, pianists, composers, artists, or mathematicians. Others, Isaac Newton, for example, are great scientists. Many geniuses are eccentric. But whether eccentric or perfectly normal, all geniuses were born as such.

Keeping this in mind, you can now begin to appreciate the phenomenon of illumination, a condition in which an even more concentrated form of cosmic prana permeates the entire brain— the Thousand-Petalled Lotus—whether the man or woman experiencing it was born with kundalini fully active or it became active at some later stage of life. As mentioned earlier, in Gopi Krishna's case, it happened when he was thirty-four.

The reason he did not become a great composer, linguist, or mathematician, or all three, as happens with some polymaths, is due to his impoverished circumstances. He was born in a mud hut in rural Kashmir, and there was never enough money to provide the necessities of life for his parents, two sisters, and himself. His mother never learned to read or write, and his own education continued only through the twelfth grade, after which he had to find full-time work as a clerk in a local government office to help care for the family.

Now try to picture several different kinds of savants all rolled up into one, and then combine some of those qualities with uncommon wisdom, genius, and prophetic vision: that is what kundalini can bestow on an ordinary person when all conditions are favorable and the Goddess is smiling. No amount of meditation, *pranayama,* or recitation of mantras can force open the door to cosmic consciousness. It has to be opened from the other side.

There is a kundalini yoga center not far from my home that regularly sends out announcements of its scheduled activities. This month's bulletin says that "Shakti or Kundalini awakening is available by appointment." Generally, *shaktipat* is harmless.

Before I met Gopi Krishna, I wasn't averse to paying for this sort of thing. I had purchased special mantras from high-level yogis, and I once traveled quite a distance to learn self-hypnosis, so I could slip through the door to superconsciousness for the equivalent of five hundred dollars in today's currency. It was the kind of superconsciousness known as "soul travel" or daydreaming. At the time, I must have thought it was worth the money, but not anymore. I have since learned something about Indian metaphysics.

The highest attainment for any human being is the experience of *samadhi,* or mystical vision. In that state, the subtle worlds of mind and prana become perceptible. Gopi Krishna describes prana as life energy, or as "the bewildering source behind the amazing organizations and instincts of living creatures." There is a different spectrum of prana for each form of life "with modifications for each individual of that form. Each distinct human personality reflects a distinct type of Pranic Spectrum. No two spectrums are alike in every respect, as there are no two personalities similar in every way."[2]

During the course of mystical ecstasy or samadhi, a new, more potent stream of prana enters the brain, creating a revolution in consciousness. "No words can express the grandeur and sublimity of the experience nor the happiness and serenity felt during Samadhi," Gopi Krishna says. "In rare cases, the experience can become a perennial feature of human life," meaning that one remains in that state during sleep and wakefulness, and even in dreams.[3] When awake in the sense that we normally understand the word, one is fully alert, just like any normal person.

In India, perennial ecstasy has been called the *Sahaja* or *Jiwan-Mukta* state. Gopi Krishna tells us that when he retired for the night to sleep, it was like waking up for the normal person. And when he awakened in the morning, it was just the opposite: as if he were dreaming. It's difficult if not impossible for us to imagine such a condition, except that we are told that in the sahaja state, one is completely different from an ordinary person but at the same time, all of the senses and the mind are superalert.

Gopi Krishna could enter another world, another dimension of consciousness, at will. Perhaps I've already said too much, because I must confess that I know nothing of mystical consciousness from my own experience. His prolific literary output itself is ample evidence of what superconsciousness can achieve in a very short period of time. Whenever he turned his attention to work, he was capable of writing on a variety of subjects: on moral values, the demands of leadership in the atomic age, and so forth.

The word *pandit* means learned man. There are countless pandits in India, but as far as I know, none is illuminated. Gopi Krishna didn't become a pandit because he earned an advanced degree at a university, as is generally the case. Rather, he became illuminated, and then it was only natural that the pandits of Kashmir would refer to him as Pandit.

Krishna says the whole ocean of prana that sustains the human race today is in a state of flux. "It is this motion in the fundamental element of life which is behind the evolution of the brain and the transformation of consciousness."[4]

The human world is advancing in knowledge because prana is moving in that direction, he has written. "And this movement or flux, in turn, causes subtle evolutionary changes in the brain which we are not able to measure but will do so when the mystery shrouding prana is solved. This will also solve the riddle of talent, genius, and extrasensory perception, because a well-marked change in prana is responsible for these conditions, too."[5]

He says further that the evolutionary change occurring in the race now is irresistible. "All of us are sailing in the same mysterious ship without knowing for which port it is bound." So, now, at last, we should know the purpose of life, which is to achieve cosmic consciousness. It may take another century or two before scientists are in on the secret. They will come to know it sooner or later, however, but only after it is common knowledge. "Many that are first shall be last; and the last shall be first." (Matthew 19:30).

We cannot imagine the mental state of a musical or mathematical genius, just as a child cannot imagine the mind of an adult. It is almost like a cat suddenly waking up from a nap with a newly planted human brain in its skull. Gopi Krishna had to deal with that kind of radical shift in his consciousness when kundalini unexpectedly shot up from the base of his spine and into his brain on Christmas Day in 1937. No wonder a decade passed before he was able to begin writing books—first his mind/brain had to become stabilized. His books, each in its own way, are of such a profound nature that one should be prepared to change his or her thinking when reading them. If the academic world were enticed into reading them, scholars, too, would find themselves as unprepared for his revelations as the cat with a human brain.

So why would anyone want to become knowledgeable about kundalini? The answer is that this kind of knowledge is more empowering than any other. It is not mere information. Words from the pen of an illuminated person are more potent than LSD. They cause major beneficial changes at the subatomic levels of the brain.

If being in the state of samadhi only meant having a blissful holiday traipsing through the galaxies, that would be one thing. But a superconscious person is able to gather up and bring back to the so-called real-world priceless gems of knowledge that could be applied to everyday life. Most of these gems have yet to be appreciated; they await the dawn of a New Age in which the significance of illumination is made the core curriculum of a doctoral program at MIT or Harvard.

Think of Nikola Tesla and countless other great inventors, writers, or engineers who received valuable hints and clues in their periods of reverie that could be incorporated into their creative projects. Once kundalini is widely understood as the biological mechanism or channel through which a person may obtain boons of every kind from the cosmic ocean of consciousness, scientists will eagerly begin to investigate the phenomenon in a serious way.

I will close this brief introduction to Gopi Krishna and his discoveries with the words of an illuminated poet who lived in the Kashmir Valley more than a thousand years ago. He wrote a hymn of praise addressed to "Super-Energy" or the Goddess Kundalini. The identity of the poet is unknown. Gopi Krishna translated the original Sanskrit text, called *Panchastavi* (a hymn in five parts), which consists of about two hundred stanzas, one of which is reproduced here. If you read it through slowly and then ponder its importance for the evolution of future generations, you will be doing your progeny a great favor:

> O, Thou, who art the Code of Conduct [in religious observances], the Repository of all Knowledge fit to be comprehended, the source of all Established Doctrines, the author and the Quintessence of the Vedas, the Mine of Wonders, the Origin of the Universe, the Controlling Power of Lord Shiva, the Spring-Head of all Morality, the Abode of Shiva-Consciousness and the Instrument of Unity with Him, O Mother, who art [inseparable from] Shiva, easily attainable through humility, bestow on us [the boon of] unparalleled devotion to Thee.
>
> —Panchastavi, V, 21

The Goal of
Consciousness Research

GOPI KRISHNA

▬▬▬▬▬▬

This interview with Gopi Krishna was conducted in New Delhi in the late 1970s by a reporter for a UNESCO publication in India. The reporter's name is unknown.

For more than a decade now, you have been writing books on consciousness and evolution and about mystical experience. Could you restate your positions in clear-cut terms and point out some of the reasons that might have stood in the way of their acceptance by scientists so far?

The main reason is that there is still a great deal of confusion about the phenomenon known as mystical ecstasy. The general impression is that it is just an altered state of awareness, comparable to the states brought about by intoxicants, mind-altering drugs, hypnosis, biofeedback, autosuggestive conditions, and the like. Even an authority like William James has been in error in the comparison he has made between mystical ecstasy and the states induced by wine and nitrous oxide.

What is the reason for this?

The reason is simple. The transcendental and transhuman nature of mystical experience are a still-uncharted province for scholars.

There is a wide gulf between scholarship and mystical vision. The staggering nature of the vision and the revolution it brings about in the life and thinking of one who is blessed with it—and the light it throws on the problems of existence—are all beyond the power of the intellect to grasp.

Can you explain this further?

Intellectual study is like the data gathered by a dreamer of the dream world in which he dwells for a while. The mystical vision is like the awareness gained by one when awake. I must make this clear, with all the emphasis at my command and in full conformity to what has been as emphatically stated by mystics of the past, that the objective world disappears, like a phantom, in the illuminating blaze of mystical consciousness. The Reality which is unveiled in the duration of the experience is beyond the grasp of the intellect and the power of language to describe.

Since it is impossible to describe, how can you hope to convince scientists that there is still something beyond their comprehension?

It is the same as though the intellectual prodigies of the past, such as Shakespeare and Bacon, were expected to know of the awful force of the atom. Most of the present-day intellectuals believe that they are almost at the frontiers of knowledge, but they have no inkling that the real quest of man has yet to begin. All the knowledge and experience they have gained, all the discoveries they have made, and all the inventions wrought, so far, have been a preparation for the next step in his progress, which is the exploration of his own mind, to answer the Riddle of his being.

It seems to me that what you are saying points to a new direction for human effort and thought.

Exactly. It is entirely beyond the imagination of our contemporaries. Hence, it is but natural that many of them should consider what I say as incredible and fantastic. We cannot expect a more favorable response from the learned, because they are no more informed about the phenomenon, on which I dwell, than the ordinary class of human beings. The intellect, proud of her knowledge, is seldom ready to believe that there are worlds and regions beyond her reach.

What about present-day research on consciousness? Isn't some progress being made in this area of science?

Research on consciousness, as it is being carried out today, can easily be compared to the investigation done by a dreamer of the mental condition of the personalities in his dream. For one who lacks the least awareness about himself, however erudite he might be, the issue will always arise—and on what? How can one who is ignorant of his own mind stalk forth to study the mind of another who is as ignorant of himself as he?

Is that why the *Upanishads* say that the efforts of the unenlightened, however scholarly they might be, are like the blind leading the blind when it comes to guiding others in the knowledge of the Self?

Yes. According to the Indian Masters who have contributed most to the study of the mind, *Turiya,* or the fourth state of consciousness, experienced in the mystical trance, is the real state of human awareness and the other three below it—namely, deep sleep, dream, and the normal wakeful state—are delusive. The normal state lends substance to a false appearance which hides the true Reality.

The research on consciousness should mean study of one's Self?

In truth, this is what the ancient sages and seers proceeded to do in their search for enlightenment. It is for this reason that during recent times there has been hardly any new addition to the brilliant galaxy of enlightened prophets and sages of the past. This is also the reason why there has been no fresh accumulation of knowledge of the mystical state of consciousness. When our study of the outer world, during the same period, has yielded such a rich harvest in transforming the life of human beings, why do we find the doors tightly shut in our exploration of the inner realm?

This is the crux of the problem, I'm sure. What is your explanation?

As one who has been granted a brief glimpse into this profound Mystery, I can say with confidence that no amount of objective study of consciousness, undertaken over the next hundreds of years, with the methods employed at present, would lead the learned any nearer to the solution of the enigma. On the contrary, except for the hundreds of volumes of confusing data that would result, the investigation would make it even more bewildering than before.

But what is the reason for this?

Research on consciousness demands a new approach because it marks a new phase in the career of humanity. Evolving man must now shift his attention from the outer to the inner world, make his own body the laboratory, and reverently approach the Spirit within to instruct him in the rudiments of this science.

Many people are eagerly waiting for this. There seems to be an instinctive longing to return to nature, for instance, and to break away from the highly complex, hectic life of today. Isn't all this an indication of a coming revolution in thinking?

The stage is being set for this radical change in the direction of human effort from the outer to the inner world. The learned are not able to read the signs, as the future is entirely shut from their view, and they have no idea of the coming revolution in the life of humanity as a complement to the evolutionary change that has occurred within.

Can you describe this evolutionary change that you believe has occurred within?

It will take some time, but it has to do with the existence of a potential in the brain that can transform human life and bestow undreamed-of intellectual, supersensory, and artistic gifts to individuals in a manner beyond imagination at present.

But as you have already said, most intellectuals have no grounding in mysticism, so they continue to apply the same methods of analysis and criticism to which they are accustomed in other branches of knowledge.

It is a sad commentary on the academic life of our time that a subject treated with respectful attention and reverential regard by the greatest intellectuals of the past, including such giants as Plato and Newton, should appear so trivial and unimportant to them that they deem it beyond their dignity to study it with the care and attention which it needs.

You are considered to be a rebel to many of the popular ideologies of our time. Perhaps if you were to put your ideas in the language of the intellectuals, they would be more acceptable to the readers in the United States.

I have made no secret in my books of the fact that my education has been poor and that all I am writing is from inspiration, which needs a dive into the depths of my own being to receive it. I have never made any claims of infallibility and have repeatedly said that every word I am writing should be weighed and put to rigid test before it is accepted. It is for this reason that I am so keen to lay the foundation of an Experimental Center, to validate my views about the evolutionary mechanism in the human frame.

Your ideas need to be expressed by scholars who are trained in the language of academics. Without such credentials, it might be impossible to make any real headway in the West.

Either that or else what we need are the resources to broadcast our views far and wide. I am putting my ideas in the language of the common man and woman rather than in that of the intellectuals for the simple reason that, in the first place, I am not capable of writing in the discursive style peculiar to scholars. Secondly, I wish my message to be easily intelligible to all those who read it.

Do you believe it is possible to communicate your ideas in the language of modern psychology?

Perhaps not. Modern psychology is bristling with internal conflicts and controversies, and also the pulls and pressures from individual authorities, each contradicting the other. How can a study based on a mistaken conception of mind, with excessive emphasis on the beast and chilling silence over the God in man, provide a suitable vehicle for explaining the profundities of consciousness or its triumphant march from the subhuman to the superhuman plane?

Then what is the solution?

The moment it is demonstrated that the human brain is still in a state of organic evolution in a preplanned direction, then not only the current theory of evolution but also psychological systems, based primarily on the animal origin of mind and not on its infinitely intelligent cosmic character, will come toppling to the earth. How can we reconcile the divine nature of consciousness with some of the revolting explanations offered by psychologists?

The universe is a vast amphitheater, and the dramas enacted by consciousness, on this stage from one end to the other, infinitely varied in plot and action, are yet closely interwoven and interconnected in a manner far beyond the grasp of the puny human intellect. Mankind will have to rise to dizzy heights of evolution before she can begin to comprehend the bewildering play of Life.

From Euclidean space we have come to the curved space of Relativity. But there are already indications to show that this is not the end. Who knows what new surprises are in store for astrophysicists in the years to come? It is a fallacy to suppose that we have come to the end of the knowledge of the mind.

You claim to be in possession of extraordinary knowledge, is that not true?

I have never laid any claim to a higher position than the one I possess. In fact, I have emphatically tried my utmost to make it clear that mystical experience does not represent a vision of God but only a passage into a new dimension of consciousness in which it wears an aspect of glory and sovereignty which is not present on the human plane. I have also repeatedly asserted that in all other aspects I belong to the class of normal human beings with the frailties and vanities common to human nature.

Nowhere in my writings have I made any claim to sainthood or nearness to God or to a superhuman stature, as is often done by godmen to point out the gulf that exists between them and the normal run of human beings.

But you do claim to reside in the transcendental state of consciousness, do you not?

Yes, but it has always been my endeavor to make it clear that the transcendental state of consciousness, experienced in the form of ecstasy by prophets and mystics throughout the past, does not signify a special favor from the Deity. It is only a more extended dimension of the perceptual faculty towards which mankind is evolving irresistibly through the operation of an evolutionary mechanism in the body, designated as Kundalini by the Indian sages of the past.

As far as I know, this is the first time that mystical consciousness, or the organic mechanism leading to it, has been defined in this way, in the language of reason, divested of the supernatural and mythical.

That is my view, exactly. I have, at the same time, made no secret of the fact that knowledge of Kundalini represents a monumental discovery of the illuminate of India, and that I am only presenting this knowledge in the language of modern science. I have also said that the interpretations I am placing on it would be beyond my capacity but for a strange dispensation of fate, beyond comprehension, by which I became the participant in an experience that unfolded the secret to me.

Secret? Can you expand on this a bit?

What I am trying to emphasize in all my work is that we have our existence in two worlds, the world of matter and the world of mind. As the result of an inquiry that has persisted through a prodigious span of time—ever since the dawn of reason—we have come in possession of a huge amount of knowledge of the material world, which is available for study by anyone. But the study of the world of spirit needs entry into a new plane of consciousness and a supersensory channel of cognition, which are slowly coming into the possession of man.

The secret, then, is that mankind is slowly coming into possession of a supersensory channel of cognition, is that correct?

Yes, through evolution. This is the purpose of the mystical trance or the transhuman states of consciousness exhibited by the prophets and mystics of the world. They sung praises to the glory of God because the plane of being where they arrived is a plane of splendor, beauty, and transport, surpassing anything conceivable by a normal mind.

But even so, if I understand you correctly, it is a plane of being just a little higher than that of normal human beings.

You are perfectly correct. Those men and women who arrogate to themselves a transhuman stature or position of authority—as incarnations of, or surrogates for, the Divine—must have a poor opinion about the staggering dimensions of the universe or the inconceivable proportions of its Almighty Creator.

Because it is simply an evolutionary advance of the normal state of consciousness?

Yes. This attitude could be justified in the prophets, sages, and seers of the past, when the earth alone bounded the vision of man and he had no idea of what gigantic worlds lie beyond, and what a countless host of colossal suns and planets dwells in space. But from a godman of today, the statements of the kind which are made in the Scriptures of the past should be an affront to the intelligence of anyone who has even a passing idea about the extent of the universe or possibility of other, far superior, forms of life residing in it. There are some, even among the learned, who believe in such self-concocted tales, but they scoff at the rational explanations which I offer.

What about the future of humankind?

From my point of view, the future luminaries of the race, adorned with transhuman consciousness, would still be occupied with the exploration of the Mystery of Creation in the higher, to us, imperceptible planes of being, in the same way as we are now occupied with the exploration of the material universe. The present-day concepts about mind, its behavior, urges, and appetites, are mere capricious intellectual excursions into a territory which needs another channel of cognition to explore.

I would like to know more about this other channel of cognition.

You said yourself that it was a plane of being that is a little higher than that of normal human beings, and that is perfectly correct. But it is nothing to merit comparison or equality with the infinite majesty and splendor of the Lord. It is a variation of almost the same kind as we observe when we rise in the scale of life from the lower species to the higher ones.

It amuses me to find that people in general, including scholars, sometimes, raise mystics and enlightened saints to the stature of gods who cease to be humans, belonging to a world of superhuman dimensions and possibilities, where they can defy the laws of nature, change the fate of common men and women, or do whatever they please.

This is a serious error which stands as an impediment in the understanding of the mystical trance and in placing this extraordinary state of mind on a rational footing. It is simply the addition of another channel of perception, designed by Nature for every human being.

But you still insist that it is necessary for science to undertake research on consciousness?

There will soon be a time when the evolution of consciousness will be taken up by scholars in all its different aspects: spiritual, psychological, sociological, and biological. When once the experiment I propose is confirmed, there will be no subject, I am sure, which will receive as much sustained attention from scholars of every shade and color, and the rank and file of science, as this.

But the most colossal task in front of the erudite would be to explain the evolution of mind in terms of the organic evolution of the brain. As far as I can see, it shall take long spans of time to cover each single step in the territory of consciousness.

Then you do welcome the efforts of scholars and psychologists to write on consciousness, to the best of their knowledge and skill.

Of course, I welcome it most certainly. But in fairness to all, I must point out that except in the case of those who have experienced the transformation, no attempt made by a scholar, merely with the exercise of his intellect, however versatile and learned he might be, can fathom the mystery.

How does Eternal Consciousness come to be embodied and then rise, step by step, through aeonian spans of time, to the realization of its own sovereignty? This is a riddle so profound that it is hard even to gauge its proportions. I must also add that present-day ideas about psychology, which emanated from Freud and others, offer only short-range explanations.

These explanations will be subject to radical change from time to time as more and more knowledge is gained by the illuminate of the future about the nature and working of the mind and the organ of its expression, the brain.

Your opinion of modern psychology is rather unflattering.

I have written extensively on this subject, but we can compare the present views of psychologists to the ideas of alchemists before the modern science of chemistry came into existence. The human intellect, not unoften, takes delight in providing explanations even for those phenomena which are beyond its probe, as, for example, the existence of God and the origin of the universe, the nature of the soul and life after death. These eternal riddles have strongly drawn the human mind from the dawn of reason to this day without ever finding the right answer that could solve them once and for all. This is also the case with the riddle of the mind.

You believe that the experiment you propose will furnish the solution?

It is my endeavor to divest mystical ecstasy of ancient superstition and modern intellectual confusion both, by drawing attention to the biological factors responsible for it. Because this objectification of the phenomenon has never been attempted before, the academic world is still unaware or incredulous of it. That shows the entirely unsuspected nature of the disclosures made.

From my point of view, mystical ecstasy is a human experience—the outcome of an organic process at work in the brain—which signifies the first beginning of transhuman capacities in man. Except for the organic changes occurring in the subtle levels of the neuronic structures, science, as it exists today, can have no direct knowledge of the subjective nature of this experience.

If that is the case, then no intellectual formulations about it are possible at this time.

That is correct.

Your writings, to summarize briefly, are primarily confined to the evolution of the mind. Isn't this what others have said?

I do not say that the human mind is evolving towards an undefined summit as, for instance, Teilhard de Chardin and others have said. What I firmly assert is that human consciousness is evolving towards a predetermined target, which I have experienced, and that this target is the mystical or illuminated state attained by thousands of mystics and enlightened human beings in the past, and that the religious scriptures of mankind are a harvest of the revelations received from a Higher Intelligence in this state of exalted being. What I further affirm is that the human brain is evolving towards this state of transhuman perception, through the activity of an organic mechanism, named Kundalini by the ancients, whose existence can be demonstrated with the methods known to science.

This is a monumental assertion. Science has been attempting to discover this organic mechanism for decades, without, insofar as I know, any success whatsoever.

From all this, it follows that I am trying to place the whole domain of religion and mystical ecstasy on the footing of a regular science, demonstrable with empirical methods of which the laboratory has to be the human body itself.

Has any thinker, scientist, or religious teacher, present or past, thrown a challenge of this kind?

I frankly know of none. There is no need for me to use dubious intellectual methods to carry my point. One successful experiment is sufficient to clear the confusion and confirm what I say.

Your writings include a good deal about other mental

phenomena in addition to mystical ecstasy. Could you elaborate on this?

My whole philosophy can be summed up in a few words. Therefore, it is not necessary that my books should be read and reread to arrive at the conclusions I have drawn from my experience. I also aver that the commonly known abnormal and paranormal states of mind—such as retardation, neurosis, or insanity, on the one hand, and exceptional talent or paranormal gifts on the other—all proceed from the working of the evolutionary mechanism; and that with advanced knowledge of this lever the aforesaid evils, resulting from its malfunctioning, can be cured or obviated and the latter highly precious attributes cultivated at will.

This is a new and original contribution to the knowledge of man, I believe.

To the best of my belief no other philosopher or mystic of the past has given the same interpretation to mystical experience and put a cut-and-dried formula before humankind. I am not putting forward an intellectual dissertation based on mere erudition and logic; I am submitting a concrete proposal based on personal study of the phenomenon, for experiment, to validate the conclusions drawn by me, which are of colossal importance for the race.

If this is the case, and I have no reason to doubt what you say, why haven't these disclosures been greeted with acclaim?

The reason is because the ideas expressed by me are new and original, which therefore need time to take root in the common mind, and, secondly, because they strongly militate against some of the current conceptions or misconceptions of both orthodox science and religion.

How can the erudite, on either side, readily swallow the utterances of one who proclaims loudly that matter is a mirage, Darwin was wrong, Freud mistaken, consciousness is All—that humanity is on her way to this awareness in the beatific state, that the great illuminate were not and could not be the favorites of the Almighty, and that mystical experience does not represent an encounter with God but only a vision of the divinity in man?

Then what is needed, urgently, as far as I can see, is something like a New Manhattan Project to try to scientifically validate your theory.

It is only by a deep study of my thesis that it can dawn on an unbiased intellect that there can be no other interpretation which can synthesize the diversity of religious experience and outlook, serve as a connecting link between religion and science, and bring science back from a lopsided, entirely materialistic view of the universe, towards a more rational and more comprehensive philosophy of Creation. This philosophy is one in which matter and mind figure as the two aspects of one incomprehensible Reality dimly perceptible in another dimension of consciousness of which religion is the still-growing child.

It must be extremely frustrating to you to spend year after year writing your views down in books, only to see decades pass without any signs of recognition on the part of the scientific community.

I have been watching the whole drama of my life without a tinge of regret for the coldness I have received for the knowledge given out by me while living virtually in the jaws of death. I am a frail human being myself, and I know the frailties of my other fellow human beings.

Had the secrets disclosed by me come from the lips of a distinguished personality in science, the discovery would have

resounded throughout the world. Or were a leading personality, like the president of the United States, to affirm publicly the
importance of the disclosure, all the newspapers of the earth
would open their columns to the message and the learned fall
over each other in expressing their high appreciation of it. It was
only through the conversion of Asoka the Great in India, and
Emperor Constantine in Rome, that Buddhism and Christianity
became dominant faiths in the East or West.

**Apparently the support of temporal authority was always
needed to push forward a spiritual creed.**

That is entirely correct. Left at the mercy of the populace, including
the learned, without the enthusiastic support of ardent protagonists,
no new idea or line of thought diametrically opposite to prevailing
conceptions can find wide acceptance. At best, it would only serve
as a topic for perfunctory discussion here and there.

Even the media, which are supposed to keep track of all new
developments, would give a wide berth to it for its uncommon
nature and touch it only if it is mentioned by one in authority, not
because they have become enamored of it but because it suits their
purpose to give publicity to the utterances of a great personage.

Such is the opacity of the human intellect when face-to-face
with a new revelation, showing the way out of a confusing labyrinth of thought. Ours is not a message that can be thoroughly
grasped or made universal in the course of a few years, but it must
roll across long spans of time to gather the momentum necessary
for it to become a universally recognized philosophy and science.

What if you had your wish, what would it be?

With all my heart, I wish that in the exploration of consciousness,
mystical tradition—not the methods of traditional psychology—
were to be followed to bring a correct awareness of its evolution to

the world. Intellectual dissertations, beyond a certain limit, would only lead to confusion and chaos in a province where firsthand experience is necessary to know the truth. Like the exploration of the sky, intellectual exercise can carry us only a short distance. After that, the use of the telescope becomes absolutely necessary for correct knowledge of the position. In the same way, for the study of the inner firmament, a dive into the depths of one's being is essential to know the reality.

The inexpressible?

Music and poetry provide a better language for expressing the profundities of consciousness than logic. This is the reason why prayers are sung. The state of mind produced under the spell of a beautifully sung prayer is more expressive of the indefinable world of consciousness than volumes of reasoned prose. The problem is that it is hard to make an intellectual accept the position that his territory ends at the very beginning of the mystical trance.

It is characteristic of the intellect that she is seldom prepared to accept defeat and is often overconfident of her ability to know all that can be known. It is only when face-to-face with the unbelievable splendor of the Mystical Vision that, hushed into silence at the awesome majesty of the Reality unfolded, the tittle-tattle of this irrepressible gossip, that always talks of this sublime experience from a distance, comes to an end and her propensity, in the words of Pascal, of putting two and two together and make it five, is lost.

Perhaps science will be forced to take up the research project, just as it was forced to experiment on the atom bomb some forty years ago, when the threat of its falling into the hands of an enemy was urgent.

Time will prove the correctness of our stand. I am not the last of the line that has already appeared to beseech their contemporaries to look within. Others will rise to repeat what has already been said and win confirmation for the disclosures made, if lacking still. No power on earth can prevent truth from spreading when time for it has come, just as no power can stop the sun from bathing the earth in light when the night is over.

The verdict on what I have revealed does not rest in the hands of a few scholars in a particular country, living now or who may rise in the future. The secret we have disclosed, not by choice but at the decree of fate, is not limited by time and place but covers the whole earth and is of everlasting value for the race.

It doesn't disturb you, then, that still more time is needed for a better grasp of your message?

Not at all. I know what I am up against in the claim I make and the truth I reveal. The day will come when those whose intuition was right in accepting this disclosure are vindicated.

Would you please close by describing your state of consciousness?

For nearly forty years, I have been undergoing a most extraordinary experience which is now a constant source of wonder and joy to me. The experience is not at all like anything I tasted of life from the day I began to remember, as a child, to my thirty-fourth year. It is not like anything of science, or art, or philosophy, of which I have read to this day. The only class of human beings in whom I find a parallel of this experience are the mystics of the East and West, but here, too, there are differences which I am trying my best to resolve.

In describing this experience, I always thoroughly weigh every word that I use, because I feel myself under a solemn obligation to give expression to what is the strictest truth. The incredible nature of my transformation lies in this, that every moment of my life I live in two worlds. One is the sensory world which we all share together—the world of sight, touch, smell, taste, and sound. My reactions to this world are the same as of other human beings. The other is an amazing supersensory world to which I first found entrance in 1937, and which, to the best of my knowledge, I share alone or, perhaps, with extremely few others unknown to me. I do not say this to claim singularity but only as a statement of fact, because to this day I have not come across any individual claiming the same peculiarity.

I am always conscious of a luminous glow, not only in my interior but pervading the whole field of my vision during the hours of my wakefulness. I literally live in a world of light. It is as if a light were burning in my interior, filling me with a luster so beautiful and so ravishing that my attention is again and again drawn towards it. In fact, it is the normal state of my perception now. Light, both within and without, and a distinct music in my ears, are the two prominent features of my transformed being. It is as if, in my interior, I live in a charming, radiant, and melodious world. A sense of its fascination is always present in me.

I do not claim that I see God, but I am conscious of a Living Radiance both within and outside of myself. In other words, I have gained a new power of perception that was not present before. The luminosity does not end with my waking time. It persists even in my dreams. In every state of being—eating, drinking, talking, working, laughing, grieving, walking, or sleeping—I always dwell in a rapturous world of light. It is obvious that the self or observer in me has experienced a change and a new being has been born who is always enwrapped in a sheath of alluring light.

If my experience were confined to the state of luminosity alone, I would, in all probability, have kept the secret to myself and not divulged it far and wide as something exceptional that deserved attention. But this inner radiance is attended by another, even more amazing feature. The enchanting light I perceive both internally and outside, is alive. It pulsates with life and intelligence.

It is like an infinite Ocean of Awareness pervading my own small pool of consciousness within and the whole universe I perceive with my senses outside.

Much as I wish to do so, it is extremely difficult for me to draw a clear picture of this aspect of my experience. For me, the universe is alive; a stupendous Intelligence that I can sense but never fathom, looms behind every object and every event in the universe, silent, still, serene, and immovable like a mountain. It is a staggering spectacle.

Nothing would grant me greater happiness than to see the start of a massive wave of interest in the internal exploration of the cerebral Temple and the Divine Light within, which has been the aim of every spiritual and occult discipline ever practiced on the earth. It is my prayer that, considering the magnitude of the phenomenon that I am relating and its paramount importance for the race, the subject may not be a topic of frivolous controversy over trifles, but an issue for sober reflection and fruitful discussion, demanding a healthy exercise of the intellect on either side.

To divert attention towards a new subject of study is a hard task to achieve. In this case, it is more so as it involves a departure from the current methods employed for the study of mind. But there always are courageous men and women who, intuitively drawn to the new idea and convinced of its importance, dedicate their lives, their time, talent, and resources, to find out and disseminate the Truth. It is by the noble effort and heroic sacrifice of this rare class of benefactors that the race has progressed, so far, and shall continue to do so in the ages to come.

PART IV

Kundalini in Motion

Kundalini Yoga and Musings from Yogis

Thoughts on Kundalini

SWAMI SIVANANDA RADHA

Swami Sivananda Radha (1911–1995) is a respected author of over ten books, several of which have become classics in the field of yoga, most notably Light & Vibration: Consciousness, Mysticism & the Culmination of Yoga; Kundalini Yoga for the West; Foundation for Character Building, Courage, and Awareness; *and* Hatha Yoga: The Hidden Language.

Kundalini Yoga for the West *is not only one of Swami Radha's most famous books, it was one of the first books of its kind. In it, she introduced what she called in the subtitle "a foundation for character building, courage, and awareness" as it related to the pursuit of kundalini. Swami Radha has been a source of information for kundalini seekers for over twenty-five years, and in the following brief excerpt from* Kundalini Yoga for the West, *she discusses what she calls, "the fire of awareness, fire of wisdom" that comes with this energetic awakening. She also answers the questions: Does kundalini energy encourage indulgence in sex? Is psychic energy kundalini? How does kundalini announce itself to the higher self?*

THE SNAKE AROUND the neck of Saddasiva and the trident in His hand indicate for the first time the possible stirring of the Kundalini energy. The fire He holds, which is also symbolic of Kundalini, reminds us that "ignorance is burned in the fire of wisdom." Such, then, is the Kundalini Fire. It is a fire of awareness that burns ignorance so that life takes on a new meaning and all previous concepts are burned up. It turns the individual upside-down, into a new being. Some Scriptures speak of being clothed with a new garment. Others speak of being touched by the Divine Light, or having Divine Mother reveal Herself in splendor. This experience may be of minutely detailed intricacy or it may suddenly sweep the aspirant to a panoramic Vision of Light, leaving him or her humbled and awed. There are no words.

It now becomes evident why the character building of the previous chakras is so important. In the early stages, the aspirant's development is a matter of awareness and of dumping those concepts that can be let go without any emotional upset. This first state of awareness may have allowed the aspirant to recognize and deal with more complicated and deep-seated beliefs, which might bring such a feeling of release that certain psychic manifestations may result. This is not Kundalini. What it means is that we have become more skillful in dealing with the sensations that exist in daily life. As an illustration, if I drive a little Volkswagen and then I buy a Lincoln, even though I have felt very comfortable with my little Volkswagen, I will now have to make adjustments for the steering, parking, speed, size, etc., of the big new car. But when I have learned to maneuver it, I will be in control of a vehicle of much greater power and quality.

To assure this kind of control, clarification of the mind is necessary. By accepting the exercises in this book, skill and awareness will be built up that will enable the aspirant to handle any experiences that come without anxiety.

In the pursuit of Kundalini, a true guru will warn against developing exclusively in one area. In other words, if intellect has been developed at the cost of the senses and particularly the emotions, even the greatest intellect will be unable to handle the impact of the emotions when they strike. It is for that reason that the emphasis is on the equal development of the five senses, with particular attention to the mind, which is the operator at the control station of all sense perception.

The Higher Self may announce or signal this stirring of the Kundalini energy ahead of time in dreams. Therefore, it is again stressed to carefully watch dreams and be consistent in noting them down. We may not understand the message of a dream, but the Higher Self derives its energy and wisdom from the Universal Intelligence, and it will find other ways and means of sending the message it intends us to have. We must pay great attention to dreams and all insights so the message will not be missed.

When the Kundalini energy stirs there is indeed a change in temperature in the body, but it is not like a high fever or an unnatural body heat, although there have been situations where that was the case. It all depends on the preparations that have been made. The many mental acrobatics, the training of the mind, are necessary to make the mind and the senses, as well as the central nervous system, pliable to deal with those incredible realities.

The question arises of whether the source of information a psychic receives is Kundalini energy. This would only be true if the term "Kundalini" were used to mean all life. Then, even functioning on the level of unawareness would be Kundalini, which would make it more difficult to understand Kundalini as a latent power within each individual or, as the old texts call it, "the coiled-up serpent." The many exercises for the attainment of the manifestation of psychic energy and spiritual experiences show that the psychic can only function within the realm of his own development of the senses and the mind. So, again we conclude, this is not Kundalini.

Experiencing lights when in a meditative state is not Kundalini, but can be taken as encouragement that we are on the right road. These experiences should be carefully observed as they are indications of the development toward the unfolding of the potential that is within everyone.

The many schools of thought concerning Kundalini make for confusion rather than clarification. However, Kundalini is the essential energy in each, and the means of reaching that state of consciousness is irrelevant. Once a path is chosen, the process becomes important and the steps laid out must be followed with care.

Any yoga singled out by itself is taking a part out of the whole and, as with any part, it is incomplete. The encouragement to sexual indulgence, alleged to be the purpose of the Kamasutra by some who teach Kundalini Yoga, is to be regretted because it means ripping out from a very beautiful and delicately balanced system some small detail and considering it the whole. It is not indulgence in sex that the Kundalini energy encourages. However beautiful sex may be, it does not open the door to a state of higher consciousness. If that were so, the majority of people who believe in sexual excesses would all have achieved enlightenment.

The part that brahmacarya plays in spiritual development can be more easily understood if we use money as a symbol for spiritual power and its hoped-for manifestation. We often scatter energy in the same way that we scatter money and it is only by holding together a large amount of either one that a large project can be undertaken.

Kundalini will have to be pursued according to the aspirant's own natural inclinations. When all the groundwork has been done, when quality has been brought into other aspects of life, which itself is a development of human potential, and when the fringe benefits have been renounced (psychic manifestations), Kundalini will begin to stir because it has been safely awakened. In the process of doing the exercises, the control of desires and all sense perceptions has increased, inner security has developed, and therefore the awakening of Kundalini will not be a frightening, but a blissful experience.

The mythology of many a culture has strenuously tried to explain not only the purpose of life but what is this God/Energy. Modern scientists continue to question this, and for each the answer is expressed differently. The human mind cannot determine what Cosmic Energy is; it can only study its manifestation. This manifestation can be brought about in oneself and studied there. Whatever the Energy is—It can only reveal Itself.

The light of the sun reveals all things,
but the light of the sun can only reveal itself.

MEDITATION ON THE LIGHT

Sit in a comfortable position or in any yogic posture, but with your ankles crossed. Close your eyes, focus them on the space between the eyebrows. Do not start until your body is quiet (perhaps with the help of a little pranayama).

In previous chapters, you have become aware of the necessity of being spine conscious. Feel your spine and as you straighten it out, putting vertebra on vertebra, see at the base of your spine a Lotus bud slowly open and, like a dewdrop, a tiny pinpoint of Light slowly emerging from it . . . floating in the very center of the spine, in that hollow part, up and up and up, passing through the respective places of the other Lotuses, finally floating to the place where the spine joins the head . . . and in a gentle curve (like a shepherd's crook) this tiny pinpoint of Light floats over the pituitary and pineal. In your mind's eye, see a flash of Light illuminating the brain matter, becoming again the pinpoint of Light and traveling, back the same way, making the gentle curve, meeting the spine and floating gently and slowly in the very center of the hollow of the spine, passing through all the Lotuses, down to the very first one. When it has touched the center of that Lotus, the four petals close as if to protect something very precious. Stay quiet and allow to come to you whatever delicate intuitive perception may want to arise. Let it happen. If nothing specific happens, that is fine too. Let yourself be absorbed in that beautiful feeling of deep peace and harmony.

Do this exercise not more than once a day. This will prevent the forcing open of the Lotuses. The experience of the arising of the Kundalini energy can take place in such small steps, so gently, as never to upset or jar you into any anxiety. Also, it takes time to reach the ability to concentrate, and to be so alert and yet so relaxed at the same time. Patience and perseverence will lead to an unfolding that can be, if the instructions are followed as given, a very beautiful experience that gives a sense of knowing of the Divine. In terms of religion, let us remember that all saints tell us that man cannot command God. To pursue the Most High we may have to learn to wait in humility.

Heart

SWAMI SIVANANDA RADHA

The following essay is an excerpt from Light & Vibration: Consciousness, Mysticism & the Culmination of Yoga, *in which Swami Radha shares a meditation on the heart, the mind, and kundalini. In it she asks questions such as: What is the guru within? What is the light within? What is the potential for the mind?*

THE HEART SYMBOLIZES an ocean of Light and Consciousness. The Heart is symbolic for the centre of the spiritual being—limitless compassion and knowledge beyond intellect. The Heart inspires and is the symbol for love, the unconditional love that is only possible through the divine source.

There is a difference between the knowing of the intellect and the knowing of the Heart. Mental acrobatics can make the mind more flexible and prepare it to leap out of its confinement of established perceptions and meanings, which are really only opinions. The Heart does not need to participate in acrobatics. The Heart is limitless.

Compassion is limitless, even within our human confinement. But sometimes we can understand that unlimited power only if we personify it, which means limiting the Energy that we do not understand by putting it into a shape and form and giving it a name. Then the path of the Heart becomes more understandable to the mind and more accessible to us as individuals. We obtain a sense of closeness.

By personalizing the Divine, we may understand the compassion in reincarnation. Like a good father or mother, the Divine will say to its child, "This is wrong. You must not do it again. I will give you another chance." To be given another chance is probably the highest expression of compassion. We may be given chance after chance, many, many times. How many lifetimes? That depends on our response to divine compassion and our willingness to increase awareness, to increase the Light of understanding, and to thereby create a source of Light within ourselves, making that source a magnet to attract more Light. For me, the evidence of divine love is being given this chance to improve and to correct mistakes, especially if we have gone against the divine law. We may not even understand all of our mistakes in one lifetime.

In Kundalini symbolism there is a small lotus called the *kalpataru*, or the Wishing Tree underneath the Heart Lotus. It is symbolic of the process of discovering the Divine within, and the mysteries and the awesome powers of the mind. Perhaps it is only when we reach a certain stage of development that we wish to know the greater wisdom. That desire to know, like any other desire, is a persistent force—we must persist until we attain the fulfillment of this desire. But this type of desire does not fulfill itself quickly. We have to be very earnest. It is like climbing a mountain. When we start off, we camp more often. When we are closer to the summit and have freed ourselves from the extra baggage —untested beliefs and opinions—we travel much lighter. The final ascent, though, may be straight up on sheer rock or ice, with nothing to hold onto. But the vibrational power that is accumulated in the Heart will serve us well enough to complete the journey.

To understand the vibrational power accumulated in the Heart, compare it to emotional power. Emotional power arms us with weapons to attain the goal of emotional satisfaction whether that is finding a partner, robbing a bank, or becoming the president of a country. If emotions can generate this much power, we cannot underestimate the power of the Heart.

If we look at the Heart as symbolic of the essence of the vibrating cosmic rhythm—because the Heart has its own rhythm—we can see that many different manifestations emanate from the Heart. There are sources from which knowledge radiates to us. Some of these sources are not to be sought outside ourselves, but rather are to be discovered in our own Heart.

To understand the Divine as rhythm, you need to personally experience the cosmic rhythm of your own pulsating consciousness. Through practice of mantra, visualization, and personal reflection, your thinking can become truly vibrant. When Consciousness becomes vibrant, you become vibrant throughout your entire body. You may feel there is a new being within you and that many of the old obstacles simply fall away.

Can the vibrant, activated Consciousness within us also be perceptible, especially when we start to ask: What is the guru within? What is the Light within? What is the innate Buddha? What is the kingdom of God within? How can we get to know that thinking being in us? How can we differentiate between it and the intellect, which can perform mental acrobatics but constantly has to revise its findings?

And if we allow the Light within us to shine through, we may radiate that Light out to others, and they will feel drawn to us. Our spiritual thinking has to become part of our Consciousness. Otherwise, we are just intellectually clever, and we end up creating conceptualizations that further armour us and prevent the Light from truly emerging.

When we investigate rhythm, we can see that life is not a straight line, but a wave, with its many ups and downs. But whether up or down, it still has the same life Energy. As human beings we need the impetus to lift out from the down to the up. It does not happen automatically. We have to contribute to it through our attitude, our emotions and our choices. The power of choice must be fully recognized.

Sometimes there can be a wave of bliss, when everything seems wonderful and our happiness can be recognized by others. If there is a Light within, we will express that Light, even if we cannot explain it. Yet nothing is permanent, and we cannot always reside in the bright Light. Sometimes we need a little shade to rest, to balance, before exposing ourselves again to this wonderful radiance of divine Knowledge, of divine vibration, so that our Consciousness will vibrate with the divine rhythm.

Practically speaking, it is important not to make major decisions when we are in the trough of the wave. From the crest, we have a different overview and are not under the pressure of the undertow of our existence.

The rhythmic beating of the physical heart can be felt as a pulse in different parts of the body. Our mental activity can also be considered a kind of pulsing. When we talk about the pulsing of the body, the pulsing of the Heart, the pulsing of the mind, what do we feel and think? What effect does reflecting have on our feelings when we have reached a certain level of spiritual awareness or even when we are just beginning to have that awareness? That awareness will sustain us in our daily life. It has to. We must not separate our daily living, with all its duties, functions, and limited choices, from our spiritual awareness. Spiritual awareness must be brought into our daily life if we are to become receptive to the radiance of that Consciousness that is pulsing with divine vibrations.

We do not need to convert from one religion to another, but rather we have to convert the darkness held in our Hearts into the Light and vibration of love.

In the struggle to control emotions that can be on the rampage, the Heart is sometimes described as a cremation ground. The Heart is where selfishness, hate, greed, and jealousy are burned away so the Heart can be filled with Light. It is in the ashes of our illusions that we find truth.

In the Heart, we sacrifice whatever prevents the Light from emerging and shining. Even today, there are some yogis in India who visit cremation grounds to meditate on the impermanence of life. My guru did not send me to the cremation ground, but asked me to reflect on my mortality. When I walked up the Ganges, where the river became much narrower, all along the banks I saw many skulls—the remnants of those pilgrims who asked that their bodies be returned to Mother Ganga's holy waters. It made me think: "What if this were the only life I had? What has to die in me so I can be free now, in this lifetime?"

Literally sitting on a corpse will not necessarily bring realization. It takes deeper thinking to understand that what needs to die is our jealousy, revenge, pride, vanity, competition. All of these personality aspects must become the corpse. Then, with the help of the Divine, we can start to see with the Light of understanding and allow the Light of knowledge to emerge.

The Heart is the cremation ground, where, for the love of God, we break our attachments and create the willingness to give up our self-will. What we cannot do for love, we cannot achieve by sheer willpower. The Heart is the cremation ground where we burn desires and imaginary needs—needs that are often not real, but illusions that we already know will not satisfy us. These are our preferences, our comfort, our attachments that we sometimes do not even know exist.

If we do not let them go voluntarily, the Divine will come along anyway—perhaps in the form of Siva, the destroyer of obstacles, and burn them away. Or as Krsna, the stealer of butter, who will steal away what we like best, as if saying, "No, that is not where you should put your Heart." When things are forcibly taken away from us, it should be a sign to start looking more clearly.

When we sacrifice our comfort, we can become independent of comfort and are no longer limited by our need for it. When we sacrifice our opinions, we may find that they were not correct anyway. When we sacrifice what we call our "security"—which, if you look at it closer, may not be real security at all—we can release a powerful Energy that leads to Liberation.

What would it mean to be truly liberated from the confinement and constriction of selfishness? Is it not selfishness, if left to run freely, that will tyrannize us? Think about the unhappiness and destroyed relationships that arise when selfishness and self-will run rampant. Nothing good comes from it. And yet many people believe their security is in getting what they want. When we burn away selfishness in the cremation ground of the Heart, we set ourselves free and set in motion a process of becoming truly human.

So do not hesitate to sacrifice whatever you hold onto tightly in the wrong belief that it is your security. It is not. True security is recognizing that there is a power greater than ourselves that can take care of us. We need to see our own evolution and how we have been cared for, almost step by step, along the way. What is important is to cultivate a commitment to giving back to life and a willingness to see how many blessings life has given us.

The practice of surrender means offering our limited understanding and limited love to the Divine in return for divine love.

The path of the Light is the path of the Heart. It can only be love that brings Light into the Heart. What else could it be? We may feel that we cannot love everybody, but we can try to understand others, especially those who give us the biggest problems. By wanting to understand, we nurture a very different attitude toward that person.

Whichever path we are on, we have to carry the Light in our Heart, even if it is just a small light. One little candle can light a whole room. From the flame of just one candle or even from the quick flare of a match, there is no longer total darkness. In the same way, we may feel elevated or inspired, but the feeling soon disappears. Yet from that instant of Light, we may see something new and experience the difference between darkness and a brilliant flicker of insight.

Whatever Light we have in ourselves, we have to fan that bit of ember until it grows into a real flame. Often we begin the path of yoga with Karma Yoga—selfless service—for purification. This path leads to the Light of the Heart and to kindling the flame of Light and love. We must protect this inner Light and not let anyone extinguish it or damage it. We are the custodians of the Light in our Heart as well as the Light in our mind.

In the Christian tradition, the Holy Spirit is the Light of the Heart. And what makes us a creation in the image of God? Divine love, and expanded Consciousness that moves us beyond our little egocentricities and daily cares, beyond the limits we set for ourselves through unproven beliefs, obligations, and ideas.

Freedom is very fragile, even the freedom of the renunciate whose aim is to be free of attachments and desires. Freedom is fragile, but at least there is freedom. The path of Light is the path of Liberation. But we have to experiment, we have to undergo the battle to break with traditions in order to know if the Power that created us in the first place will really take care of us. If we do not give people the chance to prove themselves, we do not know the truth about how they will act. If we do not give the Divine a chance, we will never know the Divine.

If we aim for the Most High, it is not easy. If we want the diamond of Higher Consciousness, it costs. There are many different diamonds, but the most expensive is the clear water diamond. It has no flaws. Costume jewellery sparkles too, but you know it is not the real thing. If you can have the real diamond that reflects the light in every facet, why be satisfied with less? Aim for the Most High. Go for the greatest Light. Become Light yourself and bring the Light to others.

The path of the Heart is the path of Light, the Light of love, and the Light of understanding. Nothing is more important. Perfection is your individual, personal relationship with the Divine, in whatever name and form you have chosen, or as the Light. If you choose the Light as your symbol of the Divine, you must love the Light, as intimately, as deeply and as intensely— much more so—as your very first love. It is your only true love.

Let Your Presence Work Through the Power of Kundalini Yoga and Meditation

GURMUKH KAUR KHALSA

━━━━━━━━━━━━

Gurmukh Kaur Khalsa, kundalini yoga teacher and cofounder and director of Golden Bridge, A Spiritual Village, was taught the way of kundalini yoga by Yogi Bhajan to help others find spiritual success. Author of two books, including The Eight Human Talents: The Yogic Way to Restoring the Natural Balance of Serenity within You, *she shares why she believes kundalini yoga is the most powerful of all yoga practices, especially at this critical time as we enter the Age of Aquarius. In the following essay she answers the questions: Are women uniquely positioned to embody the energy of the universe? What is the ultimate potential of female energy?*

THERE ARE SO many forms of yoga available these days that you might ask what makes kundalini yoga so special and different from other forms. Someone might tell you that all yoga is merely a bunch of exercises, but this is not true. There is something truly magical that takes place when a person practices kundalini yoga and meditation. This is because the impulse of the entire universe is run by the power of kundalini, and the person who practices this mystical science is able to tap into this energy. People report many illuminating experiences when their own sacred force awakens and merges with the sacred force of the universe.

Because of the far-reaching power kundalini yoga activates, it can keep you young and help you live longer.

We have been told that universal time passes through four major phases: The Golden Age, the Silver Age, the Bronze Age, and finally, the Iron Age. We are currently in the Iron Age, and are moving around once again into the Golden Age.

Long ago during the Golden Age, people were clear and awake, and peace prevailed. Knowing what was coming in the future, the sages, saints, and masters of the Golden Age left us an inheritance: kundalini yoga and meditation. For many thousands of years, these practices were kept away from the general population, until Yogi Bhajan, master of kundalini yoga, came to the United States in the 1960s and taught it openly to the public.

At that point, there were many young people who were longing for a spiritual perspective on the world, the universe, and themselves. Yogi Bhajan recognized this and began teaching these "seekers" the science and art of kundalini yoga, helping them discover a more liberated point of view than they had grown up with. I was fortunate to be among that group, and because of my teacher's love and compassion for me, I have grown by leaps and bounds. Because of his sacrifice, I am able to navigate this planet, rising above the challenges that are presented me, and I can teach others to do the same. I feel very blessed to have been able to study at the feet of such a great soul. I also feel grateful that I have the privilege to work with others to help elevate this planet.

Yogi Bhajan told us that kundalini yoga and meditation were actually for us, now, to help us move from the Piscean Age into the Age of Aquarius. He knew that this science would wake us up and help us grow into our next phase of development. Now is the time for us to evolve. Just as we humans once evolved from apelike creatures, we are now on the verge of evolving to our next phase of awareness. We have been gifted with this most powerful and sacred tool to experience the uncoiling of our souls as they blend and merge with the soul of God.

The human body has whole systems within it that many are unaware of. No one ever taught us about these things when we were growing up. Every human body is designed with a series of *chakras,* or energy centers, that are located at various points from the base of the spine to the top of the head. Once you start the practice of kundalini yoga and meditation, these chakras get charged up and begin to vibrate at a new and faster frequency. Yogi Bhajan told us, "When the Kundalini touches these lotuses, see how they open."

We have also been taught that we have only one physical body, but really we have ten, nine of which subtly surround the physical body. As our own internal Kundalini force gets awakened through the practice of the *kriyas* (exercise sets) and meditations, our different bodies are fed with new threads of life running through them. It's actually possible to begin to see them as we evolve our awareness.

One of our bodies, the aura, has become a household word as humanity's sensitivity has developed. You might not have a total understanding of what an "aura" is, but on some subtle level, you know. You may instinctively feel that someone radiates positive energy and has a "good aura." Many of our kundalini yoga sets and meditations work on the aura. Through this practice, it gets nourished with huge amounts of energy, allowing it to expand and radiate.

Why do some people have a lot of good luck? And why does one person seem brighter and more attractive than another? A lot of this can be accredited to the higher frequency of energy radiating from that person's body and into his or her aura. A really strong and well-developed auric frequency attracts opportunities to us. It is said in the yogic teachings that when you need things in life, there are two ways to get them: you can make a plan and go after them, or you can sit and vibrate and "let things come to you." This is one of the secrets to success on many levels.

A strong aura also becomes your protective shield. This radiance around you can vibrate with such powerful impulses that it connects directly to the universal impulse. But just as we clean our physical bodies, our auras and our minds also need to be cleaned daily so that old thinking and feeling patterns are cleared. Old nonuseful and painful memories can slowly be dissolved through meditation as you connect your mind to the infinite. That's why you might hear people say you can "clear your karmas" through this practice. We're doing nothing other than reconnecting to the divine light from which we came.

As humans, we need to be covered. We need protection. What protection is that? We need for our presence to work, for our auras to become activated and sensitive. Then, an intuitive understanding immediately becomes part of our knowing. That is the beauty of kundalini: it provides us with the protection of the developed intuition. And without intuition, it is as if we are driving a car with no rearview or side mirrors; we can see in one direction, but we are blinded in all others. The kundalini's unfolding protects us by developing the intuition we need.

We are moving into the Aquarian Age and nearing the awakening of a new era marked by the year 2012. An evolutionary leap is happening in much of humanity. I have been exploring this form of yoga for many years, and I have never before seen students changing, evolving, and having such profound experiences as I have of late. In all confidence, I can safely say that this evolution will pick up speed over the next few years.

As we keep doing our yoga and chanting the mantras and committing to going deeper into the experience of our expanded selves, things start happening around us. People are drawn to us, and they want to start relating to us, because as the kundalini uncoils, it goes past the aura and begins to enlighten the radiant body (one of our other bodies). This body can bring new wealth, opportunities, and friends.

Sometimes you may hear people talk about the kundalini power as the "Shakti" force, the feminine creative energy. Kundalini Yoga contains many mantras and meditations that activate this female power of the universe within. When we create a humble, prayerful attitude, we merge with the power of the Divine Mother. This ability to connect exists in men and women alike, and it is what makes us compassionate people who can radiate joy and live in happiness. We have been handed a lot of weaknesses from the past that need to be corrected. And for that, we need Shakti energy.

A woman has an especially deep and inherent link to this feminine aspect of God, often referred to as the *Adi Shakti*. Why so? Every woman is a representative of the Divine Mother; she is nothing but God's living grace. Whenever Almighty God has to take birth, he has to come through the womb of a woman. One woman, one womb, one pregnancy, one birth can deliver this entire planet to the heavens. Because of this, a woman is created sixteen times emotionally stronger than a man, sixteen times more intuitive, and has a huge impact on the environment around her. Such is the power of woman.

A woman's pure vibration can bring healing to any person or situation on earth. When she lives in her divine heritage, she becomes more than God. She actually becomes the Adi Shakti, the creative consciousness of God, and she can beam her projection of radiance and healing toward anyone. That's why a woman in a home sets the tone for all who live there. When she lives, breathes, and walks in her highest graceful power, all around her are transformed. A woman living in this state of mind and consciousness can uplift and manifest anything. A woman's sacred touch can turn all adversity into prosperity.

A woman's role is not to worship God; her role is to be the very self of God. Her oneness can affect and open every heart. Yogi Bhajan felt so strongly about the power of women that he held special trainings just for women. He would tell us, "It is the prayer of the woman that sustains the earth." With this comes a responsibility to keep her consciousness, life, and mind pure and powerful. In the kundalini yoga tradition, it is said that a woman either lives her existence as the Adi Shakti in her life or she falls flat. There's almost no in-between. Her energy is the source of creativity behind any great act of a man. Her prayers can protect the grace of mankind for centuries to come. Especially at this time in history when women have not been respected, a woman must guard and protect her own mental purity with utmost scrutiny. Her purity and prayer are called for to help deliver the planet into the Age of Aquarius, so we may transform into the tranquil and peaceful existence that is in our future.

As we move into the Aquarian Age, many people will be challenged by the changing times. Everyone's prayers are needed now to protect the grace of mankind. Out of our innocent, heartfelt projections, we can create the environments of peace and prosperity for all. Let this be a time when we visualize our radiant auric field connecting with the expanded consciousness of the universe. Then let it touch all, cover all, forgive all, and grace all with peace. Through the practice of kundalini yoga and meditation, let this be a time when we discover how to let our presence work.

Kundalini Yoga and Meditation as Taught by Yogi Bhajan

A Contemporary Approach to Human Excellence and the Thirst of the Soul

GURUCHARAN SINGH KHALSA, PHD

Gurucharan S. Khalsa, PhD, is a psychotherapist, teacher, and writer, and is a world-recognized expert in kundalini yoga as taught by Yogi Bhajan. He is the director of training for the Kundalini Research Institute, has instructed at universities—including MIT and the University of Guadalajara—and has collaborated with the Center for Psychology and Social Change at Harvard University and other institutes. He is a therapist and designs programs for the therapeutic applications of kundalini yoga and meditation. In the following essay he defines kundalini and discusses his personal experience with it. He also dismantles popular myths surrounding kundalini yoga and answers questions such as: Is kundalini yoga challenging or dangerous? Is the goal of kundalini to gain psychic or paranormal powers? What is the purpose of kundalini yoga?

"The purpose of all branches of yoga is to raise the Kundalini, to raise the dormant power of the being so that he can have excellence."

—Yogi Bhajan

WHEN WE WANT to be aware, potent, practical, and intuitive, we awaken the kundalini in our being. When we want to find the way through any block and recognize the constant guiding presence of our higher self, we awaken the kundalini within us. When we recognize our true self within the self and want our prayers and projections to be effective, we awaken the kundalini.

If we really want to experience what it is to be a human being, in all its miraculous potential, we find a way to awaken the kundalini. When this is accomplished, the first sign, as Yogi Bhajan has said,

> is that you are contained, you are content, and you are
> very continuously dependable. Your behavior reflects it.
> Your identity takes on a personality of royalty and reality.
> Royalty and reality must be in you. This is called Shakti
> Yoga. This is called Kundalini Yoga. This is called the Yoga
> of Power, Self, and Stimulation. It is also called the
> Yoga of Awareness.[1]

The kundalini is a force, a deep urge, within each of us to unfold: to express and act in our originality and uniqueness, to revel in the personal excellence that challenge evokes as we reside in the stillness that is the nucleus of our existence. It flows in each of us and in each particle of existence. It is as gentle as the fragrant blooming of each petal of a spring rose. It is as inexpressible as true love. It is as practical as a single act of kindness that is selfless, spontaneous, and effortlessly in rhythm with *all that is*. It accompanies every awakening. It cannot be forced any more than you can push the colors of dawn to hurry or to linger.

Above all, kundalini is not a property of the mind and its legions of thoughts. It is not understood by any amount of study, reading, or thinking. It can be grasped through the wisdom that comes to us through a deep experience of grace. That experience is best cultivated by consistent discipline and matured by the surrender that only love allows.

The writings of Carl Jung and Joseph Campbell popularized this sense of the fundamental importance, power, and developmental nature of kundalini. They focused on the deep psychology and symbolism of kundalini and the historical rendering of chakras, energy, and human development. And contemporary writers have greatly extended and systematized these. What was missing was wide knowledge and access to authentic disciplines. Much of the teachings of kundalini yoga and meditation (also called *Raj* yoga) were oral.

Kundalini has been a personal journey of mine as well as a discipline of study. I always had a strong urge to awaken, to know what is true, and to teach what I have experienced. By my early teens I had studied most wisdom philosophies, and I began a journey of many years through mathematics, chemistry, physics, philosophy, and psychology under the strength of that inner urge. I wanted to encounter the world and my consciousness as they are. I did not care if there was a god or not, but I wanted to act with royal and godly character. I did not care which belief I had to test or put aside, but I wanted to be believable to myself.

At thirteen, in the days before personal computers, I wandered the dusty stacks of old libraries, sought teachers, went to learn with these teachers from their teachers, and tried whatever I could find as disciplines. As I read the esoteric literature, "kundalini" or "serpent fire" was always the missing key. The knowledge surrounding kundalini at that time was necessarily secret and required initiation, lifetimes of positive karma, or the blessing of a teacher to learn. I refused all initiations; I was too much of a scientist to agree to secrecy rather than the light of shared public testing. I also thought secrecy could create issues of control, power, and blind faith, all of which I saw as contributing to the tattered and blood-stained fabric of world history. I wanted to learn, to experience, to know. And I wanted discover the inner science that could benefit everyone without restriction.

I was both delighted and shocked to find Yogi Bhajan in 1969 when I was entering graduate school in mathematics. Actually, he found me. That meeting was a synchronistic tale of a student meeting the teacher, one laced with premonitory dreams, recalcitrant efforts to avoid the messages of the portended events, and a class in kundalini yoga that was astounding and gave flesh to the philosophic skeleton of knowledge I had.

When we met, lifetimes of memories rushed into my consciousness, and I was filled with instant recognition. And the dance of teacher and student began. Yogi Bhajan taught everyone publicly. There was no initiation. He formally accepted no students and presented the techniques as a science. He did not claim perfection or to be good or bad, only that he was a master of these technologies and would produce teachers to serve, heal, and lead. I started to teach, at his direction, the very next day. I studied with Yogi Bhajan for the next thirty-five years, until he passed in 2004.

Through those years I had the opportunity to learn and teach thousands of techniques around the world—as well as to confront my own limitations. Gradually, meditation and yoga opened a space for the awareness, energy, maturity, and experiences guaranteed with kundalini yoga and meditation as Yogi Bhajan taught it. In the end, it is all about the wondrously simple reality of being a human, sharing that humanity, and witnessing the miracles of life.

Along the way I encountered and enjoyed the many myths and misconceptions about kundalini and tested the effects of this yoga in labs. I had the opportunity to collaborate with great researchers in mind-body medicine, and knew or worked alongside many well-known yogis and healers. I have also tended a broadly based psychology practice that applies meditation and yoga therapeutically.

Now, the age is changing. Knowledge is everywhere. There is no need for searching, for scrambling through old libraries or up hidden mountains. All the thousands of techniques that were hidden are now an open legacy for all. We have no excuse.

There are teachers and teachings, so anyone can tap the spark of kundalini and enter this new time with intuition, caliber, kindness, and excellence.

KUNDALINI MYTHS

I want to give you a better sense of kundalini yoga by addressing some common myths about it.

Myth #1

The first myth to put aside is that kundalini yoga is slow or takes years of practice to show results. As Yogi Bhajan said in *The Master's Touch:*

> Kundalini Yoga does not take very long—three minutes maximum, or eleven minutes, or sixty-two minutes. It creates in the brain the imprint of your self-evaluation of doing the exercises. You will find that there is no pain, just achievement within the self. And once the mind is trained to achieve, you can reach Infinity.[2]

There are guidelines on how to practice each technique. There are thousands of techniques. Some require only a few minutes, some half an hour, and some longer. When we measured effects on heart rate variation (HRV), on levels of brain activity in fMRI's, and on mood, we saw profound effects in ten to thirty minutes.

Myth #2

The second myth is that it is only for people who can simplify life, live in ashrams, or make some commitment to distance themselves from the bustle of family and business life. Yogi Bhajan repeatedly stressed that kundalini yoga is aimed at the "householder": a person who is busy and engaged in normal life pursuits. It is ideal for people who are committed to family, community, projects, business, and avocations. The techniques produce significant changes almost immediately. With regular practice, those gains in personal development and functioning stabilize and become incorporated in normal life. There is no need to retreat, to forgo an active life, or to prepare for years until one is highly qualified. The practice will qualify the practitioner. The experience opens, broadens, and consolidates the consciousness and personality of the student.

It is certainly a pleasure to enjoy a beautiful natural environment alone or with people doing a similar practice. When we share these techniques with students, we encourage periodic immersions to focus on meditation and be with a community. We have many opportunities to meditate, for one or several days. But the core practice is the daily practice in the early morning hours.

It is in that special quiet time in the morning that we cultivate the inner stillness that can guide our outer activity, that we confront and control our mind so each thought we project is more effective, and that we exercise to be physically healthy and emotionally clear. This morning *sadhana* can be done wherever we are and no matter what we do.

Myth #3

The third myth is that kundalini is raised only with kundalini yoga. Kundalini is the natural presence of awareness in our self and in all of nature. It finds its highest expression in a human being. Our nervous and glandular systems make our bodies the most complex and responsive matter in the universe. When we optimize that potential and expand our connectedness and sensitivity, kundalini increases its flow and presence. The natural results are subtle perception, intuition, and a sharpened applied intelligence. Without the normal flow of kundalini, we could only be mechanical and automatic. Wherever a prayer is effective, a mind expanded, and intuition accurate, kundalini is functioning.

Through its disciplines, kundalini yoga gives us the ability to intentionally awaken our self. We can increase our level of awareness, choice, and sensitivity through a gradual, elegant process. The graceful self-presence that comes is not reliant on chance, accident, or a special philosophy or person. It arises through the experiences that evoke in us a new level of awareness and capacity to act effectively.

Myth #4

The fourth myth is that it is dangerous. Scattered through scriptural, historical, and political writings are warnings for those who practice kundalini yoga. There were several reasons for these warnings. The matrix of energies that compose our body and mind operates by laws and is highly complex. A technology that enhances and releases those energies must be precise, and precisely managed. So there is a need for a teacher to guide or certify the teachings and how to use them.

This was a great problem for millennia. Much of what was taught was secret, restricted to privileged classes of people or passed on only orally. That has changed now. In the information age, information is no longer inaccessible. As a master of kundalini yoga, Yogi Bhajan threw aside all secrecy and recorded the techniques from many traditions that had been kept secret or transmitted only orally. He felt these techniques were a legacy that belonged to all people and would serve anyone who practiced them. He acted as a guide and certified each thing he taught, asking his students to not change those *kriyas*. As long as they are practiced as given, there can be no danger, only steady and gradual awakening. To assure this and to open the door for every person to practice without difficulty, he created the Kundalini Research Institute (KRI), a nonprofit organization to ensure authenticity of technique, provide the highest quality of teachers and instruction, and promote applications and research.

Another reason for warnings about yoga was to ensure survival under hostile political environments. Whenever strong people arise who are aware and fearless, they threaten established power.

Power depends on a story, and self-awareness lets you break the hypnosis of that story. So for protection, the practices were hidden by use of codes and special language or by interlacing them in other writings.

The greatest danger is simply that rising awareness and vitality brings new perspectives, revaluation of activities and relationships, and change. This improves many things, and it can disrupt old patterns that no longer support you. Yogi Bhajan said it clearly:

> In the beginning you are you, in the middle you are you, and in the end you are God. There's nothing else. There's nothing to it. Nothing was, nothing is, nothing shall be.
>
> For thousands of years the Piscean Age has lied to us to make us find God out there, while they knew that we are gods.
>
> Longitude and latitude are given to everybody. Altitude and attitude are given by Kundalini Yoga. When the kundalini spiral rises to penetrate through all the chakras, the man knows he's Brahma—the Divine Creative.
>
> That's why they used to warn that Kundalini Yoga is dangerous. It's dangerous because it takes away from man the ability to be exploited by another man. And for some, life without exploitation has no juice. [3]

Myth #5

The fifth myth is that yoga and meditation in the kundalini disciplines are separate—or that meditation is "higher" than the physical yoga. Body and mind are not separated. They form a seamless matrix of substance and process. Kundalini yoga uses meditation to affect the body and the body to effect meditation. Many meditations involve physical movements, posture, sound, and focus. Meditation is not restricted to attention or thought alone. It is a process that confronts the flow of thoughts and feelings and uses many techniques to create balance or change in the meridians, chakras, nerves, and glands.

The body is viewed as Guru Nanak presented it: part of the sacred pattern of the universe that enacts the highest embodiment of potential and awareness. All the resources needed to awaken our spirit and initiate profound healing are within the body in its gross and subtle structures. It was said that "the angels weep for lack of a body to experience the swirl of emotions and senses that present us with the chance for choice." There is no higher or lower between body and mind.

Myth #6

The sixth myth is that the goal of kundalini yoga is to gain psychic or paranormal powers. The goal is happiness. It is to be fulfilled as a human being. It is to awaken our potential for awareness and to synchronize our finite and infinite realms into seamless, effective action. The ultimate control we have is our attention and awareness that add choices to our life beyond the constant flow of instinctual thought, feelings, and reactions that form the habitual patterns we live.

As the energies of the body and mind grow, release, and are used in new ways, we can experience the extraordinary. We have many abilities that are dormant or unconscious. We can sense the universe. We can know many things at a distance through that sensitivity. We have unmatched capacity for empathy and mirroring others. Those same abilities let us heal each other through talk, touch, and pure awareness.

It is also possible to awaken these abilities and misuse them, like any talent. It is essential to cultivate humility and kindness along with enhanced sensitivities and energy. Instead, we sometimes attach to them and distort our ego and sense of self. Think of it as using one muscle to the extreme and neglecting the rest of the body: you can curl five hundred pounds with your biceps, but your legs are too weak to stand steady. This would make you extraordinary and limit you at the same time. Add to this ego and you might see the whole world through those biceps.

The same kind of unbalanced development can happen in the chakras and the subtle body. Then you can perform an unusual feat of strength, psychic perception, or influence on another person. It can be as tangible as an irresistible charisma so strong that others follow you without question. It can be the ability to command an element like water to heat or freeze. All wisdom schools say not to do this. The cost is the distortion of the chakras. When you die you become bound to the overdeveloped chakra. You lose authenticity and true freedom in exchange for the small gain of those paranormal tricks, and they do not make you more human, wiser, or happier.

Kundalini yoga as taught by Yogi Bhajan does develop intuition, intelligence, healing, and spiritual insight. In a steady, polite way, it can awaken natural gifts you already possess. But it only gives you to yourself instead of creating an attachment to powers.

Myth #7

The seventh myth is that once you awaken kundalini and the inner knowledge that comes with it, you can teach or practice anything that "spontaneously" arises. There is a line in classical writings that says you practice "spontaneous kriya" when kundalini rises. This is often misunderstood and misused by teachers. Spontaneous does not mean impulsive. Nor does it mean to act out your authentic emotions. It means to act from your awareness and real self. It means you can act without duality. Each action is like a kriya that blends commitment of your finite self and emotions with reliance on the infinite self. The ego is not active, so all action comes from the stillness of the self in the present. A spontaneous action or kriya is one that you will stand behind for a hundred years since there is no split, shadow, or hidden agenda interfering with the simple reality of the moment. It has a quality of action that we call *kriya*.

Each kriya—each exercise and meditation sequence—of kundalini yoga is as structured as a classical sonata and imbued with the spontaneity that comes with full presence, awareness, and commitment in each action.

Myth #8

The eighth myth is that kundalini yoga is esoteric and will never be testable or scientific. Its techniques have been discovered, used, and mastered by dedicated practitioners over centuries, and the results of this legacy are beginning to be studied. Early studies in the 1930s began a profile of the physiological changes that occur during yoga and meditation. In the early 1970s, as tools improved, the profile of changes became more extensive, and with the work of pioneers like Herbert Benson, the meditative state was recognized as a distinct, stable physiological one. Since that time, research has steadily increased, and the tools that let us explore those processes have improved exponentially.

Here are a few of the directions toward which research points to understand and apply meditation and kundalini yoga:

- The autonomic nervous system that controls excitement and relaxation can be trained, developed, and systematically influenced by breathing practices and yoga exercise.
- Kundalini yoga optimizes heart rate variation to combat depression, anxiety, and other mood disorders as well as improve cardiovascular health.[4] It is an antidote to many of the systemic effects of stress. The rhythmical exercises of kundalini yoga and Breathwalk are powerful stimulants of endogenous nitric oxide and other chemicals that interrupt the cascade of stress hormones that do damage to our body and mind.[5]
- Different meditations produce similar changes in brain function as seen in fMRI, SPECT, MEG, EEG, and other tools. But many also have distinct signatures that can lead

to targeted protocols for clinical treatments.[6] (Kundalini meditation is very effective for adjusting insomnia and many other sleep disturbances. This leads to improved health, blood pressure, and cognitive functioning.[7])

- It is very effective clinically in relieving anxiety, dysthymic disorder, mild to moderate depression, ADHD, and excessive rumination.[8] With consistent meditation, the brain responds and develops both in neurological complexity and density. This is true in specific areas related to the frontal cortex, attention, memory, and emotional regulation.
- It improves empathic capacity and interpersonal perception.
- It greatly improves the cognitive abilities to be alert and hold multiple thoughts in comparison to each other, and metacognition.

There are many researchers and thousands of papers exploring these and other facets of meditation and yoga for lifestyle, health, and clinical applications. Dr. Sat Bir Singh Khalsa, the director of research for KRI, for example, is a Harvard researcher in sleep disorders. He has become globally prominent in yoga research and has contributed to many areas of the research mentioned as well as spurring conferences and collaborations on applied yoga therapy.

Yogi Bhajan was committed to the scientific study of kundalini yoga. He supported collaborations in this and encouraged future research, although he saw his primary contributions as recording the vast number of techniques that are useful and training teachers to share them. Sometimes he would share the classical explanations and mechanisms for a kriya and stop with a laugh. He would say, "Why continue? Your understanding will completely change, and you will have a new scientific language: energy, atom, frequency, neurotransmitters, quantum, and more. Everything will have an equation. Religions and philosophy will give way to experience and science." So two things define the future: the refined experience of practitioners combined with the tools and tests of a new science of consciousness.

Myth #9

The ninth myth is that kundalini yoga is a religion or part of one religion. Techniques that raise the kundalini are part of every great wisdom tradition. They are not unique to one culture or time. In some societies, like India, they were incorporated into the mainstream culture and disseminated broadly. In others they were held tightly in special groups or classes.

Kundalini yoga is a source of experience and a discipline for mental and physical health and for spiritual development. It has never been a religion nor has it been against religion. It is only for awareness and against ignorance and pain. As Yogi Bhajan put it:

> Kundalini Yoga is not a yoga for everybody or anybody.
> The one who practices Kundalini Yoga commands
> the five tattvas, the three gunas, the seven chakras, and
> all 108 elements in the universe, including a con-
> scious creation of the Creator. Let's be clear about it.
> Kundalini Yoga is not a religion. Religions came out
> of it. Kundalini Yoga is not a fad, and it's not a cult. It's
> a practice of experience of a person's own excellence
> which is dormant and which is awakened.[9]

Myth #10

The tenth myth is that you will become perfect with kundalini yoga. You can become perfectly human and profoundly aware. You can become intuitive. You can increase your caliber, character, and effectiveness. You can be prosperous and creative. You can be humble and powerful.

You will not suddenly have a perfect personality with no flaws and irritating peculiarities. Kundalini yoga does not create "cookie cutter" people or teachers. It brings awareness to each person so that each can act from and honor his or her uniqueness and be connected to the uniqueness of the entire universe.

Kundalini yoga creates masters who master themselves. The first rule of kundalini yoga is that you do not show—obnoxiously or politely, humbly or powerfully—any power of your own. Perfection in this approach is the ability to perfectly put aside the ego you have and act from awareness. As Yogi Bhajan commented:

> The first principle of a kundalini teacher is, "I am not." If you cannot practice shuniya, you cannot be a teacher of Kundalini Yoga. "Shuniya" means zero. The moment you become zero, then all powers will prevail through you. The power of a teacher of Kundalini Yoga is in his zero, in his shuniya. In shuniya you become zero, you reduce everything to nothing: "I am nothing. Everything is nothing. There's nothing to be nothing." The moment you become that, then everything radiates from you.
>
> Second, you are a servant. The moment you become a servant, you automatically become a master. You can never become a master if you want to be a master.[10]

Myth #11

The eleventh myth is that you must be initiated or belong to something in order to learn, practice, and receive the benefit of kundalini meditations and mantras.

There is no initiation or secrecy in kundalini yoga. It is taught as a science. It is open to be experienced and tested. The only requirement is to put aside your ego and practice with precision the authentic techniques as taught. The teachings guide you, and putting aside your ego and doing them as given protect you from errors. In Yogi Bhajan's words:

We have kept the teachings of Kundalini Yoga pure from
the time we know to the time we are. That's why when
some people teach Kundalini Yoga it doesn't work. They
teach philosophy, they teach chakras, sometimes they
make up kriyas. It's a good time, but it will not touch
the core. It is as simple as that.[11]

You do not need a special person or energy from a special person.
Strong blessings and the projection of a good teacher are always
welcome, but the connection needed to practice kundalini yoga
is in the legacy of the teachings themselves and does not depend
on a personality. Yogi Bhajan emphasized this:

In Kundalini Yoga neither do we initiate the man nor do
we worship the man. We follow the Golden Chain—the
teachings. We are grateful to the Teacher—he gave us
the teachings. That doesn't mean we worship him. It is
very difficult to change this. If I am your Teacher, you
will like to love me and respect me and honor me. But
there is a way to show that you really love me, and really
exalt me, and really honor me: you will be perfect in the
teachings themselves.[12]

Myth #12
The twelfth myth, and the last, is that the practices of kundalini
yoga are daunting or severe.

In fact the practices are simple, gradual, varied, precise, and
proportional. There are exercises that are easy for beginners and
ones that require more preparation. None of them require severe
physical exertion, unnatural functions, or physical mortification
of any kind. This image arose from early contacts with India that
showed fakirs who captured popular attention by standing still
for years, eating almost nothing, walking in fire, and living in
monasteries or caves.

The actual practices are based on the concept of kriya. A kriya can be very subtle, brief or long, easy or more challenging. Each kriya is precise. Just as in music, louder is not necessarily better, so in kriya, harder and longer effort is not necessarily better. Each practice has a syntax or natural structure that aligns the body, mind, and spirit for a predictable and effective result. The exercises are not done randomly or based on personal favorites or style. Kundalini yoga practitioners are like pianists who are offered a vast array of classical music to play. Each kriya, like a composition, leads to specific states of feeling, awareness, and energy. We can pick our favorite piece and use the geometry, energy balance, and processes coded in these well-tested kriyas.

Simple kriyas may take only three minutes. Use them to breathe and break your stress at work. There are meditations that are silent; others use sound or mantra, are spoken out loud or sung. Still others are rhythmical physical movements; many use attention and mindful states alone. In eleven minutes you can significantly change your nervous system, level of energy, degree of clarity, and sense of presence and stillness. Some meditations can be done for thirty-one minutes, sixty-two minutes, or even two and a half hours.

A little at a time is often the best practice. The foundation to a serious basic practice is to exercise and meditate in the early morning. Prepare for the day as you conquer the mind and its subconscious. The period of two and a half hours before dawn is considered the ideal time and is called the time of nectar: *amrit vela.*

The practices are done as a group in the amrit vela and in classes offered by KRI and in my teachings and in the 3HO (Healthy, Happy and Holy Organization). It is also practiced individually. We also do one to three days of intensive meditations as a group in courses of white tantric yoga, which is part of kundalini yoga.

And there is Breathwalk. This is a contemplative form of walking that incorporates breathing patterns and meditation, strengthening mind and body. It awakens awareness and invites in your heart and spirit. It is the ultimate in meditation and walking for physical and mental health.[13]

You can find exercises and meditations in kundalini yoga that match your level of conditioning. Precision is more important than complexity, flow more important than level of difficulty, and steady growth more important than extreme experience. Many exercises that are done for several minutes can be physically challenging—like holding your arm out steadily. But they are normal exercises in a flow of exercises that challenge and strengthen the nervous system and focus the mind.

A central task in kundalini yoga is to conquer the mind.[14] We encounter the mind thought by thought, feeling by feeling. Each thought or feeling initiates change in our physical readiness, energy level, mood, and perception. Each thought!

The techniques bring your conscious and subconscious reactions to the natural flow of thoughts to neutral stillness. In that stillness you have a choice. You can express your true heart, your authentic self. When you experience this, it is deeply satisfying and effective your in life. Mastering the mind also opens your experience to your spirit. You act without the conflicts engendered by the ego.

In the mind, we guide each thought through its negative, positive, and neutral aspects and act with intuitive intelligence. In the body, we balance the flows of the meridians in the left (ida), right (pingala), and central (sushmana) channels. Realization comes as we act from awareness, love, kindness, and reality.

KUNDALINI IN THE AQUARIAN AGE

The age of kundalini yoga is just beginning. It is a source of strength as we face the future. It is a source of peace as we experience the present. It is a source of healing as we engage our life fully. I look forward to the ways in which we will practice and talk about these authentic technologies of human awareness as science and experience give birth to the languages of spirit in the Aquarian Age.

Find out more at kundaliniresearchinstitute.org, breathwalk.com, and Gurucharan.com.

Notes

PART I

Bonnie Greenwell

1. An annotated list of books on kundalini and many biographies can be found on my Web site: kundaliniguide.com.

2. If you take a moment when you are being very creative to sense where the focus of energy is in your body, you may find significant energy is in the neck. I can't tell you why this is, only that there appears to be a correlation between the opening of the throat chakra and creativity, a phenomenon that is recognized in yoga science.

3. Jill Bolte Taylor, *My Stroke of Insight: A Brain Scientist's Personal Journey* (New York: Viking Press, 2006), 140.

4. A modern book that beautifully demonstrates this opportunity is Kathleen Singh's *The Grace in Dying: How We Are Transformed As We Die* (New York: HarperOne, 2000).

5. Ramana Maharshi, *Ramana Gita: Dialogues with Ramana Maharshi,* third edition. English translation and commentary by A. R. Natarajan (Bangalore, India: Ramana Hamarshi Centre for Learning, 1994), 50–51. Published by the Society of Abidance in Truth. Many other books of his teachings may be found at sriramanaharshi.org/bhagvan.html.

6. Ibid., 20–22.

Penny Kelly

1. Kelly, Penny. *The Evolving Human: A True Story of Awakened Kundalini* (Lawton, Michigan: Lily Hill Publishing, 1997), 10.

PART II

Sat Bir Singh Khalsa

1. Mukta Kaur Khalsa, *Meditations for Addictive Behavior: A System of Yogic Science with Nutritional Formulas* (I Was There Press, 2008).

2. David S. Shannahoff-Khalsa, *Kundalini Yoga Meditation: Techniques Specific for Psychiatric Disorders, Couples Therapy, and Personal Growth* (New York: W. W. Norton & Co., 2006).

3. Dharma Singh Khalsa and Cameron Stauth, *Meditation as Medicine: Activate the Power of Your Natural Healing Force* (New York: Pocket Books, 2001).

4. Dharma Singh Khalsa, "An Integrative Medical Approach to Alzheimer's Disease," in *The Psychospiritual Clinician's Handbook: Alternative Methods for Understanding and Treating Mental Disorders*, ed Sharon G. Mijares and Gurucharan Singh Khalsa (New York: Haworth Press, 2005); Gurucharan Singh Khalsa, "Getting Focused in an Age of Distraction: Approaches to Attentional Disorders Using the Humanology of Yogi Bhajan," in *The Psychospiritual Clinician's Handbook*, ed. Sharon G. Mijares and Gurucharan Singh Khalsa (New York: Haworth Press, 2005); Hari Kaur Khalsa, "Yoga: An Adjunct to Infertility Treatment." *Fertility and Sterility* 80 (2003), 46–51; Manjit Kaur Khalsa, "Alternative Treatments for Borderline and Narcissistic Personality Disorders," in *The Psychospiritual Clinician's Handbook*, ed Sharon G. Mijares and Gurucharan Singh Khalsa (New York: Haworth Press, 2005); D. S. Shannahoff-Khalsa et al., "Hemodynamic Observations on a Yogic Breathing Technique Claimed to Help Eliminate and Prevent Heart Attacks: A Pilot Study," *Journal of Alternative and Complementary Medicine* 10 (2004): 757–766; David S. Shannahoff-Khalsa, "Patient Perspectives: Kundalini Yoga Meditation Techniques for Psycho-Oncology and as Potential Therapies for Cancer," *Integrative Cancer Therapies* 4 (2005): 87–100; David S. Shannahoff-Khalsa, "Complementary Healthcare Practices. Stress Management for Gastrointestinal Disorders: The Use of Kundalini Yoga Meditation Techniques," *Gastroenterology Nursing* 25 (2002): 126–129; David S. Shannahoff-Khalsa, "Kundalini Yoga Meditation Techniques for the Treatment of Obsessive-Compulsive and OC Spectrum Disorders," *Brief Treatment and Crisis Intervention* 3 (2003): 369–382; David S. Shannahoff-Khalsa, "An Introduction to Kundalini Yoga Meditation Techniques That Are Specific for the Treatment of Psychiatric Disorders," *Journal of Alternative and Complementary Medicine* 10 (2004): 91–101.

5. Sat Bir S. Khalsa et al., "Evaluation of a Residential Kundalini Yoga Lifestyle Pilot Program for Addiction in India," *Journal of Ethnicity in Substance Abuse* 7 (2008): 67–79.

6. David S. Shannahoff-Khalsa and L. R. Beckett, "Clinical Case Report: Efficacy of Yogic Techniques in the Treatment of Obsessive Compulsive Disorders," *International Journal of Neuroscience* 85 (1996): 1–17.

7. David S. Shannahoff-Khalsa et al., "Randomized Controlled Trial of Yogic Meditation Techniques for Patients with Obsessive Compulsive Disorders," *CNS Spectrums: The International Journal of Neuropsychiatric Medicine* 4 (1999): 34–46.

8. Sat Bir Singh Khalsa, "Treatment of Chronic Insomnia with Yoga: A Preliminary Study with Sleep-Wake Diaries," *Applied Psychophysiology and Biofeedback* 29 (2004): 269–278.

9. Sat Bir Singh Khalsa, "A Randomized Controlled Trial of a Yoga Treatment for Chronic Insomnia," *Applied Psychophysiology and Biofeedback* 34 (2009) (abstract in press).

10. Gurucharan Singh Khalsa and Yogi Bhajan, *Breathwalk: Breathing Your Way to a Revitalized Body, Mind and Spirit* (New York: Broadway, 2000).

11. M. Vazquez-Vandyck et al., "Effect of Breathwalk on Body Composition, Metabolic and Mood State in Chronic Hepatitis C Patients with Insulin Resistance Syndrome," *World Journal of Gastroenterology* 13 (2007): 6213–6218.

12. H. Lynton, B. Kligler, and S. Shiflett, "Yoga in Stroke Rehabilitation: A Systematic Review and Results of a Pilot Study," *Topics in Stroke Rehabilitation* 14 (2007): 1–8.

13. Sabina Sehgal, "The Effects of Kundalini Yoga on Sleep Disturbance," PhD dissertation, Sabina Sehgal, California School of Professional Psychology, Alliant International University (2007).

David Lukoff

1. J. Lewis and T. Melton, eds., *Perspectives on the New Age* (Albany, NY: State University of New York Press, 1992).

2. M. Caplan, *Halfway up the Mountain: The Error of Premature Claims to Enlightenment* (Prescott, AZ: Hohm Press, 1999), 7.

3. R. Assagioli, "Self-Realization and Psychological Disturbances," in *Spiritual Emergency: When Personal Transformation Becomes a Crisis*, eds. S. Grof and C. Grof (Los Angeles: Tarcher, 1989), 36.

4. L. Sannella, *Kundalini: Psychosis or Transcendence* (self, 1976).

5. S. Grof, "Frontiers of the Mind" (1995). healthy.net/scr/interview.asp?Id=200

6. S. Grof and C. Grof, eds., *Spiritual Emergency: When Personal Transformation Becomes a Crisis* (Los Angeles: Tarcher, 1989).

7. Silverman, J. "Shamans and Acute Schizophrenia." *American Anthropologist* 69, no. 1 (1967):21-31.

8. Lukoff, D. "Case Study of the Emergency of a Contemporary Shaman." In *Proceedings of the Ninth International Conference on Shamanism and Alternate Healing*, edited by R. I. Heinze. Berkeley, CA: Asian Scholars Press, 1993.

9. B. Cortright, *Psychotherapy and Spirit: Theory and Practice in Transpersonal Psychotherapy* (Albany, NY: SUNY Press, 1997), 161.

10. Bonnie Greenwell, "Kundalini Quest: Nighttime Shakes" (2000). realization.org/page/doc0/doc0048.htm

11. B. Greenwell, *Energies of Transformation: A Guide to the Kundalini Process* (Saratoga, CA: Shakti River Press, 1990).

12. B. Cortright, *Integral Psychology: Yoga, Growth, and Opening the Heart* (Albany, NY: SUNY Press, 2007). Used with author's permission.

13. Greenwell, "Kundalini Quest: Nighttime Shakes."

14. American Psychiatric Association, *Diagnostic and Statistical Manual, Text Revision, Fourth Edition* (Washington, DC: American Psychiatric Association, 2000).

15. R. Lim and K. Lin, "Cultural Formulation of Psychiatric Diagnosis. Case No. 03. Psychosis Following Qigong in a Chinese Immigrant," *Culture and Medical Psychiatry* 20 (1996): 373.

16. Ibid., 375-6.

17. *DSM-IV*, 488.

18. M. Epstein and S. Topgay, "Mind and Mental Disorders in Tibetan Medicine," *Revision* 5, no. 1 (1982): 27.

19. R. Walsh and L. Roche, "Precipitation of Acute Psychotic Episodes by Intensive Meditation in Individuals with a History of Schizophrenia," *American Journal of Psychiatry* 136 (1979): 1086.

20. J. Kornfield, *A Path with Heart: A Guide through the Perils and Promises of Spiritual Life* (New York: Bantam Books, 1993), 131–32.

21. Walsh and Roche, "Precipitation of Acute Psychotic Episodes," 1085–1086.

22. D. Lukoff et al., "A Holistic Health Program for Chronic Schizophrenic Patients," *Schizophrenia Bulletin* 12, no. 2 (1986): 274–282.

23. D. Lukoff, F. Lu, and R. Turner, "From Spiritual Emergency to Spiritual Problem: The Transpersonal Roots of the New *DSM-IV* Category," *Journal of Humanistic Psychology* 38, no. 2 (1998).

24. *DSM-IV*, 685.

25. E. Bragdon, *A Sourcebook for Helping People with Spiritual Problems* (Aptos, CA: Lightening Up Press, 1993), 18.

Barbara Whitfield

1. Kenneth Ring, *Heading toward Omega: In Search of the Meaning of the Near-Death Experience* (New York: Morrow, 1984).

2. B. Harris [Whitfield] and L. Bascom, *Full Circle: The Near-Death Experience and Beyond* (New York: Pocket/Simon and Schuster, 1990); B. H. Whitfield, *Spiritual Awakenings: Insights of the NDE and Other Doorways to Our Soul* (Deerfield Beach, FL: HCI, 1995); B. Whitfield, *The Natural Soul* (Pittsburg, PA: SterlingHouse, 2009).

3. C. L. Whitfield et al., *The Power of Humility: Choosing Peace over Conflict in Relationships* (Deerfield Beach, FL: HCI, 2006).

4. Ring, *Heading toward Omega*

5. Visit Gary Craig's Web site at emofree.com; it is packed with information, tutorials, case histories, and a free downloadable PDF manual.

6. B. Whitfield, *Spiritual Awakenings*. See chapter 6, "Freeing Blocked Energy."

7. B. Whitfield, *Spiritual Awakenings.* See chapter 5, "Kundalini Energy and How It Works."

8. B. Whitfield, *Spiritual Awakenings.*

9. Anonymous, *Adult Children: Alcoholic/Dysfunctional Families* (Torrance, CA: ACOA World Service Organization, 2006); adultchildren.org.

10. Ring, *Heading toward Omega.*

11. I. Bentov, *Stalking the Wild Pendulum: On the Mechanics of Consciousness* (Rochester, VT: Inner Traditions, 1977); Ring, *Heading toward Omega;* L. Sannella, *The Kundalini Experience* (Lower Lake, CA: Integral Publishing, 1987); B. Greenwell, *Energies of Transformation: A Guide to the Kundalini Process* (Cupertino: Shakti River Press, 1990); B. Whitfield, *Full Circle;* B. Whitfield, *Spiritual Awakenings.*

12. C. L. Whitfield, "Self-Realization: Entry into the Transcendent Realm of Unqualified Reality. God-Realization. Objects and States May Arise, but They Are Simply Recognized, or Their Binding Power Transcended in the Radiant Higher Power," *Alcoholism & Spirituality: A Transpersonal Approach.* Self-published. Available at cbwhit.com.

13. B. Greyson and B. Harris [Whitfield], "Clinical Approaches to the NDEr," *Journal of Near-Death Studies* 6 (Fall 1987): 41–50.

14. C. L. Whitfield, *Healing the Child Within: Discovery & Recovery for Adult Children of Dysfunctional Families* (Deerfield Beach, FL: Health Communications, 1987); C. L. Whitfield, *A Gift to Myself: A Personal Workbook and Guide to Healing the Child Within* (Deerfield Beach, FL: Health Communications, 1990); C. L. Whitfield, *Boundaries and Relationships: Knowing, Protecting and Enjoying the Self* (Deerfield Beach, FL: Health Communications, 1993).

15. C. L. Whitfield, *Boundaries and Relationships;* C. L. Whitfield, *The Truth about Mental Illness: Choices for Healing* (Deerfield Beach, FL: HCI, 2004); Whitfield et al., *The Power of Humility;* B. Whitfield, *Spiritual Awakenings;* B. Whitfield, *The Natural Soul.*

16. In Twelve-Step programs, humility is part of the solution. People might bypass humility or find false humility, which does not work. Twelve-Step fellowships believe that true humility is obtained by hitting a bottom, getting honest, and working the Twelve Steps and/or getting counseling.

17. C. L. Whitfield, et. al. *The Power of Humility.*

18. A. Newberg and J. Iversen, "The Neural Basis of the Complex Mental Task of Meditation: Neurotransmitter and Neurochemical Considerations," *Medical Hypothesis* 8 (2003): 282–291.

19. G. Vaillant, *Spiritual Evolution: A Scientific Defense of Faith* (New York: Broadway Books, 2008), 54, 183.

20. C. L. Whitfield, *The Truth about Depression: Choices for Healing* (Deerfield Beach, FL: HCI, 2003); C. Whitfield, *The Truth about Mental Illness.*

21. C. L. Whitfield, *Boundaries and Relationships;* B. Whitfield, *Spiritual Awakenings.*

22. C. Whitfield, *Boundaries and Relationships.*

23. Anonymous, *Adult Children: Alcoholic/Dysfunctional Families.*

24. C. Whitfield, *Boundaries and Relationships.*

25. Ibid.

26. C. L. Whitfield et al., *The Power of Humility.*

27. Ibid.

28. Ibid.

29. G. Vaillant, *Spiritual Evolution.*

30. B. Whitfield, *The Natural Soul.*

Charles Whitfield

1. Helen Schucman, *A Course in Miracles* (Mill Valley, CA: Foundation for Inner Peace, 1975); Charles L. Whitfield, *Choosing God: A Bird's-Eye-View of A Course in Miracles* (in pre-print draft), 1998.

2. C. L. Whitfield, *Healing the Child Within: Discovery & Recovery for Adult Children of Dysfunctional Families* (Deerfield Beach, FL: HCI Books,1987); C. L. Whitfield, *Boundaries and Relationships: Knowing, Protecting, and Enjoying the Self* (Deerfield Beach, FL: HCI Books, 1993); C. L. Whitfield, *The Truth about Depression: Choices for Healing* (Deerfield Beach, FL: HCI Books, 2003); C. L. Whitfield, *The Truth about Mental Illness: Choices for Healing* (Deerfield Beach, FL: HCI Books, 2004); C. L. Whitfield, *My Recovery: A Personal Plan for Healing* (Deerfield Beach, FL: HCI Books, 2004); C. L. Whitfield et al., *The Power of Humility: Choosing Peace Over Conflict in Relationships* (Deerfield Beach, FL: HCI Books, 2006); C. L. Whitfield, *You May NOT Be Mentally Ill* (in process.)

3. C. L. Whitfield, *Healing the Child Within;* C. L. Whitfield, *Boundaries and Relationships;* C. L. Whitfield, *My Recovery;* C. L. Whitfield, *The Truth about Depression;* C. L. Whitfield, *The Truth about Mental Illness.*

4. Peter Breggin, MD, *Brain-Disabling Treatments in Psychiatry* (New York, NY: Springer Publishing, 2nd edition, 2008).

5. Lee Sannella, MD, *Kundalini: Psychosis or Transcendence?* (Atrium Pub Group, 1976), 60.

6. Peter Breggin, MD, *Brain-Disabling Treatments in Psychiatry.*

7. C. L. Whitfield et al, *The Power of Humility;* B. Whitfield, *Spiritual Awakenings: Insights of The Near-Death Experience and Other Doorways To Our Soul* (Deerfield Beach, FL: HCI Books, 1995.) B. Whitfield, *The Natural Soul* (Pittsburgh, PA: Sterlinghouse, 2009).

8. B. Greyson and B. Harris [Whitfield], "Clinical Approaches to the NDEr," *Journal of Near-Death Studies* 6 (Fall 1987).

9. Stanislav and Christina Grof, editors, *Spiritual Emergency: When Personal Transformation Becomes a Crisis* (Los Angeles: Tarcher, 1989).

10. Barbara Harris Whitfield, *Spiritual Awakenings: Insights of the NDE and Other Doorways to Our Soul* (Deerfield Beach, FL: HCI, 1995); B. Whitfield, *The Natural Soul* (Pittsburg, PA: Sterlinghouse, 2009).

11. C. L. Whitfield et al, *The Power of Humility*.

Bruce Greyson, MD

1. Greyson, B. "Near-Death Experiences and Spirituality," *Zygon: Journal of Science and Religion,* Vol. 41, No. 2, June 2006, 393-414.

2. Kelly, E. W., Greyson, B., and Kelly, E. F., "Unusual Experiences Near Death and Related Phenomena," in Kelly, E. F., Kelly, E. W., Crabtree, A., Gauld, A., Grosso, M., and Greyson, B., *Irreducible Mind: Toward a Psychology for the 21st Century.* Lanham, MD: Rowman and Littlefield, 2007, 367-421.

3. Greyson, B., op. cit.

4. Ring, K., *Heading Toward Omega: In Search of the Meaning of the Near-Death Experience.* New York: William Morrow, 1984.

5. Blackmore, S.J., *Dying to Live: Near-Death Experiences.* Buffalo: Prometheus, 1993; Woerlee, G.M., Mortal Minds: The Biology of Near-Death Experience, Buffalo: Prometheus, 2005.

6. Helminiak, D., "Neurology, Psychology, and Extraordinary Religious Experiences," *Journal of Religion and Health*, 1984, Vol. 23, No. 1, March 1984, 33-46.

7. Ring, K., op.cit.; Ring, K., and Valarino, E.E., *Lessons From the Light: What We Can Learn From the Near-Death Experience.* New York: Plenum/Insight, 1998.

8. Grey, M., *Return from Death: An Exploration of the Near-Death Experience.* London: Arkana, 1985; Grosso, M., *The Final Choice: Playing the Survival Game.* Walpole, N.H.: Stillpoint Press, 1985; Ring, op.cit.

9. Kason, Y., Bradford, M., Pond, P., and Greenwell, B., "Spiritual Emergence Syndrome and Kundalini Awakening: How Are They Related?" *Proceedings of the Academy of Religion and Psychical Research Annual Conference*, 1992, 85-118; Kieffer, G., "Murphy's 'Impossible Dream' of a Great Evolutionary Leap," *Ascent,* Vol. 1, No. 1, 1992, 1-8; Murphy, M., *The Future of the Human Body: Explorations Into the Further Evolution of Human Nature.* Los Angeles: Tarcher, 1992; Sannella, L., *The Kundalini Experience: Psychosis or Transcendence?* Lower Lake, CA: Integral Publishing, 1987.

10. Krishna, G., *The Biological Basis of Religion and Genius.* New York: Harper and Row, 1972.

11. _____, *The Awakening of Kundalini*, New York: E.P. Dutton, 1975.

12. _____, *What is and What Is Not Higher Consciousness.* New York: Julian Press, 1974.

13. _____, *The Biological Basis of Religion and Genius*, op.cit.; Krishna, G., *The Awakening of Kundalini,* op.cit.

14. _____, *The Secret of Yoga.* New York: Harper and Row, 1972.

15. Dippong, J., "Dawn of Perception: A True Rebirth," Chimo, Vol. 8, No. 4, 1982, 31-37.

16. Kieffer, G., "Kundalini and the Near-Death Experience," *Journal of Near-Death Studies,* Vol. 12, No. 3, Spring 1994, 159-176.

17. Krishna, *The Awakening of Kundalini,* op.cit.

18. Ring, K., *Heading Toward Omega,* op cit.

19. Whitfield B.H., *Spiritual Awakenings: Insights of the NDE and Other Doorways to our Soul.* Deerfield Beach, FL: HCI, 1995.

20. Bentov, I., *Stalking the Wild Pendulum: On the Mechanics of Consciousness.* Rochester, VT: Inner Traditions, 1977; Sannella, L., *The Kundalini Experience.* Lower Lake, CA: Integral Publishing, 1987.

21. Greyson, B., "The Near-death Experience Scale: Construction, Reliability, and Validity," *Journal of Nervous and Mental Disease,* Vol. 171, No. 6, June 1983, 369-375; Greyson, B., "Near-Death Encounters With and Without Near-Death Experiences: Comparative NDE Scale Profiles," *Journal of Near-Death Studies,* Vol. 8, No. 3, Spring 1990, 151-161; Greyson, B., "Consistency of Near-Death Experience Accounts Over Two Decades: Are Reports Embellished Over Time?", *Resuscitation,* Vol. 73, No. 3, June 2007, 407-411; Lange, R., Greyson, B., and Houran, J., "A Rasch Scaling Validation of a 'Core' Near-Death Experience," *British Journal of Psychology,* Vol. 95, No. 2, May 2004, 161-177.

22. For data analysis, see Greyson, B., "Near-Death Experiences and the Physio-Kundalini Syndrome," *Journal of Religion and Health,* Vol. 32, No. 4, Winter 1993, 277-290; and Greyson, B., "The Physio-Kundalini Syndrome and Mental Illness," *Journal of Transpersonal Psychology,* Vol. 25, No. 1, 1993, 43-58.

23. Ring, K., and Rosing, C., "The Omega Project: An Empirical Study of the NDE-Prone Personality," *Journal of Near-Death Studies,* Vol. 8, No. 4, Summer 1990, 211-239.

24. Greenwell, op. cit.; Grey, op. cit.; Sannella, op. cit.

25. Gallup, G,, Jr., with Proctor, W., *Adventures in Immortality: A Look Beyond the Threshold of Death.* New York: McGraw-Hill, 1982.

26. Whitfield, B., *Full Circle: The Near-Death Experience and Beyond.* New York: Pocket Books/Simon and Schuster, 1990; Whitfield, B., *Spiritual Awakenings: Insights of the NDE and Other Doorways to our Soul,* op. cit.; Whitfield, B., *The Natural Soul.* Pittsburgh: Sterling House, 2009; Ring, K., *Heading Toward Omega,* op. cit.; Grosso, M., op. cit; Grey, op. cit.

Shanti Shanti Kaur Khalsa

1. All names and identifying details have been changed.

2. AZT is the first drug approved for the treatment of HIV. Its chemical name is Azidothymidine, and is currently manufactured as Retrovir.

3. Yogi Bhajan quoted in John White, ed., *Kundalini, Evolution and Enlightenment* (New York: Omega, 1990), 144.

PART III

Ken Wilber

1. For convenience, I am following the Vajrayana in grouping the first and second kundalini chakras into one major chakra, the first major chakra. Tibetan Buddhism recognizes five, not seven, chakras. The first and second, and the sixth and seventh, are combined.

John White

1. Gopi Krishna, "Beyond Higher States of Consciousness," *New York Times,* October 6, 1974.

2. Gopi Krishna, *The Dawn of a New Science* (Darien, CT: Institute for Consciousness Research, 1999).

Lawrence Edwards

1. Joseph Campbell, *The Hero with A Thousand Faces* (Princeton, NJ: Princeton University Press, 1973), 11.

2. Robert Bly, trans., *The Kabir Book* (Boston: The Seventies Press, 1977), 29.

3. V. K. Subramaniam, trans., *Saundaryalahari of Sankaracarya* (Delhi, India: Motilal Banarsidass, 1980).

4. M. P. Pandit, trans., *Kularnava Tantra* (Madras, India: Ganesh & Co., 1973).

5. Carl Jung, *Psychological Commentary on Kundalini Yoga, Lectures 1 & 2, 1932* (New York: Spring Publications, 1975), 18.

6. Lex Hixon, *Mother of the Universe* (Wheaton, IL: The Theosophical Publishing House, 1994), 76.

7. Lawrence Edwards, *Psychological Change and Spiritual Growth through the Practice of Siddha Yoga* (Ann Arbor, MI: University Microfilms International, 1986) unpublished doctoral dissertation.

8. Sir John Woodroffe, *The Serpent Power* (Madras, India: Ganesh and Co., 1973).

9. Aldous Huxley, *The Perennial Philosophy* (New York: Harper Colophon, 1970), 11.

10. Woodroffe, *The Serpent Power.*

11. Hixon, *Mother of the Universe,* 7.

Stuart Sovatsky

1. D. S. Radhikananda Saraswati, trans., *Dnyaneshwari once again,* (Pune, India: Swami Radhikanand, 2002).

2. D. G. White, *The Alchemical Body* (Chicago: University of Chicago Press, 1998). See *The Alchemical Body* for detailed historical study of these Tantric practices involving hatha yoga, sexo-yogic practices, and rasayana of herbal and mercuric ingestibles. White states: "Beginning in the fifth century A.D., various Indian mystics began to innovate a body of techniques with which to render themselves immortal. These people called themselves *Siddhas,* a term formerly reserved for a class of demigods revered by Hindus and Buddhists alike who were known to inhabit mountaintops or the atmospheric regions. Over the following five to eight hundred years, three types of Hindu Siddha orders emerged, each with its own specialized body of practice. These were the Siddha Kaula, whose adherents sought bodily immortality through erotico-mystical practices; the Rasa Siddhas, medieval India's alchemists, who sought to transmute their flesh-and-blood bodies into immortal bodies through the ingestion of the mineral equivalents of the sexual fluids of the god Siva and his consort, the Goddess; and the Nath Siddhas, whose practice of hatha yoga projected the sexual and laboratory practices of the Siddha Kaula and Rasa Siddhas upon the internal grid of the subtle body. For India's medieval Siddhas, these three conjoined types of practice led directly to bodily immortality, supernatural powers, and self-divinization; in a word, to the exalted status of the semi-divine Siddhas of the older popular cults."

3. While the Sikh Dharma of Kundalini Yoga taught widely in the West by Yogi Bhajan has become synonymous with the entire practice, the term Kundalini embraces all forms of hatha yoga.

4. It is assumed that the aspirant is also following the yamas and niyamas: character-cultivating first two "limbs" of the "eight-limbed" (ashtanga) path, which also includes asana, pranayama, dharana (concentration), dhyana (meditation), and samadhi (complete absorption).

5. During Kundalini activity in the highly advanced adult yogi, sweet-tasting amritas, "nectar," or soma, "elixir of immortality," will re-arouse the yogi's tongue into the tumescence of khecari mudra—"the tongue's ecstatic dance into the heaven-realm"—in mystic rapport with the matured hypothalamus, the "little wedding chamber," (as named by the ancient Greeks) or "pleasure center" (as named by modern physiologists) and also with the "seat of the soul," pineal gland.

6. V. G. Pradhan, trans., *Jnaneshvari* (Albany: State University of New York Press, 1987).

7. N. E. Sjoman, *The Yoga Tradition of the Mysore Palace* (New Delhi: Abhinav Publications, 1996).

8. G. Aurobindo and The Mother, *On Love* (Pondicherry, India: Sri Aurobindo Society, 1973).

9. S. Thirumoolar, *Thirumandiram, a Classic of Yoga and Tantra, Vol. 1-3*, trans. D. Nataranjan (Montreal: Babaji Kriya Yoga, 1993).

10. B. H. Dass, *Hariakhan Baba: Known, Unknown* (Davis, CA: Sri Rama, 1975).

11. M. Govindan, *Babaji and the 18 Siddha Kriya Yoga Tradition, 3rd edition* (Montreal: Kriya Yoga Publications, 1993).

12. S. G. B. Satyeswarananda, *Babaji: The Divine Himalayan Yogi* (San Diego, CA: The Sanskrit Classics, 1984).

13. P. Yogananda, *Autobiography of a Yogi* (Los Angeles: Self Realization Fellowship, 1977), 575.

14. Kripalu Yoga Fellowship, *Guru Prasad* (Sumneytown, PA: Kripalu Yoga Fellowship, 1982).

15. C. D. Collins, *The Iconography and Ritual of Siva at Elephanta* (Albany: State University of New York Press, 1988), 48.

Gene Keiffer

1. G. Krishna, *Secrets of Kundalini in Panchastavi* (Kundalini Research and Publication Trust, B-98, Sarvodhya Enclave, New Delhi, India,1978).

2. Ibid.

3. Ibid.

4. Ibid.

5. Ibid.

PART IV

Gurucharan Singh Khalsa

1. Yogi Bhajan, *The Master's Touch on Being a Sacred Teacher for the New Age* (Espanola, NM: Kundalini Research Institute/Sheridan Books, 1997).

2. Ibid.

3. Ibid.

4. Ary L. Goldberg, "Heart Rate Dynamics during Three Forms of Meditation," ed. C. K. Peng et al., *International Journal of Cardiology* 95, no. 1 (May 2004): 19−27.

5. A. Panduro et al., "Breathwalking Effects on the Regulation of Glucose and Insulin Tolerance in Diabetes 2," *International Diabetes Care* (2004).

6. Herbert Benson et al., "Functional Brain Mapping of the Relaxation Response and Meditation," *Neuroreport* 11, no. 7 (2000): 1–5; Manjit Kaur Khalsa, "Alternative Treatments for Borderline and Narcissistic Personality Disorders," in *The Psychospiritual Clinician's Handbook: Alternative Methods for Understanding and Treating Mental Disorders*, eds. Sharon G. Mijares and Gurucharan Singh Khalsa (New York: Haworth Press, 2005).

7. Sat Bir Khalsa, "Treatment of Chronic Insomnia with Yoga: A Preliminary Study with Sleep–Wake Diaries," *Applied Psychophysiology and Biofeedback* 29, no. 4, (2004). DOI: 10.1007/s10484-004-0387-0.

8. S. B. S. Khalsa et al., "Evaluation for a Residential Kundalini Yoga Lifestyle Pilot Program for Addiction in India," *Journal of Ethnicity in Substance Abuse* 7 (2008): 67–79.

9. Bhajan, *The Master's Touch*.

10. Ibid.

11. Ibid.

12. Ibid.

13. Yogi Bhajan and Gurucharan Singh Khalsa, *Breathwalk: Breathing Your Way to a Revitalized Body, Mind, and Spirit* (New York: Broadway Books, 2000); Gurucharan Singh Khalsa, "Getting Focused in an Age of Distraction: Approaches to Attentional Disorders Using the Humanology of Yogi Bhajan," in *The Psychospiritual Clinician's Handbook: Alternative Methods for Understanding and Treating Mental Disorders*, eds. Sharon G. Mijares and Gurucharan Singh Khalsa (New York: Haworth Press, 2005).

14. Yogi Bhajan and Gurucharan Singh Khalsa, *The Mind: Its Projections and Multiple Facets* (Espanola, NM: Kundalini Research Institute/Sheridan Books,1998).

Contributors

LAWRENCE EDWARDS, PHD, has practiced and taught meditation for over thirty-eight years. He is the founder and director of Anam Cara, Inc., a nonprofit organization dedicated to teaching meditative practices. He is also the president of the Kundalini Research Network (kundalininet.org), a nonprofit organization that provides information on kundalini and offers international conferences to gather people researching and writing on the transformative processes of kundalini awakening. His book, *The Soul's Journey: Guidance from the Divine Within,* describes this process and sets it in a context that westerners can easily understand (thesoulsjourney.com). Dr. Edwards is also trained in biofeedback and neurofeedback and has been on the faculty of New York Medical College as a clinical instructor in the Department of Community and Preventive Medicine since 1998. In 1986 he earned his doctorate in psycho-educational processes from Temple University where he was honored as a University Scholar. He was a disciple of Swami Muktananda's from 1976 until Muktananda took *mahasamadhi* in 1982. For the next twelve years he continued to study, teach, and serve under Gurumayi Chidvilasananda's tutelage. At Swami Muktananda's ashram in Ganeshpuri, India, he served as clinic manager and helped to run the mobile hospital that provided care for the desperately poor native villages in the rural area surrounding the ashram. Dr. Edwards has studied and practiced in the kundalini yoga tradition and Tibetan Buddhist and Huichol Indian shamanic traditions.

BONNIE GREENWELL PHD, is a transpersonal psychologist, writer, and educator known internationally for her specialization in assisting people in kundalini and spiritual awakening processes for over twenty-five years. She authored *Energies of Transformation: A Guide to the Kundalini Process,* based on her doctoral research, which is published in six countries. She was a founder and director of the Kundalini Research Network and frequent participant in programs of the Spiritual Emergence Network. She has worked for thirty-five years with energy and awakening systems both ancient and modern, including astanga and kundalini yoga, Jin Shin Do acupressure, Radiance and Holotropic breathwork, and Advaita Vedanta, and for the last eight years has been a student of the nondual Zen teacher Adyashanti. She now teaches in his lineage and has established Shanti River Institute in Ashland, Oregon, to support nondual students in the awakening process. She has consulted with more than a thousand people about their kundalini process through national and international seminars and programs, and on the Internet, as well as in personal counseling sessions. Currently she is writing two sequels to her groundbreaking kundalini book, *The Kundalini Guide* and *The Awakening Guide.* She can be contacted through her Web sites kundaliniguide.com and awakeningguide.com.

BRUCE GREYSON, MD, is the Chester F. Carlson Professor of Psychiatry and Neurobehavioral Sciences and director of the Division of Perceptual Studies at the University of Virginia. He was a founder and past president of the International Association for Near-Death Studies, and for the past twenty-six years has edited the *Journal of Near-Death Studies.* He was formerly on the board of directors of the Kundalini Research Network. Dr. Greyson graduated from Cornell University with a major in psychology, received his medical degree from the State University of New York Upstate

Medical College, and completed his psychiatric training at the University of Virginia. He held faculty appointments in psychiatry at the University of Michigan and the University of Connecticut, where he was clinical chief of psychiatry, before returning to the University of Virginia, where he has practiced and taught psychiatry and carried out research since 1995. His research for the past three decades has focused on near-death experiences and has resulted in more than seventy presentations to national scientific conferences, more than one hundred publications in academic medical and psychological journals, and several research grants and awards. He was coeditor of *The Near-Death Experience: Problems, Prospects, Perspectives,* and of *Near-Death Experiences: Thirty Years of Scholarly Inquiry;* and coauthor of *Irreducible Mind: Toward a Psychology for the 21st Century.*

PENNY KELLY is the owner of Lily Hill Farm and Learning Center in southwest Michigan where she teaches courses in developing the gift of consciousness, getting well again, and organic gardening. She maintains a large counseling practice, works as a consultant to schools and corporations, and raises organic vegetables. Penny is one of the founding members of the Tipping Point Network and is currently working with them to move sustainability from 2 percent to 10 percent of global market share and create a global network of consciousness centers that support the transformation to higher consciousness and sustainable living. Penny holds a degree in humanistic studies from Wayne State University, a degree in naturopathic medicine from Clayton College of Natural Health, and is currently working toward her PhD in nutrition from the American Holistic College of Nutrition. She is the mother of four children, has written five books, and is working on a sixth. Her current books in print are *The Evolving Human; The Elves of Lily Hill Farm; Robes: A Book of Coming Changes; From The Soil To The Stomach: Understanding the Connection between the Earth and Your Health;* and *Consciousness and Energy, Volume 1: Multi-dimensionality and a Theory of Consciousness.*

SAT BIR SINGH KHALSA, PHD, has practiced a yoga lifestyle for over thirty-five years and is a certified kundalini yoga instructor. He is currently the director of research for the Kundalini Research Institute and an assistant professor of medicine at Harvard Medical School at Brigham and Women's Hospital in Boston. His current research interests are in basic and clinical research on the effectiveness of yoga and meditation practices. His central research project funded by the National Center for Complementary and Alternative Medicine involves clinical research trials of a kundalini yoga treatment for insomnia. Dr. Khalsa is intimately involved with the international yoga research community and also teaches an elective course at Harvard Medical School in mind-body medicine.

GURMUKH KAUR KHALSA is the cofounder and director of Golden Bridge, A Spiritual Village both in Los Angeles and New York City. For almost four decades, students in Los Angeles and around the world have sought her classes in this most powerful style of yogas, kundalini yoga and meditation as taught by Yogi Bhajan, including pre- and postnatal classes and teacher training. This inspiring world yogini is a pioneer in yoga and the mind-body-spirit connections. She met her teacher, Yogi Bhajan, thirty-seven years ago. Under his guidance she has devoted herself to a path of helping people in many ways, from finding spiritual success in their careers and relationships, to helping them consciously deliver healthy children and start their families with a strong foundation. Gurmukh is the author of the best-selling book, *The Eight Human Talents: The Yogic Way to Restore Balance and Serenity within You,* and the must-have guide for a healthy pregnancy, *Bountiful, Beautiful, Blissful: Experience the Natural Power of Pregnancy and Birth with Kundalini Yoga and Meditation.* Her DVDs include an energizing practice, *Kundalini Yoga with Gurmukh,* and prenatal and postnatal yoga. She currently lives with her husband of twenty-six years in Los Angeles. Her daughter, age twenty-five, helps to run the Nite Moon Café and Retail Store at Golden Bridge Yoga in Los Angeles.

GURUCHARAN S. KHALSA, PhD, is a psychotherapist, teacher, and writer and is a world-recognized expert in kundalini yoga as taught by Yogi Bhajan. Dr. Khalsa is an authority in the mind and in the applied psychology of meditation and peak performance. For twenty-five years he was in clinical practice with his focus on executive coaching, conflict resolution, stress management, creativity, and the interface of high information technology with optimal human performance. He bridges two perspectives: the hard sciences, which he learned in mathematics and chemistry at Harvey Mudd College and graduate mathematic studies at Claremont Graduate School; and the human sciences, which he studied at Boston University for a master's degree in counseling. He later completed a doctorate in psychology. Gurucharan is an educator and has instructed in universities, including MIT and the University of Guadalajara, for over twenty years, and has been affiliated with the Center for Psychology and Social Change at Harvard University. He has done original research on the cognitive and physiological impact of meditation and has designed social programs. He speaks and writes on the use of yoga techniques for therapists, health care providers, and organizations. In addition, he has trained thousands of yoga teachers and conducts classes and seminars in kundalini yoga around the world. For more information go to: kundaliniresearchinstitute.org or gurucharan.com.

SHANTI SHANTI KAUR KHALSA, PhD, is founder and director of the Guru Ram Das Center for Medicine and Humanology. A yoga instructor since 1971, she began to specialize in teaching kundalini yoga and meditation to people with chronic or life-threatening illness and their family members in 1986, under the direction of Yogi Bhajan. The Center provides direct client services and yogically based programs for people with diabetes, cancer, heart disease, chronic fatigue, fibromyalgia, HIV, anxiety, depression, and life transitions. It also offers professional training and conducts outcome studies on the medical effects of yoga practice. Dr. Khalsa is a

Registered Yoga Teacher with extensive experience, a Yoga Alliance Standard, KRI-certified yoga teacher trainer, and a charter member of the International Association of Yoga Therapists. She provides training to health professionals and yoga instructors on the application of yoga and meditation to the spiritual, psychological, and behavioral aspects of getting and staying well.

GOPI KRISHNA (1903–1984) was born in a small village in India about twenty miles from the city of Srinagar, to parents of Kashmiri Brahmin extraction. He spent the first eleven years of his life growing up in the beautiful Himalayan vale of Kashmir. In 1914, his family moved to the city of Lahore in the Punjab, which, at that time, was a part of British India. He spent the next nine years completing his high school education. Illness caused him to leave the torrid plains of the Punjab and return to the cooler climate of the Kashmir Valley, where in succeeding years he secured a post in the Public Works Department of the state, married, and raised a family of two sons and a daughter. In 1967, he published his first major book in India, *Kundalini: the Evolutionary Energy in Man,* which was published a year later in Great Britain and thereafter in the United States and then in more than a dozen major languages. The work presented to the world for the first time a clear and concise autobiographical account of the awakening of kundalini, which he had experienced in 1937. In 1972 Harper & Row published his *The Secret of Yoga* and *The Biological Basis of Religion and Genius.* A forty-six-page introduction was written for the latter by Professor Carl Friedrich von Weizsäcker, the renowned German scientist and director of the Max Planck Institute at Starnberg. Gopi Krishna died of a lung infection in July, 1984, leaving a literary legacy of some eighteen books that will serve to guide scientific investigations into the phenomenon of kundalini for centuries to come.

GENE KIEFFER established the Kundalini Research Foundation, Ltd., in 1970 at the request of Pandit Gopi Krishna. The Foundation's primary mission is to make accurate and reliable information on kundalini available to the public and to scholars and scientists. He graduated from the University of Iowa with a degree in journalism and subsequently worked for more than five years at the *Des Moines Register,* after which he started an advertising/public relations agency in Des Moines. In 1969, he moved his offices to New York City, and a year later met Gopi Krishna in Switzerland. They worked together on a daily basis for fourteen years until Krishna's death in 1984. Mr. Kieffer has interviewed, in person or through correspondence, more than two thousand individuals who described their kundalini experiences to him as part of the Foundation's ongoing research project.

OLGA LOUCHAKOVA is a professor of transpersonal psychology and director of the Neurophenomenology Center at the Institute of Transpersonal Psychology. She is a master teacher of the Hridayam® School of Kundalini Yoga. Her teaching mandate came in 1988 from an underground spiritual school in the former Soviet Union. Since then, Olga has taught and studied spiritual awakening in Russia, Eastern and Western Europe, Latin America, England, India, Turkey, and the United States. In the 1980s, Olga was a neuroscientist at the Pavlov Institute of Physiology in St. Petersburg, Russia. Her pioneering work in the biotechnological diagnostics of autoimmune diseases of the nervous system was acclaimed by grants and patents, as well as published in many medical journals in Russia. Later, personal spiritual experiences led Olga to meet a spiritual elder, Vladimir Antonov. She soon afterward became a full-time spiritual teacher herself. She is a welcome teacher at the Catholic Mercy Center in Burlingame, California, at the Esalen Institute in Big Sur, California, at a phenomenological conference at Oxford University in United Kingdom, and at the conventions of the American Psychological Association and the European Association of Transpersonal Psychology. She is the founding director of the Neurophenomenology Center at

ITP, where issues connected with spiritual awakening are studied scientifically with state of the art multichanel EEG and computerized cognitive testing. Olga has established the Hridayam School in order to train professional guides in spiritual awakening. She currently offers workshops and maintains a private practice in kundalini process guidance in the San Francisco/Oakland Bay Area of northern California.

DAVID LUKOFF, PHD, is a professor of psychology at the Institute for Transpersonal Psychology and coauthor of the *DSM-IV* diagnostic category "Religious or Spiritual Problem." His areas of expertise include treatment of schizophrenia, transpersonal psychotherapy, and spiritual issues in clinical practice. He is author of seventy articles and chapters on spiritual issues and mental health and copresident of the Institute for Spirituality and Psychology and of the Association for Transpersonal Psychology, and he maintains the Spiritual Competency Resource Center at spiritualcompetency.com.

ANDREW B. NEWBERG, MD, is currently an associate professor in the Department of Radiology and Psychiatry at the Hospital of the University of Pennsylvania and is a staff physician in Nuclear Medicine. He graduated from the University of Pennsylvania School of Medicine in 1993. He is board certified in internal medicine and nuclear medicine. He has been particularly involved in the study of mystical and religious experiences as well as the more general mind-body relationship in both the clinical and research aspects of his career. Much of his research has focused on the relationship between brain function and various mystical and religious experiences, and he is the director of the University of Pennsylvania Center for Spirituality and the Mind. His research also includes understanding the physiological correlates of acupuncture therapy, meditation, and other types of alternative therapies. He is the author of a new book, *Born to Believe: God,*

Science, and the Origin of Ordinary and Extraordinary Beliefs (Free Press). He also coauthored the best-selling book, *Why God Won't Go Away: Brain Science and the Biology of Belief* (Ballantine), and *The Mystical Mind: Probing the Biology of Belief* (Fortress Press), both of which explore the relationship between neuroscience and spiritual experience.

STUART PERRIN, born in 1942, has trod the spiritual path since he was sixteen. He studied literature, philosophy, acting, and poetry and lived a Bohemian life in Europe and northern Africa until he was twenty-five years old, when he met his spiritual teacher, Albert Rudolph. Better known as Rudi, this iconoclastic spiritual teacher gave Eastern spirituality a new American slant, and Stuart has been carrying that slant forward ever since Rudi's death in 1973. His studies with Rudi gave Stuart a deep insight into how kundalini yoga can be applied in day-to-day living. The author of five books and an expert in Oriental art, Stuart ran a meditation center in Texas for nine years before moving back to New York City, where he continues to teach spiritual work in the lineage of Rudi. For more information on Stuart Perrin, go to his Web site: stuartperrin.com.

SWAMI SIVANANDA RADHA (1911–1995) is regarded as one of the most profound and practical spiritual leaders of the twentieth century. Born in Germany, Swami Radha moved to Canada after World War II, and traveled to India in the mid-fifties to meet her spiritual teacher, Swami Sivananda. Initiated into *sanyas* in 1956, she then returned to Canada and dedicated her life to selfless service and interpreting the ancient wisdom of yoga for Western minds. Swami Radha is a respected author of more than ten books, several of which have become classics in the field of yoga, most notably *Kundalini Yoga for the West* and *Hatha Yoga: The Hidden Language.* Her published works represent a living legacy of yoga practice based on forty years of personal study and compassionate teaching. Swami Radha founded the Yasodhara Ashram and a number of international Radha Yoga Centres, and has published-timeless books, and *ascent magazine*. Her work continues in the devotional spirit in which it was created, maintaining the quality and integrity that were the essence of her life.

JOHN SELBY came of age in the sixties and was lucky enough to become friends with a number of spiritual teachers from that time forward, including Krishnamurti, Ram Dass, Bhagwan Rajneesh, Alan Watts, Kriyananda, and the modern-day Sufi saint Samuel Lewis. Selby's primary spiritual teacher was the Burmese master Thakan Kung. Selby studied psychology and comparative religion at Princeton University, U.C. Berkeley, the Graduate Theological Union, and the San Francisco Theological Seminary. He completed formal research into the meditative experience at the National Institutes of Health and the New Jersey Neuro-psychiatric Institute working with Dr. Humphrey Osmond, and also conducted LSD research at the Bureau of Research in Neurology and Psychiatry. He has written more than two dozen books on yoga, meditation, spiritual awakening, and integrated wellness, including *Kundalini Awakening; Seven Masters, One Path;* and *Quiet Your Mind*. Recently, working with Senn-Delaney Leadership, he has developed awareness-management (i.e., medi-tation at work) programs for the corporate world. He currently heads Awareness Management Systems and BedRockVideo Productions. For more information please visit www.uplift.com.

STUART SOVATSKY (AB, Princeton; PhD, CIIS), a marriage thera-pist for thirty years, was first choice to codirect Ram Dass's "prison ashram" and first in the United States to bring yoga to the home-less mentally ill in the 1970s. Copresident of the Association for Transpersonal Psychology and twenty-year trustee for California Institute of Integral Studies (CIIS), he was initiating co-convener of the forty-country World Congress on Psychology and Spirituality in Delhi, India, where B. K. S. Iyengar and Sri Sri Ravi Shankar keynoted. Author of *Eros Consciousness and Kundalini, Words from the Soul:, Your Perfect Lips, Columbia Desk Companion Reference on Eastern Religion* (edited by Robert Thurman), and numerous articles and chapters on psychotherapy and tantra yoga, he has presented his work throughout the United States, India, Europe, and Russia. A thirty-year adept at *anahata-nad* spontaneous yogic chanting, he has three CDs with Axis Mundi.

DOROTHY WALTERS spent most of her professional life as a college professor of English and women's studies in various midwestern universities. She has published an account of her own kundalini awakening in *Unmasking the Rose: A Record of a Kundalini Initiation* (Hampton Roads). She has also published two books of spiritual poetry: *Marrow of Flame: Poems of the Spiritual Journey* (Hohm Press, 2000), and *A Cloth of Fine Gold: Poems of the Inner Journey* (Lulu Press, 2008). She now lives and writes in San Francisco, where she maintains a blog of poems and reflections on the spiritual path at kundalinisplendor.blogspot.com. She invites readers to contact her there and is able to offer to many advice and encouragement as they move ahead through their own awakening process. As she often remarks, "If this [spontaneous kundalini awakening] could occur to me, sitting in my living room on an elm-lined street in Kansas so long ago when little was known of this esoteric phenomenon, then what is not possible for us all?"

JOHN WHITE is an author in the fields of consciousness research and higher human development. He has published fifteen books, including *The Meeting of Science and Spirit; What Is Enlightenment?; A Practical Guide to Death and Dying;* and, for children, *The Christmas Mice.* His books have been translated into ten languages. His writing has also appeared in the *New York Times, Saturday Review, Reader's Digest, Science of Mind, Esquire, Omni, Woman's Day,* and various other newspapers and magazines. He lives in Cheshire, Connecticut.

WHITEHAWK's professional LIFE began in broadcasting and video production, then segued into software development as a writer for applications produced by Microsoft, Apple, the entertainment industry, an environmental organization, the medical field, and others. She then aligned her career more directly with her soul's calling by producing consciousness-raising media and events, and founding an organization to support wisdom sharing, networking, and peer mentoring for spiritually oriented creatives. Recently emerging from a kundalini-initiated hiatus, she anticipates continuing her immersion education with the hyper-potentiated quantum field ("deep light") taking root on earth, and exploring how to apply and assimilate the new energetic frequencies in service to personal and interpersonal healing, collaborative creativity and manifestation, community building, and peace. Contact is invited via her blog: http://wingingwithwhitehawk.wordpress.com.

BARBARA HARRIS WHITFIELD is a respiratory therapist and massage therapist. She is the author of five books: *Full Circle: The Near-Death Experience and Beyond, Spiritual Awakenings: Insights of the Near-Death Experience and Other Doorways to Our Soul, Final Passage: Sharing the Journey as This Life Ends, The Power of Humility: Choosing Peace over Conflict in Relationships,* and *The Natural Soul.* Barbara was research assistant to psychiatry professor Bruce Greyson at the University of Connecticut Medical School, studying the spiritual, psychological, physical, and energetic aftereffects of the near-death experience. She is past chair and member of the board of the Kundalini Research Network and has sat on the executive board of the International Association for Near-Death Studies. She is a consulting editor and contributor for the *Journal of Near-Death Studies.* She was on the faculty of Rutgers University's Institute for Alcohol and Drug Studies for twelve years, teaching courses on the aftereffects of spiritual awakenings. She is a faculty member of the Center for Sacred Studies where she coteaches a course with Charles Whitfield called Unity in Practice. Barbara was a key subject in Kenneth Ring's groundbreaking book on the near-death experience, *Heading Toward Omega*. He writes about her again in his latest book, *Lessons From the Light*. Barbara lives in Atlanta, Georgia, with her husband, author and physician Charles Whitfield. They share a private practice where they provide individual and group psychotherapy for trauma survivors, people with addictions and other problems in living, and spiritual seekers. For more information, see barbarawhitfield.com.

CHARLES L. WHITFIELD, MD, is a pioneer in trauma recovery, including the way we remember childhood and other trauma and abuse. A physician and frontline therapist who assists trauma survivors in their healing, he is the author of fifty published articles, and ten best-selling books on trauma psychology and recovery, including *Healing the Child Within*. He lives and practices addiction medicine, trauma psychology, and wholistic psychiatry in Atlanta, Ga. For more information please visit cbwhit.com.

KEN WILBER, author of more than two dozen published books, has created what is widely considered the first truly comprehensive Integral Map of human experience. By exploring and integrating the major insights and conclusions of nearly every human knowledge domain in existence, Ken created the AQAL Integral Framework, a framework that is grounded in millennia of human understanding and yet still grows and expands to embrace new information. In 1997 Ken founded Integral Institute (integralinstitute.org), a nonprofit think tank that brought together literally hundreds of the brightest integral thinkers alive. It was in this highly creative atmosphere that individuals shared how the integral model might be modified and improved, based on real-world application. In 2003 Ken started recording some of these cutting-edge conversations—all with people at the top of their profession, like Michael Crichton, Deepak Chopra, Tony Robbins, Genpo Roshi, Larry Dossey, and others—and made them available weekly on Integral Naked (integralnaked.org), which has nearly six years of the finest integral audio and video content available anywhere. In 2005 Ken created Integral Spiritual Center, and its yearly gatherings have consistently brought together more than forty of the world's finest spiritual teachers, all of whom are dedicated to exploring a truly integral spirituality. Wilber's latest endeavor is Integral Life (integrallife.com), with CEO Robb Smith, a for-profit extension of Integral Institute dedicated to offering practical, easy-to-understand ways to live a genuinely integral life and to create a place for integral community to take root and grow. For the latest news, blogs, and writings, check out kenwilber.com.

Credits

"Are the Chakras Real?" by Ken Wilber was excerpted from *Kundalini, Evolution, and Enlightenment,* edited by John Warren White, published by Paragon House Publishers, 1990.

"Thoughts on Kundalini" by Swami Sivananda Radha was excerpted from *Kundalini Yoga for the West: A Foundation for Character Building, Courage, and Awareness,* published by timeless books, Spokane, WA, 1996.

"Heart" by Swami Sivananda Radha was excerpted from *Light & Vibration: Consciousness, Mysticism & the Culmination of Yoga,* published by timeless books, Spokane, WA, 2007.

Portions of Swami Radhananda's, "The Subtle Path: The Web of Kundalini" appeared in *ascent magazine,* Issue 7, Autumn 2000.

Index

Note: Page numbers in italics indicate tables or figures.

3HO Foundation, 89, 336
3HO Foundation SuperHealth program, 91–92, 96
60 Minutes, 273

Abhinava-gupta, 251
Abhishiktananda, 100
abnormal states, 292
absolute being, 205
absorption, 204
academics, 283–284
active bliss, 120
acupuncture, 91, 151, 212
addiction recovery, 91–92
ADHD (attention-deficit hyperactivity disorder), 332
the Adi-Buddha, 195
Adi Shakti, 319, 320
adolescents, 258. *See also* puberty
adult child issues, 169
adult maturation, 260–265, 266–268
advaita, 251, 253
Advaita Vedanta, 32, 34, 232
Adyashanti, 30–32, 34

the Age of Aquarius, 316, 318, 320, 337–338
aggression, 134
agitation, 135–136, 137
air, *239,* 240, 256
ajna chakra, *239,* 240, 253, *254*
akashic ethers, 268
alchemy, 197, 213
alcohol, 147
alien encounters, 147. *See also* extraterrestrials
alignment, 98, 113
Alliant International University (San Diego), 95
All-That-Is, 159, 163
Alpert, Richard (Ram Dass), 268
altered perceptions, 137
Alzheimer's disease, 95, 96
Alzheimer's Research and Prevention Foundation, 95, 96
Amaurghasasana, 251
amplification, 68–69
amritas, 264, 267, 348n5
Amritsar, India, 92
amrit vela, 336
amygdala, 150
anahata chakra, *239,* 240, 252, 253, *254*

anahata-nad, 258, 259

anahata-nada, 266, 267

ananda, 213, 229

ananda-maya kosha, 253, 265

ancestors, 63–65

androgyny, 256

anima, 229

animal-like movements, 131

anja chakra, *254*

anna-maya kosha, 252, 265

Annual Convention for Adult
    Children of Alcoholics, 147

anxiety, 91–93, 122, 132, 134, 137,
    168, 198–199, 331, 332

anxiety disorders. *See* anxiety

apana-pran, 252

aphasia, 94–95

archetypes, 11

ardha-nari, 259

Arizona, 91–92

Arjuna, 109, 227–228

arousal system, 120–121

ars erotica, 261

arthritis, 122

asanas, 253, *254,* 256, 258, 259, 261,
    266

ascending bliss, 202

asceticism, 12

ashramas, 262, 264–265, 267

ashram meditation, 243. *See also*
    ashramas

ashtangha yoga, 259–260

Asoka the Great, 294

Asperger's syndrome, 274

Assagioli, Roberto, 129

asthma, 122

Atman, *162,* 163

attitude, 309

auditory hallucinations, 135

auditory meditation, 252

auditory sensations, 132

auras, 90, 267, 317–318

Aurobindo, 214, 262

authority, temporal, 294

autism, 274

autonomic nervous system, 120–121,
    331

awakening, 9–11, 17, 21–35, 118,
    120–123, 164. *See also* kundalini
    awakening; spiritual awakening;
    spontaneous awakening

    gradual, 28–29

    meditation and, 73–84, 97–115,
        127–139

    negative effects of, 123–124

    nondual aspect of, 32–35

    recovery movement and, 164–165

    spontaneous, 98–99, 101, 107, 227

    true, 82–83

    types of, 28–32

awareness, 158, 203, 298, 326–327

    focused awareness, 112

AZT (Azidothymidine), 347n2

Baba, 242, 243

Babaji, 268–269

back problems, 134

Bacon, Francis, 280

balance, 12–15, 18, 75, 77, 111–115,
    158–160, 328–329

ballet, 261

bandhas, 253

"batch karmic processing," 65

belly dancing, 260

the Beloved, 7, 11

Benson, Herbert, 331

Bentov, Itzhak, 176–177

Bentov-Sannella physio-kundalini model, 176–177

Bergson, Henri, 174

Bhagavad Gita, 109, 227–228, 261, 262

bhakti yoga, 242, 259

bhandas, 190, 191

Bharati, Agehananda, 215

bhastrika pranayama, 259

bija, 257

bindu, 210

bioenergy, 174, 202–203, 212, 219–220

bioplasma, 174, 212, 214, 216

bipolar disorder, 106–111, 151

birth. *See* childbirth

bliss, 12–13, 37–38, 120, 197–205, 202, 213, 310. *See also* pleasure

bloodstream, 221

boddhisattva, 148

bodhicitta, 229

the body, 200, 317

    the energy body, 234

    the etheric body, 215

    finality of, 99–101

    mind-body complex, 90–91, 98–101, 102

    the physical body, 99–101, 206, 234–235, 252, 317

    the radiant body, 318

    spirit and, 99–101, 102

    the subtle body, 104, 107, 203–204, 206, 214–215, 233–238, *239,* 252

body-mind-spirit, 102

Bol, Goran, 95

Book of the Dead, 33

boundaries, 153, 155, 157–158

Brahma, 104, 204–205

brahmacharya, 262–263, 304

the Brahman, 195

Brahmarandhra, 175, 214, 215

brahma randhra. See Brahmarandhra

the brain, 36, 105, 145–146, 152, 175, 215, 220, 222, 256, 274–278. *See also* the mind

    biology of, 97

    brain centers, 36

    evolution of, 276–277, 283–287, 289, 291

    kundalini flow into, 215–216

    yogic, 117–125

brain imaging studies, 119–121, 150–151, 325, 331–332

breath, 190. *See also* breathing

    breath awareness, 81

    breath technique, 191–192

breathing, 135, 144–145, 189, 190–191, 259–260

    breathing exercises, 253, *254*

    breathing meditation, 93, 94

    deep, 21

    unusual breathing patterns, 132

Breathwalk, 94, 96, 331, 336–337

Breggin, Peter, 166

"bridge pose," 95

the Bronze Age, 316

Brown, Norman O., 200

Bubba Free John, 196

Buddha, 15, 32, 80, 82, 127, 128, 216

    Buddha mind, 237

    Buddha Nature, *162,* 163

    inate, 309

    statues of, 215

Buddha's eightfold path, 247

buddhi, 103

Buddhist tradition, 32, 147–148, 150–151, 215, 260, 294

Buhnemann, Gudrun, *The Iconography of Hindu Tantric Deities,* 252

burning, 132

Bushmen, 260

caduceus, 189

Cage, Nicholas, 227

California, 93, 95

Campbell, Joseph, 8, 128, 214, 225, 323

　The Hero with a Thousand Faces, 226

cancer, 105

　kidney cancer, 113, 114

　prostate cancer, 104, 113, 114

cardiovascular health, 91, 99–106, 122, 132, 134, 325, 331. *See also* the heart; heart attacks; strokes

Castaneda, Carlos, 8

castration complex, 200

Cave of Brahma, 214. *See also* Brahmarandhra

celibacy, 131, 221–222. *See also* monastic life

　erotic, 262–263

cerebral lobes, 261

CERN, 272

chakras, 15, 28–30, 48–51, 67–68, 74, 90, 97, 103–104, 113, 117, 237, *239,* 252, 268, 317, 323, 329–330, 347n1

　balancing, 75, 77

　chakra activation, 67

　chakra meditation, 253, *254*

　chakra seven, 163

　chakra six, 163

　chakra system, 51, 53–54, 59, 106, 203, 226, 227

　character building of the, 302

　debates about the nature of the, 214–215

　existence of the, 195–206

　heart chakra, 152

　localization of the, 201–204

　opening of the, 130–131, 201–202

　root chakra, 68

　seventh chakra, 163, 214

　sixth chakra, 163

　symbolism of the, 204, 238–241

　third chakra, 49–50, 52

　throat chakra, 339n2

　unified human chakra, 68

Ch'an, 196

Chandogya Upanishad, 196

chanting, 128, 267

chemical dependence, 147. *See also* drugs

chi, 49, 174, 203, 212, 229

chih-kuan, 206

chi kung. See Qigong

childbirth, 131, 147, 266

child development, 255–258, 265–266

Children's Hospital in San Diego, 92–93

Child Within, 162, 163, 164

China, 212

choice, power of, 309

Christ. *See* Jesus Christ

Christ consciousness, 33, 45, 163, 237

Christianity, 33, 74, 212, 260, 294, 313

Christian mysticism, 106, 174

Christian saints, 11, 13, 18

chronic fatigue, 108

circulation, 256

citta, 263

clairvoyance, 67

cleansing, 62–68

codependence issues, 169

cognition, 332

   supersensory, 286–287, 288

   types of, 103

cognitive impairment, 95

colors, 58–59

compassion, 132, 141, 142, 152–153, 157–158, 307, 308

concrete thinking, 237–238

confusion, 123, 133

consciousness, 112, 134, 203, 230, 232, 236, 263, 307, 309, 310

   altered states of, 209

   cosmic, 198, 218, 274–275, 277

   development of, 198–200

   disease and, 64–65

   Divine Consciousness, 228–229, 238, 239, 245

   ego-based, 99–100

   Eternal Consciousness, 289

   expansion of, 130–131, 157

   heightened, 53

   Higher Consciousness, 205, 206, 207–224, 313

   illuminated, 271–278

   kundalini experiences and, 14, 21, 27, 32, 35–36, 37–38, 42–45, 74, 81

   kundalini yoga and, 51, 57

   mundane, 100

   mystical states of, 133, 276, 282

   ocean of, 269–275

   origin-consciousness, 268

   power of, 228–230

   primordial, 257

   process of involution and evolution through chakras, 238–241

   pure, 257

   research into, 277–298

   states of, 87

   superconsciousness, 276, 277–278

   transcendental state of, 285–286

   transformation of, 276–277

   transhuman, 288

   unitive state of, 87–88

   Unity Consciousness, 143, 230, 237–238

   universal, 217–218

   universal nature of, 104–105

   waking, 234–236

Constantine, Emperor, 294

constipation, 131

continuing pain syndromes, 94

Continuum Center for Health and Healing (New York City), 95

contraction, 196

conversion, 9

conversion disorder, 134

Core, *162*

core meditation, 77–78

cortisol, 121

Cortright, Brant, 130

Cosmic Collaboration, 62

cosmic consciousness, 198

Cosmic Energy, 304–305

countertransference, 155

courage, 252

A Course in Miracles, 163–164

Creation, 293

creative activities, 135

creative energies, 319

creativity, 339n2

the Creator, 56, 232. *See also* God

"cross the road," 186, 188–189

crown chakra, 53–54

crying, 131

"crystal children," 67

the Dark Night, 9, 13–16

Darwin, Charles, 260, 261, 293

davvening, 260

death, 147, 198–199. *See also* dying; near-death experiences

  fear of, 122–123, 198–199

delusions, 135

denial, 149, 161, 170

depersonalization disorder, 136–137

depression, 64–65, 91, 107–108, 110–111, 122–123, 132, 134, 151, 168, 331–332

depression karma, 64

derealization, 136–137

dervishes, 55

desire-self identity, 267

devotion, 252

dharana, 267

dharma, 237–238

dhrist, 190

dhyana, 267

diabetes, 65, 96, 105, 113

Diagnostic and Statistical Manual of Mental Disorders (DSM-IV), 135, 136, 138–139

diaphragm, 104, 259

diarrhea, 131

diet, 151–152

digestion, 221, 256

diksha, 24

discovery, 18

diseases. *See* illnesses

disorders, 91–92, 176

disorientation, 133

dissociation, 137

the Divine, 7, 36, 55, 227–230, 233, 293, 305–306, 309, 311. *See also* God

  awakening the, 232–233

personalization of, 308

  transforming the human into, 53–54

the Divine Beloved, 228

Divine Consciousness, 228–229, 238, 239, 245

divine destiny, 211

the Divine Feminine, 245

divine Knowledge, 310

Divine Light, 298, 302

divine love, 69, 313

the Divine Mother, 302, 319

Divine Name Betrayal, 110

Divine Names, 109–111

Divine Presence, 111–112

divine rhythm, 310

the Divine Self, 230

divinity, 293. *See also* the Divine

divya sharira, 268

DNA, 64–65, 232

Dnyaneshwari (Jnaneshvari), 250

dopamine, 121, 122

dreams, 58–59, 302–303

drug intoxication, 131

drugs, 75, 147, 151, 165–166, 168, 176. *See also specific drugs*

  prescription medication, 151, 165–166

  psychiatric, 165–166, 168, 176

  withdrawal from, 147

duality, 242, 253

duality-nonduality, oscillating, 253

Durga, 251

dvaita-advaita, 253

dying, 33. *See also* death

dysthymic disorder, 332

Dzogchen, 32, 206

Earth, 63. *See also* Gaia

earth (element), *239,* 256

eccentrcicity, 274

ecstacy, 207, 275–276, 279, 290

Edwards, Lawrence, 225–245, 351–352

ego, 141, 148–149, 156, 157–159, *162,* 163–164, 198–201. *See also* ego-mind; false self

    ego inflation, 148

    voice of the, *156–157*

ego-mind, 229, 257

Egypt, 212, 221

Einstein, Albert, 223

élan vital, 174

electroencephalography (EEG), 80–81, 119, 331

elements, *239,* 240–241, 252, 256. *See also specific elements*

the Elephanta Islands, 269

Eliade, Mircea, 8

elimination, 221, 256

Eliot, T. S., 8

embodied awakening, paradox of, 98

Emotional Freedom Technique (EFT), 146

emotions, 309, 310

    emotional health, 141–159

    emotional lineage, 63–65

    emotional strength, 319

    negative, 52–53, 62–63, 97, 132, 257

    positive, 150–151

empathy, 152–153, 155, 332

endocrine system, 215

endogenous nitric oxide, 331

energetics, 197, 202–205

energy, 6, 134, 143, 176, 213, 307, 309, 311, 323. *See also* life force

    Cosmic Energy, 304–305

    energies of low vibration, 63

the energy body, 234

energy centers, 49–51, 74, 90–91, 238, 239, 252, 317 (*See also* chakras)

energy fields, 148

energy flow, 74, 134–135

Energy of Spirit, 157

energy openings, 97

energy points, 146

energy practice, 24

energy stream, 216

energy-type massages, 151

kundalini energy, 23–32, 77–78, 87–88, 98, 103–104, 107, 161, 191, 219, 252, 301–306

    real *vs.* imagined experiences of, 77–78

    spiritual, 98, 100–101, 161–171

the energy body, 234

enlightenment, 8, 21, 48–49, 82, 103, 108, 222, 291

    false, 136–137

epilepsy, 134, 274

Epstein, Mark, 137

erotic fluids, 220–221

erotic mysticism, 207–224

Esalen Institute, 22

Eskimo shamans, 174

esoteric psychologies, 209–210

esoteric traditions, 128

essence, 220–221, 222

Eternal Consciousness, 289

eternal path, 83–84

ether, 212, *239*

the etheric body, 215

Euclindian space, 285

evolution, 3, 18, 51, 53, 83, 159, 176, 183, 256

    consciousness and, 207–224, 239, *239*

evolutionary theory, 220

of the human race, 72, 272, 276–277, 282–287, 289, 291

law of, 219

excellence, 321–338

existence, 280

existential beliefs, 103

Experimental Center, 284

extrasensory experiences, 132, 277

extra-terrestrials, 39–40, 45, 147. *See also* alien encounters

Fallacy of Simple Location, 204

false enlightenment, 136–137

false self, 148, 149, 157, 158–159, *162,* 163, 164. *See also* ego

family, 63–64, 262–265

fast food, 152

fast-food spirituality, 50

fasting, 12

fathers, 258

fatigue, 108

feelings, 203, 204

feminine energies, 69, 315–320

femininity, 251, 259

Fenichel★, 200

Ferenczi, Sándor, 200

Ferrer, Jorge, 261

fertility, 261

fibromatosis, 104

fibromyalgia, 94

fine motor coordination, 94–95

fire, *239,* 240, 252, 256

fire of yoga, 228

flamenco, 260

focused awareness, 112

focusing, 112, 119–120

focus phrases, 83–84

Forbes, James, 269

Foucault, Michel, 261

fourth vertebra, 189

Francis de Sales, Saint, 208

freedom, 313

symbols of, 225–247

Freud, Sigmund, 163, 170, 195, 197, 198, 200–201, 205, 212–213, 216, 220, 260–261, 293

frontal lobes, 119–120

function magnetic resonance imaging (fMRI), 150, 325, 331

Gaia, 63. *See also* Earth

the Ganges, 311

Garden of Eden, 11, 14, 212

gastrointestinal problems, 91, 123, 132

genetic karma, 63–64

genital sexuality, 198, 199–200, 201, 205–206, 261

genius, 216, 219, 274–275, 277. *See also* savants; talent

Genlin, Eugene, 102

gestation, 255–256, 257, 265–266

Gherand Sahmita, 251

glands, 257

glandular system, 326, 329

God, 207–208, 218, 228, 239, 241, 286–287, 293, 297, 304–306, 309, 311, 313. *See also* the Creator; the Divine; Goddess; Higher Energy

feminine aspect of, 319

five powers of, 230–232

kundalini experiences and, 13, 33, 42–43, 49, 143, 150–151, 159, 162–164, 171

women and, 319–320

God-consciousness, 206, 237, *239*

Goddess, 159, 163, 228–229, 239, 242, 243

goddesses, 11. *See also specific deities*
tantric, 252
goddess force, 18
the Godhead, 195, 239
"God particle" hunt, 272
gods, 11. *See also specific deities*
God-self, 43
God Source, 71
the Golden Age, 316
Goraksanatha, 251
Goraksha-nath, 250
Govindan, Marshall
Babaji, 268
grace, 228, 229, 233
grandparenthood, 263
granthi, 104–105, 196. *See also* knots
gratitude, 142, 170
great-great-grandparenthood, 263
the Great Lover, 229
the Great Mother, 229
the Great Retruthing, 55–71
Greece, 212
Greek mythology, 109, 228
Greenwell, Bonnie, 21–35, 131–135, 352
Energies of Transformation, 131–135
Greyson, Bruce, 144–145, 154, 173–183, 352–353
grief, 62–63
grihastha householder path, 262–265
Grihasthya Ashrama, 262
Grof, Christina, 129–130
Grof, Stanislav, 129–130
the gross body. *See* the physical body
group psychotherapy, 146
growth, 258
guilt, 132

Guru Ram Das Center for Medicine and Humanology, 90, 96
the guru within, 309
Guyon, Madame, 207–208
gymnastics, 261
gyrations, 260

hallucinations, 135
Hariakhan Baba. *See* Babaji
Hari Dass, Baba
Hariakhan Baba: Known, Unknown, 268
harmony, 98
hatha yoga, 88, 95, 206, 242, 253, 257, 258, 259, 348n2
hathayogapradipika, 251, 260
Hawking, Stephen, 272
healing, 64, 152–155, 157–158, 164, 330
through the Three Channels, 185–192
health, 97–115, 121, 122. *See also* illnesses
spirituality and, 122–125
the heart, 108, 132, 141–142, 150, 152–153, 252, 307–313. *See also* heart centers; heart chakra
as cremation ground, 310–311
development of the, 108
knowing of the, 307
spiritual, 106–111, 108
symbolism of the, 308–309
vibrational power in the, 308–309
heart activity, 221
heart attacks, 105, 134. *See also* cardiovascular health
kundalini-related, 101–102
heart centers, 99–100, 106–111. *See also* cardiovascular problems
opening of the, 99–100

perceptions associated with the, 109

heart chakra, 29, 52–53, 67, 152, 240. *See also* the heart

heart disease. *See* cardiovascular health

heartfelt experiences, 141–142, 150

Heart Lotus, 308

heart rate variation (HRV), 325, 331

heat, 130, 268

Hellenistic cultures, 106

helping professions, 153, 154–155

Hendricks, Gay, 21, 22

hepatitis C, 94

Hesychasm, 106, 260

high blood pressure, 122

Higher Consciousness, 205, 206, 207–224, 313

Higher Energy, 48, 49, 54. *See also* God

Higher Intelligence, 291

Higher Power, 150, 157, 163, 171

Higher Self, 150, *162,* 163, 302–303

high-level denial, 149, 170

Hinduism, 32, 74, 77–78, 130, 204–205, 206, 212

    Hindu mystics, 208

    Hindu mythology, xi

hippocampus, 150

Hitler, Adolf, 219

HIV (Human Immunodeficiency Virus), 187–188, 347n2

Hixon, Lex, 245–246

"Holy Ghost" dancing, 260

the Holy Spirit, 11, 163, 175, 176, 212, 228, 229, 260, 313

Homo luminous, 62, 68

Homo sapiens, 62

hormones, 121

householder path, 267, 268

Humanology, 90

humans, 51–53, 55, 125

    evolution of, 72, 211–214, 272, 276–277, 282–283, 287, 289, 291

    future of, 288

    human design, 37–45

    human development, 323

    human excellence, 321–338

    human expansion, 62

    transformation of, 62

    transformation of the human into the divine, 53–54

humility, 141–142, 149–150, 159–160, 169, 170, 343n16

    characteristics of, 155

    power of, 155–157

huo, 174

hyperactivity, 132

hypersensitivity, 132

hypoglossus, 261, 267

hypophysis, 256

hypothalamus, 120, 261, 267

the *I Am,* 42–43

"I" awareness, 108, 110, 235, 237, 241

ida, 189, 190, 218, 337

ida nadi, 190

identity, 21, 27, 198–199, 236–237. *See also* ego; self

    maturation of, 267

illnesses, 64–65, 66, 90, 91, 97, 121, 122, 176, 185–189. *See also* disorders; *specific disorders; specific illnesses*

    as a blessing in disguise, 114–115

    as a call to spiritual awakening, 112–115

    cardiovascular, 101–106 (*See also* cardiovascular health)

    kundalini-related, 101–115

psychosomatic, 101–106, 114–115

illumination, 9, 271–278

immune system, 146

Inanna, 109

incendium amoris, 174

India, 92, 264, 269, 310–311

Indian literature, 212

Indian metaphysics, 275

"indigos," 67

ineffability, 17, 18, 280, 295

infantile regression, 208, 209

infants, 197–198, 199–200, 257, 258, 266

infertility, 91

initiation, 5–6, 16, 334–335

inner heat, 268

inner life, 158

insanity, 292

insight, 204

insomnia, 93–94

insulin resistance syndrome, 94

intellectual bliss, 202

intelligence, 298, 330

Higher Intelligence, 291

Intelligent Presence, 44

International Association of Yoga Therapists, 89

International Kundalini Yoga Teachers Association, 96

intuition, 318, 319, 330

involuntary movements, xi

involution, 201, 239, *239,* 240

the Iron Age, 316

Ishvara, 259–260

Islam, 260

Iyengar, B. K. S., 261

James, William, 279

japa, 253

jati, 265

Jesus Christ, 11, 32, 33, 43–44, 45, 82, 127, 128, 207, 216

jiva, 256, 265

jiwan-mukta state, 276

jnana yoga, 206

Jnaneshvar, 251, 258

Jnaneshvar-gita, 251

jobs, 122

John of the Cross, Saint, 11, 18

journal-keeping, 154

joy, 132, 170, 229. *See also* pleasure

Judaism, 212, 259, 260

Jung, Carl, 8, 102, 163, 170, 198, 212–213, 220, 225, 233, 323

Jungian analysis, 128

Kabbalah, 197, 205

Kabir, 231

Kali, 251. *See also* Maha Kali, gifts of

kalpataru, 308

Kama-Kala-Vilasa, 251

Kamasutra, 304

kapalabhati pranayama, 259

karma, 35, 62–68, 318, 323

depression karma, 64

genetic, 63–64

karmic cleaning, 62–68

karma yoga, 266–267, 312–313

Kashmir, 274

Kashmir Shaivism, 230, 232–233

Keen, Sam, 214

Keiffer, Gene, 269–275

Kelly, Penny, 37–45, 353

keshin, 251

Khalsa, Dharma Singh, 91, 95

Khalsa, Gurmukh Kaur, 315–320, 354

Khalsa, Gurucharan Singh, 321–338, 355

Khalsa, Mukta Kaur, 91

Khalsa, Sat Bir Singh, 87–95, 332, 354

Khalsa, Shanti Shanti Kaur, 355–356

khechari mudra, 263, 264, 267

ki, 203

kidney cancer, 113, 114

Kieffer, Gene, 213, 356–357

Kinsley, David, *Tantric Visions of the Divine Feminine,* 252

kirtan, 253

Kirtan Kriya, 95

knots, 97, 103–104, 196, 197, 201, 205, 206

   knot of Brahma, 104

   knot of Rudra, 105

   knot of Vishnu, 104–105

knowledge, 277–278, 279–298, 324–325

   divine, 310

   knowing of the Heart, 264, 307

Kohut, Hanz, 107

Kornfield, Jack, 137–138

kosas, 197

Kripalvand, 269

Krishna, 11, 109, 227–228, 261, 263, 311

Krishna, Gopi, 7, 26, 27, 207, 210–224, 279–298, 356

   The Dawn of a New Science, 213

   interview with, 279–298

   introduction to, 271–278

   Kundalini: The Evolutionary Energy in Man, 210–211

   Kundalini: The Evolutionary Energy in Man, 273

Krishnamacharya, 261

Krishnamurti, 27, 75–76, 196

Kriyananda, 75

kriyas, xi, 55, 60–62, 72, 88, 132, 186, 190, 258, 317, 327, 332, 336. *See also pranic movements*

   spontaneous, 330–331

kriya yoga, 75

Krsna, 311. *See also* Krishna

kuei-hou intervals, 197

Kula-Arnava, 251

Kularnava Tantra, 232–233

kunamnama, 251

kunda, 23

kundalini, 62–63, 207–224, 221, 225–247, 228–229, 252, 260, 264, 271–272, 275, 278, 286, 291

   activities that awaken, 24–26

   in the Age of Aquarius, 337–338

   ascending, 113

   common myths about, 325–337

   definition of, 174–175, 211–212

   depiction of, 221

   dual nature of, 97–98

   embryological development and, 255–266

   examination of, 75–77

   as the "face of God," 229

   flow into the brain, 215–216

   genius and, 274

   knowledge of, 220

   as "meta-DNA," 255

   near-death experiences (NDEs) and, 175–176

   origin of the word, 23

   path of, 98

   power of, 48–49

   psychology of, 103

   safety of, 327

   showing the reality of, 219

   spontaneous awakening of, 98–99

symbolism of, 308, 323

thoughts on, 303–306

throughout the life cycle, 265–268

translation of, 211–212

true function of, 26–28

warnings about, 327–328

Kundalini (Goddess)

as the Great Lover, 229

as the Great Mother, 229

manifestations of, 250

mothering creativity of, 255–265

Mother Kundalini, 233, 252, 264, 268

kundalini awakening. *See also* kundalini process

activities that cause, 24–26

diagnosis of, 138, 139

health problems and, 101–106

improper, 218

key features of, 132–133

meditation and, 136–138

mental and emotional health and, 141–160

misdiagnosis as psychiatric disorder, 128, 129–130, 151, 165–166

negative effects of, 123–124, 218

physical symptoms of, 130–131, 132

psychological problems and, 134–135, 151

Qigong and, 135–136

resemblance to medical and psychiatric disorders, 134–135, 151

as a spiritual problem, 138–139

symptoms of, 130–131, 132, 176–177

triggers for, 131

yoga and, 130–135

kundalini consciousness, 3–19

kundalini energy, 23–32, 87–88, 98, 103–104, 107, 161, 191, 219, 252, 301–306. *See also* life-force energy

kundalini energy meditation, 75–77

real *vs.* imagined experiences of, 77–78

kundalini flow, 74–75

kundalini-gone-astray, 219

kundalini meditation, 73–84, 315–320, 321–338

brain imaging and, 331–332

clinical uses of, 331–332

kundalini energy meditation, 75–77

kundalini yoga and, 328–329

kundalini yoga meditation, 150–151

measurability of, 331–333

power of, 315–320

research on, 331–333

science and, 331–333

as taught by Yogi Bhajan, 321–338

kundalini phenomena, cross-cultural, 260–261

kundalini "popping," 56

kundalini process, 34–35, 104–105, 110–111, 213, 214, 218, 220

mental and emotional health and the, 141–159

misdiagnosis of, 165–166, 176

psychic phenomena as a by-product of, 147–148

spontaneous triggers, 146–147

symptoms of, 177–182, *178–179, 180–181*

kundalini recovery process, 161–171

kundalini-related pathology, 101–115

Kundalini Research Foundation, 213

Kundalini Research Institute, 88–89, 96, 332, 336

Kundalini Research Network, 127

Kundalini Shakti, 238

kundalini theory, 202, 206, 223

kundalini yoga, 10, 47–53, 98, 186, 203, 205, 226, 242, 261–263, 315–320, 321–338, 348n3

  accessibility of, 327

  aimed at the householder, 325–326

  aim of, 201–202

  for Alzheimer's, 95

  anatomy of, 189–191

  breath technique, 191–192

  for cognitive impairment, 95

  for continuing pain syndromes, 94

  as a coping mechanism, 122

  for diabetes, 96

  for disorders, 91–92

  effects on physical and mental health, 122–123

  for fibromyalgia, 94

  forms of, 255

  goals of, 329–330

  health effects of, 121, 122

  for HIV patients, 187–188

  illness and, 187–189, 192

  initiation and, 334–335

  for insulin resistance syndrome, 94

  kundalini meditation and, 328–329

  measurability of, 331–333

  the mind and, 337

  myths about, 325–337

  nature of practices, 335–337

  negative effects of, 123–124

  for obsessive-compulsive disorder, 92–93

  perfection and, 333–334

  positive effects of, 121, 122–123

  power of, 315–320

  practice of, 189–191

  psychic abilities and, 329–330

  psychology of, 103

  religion and, 333

  research on, 91–96, 124–125, 331–333

  safety of, 327

  science and, 331–333

  secrecy and, 334–335

  for sleep disorders, 93–94, 95

  for special populations, 91–92

  for speech disorders, 94–95

  spontaneous phenomena, 260–261

  for stroke rehabilitation, 94–95

  as taught by Yogi Bhajan, 321–338

  as therapy, 87–95

  time to results, 325

  transformational aspects of, 122–123

  warnings about, 327–328

  the yogic brain, 117–125

kundalini yoga meditation, 150–151

Kurma Purana, 269

Lakulisha, 250, 269

language, 226, 257, 284, 295

  mantric effects of sacred, 257

Large Hadron Collider, 272

lataif, 106

Latin America, 106

laughter, 131

"launching" dreams, 68

Laya Yoga, 242

left-brain activity, 30

le Saux, Henri, 100

lethargy, 132

leukemia, 113–114

liberation, 196, 233, 311

libido, 123, 199–200, 205–206, 211–212, 216, 261

Life, 42–43, 44

life-force energy, 21–35, 213, 275. *See also* kundalini energy

life goals, 122

Life Review, 143

light, 29, 132, 149, 170, 297, 303, 307, 308, 310–313
    deep light, 55–71
    of knowledge, 311
    lightbodies, 70, 71
    the Light within, 309
    "light work," 64
    meditation on the, 305–306
    of understanding, 311
    Vision of Light, 302

Lim, R., 135–136

limbic system, 145–146, 150–151, 159

limits. *See* boundaries

limpness, 131

Lin, K., 135–136

lineage, 262–263, 264, 268–269

"living electricity," 214

Living Radiance, 297–298

loneliness, 17

longing, 252, 259

loss, 147

lotus flowers, 238, 253, 274, 305–306, 308, 317

Louchakova, Olga, 97–115, 357–358

love, 29, 52–53, 131, 132, 252

lovemaking. *See* sex

loving bliss, 202

Lukoff, David, 127–139, 358

MacLaine, Shirley, 210

magnetic resonance imaging (MRI), 119

Maha Kali, gifts of, 242–247

mahamudra, 206

Mahanirvana, 251

Maharshi, 108

maha-samadhi, 264

Maha Shakti, 244–245

mahavakya, 237

maithuna, 209

manas, 103

mania, 107, 108–109, 110, 111, 151

manipura chakra, *239,* 240, 252, *254*

manomaya kosha, 253, 265

mantras, 89, 94, 186, 190, 191, 252, 253, 257, 309, 318

mantra yoga, 242

map of the psyche, 161–171, *162*

marga, 264

marriage, 262–263, 264

Martin, 187

masculine energies, 69

masculinity, 251, 259

Maslow, Abraham, 209, 220

massages, 151

masturbation, 76

materiality, 104

Matsyendra-nath, 250

Matthew, Gospel of, 277

meaning, 122

meditation, 48–49, 52–54, 73–84, 89, 93–94, 120–122, 131, 145, 147, 150–151, 209, 226, 235–236, 243, 260, 317

chakra meditations, 253, *254*
   power of, 315–320
      auditory, 252
      body-scanning, 252
      Buddhist, 77, 81, 82
      Christian, 74, 77
      Hindu, 77, 81, 82
      instruction in, 305–306
      kundalini awakening and, 136–138
      kundalini energy meditation, 75–77
      manipulative approach to, 75, 77
      meditation on the Light, 305–306
      Native American, 77
      nonstop, 79
      power of, 315–320
      psychotic episodes and, 138
      repeat experiences, 78–79
      for schizophrenic patients, 138
      Taoist, 77, 78
      as taught by Yogi Bhajan, 321–338
      visual, 252
      Zen, 78
meditation-related experiences, 136–137
MEG, 331
memory, 108, 123, 234
mental health, 105, 122, 141–159. *See also* psychological problems
mental phenomena, 291–292
meridians, 91, 97, 103–104, 191, 329, 337
mescaline, 75
metacognition, 332
metaphysics, 104, 275
Mexico, 212

the mind, 49–50, 51–53, 291. *See also* the brain
   with certainty, 103
   conquering, 337
   levels of, 103
   map of the psyche, *162,* 162–164
   mind-body complex, 90–91, 98–102
   "mind-stuff," 98
   nondual state of, 108
   quiet, 52, 53, 77, 79–82
   spirit and, 118–119
   subtle mind, *239*
   without certainty, 103
misdiagnosis of kundalini experiences, 128, 129–130, 151, 165–166, 176
mission, sense of, 142, 153–154
moksha, 268
monastic life, 264–265. *See also* celibacy
mood disorders, 331
mood swings, 107, 123, 132
mortification, 12
Mother Ganga, 311
mothering energy, 255–265
Mother Kundalini, 233, 252, 264, 268
mothers, 258
Motoyama, 27
mucopolysaccharides, 256
mudras, 132, 190, 191, 253, 258, 266
Muktananda, 27, 242, 244
mula-bandha, 259
muladhara, 238, 239
muladhara chakra, *239,* 241, 252, 253, *254,* 256
multiple sclerosis, 134
mumukshtva, 228
Mundaka Upanishad, 196
muscular problems, 123

muscular tension, 137

musculature, 259

music, 11, 295

Mystery, 163, 164, 282

Mystery of Creation, 288

Mystical Vision, 280, 295

mysticism, 8–9, 11, 17–18, 32

    Christian, 106

    erotic, 207–224

    mystical consciousness, 276

    mystical ecstasy, 279, 290

    mystical experiences, 120,
127–130, 141–142, 150, 279–280

    mystical states, 133

    mystical traditions, 128, 294–295

    mystical trance, 281, 295

mystic marriage, 11

the mystic path, 3–19

mystics, 207–208, 280, 291

myths, 11, 226–227, 228

nabho, 267

nadis, 189, 227, 236, 237, 252

Nanak, Guru Dev Jee, 329

National Center for Complementary
and Alternative Medicine, 92–93

National Institutes of Health, 92–93

National Treasure, 227

Native American tradition, 128, 191

nature, 151

nausea, 131

near-death experiences (NDEs), 141,
142–147

    definition of, 173–174

    physio-kundalini syndrome and,
173–183

    research on, 177–183

Neem Karoli Baba, 268

neo-Confucians, 197

neocortex, 152

neonatal development, 257

neo-Reichian bodywork, 21

neo-Vedanta satsangs, 108

nerve food, 220–221

nervous system, 120–121, 220–221,
222, 326, 329, 331

neurological problems, 132

neurophysiology, 119–121

neuroscience, 117–125, 150–152

neurosis, 102, 292

neurotic conflict, 102, 103, 104

neurotransmitters, 121, 122, 124

New Age Groups, 128

New Age theology, 151

Newberg, Andrew B., 117–125,
150–151, 159, 358–359

New Delhi, India, 273

"New Earth," 56, 63, 66, 68

New Mexico, 90

new self, 17

New Testament, 277

Newton, Isaac, 274, 283

New York City, 95

New York Times, 213

night moves, 60–62

nigune, 259

nirbija-samadhi, 268

nirvana, 8, 148

Nisadagatta, 32

nivritti dharma, 264–265, 267

niyamas, 266, 348n4

nocturnal phenomena, 60–62

nondrug modalities, 151–152

nonduality, 242, 253

nonstop meditation, 79

nutrition, 151–152

Obama, Barack, 83

object-relations psychology, 163

obsessive-compulsive disorder, 87, 92–93

Ocean of Awareness, 298

the Odic force, 175

the Oedipal project, 199–200, 201

old self, 17

Om Bhur Bhuva Swaha Tat Savitur Varenyam Bhargo Devasya Dhimahe Dhyo Yonah Prachodayat, 252

Omega Project, 182

Om Namo Bhagavate Vasudevaya, 252

Om Namo Shivaya, 252

oneness, 36, 55, 70–71, 72

ontogeny phylogeny recapitulation, 256

opening, 56–57

Orenstein, Robert, 214

organe energy, 174

organic syndromes, 134

orgasms, 37–38, 69

orgone, 212

origin-consciousness, 268

Ornstein, Robert, The Psychology of Consciousness, 209

Osiris, 175

out-of-body experiences (OBEs), 57, 61, 132, 144

pagan traditions, 128

pain, 6, 12–13, 123, 152–153

Panca-Tantra, 251

Panchastavi, 278

pandit, 276

Pandit, M. P., 214

paradigm shifts, 124–125

paraiyanga, 263

paranormal states, 292, 329–330. See also psychic abilities

parietal lobe, 120

partners in learning, 64

Pashupati seal, 250, 256

the past, 170. See also trauma

Patanjali, 80

pathcutters, 66–67, 68

pathcutting, 62–68

peace, 35–36

the Pearl of Great Price, 175

pelvic inflammatory syndrome, 134

Penfield, Wilder, The Mystery of the Mind, 223

Pentacostalism, 260

perception, 104–105, 221

    altered, 136–137

    extra-sensory, 277

    higher, 212

    interpersonal, 332

perceptions. See also senses

perfection, 333–334

perineum, 252, 256, 259

perineum state, 256

Perrin, Stuart, 47–53, 359

personality changes, 114–115

personal organism, 198

personal work, 112

petals, 238

la petite mort, 175

phalam, 250

phalluses, 221

Pharaoh, 212, 221

photismos, 174

the physical body, 206, 234–235, 252, 317

physical movements, 55, 60–62

physics, 285

physio-kundalini syndrome, 144–145, 173–183, *178–179, 180–181*

pineal glands, 256, 267, 268

pineal lobes, 261

pingala, 189, 190, 218, 337

pingala nadi, 190

the Piscean Age, 316

pituitary glands, 256, 267

Plato, 283

pleasure, 6, 12–13. *See also* bliss

Pleasure Principle, 197–198

the Pleiades, 60

poetry, 295

point-fixation, 82

political environment, 327–328

Porter, Katherine Anne, 5

positron-emission tomography (PET), 119, 150

possession states, 130

post-traumatic stress, 161

post-traumatic stress disorder (PTSD), 167

posture, 190

potential, hidden, 43–46

power, 327–328

power center, 211–212

prana, 90, 174–175, 190–191, 203, 212–214, 217–219, 234, 236, 252, 258, 260, 266, 274, 275–277. *See also kriyas*

   definition of, 213

   as life energy, 213

   pranic awakening, 255

   pranic movements, 132 (*See also kriyas*)

   pranic spectrum, 275

   pranic stream, 218–219

prana-maya kosha, 253, 265, 266

prana-pran, 252

pranayama, 253, 266

pranotthana, 255, 258, 259, 266

Pransali, India, 269

pratyahara, 267

pravritti, 267

prayer, 12, 120, 147

pregnancy, 258

premature transcendence, 149, 170

preparation, 10

prescription medication, 151, 165–166

presence, 315–320

present-moment awareness, 78–79, 83–84

Presley, Elvis, 260

pressure points, 91

priapic art, 221

prima materia, 213

processed food, 152

projection, 71–72

prophets, 287

proprioceptive system, disruption of the, 132

prostate cancer, 104, 113, 114

protection, 318

protoasanas, 257

protobrain, 256

protohypothalamus, 256

protolinguistic development, 257

protospine, 255–256

psyche, map of the, 161–171, *162,* 162–164. *See also* the mind

psychiatric drugs, 165–166, 168, 176

psychic abilities, 133, 147–148, 157–158, 209, 253, 292, 329–330. *See also* paranormal states

   attachments to, 147–148

psychic opening, 130

psychological problems, 136–137,
176
  kundalini awakening and,
  134–135
  psychosis, 111, 123, 128–129, 130,
  134, 135–136, 138, 151, 168
  spiritual practices and, 127–130
psychology, 165–166, 284–285,
289–290, 294, 323. *See also specific
schools*
  esoteric, 209–210
  orthodox, 208, 209
  psychological perspectives, 112,
  208
psychosis, 111, 123, 134, 135–136,
151, 168
  kundalini experiences
  misdiagnosed as, 128, 129–130
  meditation and, 138
psychosomatic illness, 101–106. *See
also* kundalini-related pathology
psychotherapy, 131, 146, 151
puberty, 261, 266, 267, 268
puja, 243
pulse, 221
pulsing, 310
purgation, 9, 12
purification, 109–110, 312–313
purity, 320
purpose, 43, 122

qalb, 108
qi, 49, 52
Qigong, 26, 36, 127, 128, 131
  kundalini awakening and,
  135–136
  Qigong psychotic reaction,
  135–136
Quakerism, 260
quaking, 260
quamaneq, 174

quiet mind, 52, 53–54, 77, 79–82
  perceptual experiences that create,
  80–81
quivering, 260
qwaali, 259

Radha, Sivananda, 301–313, 303–306,
307–313, 359–360
  Kundalinia Yoga for the West, 301
  Light & Vibration, 307–313
Radhe, 263
Radiance Breathwork, 21–22
the radiant body, 318
raja yoga, 242, 260, 323
Ramana Maharshi, 34, 36, 107, 110,
196, 202
Ram Dass, 210, 268
  Be Here Now (From Bindu to Ojas),
  210
Ramprasad Sen, 233
  Mother of the Universe, 245–246
rasayana, 251, 348n2
reality, 280, 281
  projection of, 71–72
Real Self, 162
recovery, 147, 161–171
  recovery movement, 164–165
  stages of, 167–170, *168*
red, 58–59
"red" dreams, 68
reflection, 253, 309
Reich, Wilhelm, 200, 212
reincarnation, 308
relationships, 104–105, 122, 153
Relativity, 285
relaxation, 60
religion, 333. *See also* mysticism;
  specific religions
  as evolutionary impulse, 211

religious ecstacy, 207

sexuality as religious experience, 208

Renard, Gary, *The Disappearance of the Universe,* 71

reproduction, 213. *See also* sex

reproductive energy, 213

reproductive organs, 215, 220–221

research, 91–96, 124–125, 177–183, 221, 331–333

biomedical, 91

on consciousness, 279–298

respiratory therapy, 144–145

retardation, 292

retraumatization, 167

Retrovir, 347n2

retruthing, 59–60

revelation, 17

rhythm, 309

divine, 310

right-brain activity, 29–30

rigidity, 131

Ring, Kenneth, 147, 175–176, 177, 182

Heading toward Omega, 144

ritual sexual intercourse, 209

Roberts, Jane, 8

Roche, L., 137

the Rod of Aaron, 175

root center, 256

root chakra, 59, 68, 252, 256

Rosin, Steven, 102

Rosing, Christopher, 182

Rowe, H. T., 269

ruh, 203

Rumi, 55–56, 69

rumination, 332

Rumi poems, 55–56, 69

sabija-samadhi, 268

the Sacred Fire, 175

sacred languages, 257

Sacred Person, *162,* 163, 164

Saddasiva, 301

sadhana, 326

sages, 282, 286, 287

saguna Brahman, 204–205

sahaja state, 276

sahaja yoga, 258, 262, 266

sahasrara, 202, 215, 238, 239, *239,* 240

sahasrara chakra, 253, *254*

saints, 258

Saktavijnana, 251

Sakyamuni Buddha, 196

salutary prescriptions, 259–260

salvation, 45, 46

samadhi, 33, 87–88, 275–276

samadhi state, 277–278

samana-pran, 252

samsara, 197, 205

samskaras, 236–237

Sanatana Dharma, 264

San Diego, California, 93, 95

San Francisco VA Day Treatment Center, 138

sankhocha, 196

sankini, 216

Sannella, Lee, 176–177

Kundalini: Psychosis or Transcendence?, 129, 166

sannyas, 265

sannyasa ashrama, 263–264

Sanskrit, 257

Sarah, 185–186

sat nam, 186

satori, 33

satsangs, 108

Satyeswarananda, *Babaji,* 268

Saundaryalahari, 232

savants, 274–275. *See also* genius

schizophrenic patients, 138

science, 272, 273, 277, 279, 280, 288–289, 291, 292–294, 331–333. *See also* research

Scopes "Monkey Trial," 223

Scriptures, 287, 302

seat of the soul, 189

second chakra, 53

secrecy, 334–335

seers, 287

sefiroth, 197

Selby, John, 73–84, 360
  Kundalini Awakening in Everyday Life, 74

self, 21, 27, 32–36, 34–35, 36, 106, 230
  Divine Self, 230
  false, 148, 149, 157, 158–159, *162,* 163, 164
  "false" *vs.* "true," 107
  Higher Self, 150, *162,* 302–303
  knowledge of the, 281–282
  negation of the, 105
  new, 17
  old, 17
  perceived, 106
  perceptions of, 104
  phenomenology of the, 102
  recognition of the, 113–114
  Self of All, 241
  sense of, 120, 132
  True Self, 141, 143, 149, 153, 156, 158–159, 162, *162,* 163, 164, 171
  unveiling of, 103–104
self-consciousness, 22

self-hatred, 105

self-knowledge, 9

Self of All, 241

self-psychology, 107, 108, 163

self-realization, 21–35, 233

Semela, 109

seminal fluid, 220–221

senses, 80. *See also* perceptions
  amplification of, 68–69
  sensory problems, 123

separateness, illusion of, 21, 27, 30, 32–34

serotonin, 122

serpent, 212, 232

"serpent" kundalini, 59

serpent power, 212

the Serpent power, 175

seventh chakra, 214

sex, 38, 53, 68–69, 76, 207–223, 207–224. *See also* reproduction; sexuality
  ritual sexual intercourse, 209
  sexo-yogic practices, 348n2
  sexual indulgence, 304

sex organs, 215, 220–221

sexo-yogic practices, 348n2

sexuality, 53–54, 61, 197–198, 211, 252, 261–265. *See also* libido; lovemaking
  sexual energy, 53, 205–206
  sexual essence, 220–221
  spirituality and, 207–224, 214–216
  as unexpressed or unfulfilled religious experience, 208

sexual symbolism, 245

Shabad Krya, 93

Shakerism, 260

Shakespeare, William, 280

shaking, xi, 131, 176, 260

shakptipat, 24

Shakta-Vedanta, 106

Shakti, 97–98, 175, 206, 238, 241–245, 251, 259, 263, 275, 319

shaktipat, 231–232, 232–233, 242, 253, 275

shamanica medhra, 261

shamanic traditions, 106, 128, 130, 174, 259, 260

shamanistic initiatory crisis, 130

shambhavi mudra, 268

Shams, 55–56

Shankara, 196

Shankaracharya, 232

Shannahoff-Khalsa, David, 91, 92–93

Shanti Shanti Kaur Khalsa, 185–192

Shekhinah, 229

shikantaza, 206

Shiva, 250, 251, 259, 263, 269

Shiva-Samhita, 251

Shiva-Sutra, 251

siddha-asana, 256, 259

Siddha masters, 244

siddhis, 26

Sikh Dharam, 348n3

the Silver Age, 316

simha-asana, 267

Simon, Tami, ix–xii

single photon emission computed tomography (SPECT), 119, 150, 331

Siva, 311. See also Shiva

skull chakra, 67

sleep, 38–39, 93, 95

sleep disorders, 87, 95

sleep disturbances, 123

sleeplessness, 38–39

the snake, xi, 4

So-Ham, 252

sokrlung, 137

solar plexus, 29

soma, 250

Somananda, 251

somas, 267, 348n5

somatic personhood, 107–108, 110–111

somatized awakening, 112

sorrow, 131

the soul, 143, 162, 256

seat of, 189

thirst of, 321–338

voice of, 141, 156–157

yearning of, 228

soul contracts, 64

soul-self identity, 267

soul travel, 275

sounds, 131

the Source, 41–42, 201

South America, 212

Sovatsky, Stuart, 247–267, 360–361

Special K, 58–59, 65

special populations, 91–92

speech disorders, 94–95

sphincter, 259

spinal column, 87, 189–191, 214–215, 218, 221, 238, 255–256, 259, 261, 265–266

spinal problems, 132

spinal-rocking, 260

spirit, 97–98, 158. See also the Holy Spirit

body and, 99–101

immensity of the, 99–101

mind and, 118–119

spiritual awakening, x, 21–35, 37–46, 97–115, 98–99, 101, 103–105, 147, 161–162. *See also* awakening; kundalini awakening

bipolar disorder and, 106–111

disease and, 112–115

physical and mental health aspects of, 111–115

recovery movement and, 164–165

traps in, 165–167

the spiritual body, maturation of the, 247–267, 248–269

spiritual bypass, 141, 142, 148–149, 167

spiritual emergence, 130, 139–140

Spiritual Emergence Network. *See* Spiritual Emergency Network (SEN)

Spiritual Emergence Network Newsletter, 131

spiritual emergencies, 130, 131, 137–138. *See also* kundalini awakening; spiritual emergence

Spiritual Emergency Network (SEN), 127, 129

spiritual energies, 98, 100–101, 161–171

spiritual entities, 132

spiritual heart, 108

problems associated with the, 106–111

spirituality, 159

health and, 122–125

sexuality and, 207–224, 214–216

spiritual growth, 206

spiritual insight, 330

spiritual problems, 138

spiritual masturbation, 76–77

spiritual paths, 74–75

spiritual practices, 169–170

neurophysiology and, 119–121

psychological problems and, 127–130

spontaneous awakening, 98–99, 101, 107, 227

spontaneous healing, 68

spontaneous inner transformation, 17

spontaneous *kriyas,* 330–331

spontaneous movements, 258

spontaneous sounding, 258

spontaneous triggers, 146–147

sri yantra, 252

Stages of Recovery, 146

Steindl-Rast, David, 139–140

still-sitting, 260

stress, 331

strokes, 29, 105

kundalini-related, 101–103

stroke rehabilitation, 94–95

sublimation, 205, 216

substance abuse, 91–92

the subtle body, 104, 107, 203–204, 206, 214–215, 233–238, *239,* 252

subtle channels, 252

subtle energetic anatomy, 252

subtle energy fields, 90, 148

subtle energy systems, 90–91

subtle judgement, 253

subtle mind, *239*

Sufism, 9–10, 106, 108, 109, 208, 259

sukshmasharira, 252

Sumer, 212

the Sun Behind the Sun, 175

sunlight, inner, 250

superconsciousness, 275, 276, 277–278

"superintelligent energy," 214

Supreme Identity, 198, 201

Surangama Sutra, 196

surrender, 9, 312

sushanna nadi, 236, 238, 241

sushmana, 337

sushumna, 189–190, 214, 255–256

sushumna nadi, 241

svadhishthana chakra, *239,* 240, 252, *254*

symbols, 132, 226–227, 308

Symptom Checklist-90-Revised Obsessive Compulsive Scale, 93

synergy, 68

synesthesia, 274

tai chi, 128, 260

Taittiriya-Upanishad, 252

talent, 277, 292. *See also* genius; savants

Tammet, Daniel, *Born on a Blue Day,* 273–274

Tantraloka, 251

tantras, 197, 205, 209, 212, 251

Tantra-Tattva-Tantra, 251

tantric tradition, 215, 245, 253, 348n2

tantric sex, 69, 245, 348n2

tantric yoga, 53

Taoism, 8, 197, 260

Taylor, Jill Bolte, 29

Teilhard de Chardin, Pierre, 291

tejas, 267

telepathy, 67, 68, 114

television viewing, elimination of, 151

Teresa of Avila, Saint, 11, 18, 207

Terry, 133–134

Tesla, Nikola, 278

Thakan Kung, 75

thalamus, 119–120

thatagatas, 229

theology, 151

The Void, 42

third chakra, 49–50, 52–53, 53–54

third eye, 29, 240

Thirumandiram, 251

Thirumoolar, 263

Thousand-Petalled Lotus, 274

Thousand-Petalled lotus, 253

the Three Channels, 185–192

thresholds, 97, 103–104

throat chakra, 339n2

thxiasi num, 260

thymus gland, 67

Tibet, 212

Tibetan Buddhism, 150–151, 174, 260, 347n1

Tiller, William, 214–215

Tolle, Eckhart

The Power of Now, 113–114

"tonal transmissions," 55, 60

tongues, talking in, 131, 267

toxicity, 158

toxic people, 158

trance-dances, 260

trances, 281, 295

trance singing, 259

tranformation, 225–247, 227

transcendence, 33–34, 36, 142, 149, 170, 201–202, 279–280, 285–286

transcendent bliss, 202

transference, 155

transformation, 17

symbols of, 225–245

transhuman consciousness, 288

transhuman nature, 279–280, 287

transmutation, 66

transpersonal psychology, 209, 220, 261

traps, 165–167

trauma, 161, 164, 167, 169

tremors, 130

triggers, 146–147

Tripuropanishad, 251

true love, 313

True Self, 141, 143, 149, 153, 156, 158–159, 162, *162,* 163, 164, 171

truth, 43–44, 231–232, 298

Tucson, Arizona, 91–92

tumo heat, 260

Turiya, 281

Twelve-Step programs, 147, 154, 164–165, 171, 343n16

twisting, 176

"tyranny of genital organization," 199–200

udan-pran, 252

uddiyana-bandha, 259

uju kaya, 259

unconditional love, 41

Underhill, Evelyn, 8–9, 12, 13, 17

unified human chakra, 68

union, 9, 259

Unity Consciousness, 143, 230, 237–238

Universal Intelligence, 303

University of California, San Francisco, 138

University of Connecticut Medical School, 144–145

University of Guadalajara, 94

University of Pennsylvania, 95, 150

University of Utah Pain Center, 94

unmani mudra, 268

unrequited love, 131

Upanishads, 281

urdhva-retas, 267

Usha-Nisha-Kamala, 215

uterine conditions, 104

Vaillant, George

  Spiritual Evolution, 159

vajra, 5

Vajrayana, 206, 347n1

Vamakeshvara-tantra, 251

vanaprasthya ashrama, 263

Vasudhaiva kutumbakam, 264

Vaya Purana, 269

vayu, 250–251

Vedanta, 197, 206

Vedas, 237

Vedic Age, 222

Vedic tradition, 212, 250–251

vertigo, 105

vibration, 63, 64–65, 66, 68, 176, 203, 204, 258, 319

  divine, 310

vijnana-maya kosha, 253, 265

vijnanas, 197

Vinit-muni, 269

the virgin, 11

virya, 267

viscera, 259

Vishnu-granthi, 104–105

vishuddha chakra, *239,* 240, 253, *254*

Vision of Light, 302

visions, 136–137

visualization, 309

vital force, 204

viveka, 227

voice of the soul, 141

voudoo, 260

vya-pran, 252

Vyasa, 216

Walsh, R., 137

Walters, Dorothy, 3–19, 361

Washburn, Michael, 261

water, *239,* 240–241, 252, 256

waves, 231

way of the bodhisattva, 18

White, D. G.

The Alchemical Body, 348n2

White, John, 207–223, 361

Future Science, 213

Whitehawk, 55–71, 362

Whitfield, Barbara Harris, 141–159, 170, 362–363

The Power of Humility, 155

"The Emotional Needs of Critical Care Patients," 144

Whitfield, Charles L., 146, 161–171, 363

Wilber, Ken, 112, 195–206, 261, 363–364

willfulness, 252

Wishing Tree, 308

withdrawal, 147

women, 315–320, 319, 320

Woodroffe, John

Serpent Power, 241

Yale-Brown Obsessive Compulsive Scale, 93

yamas, 259–260, 266, 348n4

year 2012, 318

yearning, 9–10, 261

Yeats, W. B., 8

yoga, 131, 209, 232, 242, 259, 260. *See also* kundalini yoga; *specific types of yoga*

of devotional moods, 259

erotic, 263

fire of, 228

in India, 89

kundalini awakening and, 130–135

power of, 315–320

problematic kundalini awakening and, 129

the secret behind, 217–219

as taught by Yogi Bhajan, 321–338

as therapy, 87–96

types of, 88

as union of Shakti and Shiva, 259

Yogacara, 197

Yogananda, Paramahansa, 268–269

yoga postures, 254, 255, 258

yoga practice, 24, 255

Yogi Bhajan, 87–95, 191, 315–317, 319–320, 321–338, 348n3

The Master's Touch, 325

the yogic brain, 117–125

yogic breathing practices, 135

yogic phenomenoa, 132

yogic theory, 90–91

yogic tradition, 228–229

Zen Buddhism, 32, 34

Zen masters, 196

Zen meditation, 30–32

Zeus, 11, 109

zikr, 260